4th Workshop on Natural Language Processing and Computational Social Sciences (NLP+CSS 2020)

Online
20 November 2020

ISBN: 978-1-7138-1998-1

NLP+CSS 2020

**Natural Language Processing
and Computational Social Sciences**

Proceedings of the Fourth Workshop

November 20, 2020
Online

Introduction

Welcome to the Fourth Workshop on Natural Language Processing (NLP) and Computational Social Science (CSS)! This workshop series builds on a successful string of iterations, with dozens of interdisciplinary submissions to make NLP techniques and insights standard practice in CSS research—as well as improve NLP through insights from Social Science.

We received a record 61 submissions and after a rigorous review process by our committee, we accepted 23 archival entries, and 4 non-archival abstracts. In a time of uncertainty and a global pandemic, we are heartened to see strong interest and genuinely excited to share these fantastic works. Due to the conference shifting to a virtual format, all papers will be presented with pre-recorded videos during two sessions of the workshop, allowing authors to engage through chat and video throughout the workshop. We are especially excited to see so many submissions from outside of NLP, and hope to continue the tradition to foster a dialogue between researchers in NLP and these other fields.

We are glad to present a fantastic selection of invited speakers from various aspects of computational social science: Elizabeth E. Bruch (University of Michigan), Dong Nguyen (Utrecht University), Jesse Shapiro (Brown University), and Diyi Yang (Georgia Institute of Technology). This year, we recognize the growing role of NLP+CSS technology outside of academia and aimed to highlight opportunities for students and practitioners outside of academia. To help this effort, we are thrilled to host a panel discuss NLP and CSS in industry with amazing speakers from a variety of tech companies: Kristin Althenburger (Facebook), Jason Baldridge (Google), Glen Coppersmith (Qntfy), Emre Kiciman (Microsoft Research), and Umashanthi Pavalanathan (Twitter).

Recognizing the growing community of CSS researchers outside of NLP, as well as new researchers starting out in NLP+CSS, we introduced a new mentoring program that connected volunteers from our Program Committee to authors wanting additional guidance. We are especially grateful for their time and guidance.

We would like to thank the Program Committee members who reviewed the papers this year. We would also like to thank the workshop participants. Last, a word of thanks also goes to our sponsors Microsoft Research and Facebook, who enabled us to support a record number of students this year.

David Bamman, Dirk Hovy, David Jurgens, Brendan O'Connor, and Svitlana Volkova (Co-Organizers)

Organizers:

David Bamman, University of California, Berkeley
Dirk Hovy, Bocconi University
David Jurgens, University of Michigan
Brendan O'Connor, University of Massachusetts Amherst
Svitlana Volkova, Pacific Northwest National Laboratory

Program Committee:

Natalie Ahn
Nikolaos Aletras
Kristen M. Altenburger
Vijjini Anvesh Rao
Alexandra Balahur
Timothy Baldwin
Alon Bartal
Eric Bell
Laura Biester
Michael Bloodgood
Chris Brew
Julian Brooke
Aron Culotta
Steve DeNeefe
Matthew Denny
A. Seza Doğruöz
Jonathan Dunn
Valery Dzutsati
Jacob Eisenstein
Jason Eisner
Micha Elsner
Alex Fine
Tommaso Fornaciari
Kathleen C. Fraser
Jesse Freitas
Juri Ganitkevitch
Dan Goldwasser
Yvette Graham
Andrew Halterman
Oul Han
Marti A. Hearst
Michael Heilman
Loring Ingraham
Molly Ireland
Anders Johannsen
Kristen Johnson
Kenneth Joseph
Brendan Kennedy
Sunghwan Mac Kim
Vivek Kulkarni

Jonathan K. Kummerfeld
Alessandro Lenci
Mingyang Li
Nikola Ljubešić
Josephine Lukito
Teresa Lynn
Elijah Mayfield
Diana Maynard
Paul McLachlan
Julia Mendelsohn
Ben Miller
David Mimno
Shubhanshu Mishra
Aida Mostafazadeh Davani
Dong Nguyen
Pierre Nugues
Stephan Oepen
Miles Osborne
Sebastian Padó
Shriphani Palakodety
Ted Pedersen
Viktor Pekar
Barbara Plank
Massimo Poesio
Thierry Poibeau
Daniel Preoţiuc-Pietro
Afshin Rahimi
Sravana Reddy
Ellen Riloff
Anthony Rios
Carolyn Rosé
Alla Rozovskaya
Derek Ruths
Asad Sayeed
Natalie Schluter
Djamé Seddah
Felix Soldner
Vivek Srikumar
Ian Stewart
Oren Tsur
Lyle Ungar
Esther van den Berg
Zijian Wang
Swede White
Steven Wilson
Wei Xu
Michael Yeomans
Shuang (Sophie) Zhai

Invited Speakers:

Elizabeth E. Bruch, University of Michigan
Dong Nguyen, Utrecht University
Jesse Shapiro, Brown University
Diyi Yang, Georgia Institute of Technology

Panelists:

Kristin Althenburger, Facebook
Jason Baldridge, Google
Glen Coppersmith, Qntfy
Emre Kiciman, Microsoft Research
Umashanthi Pavalanathan, Twitter

Table of Contents

Conference Program

Friday, November 20, 2020 (All times PST; UTC-8)

07:00–07:15 *Introductory Remarks*

07:15–09:00 **Session 1**

07:15–08:00 *Invited Talk 1: When NLP Meets Language Variation*
Dong Nguyen

08:00–09:00 *Paper Session and Discussion 1*
All papers

08:00–09:00 *Measuring Linguistic Diversity During COVID-19*
Jonathan Dunn, Tom Coupe and Benjamin Adams

08:00–09:00 *How Language Influences Attitudes Toward Brands*
David DeFranza, Arul Mishra and Himanshu Mishra

08:00–09:00 *Using BERT for Qualitative Content Analysis in Psychosocial Online Counseling*
Philipp Grandeit, Carolyn Haberkern, Maximiliane Lang, Jens Albrecht and Robert
Lehmann

08:00–09:00 *Swimming with the Tide? Positional Claim Detection across Political Text Types*
Nico Blokker, Erenay Dayanik, Gabriella Lapesa and Sebastian Padó

08:00–09:00 *Does Social Support (Expressed in Post Titles) Elicit Comments in Online Substance
Use Recovery Forums?*
Anietie Andy and Sharath Chandra Guntuku

08:00–09:00 *I miss you babe: Analyzing Emotion Dynamics During COVID-19 Pandemic*
Hui Xian Lynnette Ng, Roy Ka-Wei Lee and Md Rabiul Awal

08:00–09:00 *Assessing population-level symptoms of anxiety, depression, and suicide risk in real
time using NLP applied to social media data*
Alex Fine, Patrick Crutchley, Jenny Blase, Joshua Carroll and Glen Coppersmith

08:00–09:00 *Topic preference detection: A novel approach to understand perspective taking in
conversation*
Michael Yeomans and Alison Wood Brooks

08:00–09:00   *Foreigner-directed speech is simpler than native-directed: Evidence from social media*
Aleksandrs Berdicevskis

08:00–09:00   *Diachronic Embeddings for People in the News*
Felix Hennig and Steven Wilson

08:00–09:00   *Social media data as a lens onto care-seeking behavior among women veterans of the US armed forces*
Kacie Kelly, Alex Fine and Glen Coppersmith

08:00–09:00   *Understanding Weekly COVID-19 Concerns through Dynamic Content-Specific LDA Topic Modeling*
Mohammadzaman Zamani, H. Andrew Schwartz, Johannes Eichstaedt, Sharath Chandra Guntuku, Adithya Virinchipuram Ganesan, Sean Clouston and Salvatore Giorgi

08:00–09:00   *Emoji and Self-Identity in Twitter Bios*
Jinhang Li, Giorgos Longinos, Steven Wilson and Walid Magdy

08:00–09:00   *Analyzing Gender Bias within Narrative Tropes*
Dhruvil Gala, Mohammad Omar Khursheed, Hannah Lerner, Brendan O'Connor and Mohit Iyyer

08:00–09:00   *An Unfair Affinity Toward Fairness: Characterizing 70 Years of Social Biases in B^Hollywood*
Kunal Khadilkar and Ashiqur KhudaBukhsh

09:00–09:15   **Break**

Measuring Linguistic Diversity During COVID-19

Jonathan Dunn
Department of Linguistics
University of Canterbury
Christchurch, New Zealand
jonathan.dunn@canterbury.ac.nz

Tom Coupe
Department of Economics
University of Canterbury
Christchurch, New Zealand
tom.coupe@canterbury.ac.nz

Benjamin Adams
Department of Computer Science and Software Engineering
University of Canterbury
Christchurch, New Zealand
benjamin.adams@canterbury.ac.nz

Abstract

Computational measures of linguistic diversity help us understand the linguistic landscape using digital language data. The contribution of this paper is to calibrate measures of linguistic diversity using restrictions on international travel resulting from the COVID-19 pandemic. Previous work has mapped the distribution of languages using geo-referenced social media and web data. The goal, however, has been to describe these corpora themselves rather than to make inferences about underlying populations. This paper shows that a difference-in-differences method based on the Herfindahl-Hirschman Index can identify the bias in digital corpora that is introduced by non-local populations. These methods tell us *where* significant changes have taken place and whether this leads to increased or decreased diversity. This is an important step in aligning digital corpora like social media with the real-world populations that have produced them.

1 Biases in digital language data

Data from social media and web-crawled sources has been used to map the distribution of both languages (Mocanu et al., 2013; Gonçalves and Sánchez, 2014; Lamanna et al., 2018; Dunn, 2020) and dialects (Eisenstein et al., 2014; Cook and Brinton, 2017; Dunn, 2019b,a; Grieve et al., 2019). This line of research is important because traditional methods have relied on census data and missionary reports (Eberhard et al., 2020; IMB, 2020), both of which are often out-of-date and can be inconsistent across countries. At the same time, we know that digital data sets do not necessarily reflect the underlying linguistic diversity in a country: the actual

population of South Africa, for example, is not accurately represented by tweets from South Africa (Dunn and Adams, 2019).

This becomes an important problem as soon as we try to use computational linguistics to tell us about *people* or *language*. For example, if an application is using Twitter to track sentiment about COVID-19, that tracking is meaningless without good information about how well it represents the population. Or, if an application is using Twitter to study lexical choices, that study depends on a relationship between lexical choices on Twitter and lexical choices more generally. In other words, the more we use digital corpora for scientific purposes, the more we need to control for *bias* in that data. There are four sources of diversity-related bias that we need to take into account.

First, *production bias* occurs when one location (like the US) produces so much digital data that most corpora over-represent that location (Jurgens et al., 2017). For example, by default a corpus of English from the web or Twitter will mostly represent the US and the UK (Kulshrestha et al., 2012). It has been shown that this type of bias can be corrected using population-based sampling (Dunn and Adams, 2020) to enforce the representation of all relevant populations.

Second, *sampling bias* occurs when a subset of the population produces a disproportionate amount of the overall data. This type of bias has been shown to be closely related to economic measures: more wealthy populations produce more digital language per capita (Dunn and Adams, 2019). By default, a corpus will contain more samples representing wealthier members of the population. Thus,

1

Proceedings of the Fourth Workshop on Natural Language Processing and Computational Social Science, pages 1–10
Online, November 20, 2020. ©2020 Association for Computational Linguistics
https://doi.org/10.18653/v1/P17

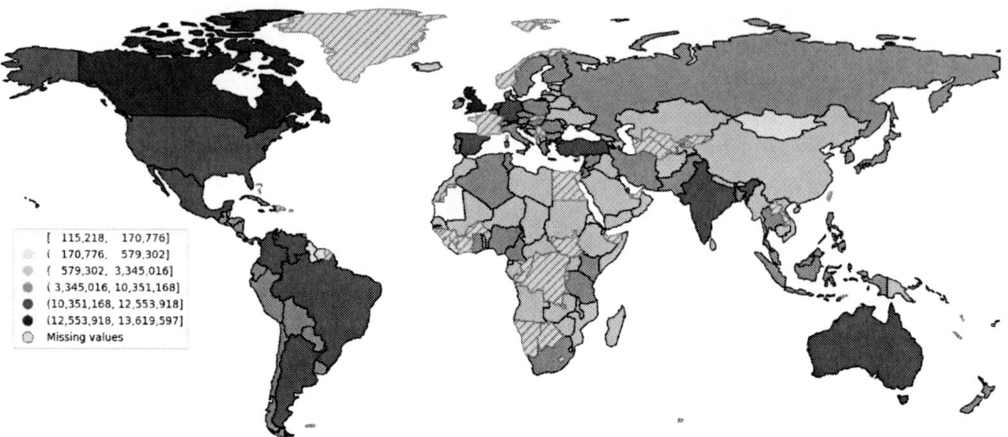

Figure 1: Number of observations per country.

this is similar to production bias, but with a demographic rather than a geographic scope.

Third, *non-local bias* is the problem of over-representing those people *in* a place who are not *from* that place: tourists, aid workers, students, short-term visitors, etc. For example, in countries with low per-capita GDP (i.e., where local populations often lack internet access) digital language data is likely to represent outsiders like aid workers. On the other hand, in countries with large numbers of international tourists (e.g., New Zealand), data sets are likely to instead be contaminated with samples from these tourists.

Fourth, *majority language bias* occurs when a multi-lingual population only uses some of its languages in digital contexts (Lackaff and Moner, 2016). Most often, majority languages like English and French are used online while minority languages are used in face-to-face contexts. The result is that even though an individual may be represented in a corpus, the full range of their linguistic behaviours is *not* represented. This is the only type of bias not quantified in this paper. For example, it is possible that changes in linguistic diversity are caused by a shift in behaviour, rather than a shift in population characteristics.

Of the three sources of bias that we examine here, non-local bias is the most difficult to uncover (Graham et al., 2014; Johnson et al., 2016). We can identify production bias when the amount of data per country exceeds that country's share of the global population. In this sense, the ideal corpus of English would equally represent each country according to the number of English speakers in that country. Within a country, we can measure the amount of sampling bias by looking at how economic measures like GDP and rates of internet access correspond with the amount of data per person. Thus, we could use median income by zip code to ensure that the US is properly represented. But non-local bias is more challenging because we need to know which samples from a place like New Zealand come from those speakers who are only passing through for a short time.

Only with widespread restrictions on international travel during the COVID-19 pandemic do we have access to a collection of digital language from which non-local populations are largely absent (Gössling et al., 2020; Hale et al., 2020). This paper uses changes in linguistic diversity during these travel restrictions, against a historical baseline, to calibrate computational measures that support language and population mapping. This is a part of the larger problem of estimating population characteristics from digital language data.

We start by describing the data used for the experiments in the paper (Section 2), drawn from Twitter over a two-year period. We then explore sources of bias in this data set by looking at production bias and sampling bias (in Section 3) and then developing a baseline of temporal variation in the data (in Section 4). We introduce a measure of geographic linguistic diversity (Section 5). Then we use this measure to find which countries and languages are most contaminated by non-local populations (in Section 6). Finally, we examine the results to find where the linguistic landscape has changed during the COVID-19 pandemic.

Region	N.	Pop	Data
Africa, Southern	12.28m	1.0%	2.0%
Africa, Sub	43.87m	10.1%	7.0%
Africa, North	16.60m	3.4%	2.7%
America, Brazil	10.96m	2.8%	1.8%
America, Central	66.12m	2.9%	10.6%
America, North	24.64m	4.8%	4.0%
America, South	77.79m	2.9%	12.5%
Asia, East	15.88m	22.3%	2.6%
Asia, Central	15.08m	2.7%	2.4%
Asia, South	30.06m	23.3%	4.8%
Asia, Southeast	31.88m	8.4%	5.1%
Europe, East	51.48m	2.4%	8.3%
Europe, Russia	9.38m	2.0%	1.5%
Europe, West	155.74m	5.7%	25.0%
Middle East	36.58m	4.5%	5.9%
Oceania	24.92m	0.8%	4.0%
Total	**623.33m**	**100%**	**100%**

Table 1: Distribution of data by region.

2 Data sources

We draw on Twitter data sampled globally from 10k cities over a 25-month period (July 2018 through August 2020). This city-based collection reduces production bias from the start (as opposed to collecting data by user or search term) because it forces non-central cities to be included. The cities are selected to represent the global population and all retweets are removed. This provides 623 million tweets, distributed across regions as shown in Table 1 with each region's share of the data and of the world's population.

This table provides a clear illustration of production bias. East Asia, for example, accounts for 22.3% of the world's population but only 2.6% of the data. We see the reverse in Western Europe, which provides 25% of the data but only 5.7% of the population. Population-based sampling is an effective method for correcting this bias (Dunn and Adams, 2020), if the goal is to produce a corpus representing the actual distribution of speakers. Our goal here is to find which countries contain data from non-local populations. To do this, we need to find out if the data has a stable geographic distribution that is driven by the underlying population.

The idNet language identification package is used to provide language labels (Dunn, 2020). Any tweet under 40 characters (after cleaning URLs and hashtags) is removed because of reduced identification accuracy below this threshold. The average tweets per month per country is visualized in Figure 1. Because we are looking at change over time by country, the data is binned into potentially small categories (e.g., Nigeria in July 2019). Both the table and the map show that countries in East Asia are under-represented. Thus, we use significance testing *within* countries when looking for change over time.

3 Demographics and language use

The next question is the degree to which the production of this data is driven by underlying populations (potential production bias) and by demographic factors like GDP (potential selection bias). We start, in Figure 3, by looking at the relationship between each country's population and share of the corpus. This expands on the region aggregations in Table 1 by dividing regions into countries. Each country is an observation that is represented by its average monthly data production and several demographic factors. Overall, there is a very significant correlation (Pearson) between population and the amount of data from each country (0.46). Thus, the number of people in a country is an important factor explaining how much data that country produces. While this is significant, however, it also means that there are many other factors that influence the geographic distribution of the data.

To better understand the factors influencing the geographic distribution of the data, we work with three variables: *population*, the number of people in each country; *internet population*, the number of internet users in each country; and *GDP*, a measure of each country's economic output (United Nations, 2011, 2017b,a). Figure 3 shows three regression plots in which these variables (on the y axis) are compared with the average monthly data production per country (given in number of tweets per month on the x axis).

In each case, there is a close relationship between data production and demographics, with several extreme outliers. For *population*, the outliers are China and India. Both are highly populated countries with significantly lower than expected data production (especially China). Both countries have relatively low rates of internet access: 38% for China and 11% for India; this lowers the total population in each country. Thus, although the populations are quite large, most of the population is not able to produce digital language data. For the influence of GDP, the outliers are the US and China.

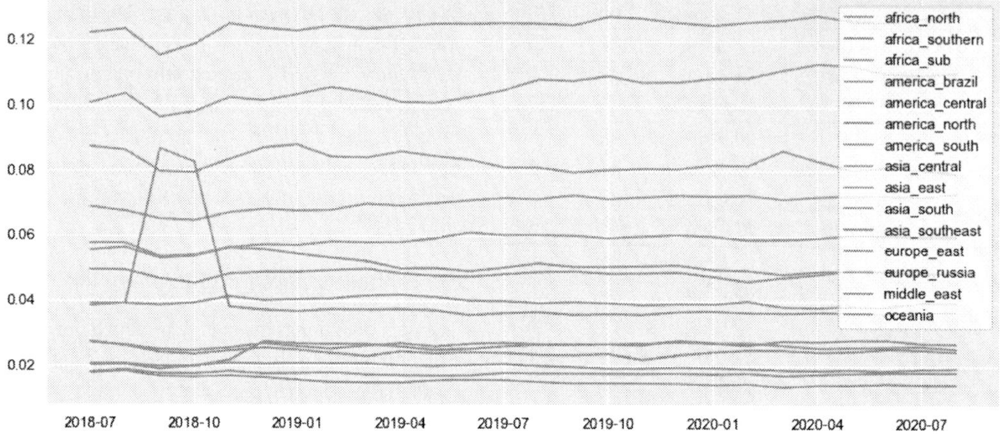

Figure 2: Geographic distribution of data by region by month.

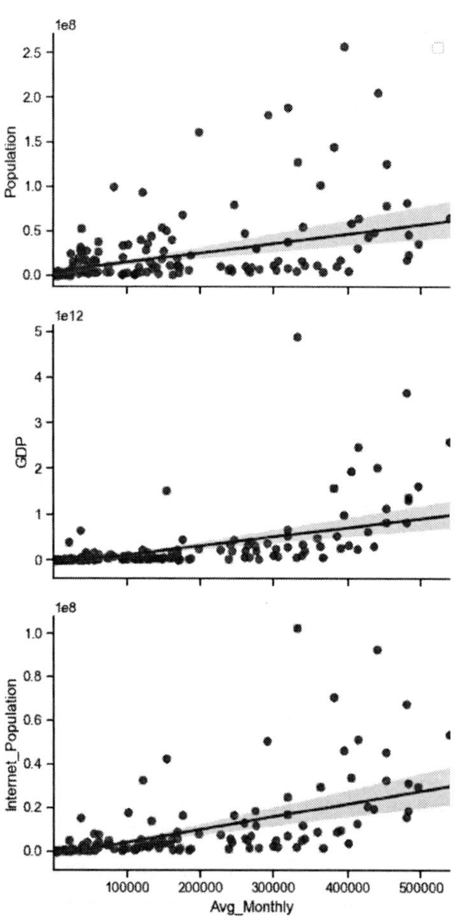

Figure 3: Relationship between data and demographic factors: *Population*, *Internet Access*, and *GDP* (With Outliers Removed).

For the US, in particular, the GDP is quite high: there seems to be a ceiling after which increased GDP is unlikely to influence digital behaviours. Further, that GDP is not evenly distributed across the entire population. For the influence of internet access, the outliers are again China and the US. With a few notable exceptions there is a relatively close relationship between data production and the demographic factors of each country.

With these three outliers removed (the US, China, India), there are very significant correlations between these three variables and the geographic distribution of the data: 0.46 (population), 0.61 (population with internet access), and 0.59 (GDP). This leaves some unexplained production factors. The most obvious missing factor here is social media platforms specific to given countries (e.g., Sina Weibo). These alternative platforms will siphon away enough users to distort the representation of a population given access only to other platforms. Further, Twitter is banned in China: because only some companies are allowed to use it through specific VPNs, the text is not representative of language use in China. Casual users of Twitter will use a VPN through another country which would distort this method of data collection.

Regardless, this section has shown that we can explain a significant portion of the geographic distribution of the data. This is important because we want to describe *populations* by observing *digital corpora*. If there is no relationship between the two in terms of distribution, it is difficult to make such inferences. What we have seen, however, is that there is a very significant relationship. What

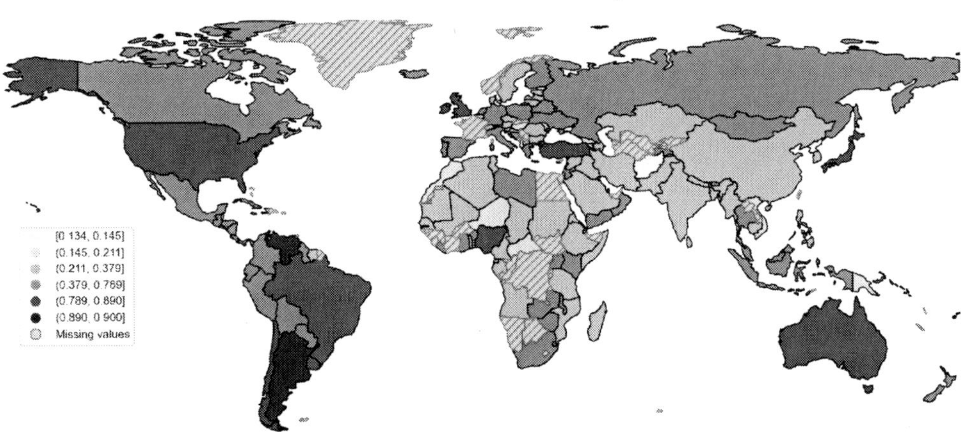

Figure 4: Herfindahl-Hirschman Index of the distribution of languages by country.

is the required threshold for establishing a relationship like this? We should think about this as a metric for evaluating digital corpora: data with a stronger relationship to demographic variables are more representative. The next question is whether this relationship remains stable over time: can we depend on these demographic factors across the entire period?

4 Controlling for temporal variation

The next question is whether these production factors are stable over time. Here we build a baseline for temporal variation: to what degree is the data subject to unrelated fluctuations that will reduce our ability to assign a cause-and-effect relationship to linguistic diversity during travel restrictions?

Although the same collection and processing methods are maintained over the two-year period, there is variation in the total number of observations (tweets) per month. There are many reasons why this might be the case. What matters to us, though, is the relative share of each country. In other words, the population does not change from month to month in the same way that the number of tweets changes. Regardless of the total amount of data collected per month, is the geographic distribution consistent? Figure 2 shows stability over time by representing the relative proportion of observations per region by month. Western Europe is removed for the sake of clarity, as it represents a significantly higher share (roughly 25%). The distribution of samples is consistent over time. The main exception is that, for a two-month period in 2018, there is much more data from Oceania.

We use a t-test to find out if the share of each region is stable over time. If the distribution changes significantly, then it may be hard to determine the cause of any individual change. None of the regions show a significant fluctuation; this is helpful because it shows that there is not random noise in the data that could interfere with measures of linguistic diversity. The difference-in-differences methods we use in Section 8 would control for such noise, but this gives us further confidence. We use a t-test, rather than a time-specific test like Dickey-Fuller, because we are interested in consistency rather than in non-stationarity. These results show that, in the aggregate, the distribution of samples remains constant. But how much variation within individual countries does this region-based measure disguise? To answer this, we look at the same t-test approach by country: do individual countries vary widely in their relative production? No countries show a significant change.

These findings show that we can largely focus on diversity, the distribution of languages within a country by month, rather than on the production of data over month as in Section 3. There is natural variation in the data, of course, and this is taken into account in our later approaches. For example, if we compute the correlation between population and language production (as in Section 3) for each month in isolation, there is no significant difference over time. This stability is important for creating a baseline against which to understand demographic changes during travel restrictions. Because the relationship between demographics and the data set remains stable, we can focus specifically on changes in linguistic diversity.

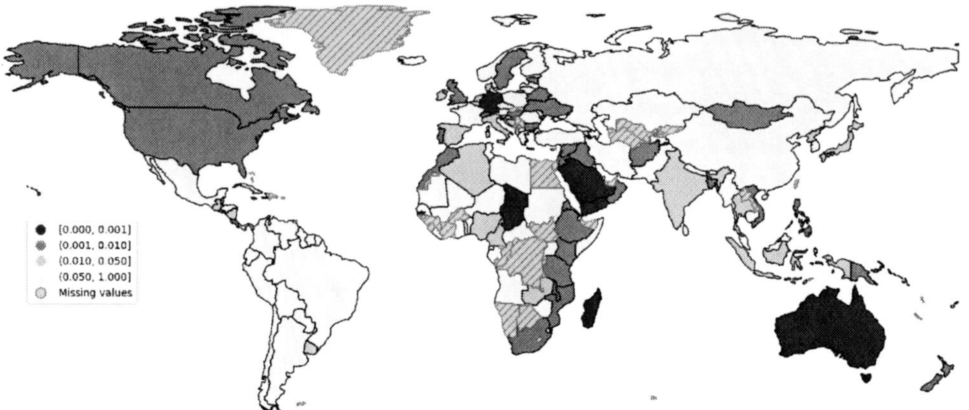

Figure 5: Countries with significant change in linguistic diversity during travel restrictions.

5 Measuring linguistic diversity

Linguistic diversity is an important part of accurate language and population mapping. The goal is to have a single measure that can tell us how much language contact is taking place and which communities are multi-lingual. To do this we must generalize across specific languages: linguistic diversity in the US might involve English and Spanish, but it might involve Portuguese and Spanish in Brazil.

We measure linguistic diversity as a probability distribution over languages for each country. Drawing on previous work on short-sample language identification, this paper includes 464 languages across 157 countries. For each country, then, we have a relatively accurate identification of which languages are used on Twitter. Given this probability distribution for each country, we compare countries using the Herfindahl-Hirschman Index (HHI) as shown in Figure 4. The HHI was developed in economics to measure market concentration: the more of a given industry is dominated by a small number of companies, the higher the HHI (Hirschman, 1945). The measure is derived using the sum of the square of shares, in this case the share of each language in each country. The higher the HHI (the darker red) for a country, the more one language dominates the linguistic landscape.

Thus, the HHI is higher when the distribution is centered around just a few languages. For example, in Table 2 we focus on three countries that show a range of linguistic diversity: Israel, India, and the US. Israel has the lowest HHI (0.207). Looking at the share of the top five languages, we see roughly equal usage of three languages (in the 20s)

	ISR	IND	USA
HHI	0.207	0.356	0.852
L1	27.3%	50.8%	92.3%
L2	25.9%	30.8%	2.6%
L3	23.5%	3.4%	0.6%
L4	7.5%	2.5%	0.6%
L5	5.3%	1.4%	0.4%

Table 2: Sample language distributions by country.

followed by two significant minority languages. This lower HHI reflects the fact that a number of languages are being used together: no language has a monopoly. On the other extreme, the US has one of the highest values for HHI (0.852). There is one very dominant language (92%), one significant minority language (2.6%), and a number of very insignificant languages. English has a metaphoric monopoly on the linguistic landscape of the US.

Figure 4 shows linguistic diversity across the world: lighter countries (like Israel) have a mix of languages while darker countries (like the US) are mostly monolingual. There are many linguistic landscapes around the world, ranging from multi-lingual to monolingual. This Figure 4 is a baseline representation, averaged across the entire time period (July 2018 to August 2020). It is possible that this averaged representation disguises temporal fluctuations. We have already seen that there are only a few changes in the share of data per country per month, and no significant change in the relationship between the data set and demographic factors like GDP. The question here is whether there is arbitrary variation in the linguistic diversity per country

6

Figure 6: Increasing vs. decreasing HHI during travel restrictions.

per month. In other words, if Israel becomes significantly more diverse every three months, it will be difficult to find out what is causing those changes. We use a a t-test for the mean of each country to determine if each country's diversity is actually a single group. There are no significant fluctuations across the period as a whole.

6 Finding non-local populations

To what degree do countries change during travel restrictions resulting from COVID-19? We have a measure of diversity (the HHI) and data collected by month. The basic approach is to create two groups of samples: first, months during the pandemic (March through August, 2020); second, months not during the pandemic (March through August, 2019). These two groups are aligned by month so that seasonal fluctuations are taken into account (e.g., tourism high season in February for New Zealand and in July for Italy). Given these two groups of samples, we use a t-test for two independent samples to determine whether these groups are, in fact, different. If we reject the null hypothesis, it means that linguistic diversity during travel restrictions is significantly different than the seasonally-adjusted baseline.

The results show that 70 countries have a changed linguistic landscape during the pandemic. This is visualized in Figure 5, with p-values classed into highly significant (under 0.001), very significant (under 0.01), and significant (under 0.05). We see, for example, that the US and Canada undergo significant change, but not Mexico and South America. There are clear geographic patterns in linguistic change: North but not Central or South America; East Africa but not West Africa; South/east Asia but not East Asia; Europe but not Russia. We will examine in more detail how and why the linguistic landscape changes in Section 7.

These significant changes during international travel restrictions show that our measure (the HHI) and our data (tweets) offer a meaningful representation of underlying populations. If the data did not represent populations, we would not see the relationships examined in Section 3. There are no random fluctuations in the distribution of the data across countries or in the distribution of languages within countries. At the same time, given a massive social change (i.e., the COVID-19 pandemic), the measure clearly identifies changes in the linguistic landscape. Thus, the measure is both precise (not disguised by noise) and accurate (observing change where we expect it). The key point is that the change in diversity during the COVID-19 period is identifiable against the background noise.

A country's linguistic landscape could change by becoming more diverse (i.e., with more languages) or by becoming less diverse (i.e., with fewer languages). Which is causing the significant changes that we are observing? Figure 6 distinguishes between countries with an increasing HHI (becoming more monolingual) and a decreasing HHI (becoming more multilingual). We can think about two contexts in which this change can take place: a country like India might look more multilingual because non-local tourists who speak English are no longer creating noise in the data; or, a country like South Africa might look more monolingual

Country	Normal	COVID
Eritrea	63.16%	41.94%
Samoa	45.00%	30.18%
Cabo Verde	27.78%	16.63%
Equatorial Guinea	33.08%	24.40%
Madagascar	53.08%	44.87%
Kiribati	31.10%	23.56%
Tanzania	34.43%	27.35%
Mongolia	30.32%	23.52%
Chad	45.48%	39.71%
Sao Tome	12.57%	7.14%
Yemen	14.44%	9.20%

Table 3: Major reductions in English.

Country	Language	Normal	COVID
Belarus	Russian	69.05%	66.13%
Ukraine	Russian	54.60%	50.06%
Lithuania	Russian	20.09%	15.72%
Latvia	Russian	10.43%	8.26%
Algeria	Arabic	51.56%	46.77%
Morocco	Arabic	33.75%	28.53%
Israel	Arabic	27.75%	26.08%
Tunisia	Arabic	24.24%	19.65%
Bhutan	Arabic	6.25%	2.55%
Moldova	Arabic	2.71%	0.79%

Table 4: Major reductions in Russian and Arabic.

Country	Language	Normal	COVID
SAU	Arabic	70.10%	81.87%
SAU	English	12.18%	7.35%
SAU	Turkish	4.34%	2.12%
SAU	Greek	2.55%	1.65%
BEL	French	28.64%	34.72%
BEL	English	31.01%	26.83%
BEL	Dutch	27.08%	25.12%
BEL	German	2.26%	1.93%
BEL	Portuguese	1.51%	1.68%

Table 5: Changing landscape in Saudi Arabia and Belgium.

because its own English-speaking citizens abroad are returning home. The flow of international travellers changes the balance of locals and non-locals in both directions (leaving and coming home).

7 Identifying out-of-place populations

Our task now is to use these changes during travel restrictions to identify which populations are out-of-place in ordinary times. In other words, if India has decreasing English use during the pandemic period, then we know that English is over-represented in the country as a result of non-local populations. We find these languages by repeating the comparison of pandemic vs. normal periods per country per month, but now we look at the share of individual languages rather than the HHI (in countries with a significant change). We are only interested in languages which account for at least 1% of a country's usage. Less commonly used languages may be changing significantly but have less influence on a country's overall linguistic landscape.

We start by looking at countries where the use of English falls dramatically during the pandemic period, in Table 3. These dramatic reductions suggest that much of the population represented on Twitter is non-local: there is a change from 63% to 42% in Eritrea and from 53% to 44% English use in Madagascar. If the local population was well-represented on Twitter, we would not see this dramatic reduction in an international language. Thus, here we see an example of how digital data is biased towards non-local populations in countries where the local population has reduced internet access.

The influence of non-local populations returning home is shown for Russian and Arabic in Table 4. We see a major reduction in the use of Russian in countries like Ukraine that have had a strong Russian influence (from 54% to 50%). In both Ukraine and Belarus, there are other social and political factors that could influence the shift, since much of the population is bilingual (e.g., bilingual speakers in Ukraine putting aside the use of Russian for political purposes). But we also see similar changes in the use of Arabic. In Algeria it falls from 51% to 46% and in Morocco from 33% to 28%. These countries do not have the same political factors as Ukraine and Belarus, thus providing a clearer example of the exodus of non-local populations.

We get a different view by looking at the change of languages *within* a country, as with Belgium and Saudi Arabia in Table 5. In Saudi Arabia we see a rise in Arabic at the expense of English, Turkish, and Greek. This reflects the exodus of non-local tourists and workers; but it also likely reflects the return of Saudi Arabians from countries like Algeria and Morocco that is suggested by Table 4. In Belgium, we see a rise in French at the expense of English, Dutch, German, and Portuguese. This is a reflection of a reduction in non-local tourists.

However, we see the opposite effect of tourists

Country	Language	Normal	COVID
NZL	English	86.26%	84.13%
NZL	Spanish	2.13%	3.37%
NZL	Portuguese	2.30%	2.82%
NZL	Indonesian	0.89%	1.27%
AUS	English	89.51%	87.45%
AUS	Portuguese	1.83%	2.52%
AUS	Spanish	1.52%	2.08%
AUS	Japanese	0.99%	1.32%

Table 6: Changing landscape in Oceania.

leaving when we look at New Zealand and Australia, two countries which have had closed borders (Table 6). Here there is a *reduction* in English usage within English-majority countries that takes place when international tourists stop arriving. The situation here is that there are so many English-speaking tourists (i.e., from the US and UK) that local immigrant languages like Spanish and Portuguese (part of the long-term local population) are drowned out by non-local tourists using English. Another possible explanation is that immigrant populations are increasingly using Twitter to communicate with non-local populations (e.g., with family and friends in their previous country).

8 Sources of Change

This paper has shown that there is a significant change in the linguistic diversity of many countries *during* the travel restrictions caused by COVID-19. But to what degree are these changes *related* to the travel restrictions themselves? For example, we could imagine a population that is changing over time which we just happen to observe in mid-change. It could be the case that a country has been becoming less diverse over the past decade because of fewer incoming immigrants; the approach taken so far in this paper would misinterpret such macro-trends to be a direct result of COVID-19.

We use a difference-in-differences method (Card and Krueger, 1994) to correct for this. The basic idea behind a difference-in-differences approach is to conduct a *natural experiment* with a control group (here, data from 2018) and an effect group (here, data from 2020) differentiated by time. We have three months (July, August, September) that are shared across 2018, 2019, and 2020. So, using the same methods described above, we find out which countries have a significant change between 2019 and 2020. This is the period that takes place

during travel restrictions. If travel restrictions influence linguistic diversity, we would expect such influence to take place during this period. We then find out if the countries which show a significant change in 2020 also show a significant change from 2018 to 2019. This provides a baseline: removing any country whose linguistic diversity was already in the process of changing.

Over this three-month period (July through September), 58 countries show a change in linguistic diversity during the pandemic. This is a smaller number than the main results reported above for two reasons: (i) the time span is shorter, giving less robust results and (ii) this particular time span came after some travel had resumed. Of these 58 countries that show a significant change in diversity, most (38) show no difference at all in the baseline period before the pandemic. Another eight show a much greater difference during the COVID-19 period (e.g., p-values of 0.03 vs 0.004 for baseline and COVID-19, respectively). This means that the pandemic has either created or has significantly contributed to 79.3% of the cases of changing linguistic diversity. The remaining 20.7% of changes, then, must have been created by macro-trends like immigration or changes in bilingual behaviour. The main conclusion from this difference-in-differences examination, however, is that most of these changes can be specifically connected to COVID-19.

9 Conclusions

The goal of this paper is to validate measures of linguistic diversity using changes in underlying populations during the COVID-19 pandemic. We have shown that there is a significant relationship between our data and the underlying population. Thus, what we are observing (tweets) can tell us about the people we want to study. At the same time, both the distribution of the data across countries and the distribution of languages within countries are stable. Thus, the data does not have random fluctuations that will get in the way. Using the HHI as a measure of diversity, there is a significant change in the linguistic landscape of 70 countries against a seasonally-adjusted baseline. This reflects non-local populations (e.g., the impact of tourists leaving a country or short-term visitors returning to their own countries). These results validate a measure of linguistic diversity that is based on digital language data and shows that we can correct for the bias introduced by non-local populations.

References

David Card and Alan Krueger. 1994. Minimum wages and employment: A case study of the fast-food industry in new jersey and pennsylvania. *American Economic Review*, 84.

Paul Cook and Laurel J Brinton. 2017. Building and evaluating web corpora representing national varieties of English. *Language Resources and Evaluation*, 51(3):643–662.

Jonathan Dunn. 2019a. Global Syntactic Variation in Seven Languages: Towards a Computational Dialectology. *Frontiers in Artificial Intelligence*, 2:1–15.

Jonathan Dunn. 2019b. Modeling Global Syntactic Variation in English Using Dialect Classification. In *Proceedings of NAACL 2019 Sixth Workshop on NLP for Similar Languages, Varieties and Dialects*, pages 42–53. Association for Computational Linguistics.

Jonathan Dunn. 2020. Mapping languages: the Corpus of Global Language Use. *Language Resources and Evaluation*.

Jonathan Dunn and Benjamin Adams. 2019. Mapping languages and demographics with georeferenced corpora. In *Geocomputation 2019*.

Jonathan Dunn and Benjamin Adams. 2020. Geographically-balanced gigaword corpora for 50 language varieties. In *Proceedings of The 12th Language Resources and Evaluation Conference*, pages 2528–2536. European Language Resources Association.

David M. Eberhard, Gary F. Simons, and Charles D. Fennig. 2020. *Ethnologue: Languages of the World. Twenty-third edition.* SIL International, Dallas, TX.

Jacob Eisenstein, Brendan O'Connor, Noah A Smith, and Eric P Xing. 2014. Diffusion of lexical change in social media. *PloS one*, 9(11):e113114.

Bruno Gonçalves and David Sánchez. 2014. Crowdsourcing dialect characterization through Twitter. *PloS one*, 9(11):e112074.

Stefan Gössling, Daniel Scott, and C Michael Hall. 2020. Pandemics, tourism and global change: a rapid assessment of COVID-19. *Journal of Sustainable Tourism*, pages 1–20.

Mark Graham, Scott Hale, and Devin Gaffney. 2014. Where in the World are You? Geolocation and Language Identification on Twitter. *The Professional Geographer*, 66(4):568–578.

Jack Grieve, Chris Montgomery, Andrea Nini, Akira Murakami, and Diansheng Guo. 2019. Mapping lexical dialect variation in British English using Twitter. *Frontiers in Artificial Intelligence*, 2:11.

Thomas Hale, Anna Petherick, Toby Phillips, and Samuel Webster. 2020. Variation in government responses to COVID-19. *Blavatnik school of government working paper*, 31.

Albert O Hirschman. 1945. *National power and the structure of foreign trade.* Univ of California Press.

IMB. 2020. *People Groups Data, 2020-08.* International Missionary Board: Global Research, Richmond, VA.

Isaac L Johnson, Subhasree Sengupta, Johannes Schöning, and Brent Hecht. 2016. The geography and importance of localness in geotagged social media. In *Proceedings of the 2016 CHI Conference on Human Factors in Computing Systems*, pages 515–526. Association for Computing Machinery.

David Jurgens, Yulia Tsvetkov, and Dan Jurafsky. 2017. Incorporating Dialectal Variability for Socially Equitable Language Identification. In *Proceedings of the Annual Meeting of the Association for Computational Linguistics*, pages 51–57. Association for Computational Linguistics.

Juhi Kulshrestha, Farshad Kooti, Ashkan Nikravesh, and Krishna P Gummadi. 2012. Geographic dissection of the Twitter network. In *Sixth international AAAI conference on weblogs and social media*, pages 202–209. Association for the Advancement of Artificial Intelligence.

Derek Lackaff and William J Moner. 2016. Local languages, global networks: Mobile design for minority language users. In *Proceedings of the 34th ACM International Conference on the Design of Communication*, pages 1–9. Association for Computing Machinery.

Fabio Lamanna, Maxime Lenormand, María Henar Salas-Olmedo, Gustavo Romanillos, Bruno Gonçalves, and José J Ramasco. 2018. Immigrant community integration in world cities. *PloS one*, 13(3):e0191612.

Delia Mocanu, Andrea Baronchelli, Nicola Perra, Bruno Gonçalves, Qian Zhang, and Alessandro Vespignani. 2013. The Twitter of Babel: Mapping world languages through microblogging platforms. *PloS one*, 8(4):e61981.

United Nations. 2011. *Economic and Social Statistics on the Countries and Territories of the World, with Particular Reference to Childrens Well-Being.* United Nations Children's Fund.

United Nations. 2017a. *National Accounts Estimates of Main Aggregates. Per Capita GDP at Current Prices in US Dollars.* United Nations Statistics Division.

United Nations. 2017b. *World Population Prospects: The 2017 Revision, DVD Edition.* United Nations Population Division.

Using BERT for Qualitative Content Analysis in Psycho-Social Online Counseling

Philipp Grandeit, Carolyn Haberkern, Maximiliane Lang,
Jens Albrecht, Robert Lehmann
Nuremberg Institute of Technology Georg Simon Ohm, Nuremberg, Germany
`{grandeitph64509, haberkernca76525, langma76539,`
`albrechtje, lehmannro}@th-nuernberg.de`

Abstract

Qualitative content analysis is a systematic method commonly used in the social sciences to analyze textual data from interviews or online discussions. However, this method usually requires high expertise and manual effort because human coders need to read, interpret, and manually annotate text passages. This is especially true if the system of categories used for annotation is complex and semantically rich. Therefore, qualitative content analysis could benefit greatly from automated coding. In this work, we investigate the usage of machine learning-based text classification models for automatic coding in the area of psycho-social online counseling. We developed a system of over 50 categories to analyze counseling conversations, labeled over 10.000 text passages manually, and evaluated the performance of different machine learning-based classifiers against human coders.

1 Introduction

1.1 Psycho-Social Online Counseling

Online counseling has developed into a full-fledged psycho-social counseling service in Germany since the 1990s. Today, people can get advice on a wide variety of psycho-social topics in web forums and dedicated text-based counseling platforms. Online counseling is provided by psycho-social professionals who have received special training in this method. Similar to face-to-face psycho-social counseling, some aspects are known to make up high-quality online counseling, but there is few empirical evidence for special impact factors (Fukkink et al 2009, Dowling & Rickwood 2014).

Due to the complexity of the content, quantitative approaches have not been able to analyze the meaning and significance of methodical patterns in large numbers of consulting communications (Navarro et al. 2019). It is, however, possible to understand and describe the meaning of online counseling content with qualitative approaches (Bambling et al. 2008, Gatti et al. 2016).

This allows linking certain interventions of the counselors to the reactions of the clients on a case-by-case basis. But generalized statements on causal relationships are not possible with the small number of cases from qualitative studies (Ersahin & Hanley 2017).

An analysis of large numbers of counseling conversations using qualitative social research tools would help to better understand how successful online counseling works. Few related studies on these topics are available. Althoff et al. (2016) defined different models to measure general conversation strategies like adaptability, dealing with ambiguity, creativity, making progress or change in perspective and illustrated their applicability on a corpus of data from SMS counseling. Pérez-Rosas et al. (2019) analyzed the quality of consulting communications based on video recordings. Their automatic classifier used linguistic aspects of the content and could predict counseling quality with relatively good accuracy. However, neither of the mentioned approaches had the intention to recognize the meaning of individual phrases even though this deep understanding is crucial to eliminate weaknesses in the education of online counselors (Luitgaarden et al. 2016, Niuewboer et al. 2014). In addition, systems could be developed to provide online advisors with practical suggestions for improving their work.

1.2 Qualitative Content Analysis

Qualitative social research is a generic term for various research approaches. It attempts to gain a better understanding of people's social realities and to draw attention to recurring processes, patterns of

Proceedings of the Fourth Workshop on Natural Language Processing and Computational Social Science, pages 11–23
Online, November 20, 2020. ©2020 Association for Computational Linguistics
https://doi.org/10.18653/v1/P17

interpretation, and structural characteristics (Kergel, 2018).

One such research approach deals with the content analysis of texts, the so-called qualitative content analysis according to Mayring (2015). It is a central source of scientific knowledge in qualitative social research. It tries to determine the subjective meaning of contents in texts. For this purpose, categories are formed based on known scientific theories on the topic and the discursive examination of the content. The definitions of those categories along with representative text passages are summarized in a codebook.

Then, human coders are coached in using the codebook. The coaching process and the implementation of the coding require high human expertise and manual effort because the coders must read, interpret, and annotate each text passage. Thus, qualitative studies can only be applied to a limited number of texts. Furthermore, it is hardly possible to define the categories so precisely that all coders find identical results, as human language is inherently ambiguous and its interpretation always partly subjective.

Machine learning could be a solution to the dilemma: If a trained model was able to categorize parts of the conversations according to a given codebook with similar accuracy as a human, the time-consuming text analysis could be automated.

1.3 Machine Learning for Qualitative Content Analysis

Previous studies have shown that supervised machine learning is generally suitable for qualitative content analysis (Crowston e.a. 2010, Scharkow 2013). However, these studies used only a few categories that could be distinguished relatively good, e.g. news categories like sports and business.

Online counseling, in contrast, is a complex domain. A detailed system of categories is necessary to identify impactful patterns in counseling conversations. Additionally, many categories such as "Empathy" or "Compassion" are quite similar in terms of the words used and can only be distinguished if the model is able to somehow "understand" the meaning of the texts.

Recent neural models have drastically outperformed previous approaches for sophisticated problems like sentiment analysis and emotion detection (Howard&Ruder 2018, Devlin e.a. 2018, Chatterjee e.a. 2019). We wanted to investigate if these models can be used for qualitative content analysis of online counseling conversations.

1.4 Research questions / Contribution

Our *first research question* is whether it is possible to train a model to identify psycho-social codes with a human-like precision. It also needs to be clarified whether a certain machine learning approach is particularly well suited for certain topics.

It is assumed that this training does not work equally well with all codes of the codebook. Therefore, *the second question* is which characteristics codes must have in order to be learned particularly well or particularly poorly.

In social science research, the discussion of different assessments of text passages is an important part of the scientific process. Therefore, the analysis of codes incorrectly assigned by a model is an important part of this work. The *third research question* is, therefore: What differences can be observed between the machine and human coding of text passages? If the deviations are plausible, they can be perceived as enriching the discursive process.

1.5 Methodology and Structure of the Paper

For the experimental evaluation, the social scientists in our interdisciplinary team created a codebook consisting of over 50 fine-grained categories and labeled over 10.000 text sequences of psycho-social counseling conversations (described in Section 2). The computer scientists then trained and evaluated a support-vector machine and different state-of-the-art models (e.g. ULMFit and BERT) on the provided data set (Section 3). Finally, the team investigated how human coders from the social sciences perform in comparison to the BERT model on a subset of the data (Section 4).

2 Creating the Data Set

Online forums for psycho-social counseling provide a good basis for an empirical evaluation because they contain large amounts of publicly accessible data. For our study, we used posts from a German site for parent counseling. Here, parents who have problems in bringing up their children are seeking advice. Possible topics are, for example, drug abuse by the child or inadequate school performance. A user can start a new thread with a problem description. Professional counselors reply and discuss solution approaches with the initial

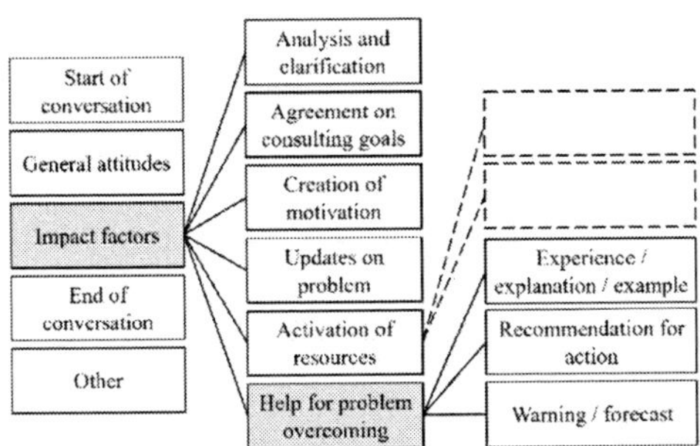

Figure 1: Illustration of the codebook with an exemplary breakdown of the categories

user and others. Thus, each thread contains a series of posts with questions and suggestions about the initially described problem. Since we are especially interested in counseling patterns, we focused on the posts of professional counselors in our analysis.

2.1 Development of the Codebook

Based on existing scientific theories (Fukkink et al 2009, Dowling & Rickwood 2014) on online counseling and first analyses of the text content, a first version of the codebook was created. The various aspects expected in counseling conversations were mapped to a logical hierarchical structure (see Figure 1). The top-level covers general counseling aspects, such as "General attitudes" or "Impact factors". On the intermediate level, these aspects were distinguished more finely, e.g. "Help for problem overcoming". The categories at the lowest level are the ones to be used for the annotation of the text passages, such as "Recommendation for action" or "Warning / forecast".

The different codes were defined as precisely as possible and provided with typical examples. The team of coders applied this codebook to the counseling texts in several turns and iteratively improved the codebook. The final version consists of 51 granular categories (see Appendix A).

2.2 Data Labeling

Based on the codebook described in Section 2.1, a team of coding social scientists manually labeled over 10.000 text sequences in 336 threads. Such a sequence can consist of only a few words (e.g. a greeting) or even multiple sentences (e.g. a recommended action). Sequences, however, do not overlap, i.e. each word should be part of only one labeled sequence. See Figure 2 to get an idea.

Figure 2: Example of three labeled sequences. The original texts are in German.

In the end, we obtained a heavily imbalanced data set: The average number of samples per category is about 200, but the numbers vary greatly (see Appendix A for more details). For some categories in the area "Impact factors", e.g. "Evaluation / understanding / calming" or "Experience / explanation / example" we obtained over 1000 samples, whereas other categories including "Change" or "Suggestion to put oneself in a problem situation physically" are barely represented. Such an unequal distribution of the frequencies of single codes is not unusual in the social sciences. Since there is no statistical analysis in qualitative research, this is usually not a problem. There are even some research approaches that consider the analysis of very rare codes, in particular, to be extremely insightful (Glaser 2017).

2.3 Data Preparation and Preprocessing

After labeling, we tested the impact of common preprocessing techniques like lemmatization and the removal of usernames. It turned out that both, the support-vector machine classifier as well as the BERT model work best without any of these techniques. Therefore, we used the labeled data without such modifications.

Sequence Length (WordPiece Tokens)	Number of Text Sequences in the Data Set
0-64	8846
65-128	814
129-256	310
257-512	101
>512	16

Table 1: Distribution of text sequence lengths (in WordPiece tokens) in the data set.

However, the BERT model can only process fixed-length sequences consisting of at most 512 subword units called WordPiece tokens (Vaswani et al., 2017). Thus, we restricted the sequence length for all training data. We decided to work with a limit of only 256 WordPiece tokens. This value provides a good trade-off between performance and resource consumption in our setting. Longer sequences yield potentially more accurate results but generate a high overhead because all sequences must be padded to the specified length. Since only a little more than 1% of the complete data samples contain more than 256 WordPiece tokens, we did not lose much information (cf. Table 1). Instead, the trade-off in length allowed using higher batch sizes and faster training.

To make the results of the different classifiers comparable and to take the data set imbalance into account, a stratified 70-30-train test split was performed on the data set. This results in a training data set with 7169 samples and a test data set with 3072 samples in total. See Appendix A for the number of samples in each category.

3 Model-Based Classification of Psycho-Social Text Sequences

As a result of the created codebook and the collected data, our classification task consists of classifying psycho-social text sequences into one of 51 categories. For the training of the classifiers, the data set described in the previous section with 7169 samples is used. The created models are then evaluated against the 3072 samples in our test data set.

3.1 Support-Vector Machine as a Baseline

The support-vector machine (SVM) is a commonly used classifier due to being lightweight, benefitting from fast training times, and still achieving good results in text classification tasks (Aggarwal, 2018, pp. 12). Therefore, the SVM was chosen as a baseline model. The prepared data was transformed into TF-IDF vectors (bag-of-words) for training and evaluation (Aggarwal, 2018, pp. 24-26).

The model was implemented using the scikit-learn library. The hyperparameters used were chosen according to the results of our hyperparameter tuning. Apart from the default parameters of the TF-IDF-vectorizer, a max_df-value of 0.5 and a min_df-value of 0 was used. Additionally, the inverse-document-frequency reweighting was enabled and unigrams, as well as bigrams, were considered. The support-vector classifier itself used a sigmoid kernel with the gamma value set to "scale", a C-value of 10, and enabled probability estimates which internally enables 5-fold cross-validation.

The SVM achieved a total accuracy of 68.8% on the test data (cf. Table 2). Due to the heavily imbalanced data set, however, the total accuracy is not a good indicator of the model's performance. Thus,

Metric	SVM	BERT
Accuracy	68.8%	75.8%
Macro F1 score	39.7%	29.2%
Weighted F1 score	68.0%	74.4%

Table 2: Evaluation metrics on the test data set

we also calculated the macro and weighted F1 scores. The SVM achieves a weighted F1 score of 68.0% (close to the accuracy) and a macro F1 score of 39.7%. The low macro F1 indicates, that classes with little support are frequently misclassified.

A detailed analysis of the results shows that the SVM achieves quite good results in categories with a large number of training samples. For instance, an F1 score of 76.2 % is achieved in the category "Experience / explanation / example" with 1398 training and 599 test sequences. Furthermore, simple sequences that only contain few keywords, such as greeting phrases in the category "Start of conversation", can also be identified quite well, even though only a few training samples exist. In particular, the category "General salutation" achieves an F1 score of 75.0% while only having 22 training and 9 test samples. More complex categories, such as the expression of "Empathy for others", however, achieve lower F1 scores of 59.8% even with a relatively high number of 118 training and 51 test samples. Other categories like "Warning / forecast" achieve even lower F1 scores of only 29.3% even though having 71 training and 30 test samples.

3.2 BERT as Advanced Classifier

BERT is a multi-layer bidirectional Transformer encoder based on the original Transformer implementation described in Vaswani et al. (2017). BERT is typically pre-trained on two unsupervised learning tasks. After the pre-training, the model can be fine-tuned according to the downstream task (Vaswani et al., 2017).

For the classification task in our approach, we used the BertForSequenceClassification implementation from the Hugging Face's Transformers library (Wolf et al., 2019) that combines the BERT Transformer model with a sequence classification head on top (Hugging Face, 2020).

In total, we tested thirteen pre-trained BERT models. Among the ten tested German language models, the results varied between a weighted F1 score of 69.3% and 74.4% on the test data set, whereby the best result was achieved with the pre-trained uncased language model of the Bavarian State Library (DBMDZ, 2019). The three multilingual models achieved weighted F1 scores as high as 71.0% with the pre-trained language model by DeepPavlov (DeepPavlov, n. d.).

All of the following analyses are, therefore, based on the best performing DBMDZ BERT model.

The hyperparameters used for the fine-tuning were taken from the original BERT publication (Devlin e.a., 2018). Since we are using text sequences with a length of 256 WordPiece tokens, a batch size value of no more than 16 was possible due to GPU memory limitations. Larger models, especially multi-lingual models, even only allowed a batch size of 8. Further testing has shown that the best results can be achieved with a learning rate of 2e-5 and 4 epochs.

3.3 Analyzing the Classification Results

Table 2 shows the different evaluation metrics for both, the SVM and the best BERT classifier.

The low macro F1 score with 29.2% of the BERT classifier compared to the 39.7% of the SVM classifier shows that the BERT classifier performs significantly worse on classes with few samples than the SVM classifier. The result of the weighted F1 score of 74.4% of the BERT model compared to the 68.0% of the SVM model, however, indicates that the BERT classifier outperforms the SVM if the whole data set is considered.

Category	F1 score		Support (Training)
	SVM	BERT	
Other introduction	27.3%	11.8%	37
Activation of resources (professional level)	43.2%	42.1%	49
Wish	63.8%	75.9%	80
Empathy for others	59.8%	49.5%	118
Evaluation / understanding / calming	59.0%	67.0%	1136
Experience / explanation / example	76.2%	83.1%	1398

Table 3: Extract of the classification report

Table 3 shows an extract from the classification report. In general, the BERT classifier improves in its performance with the increase in available training samples for each class.

In specific categories, such as "Empathy for others", this observation is not true. Categories with this behavior often contain previously mentioned category-specific keywords or phrases which is why the simple bag-of-words approach outperforms the more complex BERT techniques from a statistical point of view. A detailed analysis of the misclassified sequences by the BERT model, however, has shown that the classification of these sequences is not inherently wrong but rather shows suitable alternative affiliations to categories. This behavior is examined in greater detail in Section 3.6.

3.4 Examining other Classification Models

In addition to BERT, other classification models, such as DistilBERT (Sanh et al., 2019), XLM-RoBERTa (Conneau et al., 2019), XLM (Lample and Conneau, 2019), and ULMFit (Howard and Ruder, 2018) were examined in our study as well.

Classification Model	Weighted F1 score
SVM (baseline)	68.0%
BERT (best model)	74.4%
DistilBERT	70.4%
XLM-RoBERTa	70.5%
XLM	65.1%
ULMFit	71.2%

Table 4: Weighted F1 scores of all evaluated classification models

Table 4 shows the best weighted F1 scores of each model. The DistilBERT model performs around 4% worse than the best BERT model on our test data set. This difference lies around the range described by the authors of the DistilBERT paper (Sanh et al., 2019). In addition to that, both the XLM-RoBERTa and XLM models also perform worse than the best BERT classifier. Apart from the Transformer approaches, the bidirectional RNN model called ULMFit was also analyzed. The results show that the different Transformer models as well as the ULMFit model generally perform quite similar on our classification task, except for the XLM model that performs even worse than the simple SVM approach.

3.5 Explaining the Classifiers

Since predictions of BERT, or Transformer models in general, are often untransparent and difficult to

Expert assessment	Number of Samples	Percentage
(I) Both, actual and predicted label would fit	62	32.4%
(II) Predicted label fits better than actual label	49	25.7%
(III) Similar choice of words between actual and predicted classes	29	15.2%
(IV) Sequence contains keywords from other classes	16	8.4%
(V) Assignment cannot be explained by the experts	14	7.3%
(VI) Incorrect sequence	12	6.3%
(VII) Special sequence (uncommon words; not enough context)	6	3.1%
(VIII) Multiple sentences with multiple categories	3	1.6%

Table 5: Expert assessment of incorrectly classified text sequences

justify, different approaches, such as LIME (Ribeiro et al., 2016) or Attention Flow (Abnar and Zuidema, 2020), can be used to generate model insights.

While LIME takes a retrospective approach that can be applied to any classification model, Attention Flow tries to visualize the actual attention maps of Transformer models. Both approaches provide insights that can be used to explain the classification predictions of the models. Since we want to generate model insights regardless of the approach used to create the model, we decided to use LIME as our analyzing tool of choice.

For example, the analysis of the sentence "Have you ever spoken to the kindergarten teachers?" (cf. original German sentence in Figure 3) helps to further understand the model. Originally, the sequence was coded as "Follow-up question" by the expert coders. The BERT classifier did correctly classify this sequence, whereas the SVM classifier classified this sequence as a "Questions about possible support resources".

While both assignments might sound reasonable at first, the question arises why each classifier performed its prediction. To answer this question, the text-heatmaps in Figure 3 were generated with LIME. The percentage values indicate how important the LIME model considers the corresponding word for the classification.

Text with highlighted words

9% 4%   4% 5%   <1%
BERT: Hast Du mal mit den Erzieherinnen gesprochen ?
SVM: Hast Du mal mit den Erzieherinnen gesprochen ?
2% 3% 8% 6% 1%   4%   2%

Figure 3: Text heatmaps highlighting the determining words for the classification decision

The BERT heatmap shows that the model mainly focuses on the words that form the question "Hast", "Du", "mit", "den", "Erzieherinnen" (Engl. "have", "you", "with", "kindergarten teachers") while the SVM heatmap shows that the SVM classifier considers all words as important for the classification but with high focus on the word "Erzieherinnen" (Engl. kindergarten teachers) which is a possible support resource.

This strong focus on individual keywords from the SVM can be explained by the operating principle of the bag-of-words approach and verifies the assumption from Section 3.3 that the SVM performs well in classes with distinctive keywords. But examples like this show that this simple approach can also be misled when such distinctive keywords appear in more complex sequences in which the keyword is not decisive for the correct class and the context has to be considered as well for the correct classification.

Since LIME follows a bag-of-words evaluation model, it cannot provide additional insights on how our BERT model exactly handles context. Thus, we can only use LIME to illustrate whether the models' decisions are reasonable, or not.

3.6 Analyzing Misclassified Sequences

To better understand our model and to identify further potential for improvement, the incorrectly classified test data were analyzed.

Out of the 3072 test sequences, the BERT model classified 2325 sequences correctly. Out of the 747 incorrectly classified sequences, our team of social scientists manually examined a sample of 191 sequences. The inspected samples were randomly chosen based on conspicuous categories that were not in the diagonal of the confusion matrix. The summarized results of this examination are shown in Table 5.

The general conclusion of this analysis is that 58.1% (Table 5, I+II) of the incorrectly classified sequences are not inherently wrong but their assigned category depends on the different points of view of the coders. For example, the sequence "Have you ever talked to a pediatrician? Or do you have a family counseling center?" was initially encoded as a "Question about possible support resources" by the human encoder, whereas the BERT model associated the sequence with a "Follow-up question". In our analysis, the experts concluded that both categories would fit. Another example in which the predicted label would fit even better than the actual label is the sequence "This has to be done consequently, even if screaming is annoying. You have to go through it – sometime." This sequence was initially encoded as a "Warning / forecast" by the human experts. The BERT model, however, assigned this sequence to the category of "Recommendation for action". Since these different interpretation options are not only a technical issue but can also be observed in human coders, the intercoder reliability between an expert coder, an untrained human coder ("novice"), and BERT is analyzed in Section 4.

For another 23.6% of the analyzed sequences (Table 5, III+IV), we were able to trace back the incorrect classification to the use of keywords or similar terms between different categories. For example, the simple sequence "good luck" is considered to be a "Wish" by the human encoders, whereas our BERT model mistakes this sequence for a traditional farewell phrase (category "Other farewell"). This behavior of the BERT model can be explained by the fact that some sequences in the training data contain closing phrases, such as "Good luck [user]".

In 14 more cases (Table 5, V) the experts were unable to identify any distinctive features that caused the sequences to be classified incorrectly by the BERT model.

Apart from these technical insights, in 12 cases (Table 5, VI) weaknesses in the training data set were identified, such as incorrect assignments of the actual label previously made by the human coder, sequences composed by clients rather than counselors, or sequences that only contain single characters.

Furthermore, in a total of nine sequences (Table 5, VII+VIII), the experts declared the sequences as "hard to assign for humans" due to the usage of uncommon words, not enough context, or since the sequence consists of multiple sentences with multiple categories.

To estimate the impact of the interpretation options during the classification regarding the evaluation metrics, an adjusted accuracy can be estimated. This adjusted accuracy is calculated by transferring the proportion of analyzed incorrectly classified sequences that are not inherently wrong (Table 5, I+II) to the total of the 747 incorrectly classified sequences. This means that 58.1% of the originally incorrectly classified sequences can be considered as correct. This leads to an increase of the correctly classified sequences from 2325 to 2759 which corresponds to a more than satisfying accuracy of 90%, respectively. Since this is only an overall estimation, adjusted F1 scores cannot be calculated.

3.7 Discussion about Improving the Model

To understand the influence of the availability of training samples, we ran multiple tests in which the number of training samples in a specific category was reduced. Hereby, we tested all categories that achieve an F1 score of 70% or higher. For each of the categories, six models were trained with a restricted number (10, 20, 50, 100, 250, and 500) of randomly selected training samples. All models were then evaluated on our test data set. Results have shown that simple categories, such as "General salutation", "Familiar salutation (without name)", "Welcoming", or "Follow-up question", only require about 50 training samples to achieve F1 scores of 0.71 or higher. However, categories that contain text sequences with more complex structures, such as "Experience / Explanation / Example" or "Recommendation for action", still show significant improvements when using 250, 500, or all available text sequences for training.

As described in Section 2, our training data set is unevenly distributed. Data set imbalance is a well-known problem in machine learning (He and Garcia, 2009) and in our case is due to the annotation process. Hereby, available forum posts were annotated without specifically having the category distribution in mind. Typical techniques to reduce the data set imbalance, such as random oversampling or synthetic sampling with data generation (He and Garcia, 2009), cannot easily be applied to textual data, especially not when precise phrasing and wording is important for the classification as in our case. One technique that might, however, lead to improvements is generating new text sequences by randomly combining sentences from other sequences of the same category. Other possible approaches such as aggregating categories with few examples to their superset-level were also considered but dismissed since our goal is to predict categories on a detailed level.

With the approximate number of required samples per category, we think that manually creating additional training data in especially underrepresented classes and edge-cases will, therefore, help to improve the model in the future.

Another idea to improve the model is by taking the model's first and second prediction into account. Human coders can then be supported with suggestions by the model during coding tasks and choose the best fitting label. This feedback can then be used to further improve the model.

4 BERT vs. Human Coders

Coding of text passages is to some degree dependent on the subjective perception of the coders. Especially for similar categories like "Empathy" and "Compassion", different coders will sometimes assign different labels to the same text. Thus, even human coders which were trained on the usage of the codebook will not reach 100% agreement. To get a better understanding of the applicability of our model for automatic coding, we compared the coding performance of BERT against a trained human coder familiar with the codebook ("expert") and an untrained human coder ("novice").

4.1 Intercoder Reliability between Experts

The degree of consensus among coders, the intercoder reliability, is often measured by Cohen's κ (kappa) coefficient (Cohen 1960, Burla et al. 2008). The maximum value of κ is 1, $\kappa > 0.8$ indicates almost perfect, and $\kappa > 0.6$ indicates substantial agreement.

During the creation of the training data, our experts regularly coded the same texts and aligned their coding style. After coding was finished, we calculated the κ coefficient between those two coders who had coded the most samples. Thereby, we considered only posts coded by both coders and text sequences with at least 75% overlap regarding the first and last word. We determined a κ coefficient of 0.73 between those two experts. This value is relatively high given our complex codebook with over 50 categories.

4.2 Intercoder Reliability between an Expert, a Novice, and BERT

To understand how our BERT model performs compared to human coders, we benchmarked the performance of the following three participants: The expert was one of the coders observed in the intercoder reliability measurement. The novice had only a little experience in text annotation and had just recently familiarized herself with the codebook and typical examples for each category. The third participant was our BERT classification model.

All participants had the task to annotate the same 50 text passages. Each text passage was randomly chosen from the set of previously unlabeled forum posts.

Besides measuring the intercoder reliability among the participants, we also wanted to generate indications about which sequence length is best suited for the application of the BERT model. For typical coding tasks in the social sciences, the length of a sequence to be coded is defined by a change in the occurring category. This contrasts with most machine-based classifiers which expect a defined sequence of words as input. The choice of start and end for a label in continuous text is usually not part of the classification task.

Therefore, we generated three variants of the 50 text sequences for coding: The first data set consists of single sentences only, the second data set includes, if existing, the following sentence for each sample, and the third data set contains sequences of at most three consecutive sentences. Figure 4 illustrates the breakdown of an exemplary post.

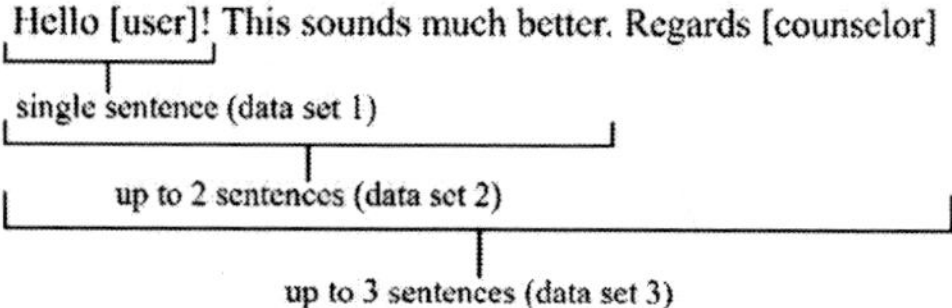

Figure 4: Exemplary structure of the sequences within the different data sets

All three data sets were then coded independently by the participants. As before, the agreement between the different coders was measured using the κ coefficient (see Table 6).

Surprisingly, the intercoder reliability between BERT and the human expert is higher than the intercoder reliability between the expert and the novice, regardless of the sequence length. In its best case, the BERT classifier achieves nearly expert-expert-like intercoder reliability with a value as high as 0.64 in comparison to the earlier calculated expert intercoder reliability of 0.73. It seems that the BERT model has learned the expert style of

Sequence Length	k coefficient		
	Expert-Novice	Expert-BERT	Novice-BERT
Single sentence	0.55	0.64	0.53
Up to 2 sentences	0.53	0.60	0.43
Up to 3 sentences	0.50	0.50	0.38

Table 6: κ coefficient of the participants

coding from the training data better than an untrained human coder using the codebook.

While classifying sequences that contain only one sentence was rated difficult by the human coders due to the missing context, sequences with up to 3 sentences were rated as too long since they often contained patterns from multiple categories. Therefore, sequences with the length of two sentences were rated as best fitting lengths for classifying sequences by both the novice and the expert coder. In contrast to the ratings of the coders, the intercoder reliability shows the highest values when encoding sequences with the length of only one sentence.

5 Conclusion

It has been shown that machine-based classifiers can reach human-like performance for the annotation of complex categories in psycho-social texts. The results indicate that the models learn to mimic the coding style of the initial creators of the training data. The trained BERT model was even better in coding than a human novice. As in other areas of machine learning, this bears the risk that a model also learns the bias from the training data. Therefore, it is important to understand and regularly check the decisions of the model by human experts.

High coding quality could not be achieved for all codes, however. Especially underrepresented categories, which are common in social sciences, are problematic. Thus, a sufficient number of training samples is an obvious prerequisite for good results.

The typical approach of social sciences in analyzing text corpora consists of coding one text after the other and ignoring unequal frequencies of the individual codes. Our study shows that when using machine learning methods, it is better to generate training examples for as many categories as possible and pay less attention to the complete coding of individual texts. This is an important finding for the organization of future studies in this field.

The investigation of misclassified sequences showed that many recorded misclassifications actually were minor mistakes. The model frequently chose not the actual but a very similar category such that even human experts would regard the assignment plausible. Thus, codes with very similar meanings must be distinguished more sharply to give the model a chance to learn to differentiate.

The analysis of the misclassified sequences of BERT opens up new perspectives for the social sciences: More than half of the "incorrectly classified sequences" appeared to the human expert to be plausible or at least worthy of consideration. Since the discussion of the understanding of individual text passages is an important element of social science research, such plausible misinterpretations can enrich the research process. They offer an alternative way of looking at reality and force the human coder to either rethink his assessments or to better justify them.

Currently, we are working on improving the classification performance. One approach is the generation of additional training data for underrepresented categories. Another idea is using an ensemble of SVM and BERT as a classifier to better utilize the individual strengths of the different models. In any case, the findings on how the models work and perform help to consider such technical aspects in future social science research.

With regard to the application domain, we can conclude that it is definitely possible to analyze online counseling conversations with the help of machine learning. We intend to use machine learning in future research projects to investigate correlations between the different techniques used by counselors and the characteristics and reactions of clients. In addition to the question of whether successful counselors use certain techniques significantly more often than others, it can now be clarified if certain approaches are particularly promising for certain target groups or specific problems. These findings can be integrated into the education of online counselors. Furthermore, assistance systems are conceivable that support online counselors in real-time with information generated from this data.

In any case, the results of this study have shown that it is possible to merge the advantages of qualitative and quantitative approaches in social science with the help of machine learning. Automated data annotation for qualitative analysis is the cornerstone for future insights on an unprecedented level.

References

Abnar, S. and Zuidema, W. (2020) Quantifying Attention Flow in Transformers [Online]. http://dx.doi.org/10.18653/v1/2020.acl-main.385.

Aggarwal, C. C. (2018) Machine Learning for Text, Springer [Online]. https://doi.org/10.1007/978-3-319-73531-3.

Althoff, T., Clark, K. and Leskovec, J. (2016) Large-scale Analysis of Counseling Conversations: An Application of Natural Language Processing to Mental Health [Online]. http://dx.doi.org/10.1162/tacl_a_00111.

Bambling, M., King, R., Reid, W. & Wegner, K. (2008) Online counselling: The experience of counsellors providing synchronous single-session counselling to young people, *Counselling and Psychotherapy Research*, vol. 8, no. 2, pp.110–116 [Online]. https://doi.org/10.1080/14733140802055011.

Burla, L., Knierim, B., Barth, J., Liewald, K., Duetz, M. and Abel, T. (2008) From Text to Codings: Intercoder Reliability Assessment in Qualitative Content Analysis, *Nursing research*, vol. 57, no. 2, pp. 113–117 [Online]. https://doi.org/10.1097/01.nnr.0000313482.33917.7d.

Cameron, G., Cameron, D. M., Megaw, G., Bond, R. B., Mulvenna, M., O'Neill, S. B. et al. (2017) Towards a chatbot for digital counselling, *Proceedings of the 31st International BCS Human Computer Interaction Conference (HCI 2017)*. BCS Learning & Development [Online]. https://doi.org/10.14236/ewic/HCI2017.24.

Chardon, L., Bagraith, K. S. & King, R. J. (2011) Counseling activity in single-session online counseling with adolescents: An adherence study, *Psychotherapy Research*, vol. 21, no.5, pp. 583–592 [Online]. https://doi.org/10.1080/10503307.2011.592550.

Chatterjee, A., Narahari, K.N., Joshi, M., and Agrawal, P. (2019) SemEval-2019 Task 3: EmoContext - Contextual Emotion Detection in Text. In: *Proceedings of the 13th International Workshop on Semantic Evaluation* (SemEval-2019), pp. 39–48 [Online]. http://dx.doi.org/10.18653/v1/S19-2005.

Cohen J. (1960) A Coefficient of Agreement for Nominal Scales. In: *Educ Psychol Meas.* 20:37–46 [Online]. https://doi.org/10.1177/001316446002000104.

Conneau, A., Khandelwal, K., Goyal, N., Chaudhary, V., Wenzek, G., Guzmán, F., Grave, E., Ott, M., Zettlemoyer, L. and Stoyanov, V. (2019) Unsupervised Cross-lingual Representation Learning at Scale [Online]. http://dx.doi.org/10.18653/v1/2020.acl-main.747.

Crowston, K., Liu, X. and Allen, E.E. (2010) Machine learning and rule-based automated coding of qualitative data, *Proc. Am. Soc. Info. Sci. Tech.*, vol. 47, pp. 1-2 [Online]. https://doi.org/10.1002/meet.14504701328.

DBMDZ (2019) German BERT [Online]. https://huggingface.co/dbmdz/bert-base-german-uncased.

DeepPavlov (n. d.) Sentence Multilingual BERT [Online]. https://huggingface.co/DeepPavlov/bert-base-multilingual-cased-sentence.

Devlin, J., Chang, M.-W., Lee, K. and Toutanova, K. (2018) BERT: Pre-training of Deep Bidirectional Transformers for Language Understanding [Online]. http://dx.doi.org/10.18653/v1/N19-1423.

Dowling, M. J. & Rickwood, D. J. (2014) Experiences of counsellors providing online chat counselling to young people, *Journal of Psychologists and Counsellors in Schools*, vol. 24, no.2, pp. 183–196. Cambridge University Press, Cambridge, UK [Online]. https://doi.org/10.1017/jgc.2013.28.

Dowling, M. & Rickwood, D. (2015) Investigating individual online synchronous chat counselling processes and treatment outcomes for young people, *Advances in Mental Health*, vol. 12, no. 3, pp. 216-224 [Online]. https://doi.org/10.1080/18374905.2014.11081899.

Ersahin, Z. & Hanley, T. (2017) Using text-based synchronous chat to offer therapeutic support to students: A systematic review of the research literature, *Health Education Journal*, vol. 76, no. 5, pp. 531–543 [Online]. https://doi.org/10.1177/0017896917704675.

Fukkink, R. G. & Hermanns, J. M. A. (2009) Children's experiences with chat support and telephone support, *Journal of Child Psychology and Psychiatry*, vol. 50, no. 6, pp.759-766 [Online]. https://doi.org/10.1111/j.1469-7610.2008.02024.x.

Gatti, F. M., Brivio, E. & Calciano, S. (2016), "Hello! I know you help people here, right?": A qualitative study of young people's acted motivations in text-based counseling, *Children and Youth Services Review*, vol. 71, pp. 27-35 [Online]. https://doi.org/10.1016/j.childyouth.2016.10.029.

Glaser, B. G. & Strauss, A. L. (2017). Discovery of grounded theory: Strategies for qualitative research. Routledge.

Hanley, T. (2012) Understanding the online therapeutic alliance through the eyes of adolescent service users, *Counselling and Psychotherapy Research*, vol. *12, no.*1, pp. 35–43 [Online]. https://doi.org/10.1080/14733145.2011.560273.

He, H. and Garcia, E. A. (2009) Learning from Imbalanced Data, IEEE Transactions on Knowledge and Data Engineering, vol. 21, no. 9, pp. 1263–1284 [Online]. https://doi.org/10.1109/TKDE.2008.239.

Howard, J. and Ruder, S. (2018) Universal Language Model Fine-tuning for Text Classification [Online]. http://dx.doi.org/10.18653/v1/P18-1031.

Hugging Face (2020) BertForSequenceClassification [Online]. https://huggingface.co/transformers/model_doc/bert.html#transformers.BertForSequenceClassification.

Kergel D. (2018) *Qualitative Bildungsforschung – Ein integrativer Ansatz*. Wiesbaden, Springer VS [Online]. https://doi.org/10.1007/978-3-658-18587-9.

King, R., Bambling, M., Reid, W. & Thomas, I. (2006) Telephone and online counselling for young people: A naturalistic comparison of session outcome, session impact and therapeutic alliance, *Counselling and Psychotherapy Research*, vol. 6, no. 3, pp. 175–181 [Online]. https://doi.org/10.1080/14733140600874084.

Lample, G. and Conneau, A. (2019) Cross-lingual Language Model Pretraining [Online]. http://arxiv.org/pdf/1901.07291v1.

van de Luitgaarden, G. & van der Tier, M. (2018) Establishing working relationships in online social work, *Journal of Social Work*, vol.18 no.3, pp. 307–325 [Online]. https://doi.org/10.1177/1468017316654347.

Mayring, P. (2015) Qualitative Content Analysis: Theoretical Background and Procedures (Advances in Mathematics Education), *in* A. Bikner-Ahsbahs, C. Knipping & N. Presmeg (eds), *Approaches to Qualitative Research in Mathematics Education: Examples of Methodology and Methods*. Dordrecht, Springer Netherlands, pp. 365-380 [Online]. https://doi.org/10.1007/978-94-017-9181-6_13.

Navarro, P., Bambling, M., Sheffield, J. & Edirippulige, S. (2019) Exploring Young People's Perceptions of the Effectiveness of Text-Based Online Counseling: Mixed Methods Pilot Study, JMIR Mental Health, vol. 6, no. 7, e13152 [Online]. https://doi.org/10.2196/13152.

Nieuwboer, C. C., Fukkink, R. G. & Hermanns, J. M. A. (2015) Single session email consultation for parents: an evaluation of its effect on empowerment, *British Journal of Guidance & Counselling*, vol. 43, no. 1, pp. 131–143 [Online]. https://doi.org/10.1080/03069885.2014.929636.

Pérez-Rosas, V., Wu, X., Resnicow, K. and Mihalcea, R. (2019) What Makes a Good Counselor? Learning to Distinguish between High-quality and Low-quality Counseling Conversations, Proceedings of the 57th Annual Meeting of the Association for Computational Linguistics. Florence, Italy. Stroudsburg, PA, USA, Association for Computational Linguistics, pp. 926–935 [Online]. https://doi.org/10.18653/v1/P19-1088.

Ribeiro, M. T., Singh, S. and Guestrin, C. (2016) "Why Should I Trust You?": Explaining the Predictions of Any Classifier [Online]. http://dx.doi.org/10.18653/v1/N16-3020.

Rodda, S. N., Lubman, D. I., Cheetham, A., Dowling, N. A. & Jackson, A. C. (2015) Single session web-based counselling: a thematic analysis of content from the perspective of the client, *British Journal of Guidance & Counselling*, vol. 43, no.1, pp. 117–130 [Online]. https://doi.org/10.1080/03069885.2014.938609.

Sanh, V., Debut, L., Chaumond, J. and Wolf, T. (2019) DistilBERT, a distilled version of BERT: smaller, faster, cheaper and lighter [Online]. http://arxiv.org/pdf/1910.01108v4.

Sefi, A. & Hanley, T. (2012) Examining the complexities of measuring effectiveness of online counselling for young people using routine evaluation data, *Pastoral Care in Education*, vol. 30, no. 1, pp. 49–64 [Online]. https://doi.org/10.1080/02643944.2011.651224.

Vaswani, A., Shazeer, N., Parmar, N., Uszkoreit, J., Jones, L., Gomez, A. N., Kaiser, L. and Polosukhin, I. (2017) Attention Is All You Need [Online]. http://arxiv.org/pdf/1706.03762v5.

Wolf, T., e.a. (2019) HuggingFace's Transformers: State-of-the-art Natural Language Processing [Online]. http://arxiv.org/pdf/1910.03771v5.

Appendix A. Codebook Including Number of Samples and Classification Results

Top Level	Superset Level	Category Level	Training Support	Test Support	SVM F1 Score	BERT F1 Score
Start of conversation	Salutation	General salutation	22	9	75.0%	82.4%
		Formal salutation (without name)	2	1	0.0%	0.0%
		Formal salutation (with name)	4	1	100.0%	0.0%
		Familiar salutation (without name)	139	59	71.7%	98.3%
		Familiar salutation (with name)	579	248	89.5%	98.6%
		Other salutation	8	3	0.0%	0.0%
	Welcoming	Welcoming	102	44	91.3%	93.5%
		Introduction institution / consultant	5	2	0.0%	0.0%
		Other introduction	37	16	27.3%	11.8%
	Conversation management	Conversation management	1	0	0.0%	0.0%
		Organizational issues	14	6	0.0%	0.0%
		Technical issues	6	2	66.7%	0.0%
		Reference to post	190	81	53.2%	52.5%
		Explanatory modalities	4	1	0.0%	0.0%
General attitudes	Empathy	Empathy	1	0	0.0%	0.0%
		Empathy for others	118	51	59.8%	49.5%
		Compassion	17	7	72.7%	0.0%
		Concern for others	3	2	0.0%	0.0%
	Appreciation	Congratulations	1	1	0.0%	0.0%
		Praise / acknowledgement	43	18	38.5%	30.8%
		Gratitude / appreciation	8	3	0.0%	0.0%
	Congruence	Wish	80	34	63.8%	75.9%
Impact factors (1 of 2)	Analysis and clarification	Analysis and clarification	3	2	66.7%	0.0%
		Follow-up question	491	211	65.3%	85.1%
		Communication of grasp	176	75	42.5%	49.3%
		Evaluation / understanding / calming	1136	487	59.0%	67.0%
	Agreement on consulting goals	Demand for concern	1	1	0.0%	0.0%
		Encouragement to think about the concern	2	1	0.0%	0.0%
		Definition of the objective	1	1	0.0%	0.0%
	Creation of motivation	Encouragement	134	57	36.6%	34.2%
		Change	1	0	0.0%	0.0%
	Update on problem	Request for detailed description	10	5	25.0%	0.0%
		Suggestion to put oneself in a problem situation physically	1	1	100.0%	0.0%
		Suggestion to put oneself in a problem situation mentally	2	1	0.0%	0.0%

Top Level	Superset Level	Category Level	Training Support	Test Support	SVM F1 Score	BERT F1 Score
Impact factors (2 of 2)	Activation of resources	Question about possible support resources	15	6	16.7%	0.0%
		Activation of resources (family)	4	2	0.0%	0.0%
		Activation of resources (friends)	2	1	100.0%	0.0%
		Activation of resources (professional level)	49	21	43.2%	42.1%
		Activation of resources (uncertain level)	3	2	0.0%	0.0%
	Help for problem overcoming	Experience / explanation / example	1398	599	76.2%	83.1%
		Recommendation for action	1372	588	68.1%	75.5%
		Warning / forecast	71	30	29.3%	12.1%
End of conversation	Suggestion for private exchange	Suggestion for private exchange	8	4	0.0%	0.0%
	Suggestion for further forum exchange	Suggestion for further forum exchange	51	22	52.9%	50.0%
		Formal farewell (with a name)	3	2	50.0%	0.0%
		Familiar farewell (without a name)	21	9	57.1%	71.4%
		Familiar farewell (with a name)	629	269	90.2%	92.7%
		Other farewell	135	58	52.7%	53.2%
Other	Typographical error	Typographical error	1	1	0.0%	0.0%
	Inappropriate comment	Inappropriate comment	10	4	0.0%	0.0%
	Emotional clarification	Emotional clarification	55	23	64.6%	90.9%

Swimming with the Tide?
Positional Claim Detection across Political Text Types

Nico Blokker[1], Erenay Dayanik[2], Gabriella Lapesa[2], and Sebastian Padó[2]

[1]SOCIUM, University of Bremen, Germany
[2]IMS, University of Stuttgart, Germany
{*blokker*}*@uni-bremen.de*
{*erenay.dayanik, gabriella.lapesa, sebastian.pado*}*@ims.uni-stuttgart.de*

Abstract

Manifestos are official documents of political parties, providing a comprehensive topical overview of the electoral programs. Voters, however, seldom read them and often prefer other channels, such as newspaper articles, to understand the party positions on various policy issues. The natural question to ask is how compatible these two formats (manifesto and newspaper reports) are in their representation of party positioning. We address this question with an approach that combines political science (manual annotation and analysis) and natural language processing (supervised claim identification) in a cross-text type setting: we train a classifier on annotated newspaper data and test its performance on manifestos. Our findings show a) strong performance for supervised classification even across text types and b) a substantive overlap between the two formats in terms of party positioning, with differences regarding the salience of specific issues.

1 Introduction

Electoral programs described in party manifestos are official documents of political parties. Not only do they capture their positions on a broad variety of policy issues, but they are also authoritative for the entire party. In this sense, they are fundamentally different from statements issued only by factions or solitary members of a party (Budge et al., 2001, p. 216). Ordinary citizens, however, rarely read the manifestos (Budge, 1987; Volkens and Bara, 2013). Arguably, an informed voter is more likely to be exposed to electoral programs indirectly through another medium, namely the newspaper. News articles present the reader with the *political claims* put forward by different parties and often directly contrast them. More specifically, we adopt the definition of claims as any form of politically motivated demand or action (both verbal and non-verbal) of deliberate actors (Koopmans and Statham, 1999).

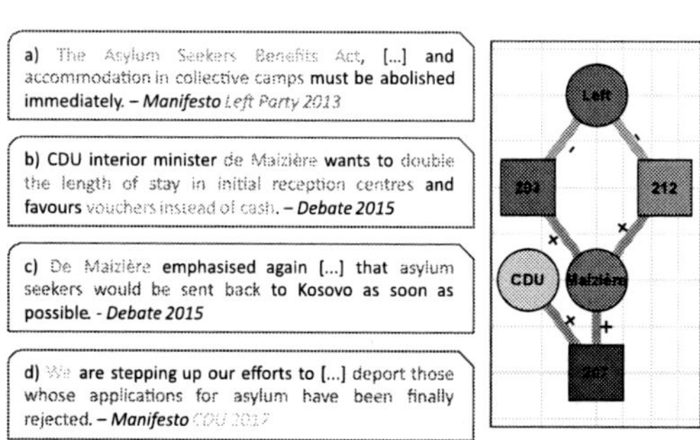

Figure 1: Mapping cross-genre policy proposals

Information about claims is routinely used by readers to infer the parties' standpoints. This places parties in a delicate situation: They largely rely on newspapers and other media to convey their claims to the voter to gain their approval in elections (Robertson, 1976).

Recent advances in the application of NLP methods to political reporting can reliably extract such claims with models trained on manually annotated claims in newspapers (Dayanik and Padó, 2020; Haunss et al., 2020). From a NLP perspective, this gives rise to the following question which we will address in this paper: Can we transfer existing models for claim identification to party manifestos without substantial loss of performance? If so, this would enable political scientists to address substantive questions such as: To what extent do manifestos of specific parties and the positions of their members as reported in newspaper articles overlap? How do differences articulate themselves in practice?

One way to address these questions is to directly compare the agreement between claims from the two formats[1]. Figure 1 (left panel) shows four sentences containing political claims on the pol-

---

[1]We use *format* and *genre* interchangeably to describe *text types*.

Proceedings of the Fourth Workshop on Natural Language Processing and Computational Social Science, pages 24–34
Online, November 20, 2020. ©2020 Association for Computational Linguistics
https://doi.org/10.18653/v1/P17

icy issue of migration. While the first sentence is translated from the party manifesto of the German left-wing party *Linke* (Left) from the federal election 2013, the last one is from the 2017 manifesto of the conservative *Christian Democratic Union* (CDU). Both sentences in the middle are statements from the German minister of the interior (CDU) published in newspaper articles in 2015.

Despite the discrepancy in time and genre, a) and b) as well as c) and d) encode the same political claims: In b) the minister supports (+) the idea to give refugees vouchers instead of cash (claim category 212[2]), and he proposes to extend the length of central accommodation of refugees (203). In a) both claims are opposed (-) by the Left party (benefits in kind are regulated by the 'Asylum Seekers Benefits Act' in Germany). Analogously, in c) and d) the minister and his party CDU both express support to deport asylum seekers (claim 207).

On a substantive level, the sentences are very similar. Yet linguistically, they are quite different. While manifestos are written in direct speech and express the will of the party, the quotes from the public (newspaper) debate hold indirect speech that can be attributed to an individual actor. Besides, they often differ in the lexical choices, e.g. colloquial vs. technical terms, as in "sent back" vs. "deport" in Figure 1 c) and d). To exacerbate matters, differences exist within genres in addition to the variability between them.

The purpose of this paper is to determine whether computational models for claim detection in newspaper articles (Dayanik and Padó, 2020) can be applied directly to party manifestos. Our findings indicate that there is indeed a strong transferability and a substantive overlap between estimated party positions between the text types on the issue of migration. These findings are limited in scope to the German case and require further validation given the heterogeneity of both parties and policy issues.

Nevertheless, the contributions of our work address several points. First, we take a further step in the strive for scaling up the semi-automatic identification of tangible policy instruments in political texts (Haunss et al., 2020) by introducing cross-

text type evaluation. Second, at a theoretical level, we provide further experimental insights into the relationship between party manifestos and newspaper debates: we analyse the substantive overlap of both formats considering the underlying claim-distribution per party in the two most recent federal elections in Germany (2013 and 2017) and the interim public newspaper discourse (2015) to see whether previous findings from the political science literature (cf. Section 2) hold. Third, we extend the scope of our investigation to a concrete application scenario, namely a discourse network analysis of the debate at issue (right panel, Figure 1). In this relational approach, the actor-claim-dyad is the first building block of a more complex, bipartite network structure. By abstracting from the actual text it is possible to directly contrast, compare, and even combine the two different formats on a network level. In this perspective, individual actors/parties and claims are two distinct types of vertices that are connected via edges that express support or opposition (Leifeld, 2009, 2016). We use this to demonstrate how our approach translates from newspaper data to party manifestos and how it leads to deeper conceptual insights.

Section 2 illustrates how our approach relates to the literature and compares characteristics of the distinct data sources. Section 3 examines existing modeling approaches to claim identification. The results are presented in Section 4 and 5 and their relevance is discussed in Section 6.

2 Related Work: Debate and Manifestos

Political Science. The inter-linkage of public (newspaper) debates and party documents is currently widely investigated (Schwarzbözl et al., 2019; Haselmayer et al., 2019; Merz, 2018). Political parties rely on mass media to distribute their declarations of intent to the voter (Robertson, 1976; Bara, 2006), who in turn holds the party responsible for the promises made (American Political Science Association, 1950; Thomassen, 1994; Adams, 2001, for a critical discussion see Mair, 2009). Given these assumptions, it is natural to infer a substantial overlap between the content of domain-specific newspaper articles and the corresponding sections in party manifestos. Therefore, the identification of proposed policy instruments – *political claims*, or, in the electoral context, *pledges* (Rallings, 1987), in one of the text types arguably parallels the existence in the other.

---

[2]We use the claim categories and codes for the migration debate proposed by Lapesa et al. (2020). The data set can be found here: `hdl.handle.net/11022/1007-0000-0007-DB07-B` and the coding scheme here: `https://github.com/mardy-spp/mardy_acl2019/blob/master/codebook.pdf`

Despite the mediating role played by newspapers in the diffusion process of disseminating party visions, vast differences between the text types exist on a conceptual level. While electoral programs paint a cohesive and unified picture of the party line, media coverage highlights conflict within parties. Parties do not control the content written in newspaper articles. Instead, their message is filtered and interpreted by editors and authors. In the news, parties compete with each other, trying to establish themselves and appeal to the reader (Helbling and Tresch, 2011; Green-Pedersen and Mortensen, 2015).

Hence, existing studies measure and validate the substantive agreement between several (media) genres both in respect to party positioning on certain policy issues as well as the amount of attention (salience) these issues receive (Ray, 2007; Netjes and Binnema, 2007). For instance, comparisons are carried out between expert survey and party manifestos (Benoit and Laver, 2007; Marks et al., 2007) and, more recently, with the addition of newspaper articles as a third data source. Helbling and Tresch (2011) find that while party positions are mostly congruent between manifestos and media coverage in the same election campaign, they differ when it comes to the salience of specific issues. Thus, the media bias appears to have a stronger impact on the selection of certain topics than on the content's accuracy regarding party positions (Helbling and Tresch, 2011, p. 180). One natural characteristic is that the substantive density (e.g. as a ratio of claims to text) is much higher in electoral programs than in newspaper articles.

Natural Language Processing. The literature concerning NLP support corpus-based investigations in political (and more broadly social) science is quite heterogeneous. The first group of approaches targets the facilitation of the annotation procedure (traditionally carried out by hand) with argument mining or machine learning. The goal is to speed up annotation without losing in quality (Cabrio and Villata, 2018; Lippi and Torroni, 2015, 2016). The second line of research targets the direct automatic analysis of politic debates in textual form. As far as political claim analysis in newspaper articles is concerned, Padó et al. (2019) have developed relatively simple embedding-based models for claim identification and classification. The experiments presented in this paper are based on their model architecture. As for party manifestos,

NLP methods have been developed for automatic topic analysis (Glavaš et al., 2017). They have been investigated in a comparative fashion due to the textual and conceptual similarity to parliamentary speeches, which creates fertile grounds for domain adaptation (Daumé III, 2007) and cross-topic argument mining (Stab et al., 2018). For example, Abercrombie et al. (2019) apply the annotation scheme of the MARPOR project[3] to a corpus of parliamentary speeches to automatically label policy preferences. To the best of our knowledge, this work is the first study that attempts to establish a direct comparison between manifestos and newspaper reports of the political debates while being grounded in the application of automatic classification methods.

3   Methodology

In what follows, we spell out the two steps of our methodology underlying the experiments presented in the subsequent sections.

Step 1: Automatic claim detection   For our machine learning experiments, we employ the political claim detector from Dayanik and Padó (2020). It models claims detection as a binary classification task at the sentence level where the goal is to decide whether each input sentence contains a claim or not. The architecture is shown in Figure 2. It is based on the BERT architecture (Devlin et al., 2019) which is used to generate sentence representations by computing an embedding for the special [CLS] token used to indicate sentence breaks. We use a language specific BERT that is trained on German corpora[4] since it is better at finding subword units for German than the multilingual BERT model (Rönnqvist et al., 2019). A softmax classifier is then placed on top of BERT. It takes the [CLS] embedding performs the claim/no-claim classification.

The model is trained using the DEbateNet-mig15 (Lapesa et al., 2020) data set. This data set contains about 2.000 claims from over 450 articles on the domestic discourse of migration in the German quality newspaper *taz* in the year 2015. We use 10 random train, development, and test splits and report the average. Following recommendations made by Devlin et al. (2019), we use the Adam optimizer with learning rates of $5 \cdot 10^{-5}$, $\beta_1 = 0.9$, β_2

[3]Manifesto Research on Political Representation, https://manifesto-project.wzb.eu/

[4]https://deepset.ai/german-bert

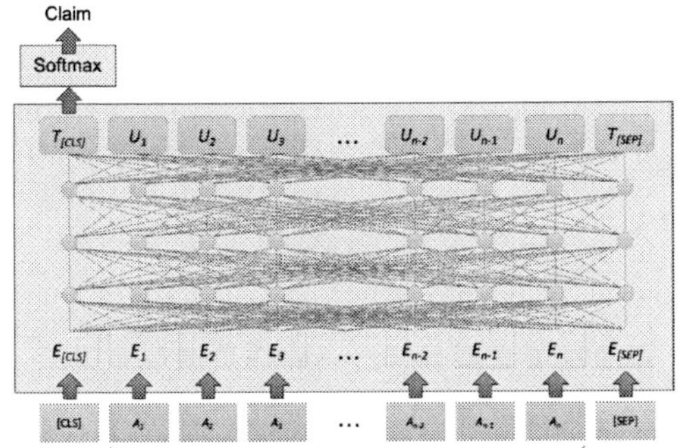

Figure 2: Model architecture of political claims detector (from Dayanik and Padó, 2020)

party	# analyzed text spans	# annotated claims	ratio
AfD	118	63	0.53
CDU	114	63	0.55
Green	427	276	0.65
Left	257	159	0.62
SPD	247	161	0.65
total	1163	722	0.62

Table 1: Annotation statistics on the Manifesto data set (ratio: claim "density")

= 0.999, a batch size of 32, a gradient clip threshold of 1.0, dropout with p=0.1, and 15 epochs. With this configuration, our model achieves an F1 score of 52.2 on the debate test set (P=40.1, R=74.7). This classifier will be applied and evaluated in Section 4.2.

Step 2: Semi-Automatic Analysis for Discourse Network Construction. The NLP approach to the evaluation of a classifier just outlined assumes that the final goal is to detect every single claim correctly. However, in the political science community it has been argued recently that the core of a debate can be perfectly captured even from imperfectly analyzed data (Haunss et al., 2020). An important factor is *redundancy*: the core claims of debates tend to be mentioned multiple times in an article, and thus not every occurrence must be identified. This is particularly true for newspaper reporting, but also holds for party manifestos. This realization motivates our attempt, even in the face of a relatively modest performance of the claim classifier, to construct *discourse networks* of political debates based on newspaper and manifesto texts (cf. Section 1).

That being said, the classifier described above only provides part of the information necessary to create discourse networks. We therefore set up a semi-automatic analysis procedure which we will apply in Section 4.3. First, the researcher runs the automatic claim identifier. They then manually add the polarity (agreement or rejection of claim), identify the actor (in the case of manifestos, this is always the party), filter the false positives from the automatically identified suggestions, and categorize the remaining claims according to the codebook of Lapesa et al. (2020). Under the assumption that claim identification is the most time-consuming of the steps mentioned above our hypothesis is that this semi-automatic procedure allows us to save a significant amount of time and effort. Indeed, analysis proceeds faster because it is not necessary to read large portions of text (or, potentially, entire articles) which do not contain any claims.

4 Experiments

This section introduces the manifesto data (Section 4.1) and presents results for fully automatic model performance in the cross-text type setting (Section 4.2). We then carry out a more substantive comparison in terms of discourse networks and party positions that combines automatic analysis with manual post-processing (Section 4.3).

4.1 Manifesto Data Set

The manifesto data set we use encompasses the electoral programs of five German parties from the preceding (2013) and succeeding (2017) election campaigns as collected by the MARPOR project (Volkens et al., 2019).[5] We restricted ourselves to those manifesto sections that dealt with migration-related topics. We built on the MARPOR segmentation of the manifestos into text spans, which often, but not always, correspond to sentences.

We re-used the annotation scheme and predefined categories ("codebook") proposed by Lapesa et al. (2020) for the Manifesto data set in order to transfer and compare results from one

---

[5]We considered all parties represented in the German Bundestag in both legislative periods: The Christian Democratic Union (CDU), the Social Democratic Party (SPD), the Green Party (Green), the Left Party (Left). We added the migration-skeptic Alternative for Germany (AfD).

	$M \cup D$	$M \cap D$	$D - M$	$M - D$
manual	98	71	13	14
semi-auto.	97	70	14	13

Table 2: Relationships among sets of claim categories in debates (D) and manifestos (M)

text type to the other. The codebook itself consists of eight higher-level categories (e.g. controlling migration, residency, and foreign policy), which in turn are divided into over 100 smaller sub-categories of political claims (e.g. central accommodation, contributions in kind; cf. Figure 1).

The resulting data set contains 722 sentences enclosing at least one claim (on average 144 per party) spread over 1.163 text spans; Table 1 shows details per party. In other words, roughly every other text span contains a migration claim.[6]

Comparison to debate data. The empirical overlap between the text types can be described on two levels: On the level of claim categories per genre and on the level of claim categories per genre *and* political party. Table 2 shows the relationships between sets of unique claim categories in the two data sets both for manual and semi-automatic analysis (see Section 4.3). The first row indicates that 98 distinct claim categories exist in total, from which 71 appear in both formats. 13 are unique to the newspaper debate and 14 only appear in electoral programs. The latter appear to be mostly categories that were added during codebook revisions and which may not have been existent for the full period of the annotation of the debate data. Therefore, the difference may be artificially overestimated. Conversely, claims specific to the debate texts deal, e.g., with acute issues related to first admission and accommodation of refugees that were not deemed general enough for inclusion in electoral manifestos.

4.2 Step 1: Automatic Claim Identification

To quantify the performance of automatic claim identification, we report precision, recall, F1-score, and accuracy for the model trained on the 2015 debate corpus used to classify each manifesto corpus text span. We break down results by manifesto year (2013 vs. 2017). We expect systematic misclassifications, given that the move from newspaper articles to party manifestos involves shifts both conceptually and linguistically.

Overall, the F1-score ranges on a high level from 0.78 in 2017 to 0.86 in 2013 (cf. Table 3). The model also retains a high recall (0.84 in 2013 / 0.79 in 2017) as well as precision (0.88 / 0.77) and accuracy (81.31 / 73.63).

This is bolstered by the second row of Table 2, which shows that all but one claim categories have been identified by the automatic model at least once. Apparently, the model trained on newspaper debate data transfers well to the manifesto corpus and is able to reliably detect political claims in both text types even though the test data is considerably different from the training data. This is positive and encouraging news; we attribute this primarily to the higher density of claims in the manifestos. Additionally, manifestos seem to express their claims in a more concise and unembellished language compared to newspaper articles, sometimes even using enumerations with claims back to back. As a consequence, the performance obtains a better fit than on the original training data set, especially since we narrowed it down to relevant sections of the manifestos beforehand.

Given that recall is generally lower than precision, a remaining question is why, and in what instances, the detection model fails to identify claims correctly. One reason is the difference in coding units (complete sentences in the debate vs. subsentential spans (sub) in the manifestos, see Table 4 for examples). Another is simply the usage of exclamation marks in electoral programs that are uncommon for claims reported in newspapers (*'Stop the harassment of refugees!'* - Manifesto of the Left party, 2013).

Yet, there are further possible causes. For this we turn to the striking difference in performance in both precision and recall between 2013 and 2017: The claim detection model achieves better results for the time period before the training data than after. One possible explanation is that the focus on the content of the 2013 manifestos carries over into the early stages of the 2015 debate and fades away by the end of the year. To rule out this hypothesis, we trained one detector-model on the discourse data from the beginning of the year up until shortly before the peak of the crisis (January to August), and another from there to the end of the year (September to December). Each model still performed better in terms of F1 score on the electoral

---

[6]The manifesto data set is available as a CLARIN resource at the **PID** `http://hdl.handle.net/11022/1007-0000-0007-E7E7-0`.

| | 2013 | | | | 2017 | | | |
	recall	precision	F1	accuracy	recall	precision	F1	accuracy
AfD	0.83	1.00	0.91	85.71	**0.70**	0.82	0.75	76.58
CDU	0.83	0.83	0.83	80.82	0.73	**0.55**	0.63	53.66
Green	0.80	0.90	0.85	77.97	0.86	0.80	0.83	78.32
Left	0.88	0.91	0.90	85.71	0.82	0.77	0.80	74.52
SPD	0.90	0.86	0.88	83.78	**0.70**	0.77	0.73	67.05
total	0.84	0.88	0.86	81.31	0.79	0.77	0.78	73.63

Table 3: Precision, Recall, and F1-Score for claim identification on manifesto data

programs of 2013 than those from 2017, making a seasonal after-effect unlikely.

This begs the question of where the difference in performance between years stems from: Given that the unit of interest is unchanged and it is plausible to assume that the perceived crisis situation of 2015 left a formative imprint in the succeeding manifestos, one might expect better results for 2017.

One explanation applies to the level of machine learning: statistical models tend to decrease in performance with temporal distance from their training data due to the changes in the underlying distribution, a phenomenon known as concept drift (Gama et al., 2014). Arguably, extrapolating into the future should be more difficult than extrapolating into the past, even though we are not aware of specific studies in NLP on this aspect.

Another set of explanations can however be found in the political circumstances and outcomes accompanying the different elections. As a result of the federal elections in 2013, the government coalition changed and the newly founded far-right AfD entered the political landscape in Germany.

Incidentally, the parties most affected by this are the parties in government (SPD and CDU) and the AfD (see bold numbers in Table 3). We propose three plausible explanations for this behaviour:

- The first one is connected to linguistic changes in electoral programs from 2013 to 2017. The SPD's new position in government is reflected in such changes: a) The precondition of re-election is sometimes omitted, making claims sound factual instead of prospective (mood, see Table 4); and b) we observe an increased use of the passive voice (PV). The AfD, too, uses this deviant linguistic style. Since this is very different from the usual language newspapers use to report demands and intentions of political actors, those claims are not reliably recognized by our models. This is due to the fact that political claims analysis, both by definition and concretely in our coding scheme, requires an attributable actor. As a consequence, our models overlook claims, and recall drops.
- The CDU on the other hand keeps reminding the voter of how well they handled the crisis, signaling a claim to our identifier, even though

Party	Quote	Class	Reason
AfD	All rejected asylum seekers must be returned to their countries of origin.	FN	PV
SPD	[...] asylum procedures will continue to be conducted on European soil.	FN	PV
CDU	We have effectively reduced the number of those who do not have the right to stay.	FP	CA
CDU	We have helped many people in need and offered them hospitality and shelter.	FP	CA
SPD	In this [*proposed*] procedure, people make the application before entering Europe.	FN	mood
SPD	In this way, the identity is [*will be*] also determined in advance and registration is carried out.	FN	mood
AfD	We [...] demand mandatory age tests in cases of doubt,	TP	sub I
AfD	[*and*] the exclusion of family reunification.	FN	sub II
CDU	Especially in times of uncertainty, we need public institutions [...]	FP	NM
SPD	We are therefore committed to a new disarmament initiative.	FP	NM

Table 4: Examples of misclassifications from 2017

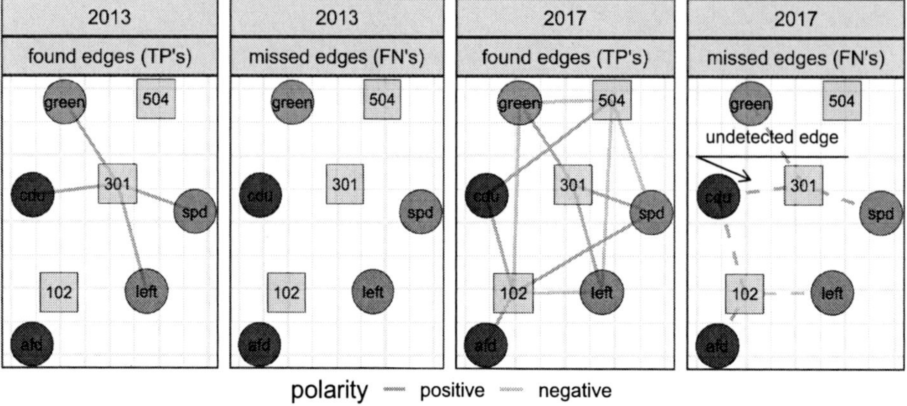

Figure 3: Identifying discourse networks in manifesto data

it is no longer an active demand but rather an already completed action (CA). This increases the number of false positives and results in a lower recall value.

- The most important difference, however, is that across all programs, parties expanded their treatment of migration and the topic started to permeate other subjects: In 2017, migration has become the justification for a lot of claims that were previously unrelated or peripheral (NM, cf. Table 4). Thus, the false positive rate increases and precision declines.

In conclusion, despite considerable textual and conceptual peculiarities, model performance in both years is on a surprisingly high level, modulated by ongoing political shifts.

4.3 Step 2: From Claims to Discourse Networks

Given the relatively robust performance of the computational model as well as the high overlap between correctly identified categories, we proceed to apply our model to a more substantive use case, namely the creation of discourse networks (see Figure 3). These networks harbour the potential to – at least partially – explain shifts in party position in their corresponding manifesto with shifts during the debate and vice versa.

Methodologically, discourse network analyses (DNA) aim to reveal discursive patterns of policy debates by focusing on the relations (edges) between actors and claims (vertices, cf. Figure 1) over time (Leifeld, 2016). In other words, the networks tie political to textual entities (concepts) to trace how a political discussion evolves, and how

influence is exerted to shape the direction of the discourse without directly addressing the political counterpart. Therefore, it is also particularly suitable for party manifestos, in which an open exchange of blows is neither possible nor desirable for most parties (Budge et al., 2001).

To carry out a discourse network analysis of the manifesto data, we employ the semi-automatic approach outlined in section 3.

We trace the development of prominent claims (upper limit - 102, integration offers - 301, safe countries of origin - 504) in 2013 and 2017 in Figure 3. Panels 1 and 2 describe the year 2013. Panel 1 shows the edges that are both manually and automatically identified (TPs): apparently only one claim of the three is supported by the four established parties. The empty Panel 2 shows that no such edges have been missed by the model. The picture changes once we move to 2017: Not all edges identified in 2017 (Panel 3) have also been identified each time (dashed lines, Panel 4).

However, as can be seen in the last panel, 5 out of 6 times this bears no consequence for the network topography, because the claim has already been found in another instance. Only in the case of the CDU's support of integration offers, the model failed to detect a claim and thus the network misses an edge. Auspiciously, this is rather the exception than the rule: For all claims in the entire network, only 7 percent of edges are missed by the semi-automatic approach (22 cases out of 333). We thus conclude that the claim identifier trained on newspaper data is a surprisingly good fit for party manifestos, due to the informational redundancy.

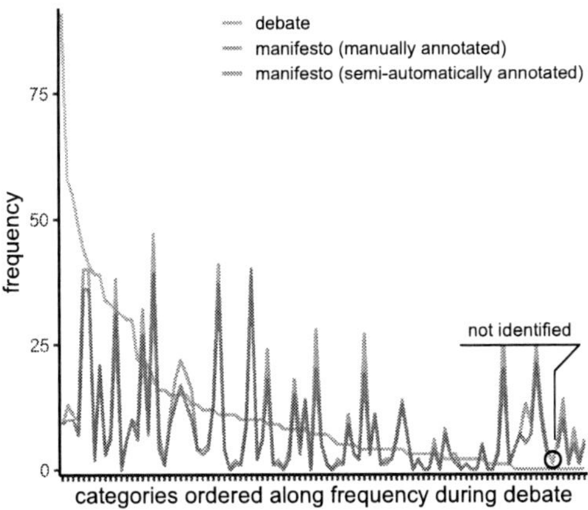

Figure 4: Claim category distribution in debates and manifestos

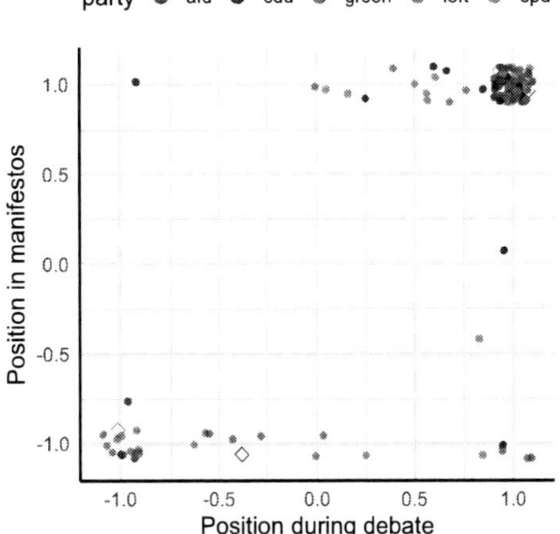

Figure 5: Scatterplot of positions (with jitter for clarity)

5   Issue salience and party position

In light of the promising performance, we now turn to the two remaining questions of substantive overlap between newspaper debate and party manifestos from the literature (cf. Section 2).

Salience.   The first one is: Can we in fact observe a different focus in terms of salience between formats? Figure 4 depicts the frequency distributions of (manually annotated) claim categories across public newspaper debate (red) and manifestos (blue), sorted by debate frequency. We observe considerable differences: popular categories during the 2015 debate are by no means also predominant in the party manifestos of 2013 and 2017. The correlation between genres amounts to only $r = 0.01$ ($p = 0.91$; for 2013 and 2017 alone $r = 0.28$ and $r = 0.1$, respectively), once one takes party specific salience into account. These results align well with findings from the literature on party salience. In contrast to the debate–manifesto split, the manually annotated distribution in the manifestos (blue) correlates extremely highly with the semi-automatic distribution (purple). ($r = 0.99$, $p < 0.01$), carrying over to individual parties as well, ranging from $r = 0.91$ to $r = 0.98$. This underlines again the usefulness of automatic analysis.

Positions.   A final question is whether the positions of parties regarding certain categories are similar across formats and whether a semi-automatic approach captures complementary tendencies. Po-

sitions (P) can be calculated as the difference between all positive and negative referrals to a certain claim C divided by their sum (Kim and Fording, 2003, p. 97-98):

$$P = \frac{\left(\sum C_{pos} - \sum C_{neg}\right)}{\left(\sum C_{pos} + \sum C_{neg}\right)} \tag{1}$$

Figure 5 shows the positioning of parties on different claims in the 2015 debates (x-axis) as well as the union of their 2013 and 2017 manifestos (y-axis), ranging from -1 (total opposition) to 1 (total support). This translates into a scale with the endpoints acceptance or rejection regarding a certain political demand with more moderate positions in between. The four uncoloured squares mark claims which were not automatically identified for this particular party in their manifesto. Most observations are aligned perfectly across genres and located in two clusters (bottom left and top right corner). This indicates consistent party positions between text types (and also years) with occasional moderate changes and very few volte-faces.

Again, this confirms findings from the literature: The positions derived from manifestos are a strong indicator of positioning during discourse and vice versa ($r = 0.79$, $p < 0.01$; for 2013 and 2017 alone $r = 0.69$ and $r = 0.83$, respectively). Unsurprisingly, we observe more variance in the position of parties during the debate (x-axis, Figure 5), since it displays the aggregated and at times contradictory position of individual party members instead of an unified party.

It is also noteworthy that 62% of party specific claims appear in one text type but not the other. This fact diminishes the party-specific overlap between formats quite a lot and also impacts the meaningfulness of the correlation. Interestingly enough, the correlation between manually and semi-automatically estimated positions (excluding the missing claims) appears unaffected by this bias and amounts to $r = 0.99$ ($p < 0.01$). Analogous to the application scenario in 4.3, this can to a great extend be explained by textual redundancy: Assuming that parties emphasize claims multiple times and streamline their texts to avoid contradictions, we only need to find a single repetition of a specific claim to find the correct representation of that position. That makes a semi-automatic approach to positions much less demanding than to salience, because in the latter case every instance matters. In summary, while parties did not put the same emphasis on categories across text types, their standpoints appear to be consistent over the short time window under investigation.

6 Conclusion

In this paper, we have explored whether computational models for claim detection trained on newspaper data could be applied to party manifestos as well. We found both high numeric performance, with F1 scores in the range of 0.80, and substantive overlap between manual and semi-automatically annotated sections in electoral programs.

A first surprise was that the claim detection model achieved better results for the 2013 than for the 2017 manifesto. We have offered a machine learning-based explanation, and a set of three political ones: The first two were connected to deviant linguistic styles, and the third to the increasingly ubiquitous nature of the migration topic after the so-called 'refugee crisis' of 2015. These hypotheses can clearly benefit from a future more systematic re-examination on a larger scale.

Assessing the perspectives for building discourse networks from the party manifestos, we were able to semi-automatically identify 93% of the edges by taking advantage of textual redundancy. With this in mind, we were able to confirm existing findings from the political science literature on party position and issue salience. While the positions of different parties on distinct claims are mostly congruent between formats, salience turned out to be largely uncorrelated.

Clearly, our current approach has further limitations. First, we only focus on one of many potential policy issues (migration) within a very short time-frame. This begs the question of generalizability, which we aim to address in three ways in future research: Concretely, ongoing work extends our analysis to different years (2005 and 2010), to the issue of pensions, and to another newspaper to validate our findings as well as to account for issue-specific characteristics (such as the degree of polarization or the granularity of proposed policy instruments).

Second, even though we already reduced it considerably, we still rely on human intervention for the semi-automatic annotation. Yet, from a mixed-methods perspective, this approach highlights the mutual benefit of interleaving political science and NLP. On the one hand the cross-validation of discourse networks with networks based on electoral programs could open up new venues for DNA and, conversely, explore the role public discourse plays in the formation of these programs. On the other hand, a still open question is whether training and test data can be reversed. To answer this question additional labeled material is needed. Positive results might prove as a welcome shortcut to the creation of comprehensive codebooks for political claims analysis given the much higher ratio of claims to text in manifestos. Both approaches would require computational assistance and thus enable further integration of NLP and CSS.

Acknowledgments

We acknowledge funding by Deutsche Forschungsgemeinschaft (DFG) through MARDY (*Modeling Argumentation Dynamics*) within SPP RATIO and by Bundesministerium fur Bildung und Forschung (BMBF) through E-DELIB (*Powering up e-deliberation: towards AI-supported moderation*).

References

Gavin Abercrombie, Federico Nanni, Riza Batista-Navarro, and Simone Paolo Ponzetto. 2019. Policy Preference Detection in Parliamentary Debate Motions. In *Proceedings of the 23rd Conference on Computational Natural Language Learning (CoNLL)*, pages 249–259, Hong Kong, China. Association for Computational Linguistics.

James Adams. 2001. *Party Competition and Respon-*

sible Party Government. University of Michigan Press.

American Political Science Association. 1950. *Toward a More Responsible Two-Party System. A Report of the Committee on Political Parties*. Menasha, Wis.

Judith L. Bara. 2006. The 2005 Manifestos: A Sense of Déjà Vu? *Journal of Elections, Public Opinion and Parties*, 16(3):265–281.

Kenneth Benoit and Michael Laver. 2007. Estimating party policy positions: Comparing expert surveys and hand-coded content analysis. *Electoral Studies*, 26(1):90 – 107.

Ian Budge. 1987. The internal analysis of election programmes. In David Robertson, Derek Hearl, and Ian Budge, editors, *Ideology, Strategy and Party Change: Spatial Analyses of Post-War Election Programmes in 19 Democracies*, pages 15–38. Cambridge University Press, Cambridge.

Ian Budge, Hans-Dieter Klingemann, Andrea Volkens, Judith Bara, and Tanenbaum. 2001. *Mapping Policy Preferences: Estimates for Parties, Electors, and Governments, 1945-1998*. Oxford University Press.

Elena Cabrio and Serena Villata. 2018. Five Years of Argument Mining: A Data-driven Analysis. In *Proceedings of the Twenty-Seventh International Joint Conference on Artificial Intelligence*, pages 5427–5433, Stockholm, Sweden. International Joint Conferences on Artificial Intelligence Organization.

Hal Daumé III. 2007. Frustratingly easy domain adaptation. In *Proceedings of the 45th Annual Meeting of the Association of Computational Linguistics*, pages 256–263, Prague, Czech Republic. Association for Computational Linguistics.

Erenay Dayanik and Sebastian Padó. 2020. Masking actor information leads to fairer political claims detection. In *Proceedings of the 58th Annual Meeting of the Association for Computational Linguistics*, pages 4385–4391, Online. Association for Computational Linguistics.

Jacob Devlin, Ming-Wei Chang, Kenton Lee, and Kristina Toutanova. 2019. BERT: Pre-training of deep bidirectional transformers for language understanding. In *Proceedings of the 2019 Conference of the North American Chapter of the Association for Computational Linguistics: Human Language Technologies, Volume 1 (Long and Short Papers)*, pages 4171–4186, Minneapolis, Minnesota. Association for Computational Linguistics.

João Gama, Indrė Žliobaitė, Albert Bifet, Mykola Pechenizkiy, and Abdelhamid Bouchachia. 2014. A survey on concept drift adaptation. *ACM Computing Surveys*, 46(4).

Goran Glavaš, Federico Nanni, and Simone Paolo Ponzetto. 2017. Cross-lingual classification of topics in political texts. In *Proceedings of the Second Workshop on NLP and Computational Social Science*, pages 42–46, Vancouver, Canada. Association for Computational Linguistics.

Christoffer Green-Pedersen and Peter B. Mortensen. 2015. Avoidance and Engagement: Issue Competition in Multiparty Systems. *Political Studies*, 63(4):747–764.

Martin Haselmayer, Thomas M Meyer, and Markus Wagner. 2019. Fighting for attention: Media coverage of negative campaign messages. *Party Politics*, 25(3):412–423.

Sebastian Haunss, Nico Blokker, Andre Blessing, Erenay Dayanik, Gabriella Lapesa, Jonas Kuhn, and Sebastian Padó. 2020. Integrating manual and automatic annotation for the creation of discourse network data sets. *Politics and Governance*, 8(2):326–339.

Marc Helbling and Anke Tresch. 2011. Measuring party positions and issue salience from media coverage: Discussing and cross-validating new indicators. *Electoral Studies*, 30(1):174–183.

Heemin Kim and Richard C. Fording. 2003. Voter ideology in Western democracies: An update. *European Journal of Political Research*, 42(1):95–105.

Ruud Koopmans and Paul Statham. 1999. Political Claims Analysis: Integrating Protest Event and Political Discourse Approaches. *Mobilization: An International Quarterly*, 4(2):203–221.

Gabriella Lapesa, Andre Blessing, Nico Blokker, Erenay Dayanik, Sebastian Haunss, Jonas Kuhn, and Sebastian Padó. 2020. DEbateNet-mig15:tracing the 2015 immigration debate in Germany over time. In *Proceedings of The 12th Language Resources and Evaluation Conference*, pages 919–927, Marseille, France. European Language Resources Association.

Philip Leifeld. 2009. Die Untersuchung von Diskursnetzwerken mit dem Discourse Network Analyzer (DNA). In Volker Schneider, Frank Janning, Philip Leifeld, and Thomas Malang, editors, *Politiknetzwerke. Modelle, Anwendungen Und Visualisierungen*, pages 391–404. VS Verlag für Sozialwissenschaften, Opladen.

Philip Leifeld. 2016. *Policy Debates as Dynamic Networks: German Pension Politics and Privatization Discourse*. Campus Verlag, Frankfurt/New York.

Marco Lippi and Paolo Torroni. 2015. Context-independent claim detection for argument mining. In *Proceedings of the 24th International Conference on Artificial Intelligence*, page 185–191. AAAI Press.

Marco Lippi and Paolo Torroni. 2016. Argument mining from speech: Detecting claims in political debates. In *Proceedings of the Thirtieth AAAI Conference on Artificial Intelligence*, page 2979–2985. AAAI Press.

Peter Mair. 2009. Representative versus responsible government. Working Paper 09/8, MPIfG working paper.

Gary Marks, Liesbet Hooghe, Marco R. Steenbergen, and Ryan Bakker. 2007. Crossvalidating data on party positioning on European integration. *Electoral Studies*, 26(1):23–38.

Nicolas Merz. 2018. *The Manifesto-Media Link: How Mass Media Mediate Manifesto Messages*. Ph.D. thesis, Humboldt-Universität zu Berlin, Kultur-, Sozial- und Bildungswissenschaftliche Fakultät.

Catherine E. Netjes and Harmen A. Binnema. 2007. The salience of the european integration issue: Three data sources compared. *Electoral Studies*, 26(1):39–49.

Sebastian Padó, Andre Blessing, Nico Blokker, Erenay Dayanik, Sebastian Haunss, and Jonas Kuhn. 2019. Who Sides with Whom? Towards Computational Construction of Discourse Networks for Political Debates. In *Proceedings of the 57th Annual Meeting of the Association for Computational Linguistics*, pages 2841–2847, Florence, Italy. Association for Computational Linguistics.

Colin Rallings. 1987. The influence of election programmes: Britain and Canada 1945–1979. In David Robertson, Derek Hearl, and Ian Budge, editors, *Ideology, Strategy and Party Change: Spatial Analyses of Post-War Election Programmes in 19 Democracies*, pages 1–14. Cambridge University Press, Cambridge.

Leonard Ray. 2007. Validity of measured party positions on european integration: Assumptions, approaches, and a comparison of alternative measures. *Electoral Studies*, 26(1):11 – 22.

David Bruce Robertson. 1976. *A Theory of Party Competition*. J. Wiley.

Samuel Rönnqvist, Jenna Kanerva, Tapio Salakoski, and Filip Ginter. 2019. Is multilingual BERT fluent in language generation? In *Proceedings of the First NLPL Workshop on Deep Learning for Natural Language Processing*, pages 29–36, Turku, Finland. Linköping University Electronic Press.

Tobias Schwarzbözl, Matthias Fatke, and Swen Hutter. 2019. How party-issue linkages vary between election manifestos and media debates. *West European Politics*, pages 1–24.

Christian Stab, Tristan Miller, Benjamin Schiller, Pranav Rai, and Iryna Gurevych. 2018. Cross-topic Argument Mining from Heterogeneous Sources. In *Proceedings of the 2018 Conference on Empirical Methods in Natural Language Processing*, pages 3664–3674, Brussels, Belgium. Association for Computational Linguistics.

Jacques J. A. Thomassen. 1994. Empirical Research into Political Representation: Failing Democracy or Failing Models? In M. Kent Jennings and T.E. Mann, editors, *Elections at Home and Abroad, Essays in Honor of Warren Miller*, pages 237–265. Michigan University Press.

Andrea Volkens and Judith Bara. 2013. Presidential Versus Parliamentary Representation: Extending the Manifesto Estimates to Latin America. In Andrea Volkens, Judith Bara, Ian Budge, Michael D. McDonald, Robin Best, and Simon Franzmann, editors, *Mapping Policy Preferences From Texts: Statistical Solutions for Manifesto Analysts*, chapter Mapping Policy Preferences From Texts, pages 277–298. Oxford University Press.

Andrea Volkens, Werner Krause, Pola Lehmann, Theres Matthieß, Nicolas Merz, Sven Regel, and Bernhard Weßels. 2019. The Manifesto data collection, version 2019b.

Does Social Support Expressed in Post Titles Elicit Comments in Online Substance Use Recovery Forums?

Anietie Andy[1], Sharath Chandra Guntuku[2]
[1]Penn Medicine [2]Computer and Information Science
University of Pennsylvania
{anietie.andy@pennmedicine,sharathg@cis}.upenn.edu

Abstract

Individuals recovering from substance use often seek social support (emotional and informational) on online recovery forums, where they can both write and comment on posts, expressing their struggles and successes. A common challenge in these forums is that certain posts (some of which may be support seeking) receive no comments. In this work, we use data from two Reddit substance recovery forums: */r/Leaves* and */r/OpiatesRecovery*, to determine the relationship between the social supports expressed in the titles of posts and the number of comments they receive. We show that the types of social support expressed in post titles that elicit comments vary from one substance use recovery forum to the other.

1 Introduction

In the United States (US), substance use disorder (SUD) is one of the main causes of premature death (Johnston et al., 2003; Schulte and Hser, 2013). Social media is often used by people with SUD to seek support (MacLean et al., 2015). Online substance use recovery forums such as the Reddit forum, */r/Leaves* - which focuses on discussions around quitting marijuana, provide a "safe space" where members - some of whom may be struggling with substance use, can freely communicate and seek help from other members.

Prior work showed that 10% of support-seeking messages on a forum focused on discussions around cancer received no comments (Wang et al., 2015; Yang et al., 2019a). We find that support-seeking posts (across a 3 months time period) from */r/Leaves* follow a similar trend with 11% of posts receiving no comments, thereby leaving some users seeking support without adequate support.

The following social supports: emotional and informational are crucial in online forums focused on discussions around health and well-being (Wang et al., 2012; Yang et al., 2017), where similar to prior work (Wang et al., 2012), emotional support sought in posts seek affirmation, encouragement, and compassion, while informational support sought in posts seek information or advice.

Reddit posts are made up of two sections: the *title* - which briefly describes the post, and the *selftext* - which describes the post in more detail. Glenski and Weninger (2017) demonstrated that on Reddit, user interactions such as voting and commenting on posts is guided by the title of the post (post-titles); thereby implying that readers utilize linguistic cues in the post-titles on Reddit to decide whether to respond to posts. Hence, in this work, we focus on analyzing the post-titles in two Reddit substance use recovery forums */r/Leaves* and */r/OpiatesRecovery*. We measure the extent to which these post-titles seek emotional support and informational support and analyze their relationship with the number of comments they receive. We hypothesize that since the interests of users who belong to different forums focused on similar discussions differs Tran and Ostendorf (2016), the type of social support (expressed in post-titles) that elicits comments may differ from one online substance use recovery forum to the other.

Understanding the relationship between the social supports (emotional and informational) sought in post-titles published in substance use recovery forums and the number of comments these posts receive is important partly because users join online health forums when going through a health care event such as cancer (Wen and Rosé, 2012; Yang et al., 2019a) or recovering from substance use (MacLean et al., 2015); therefore, posts not receiving comments in these forums means that some users are not getting the necessary support they need.

Proceedings of the Fourth Workshop on Natural Language Processing and Computational Social Science, pages 35–40
Online, November 20, 2020. ©2020 Association for Computational Linguistics
https://doi.org/10.18653/v1/P17

2 Related Work

Some prior work focused on non-health related forums while others focused on health related forums.

In non-health related forums, Althoff et al. (2014) studied a Reddit forum to determine the social and linguistic factors associated with posts in the forum that elicit responses. Tran and Ostendorf (2016) explored several Reddit forums and determined that different forums use different language styles and there was a correlation between a forums language style and the responses to comments. Jaech et al. (2015) examined the effect of language use in online forums on the reaction of members of the forums to comments. Hessel et al. (2017) studied if incorporating multimodal features attracted user attention (Horne et al., 2017).

In health related forums, Wang et al. (2012) examined the effect of different social supports users are exposed to in an online cancer forum and its effect on the duration of user membership in the forum. Wang et al. (2015) demonstrated that in an online cancer forum, members tend to respond with emotional support when users self-disclose negative information about themselves. Yang et al. (2019b) studied communication in an online cancer forum and determined that members of the forum tend to disclose more negative information about themselves in public domains provided by the forums compared to the forums private domains. Yang et al. (2017) examined the relationship between the kind of communication received by members of an online cancer forum and their commitment to the forum. Yang et al. (2019a) determined that over time, members of an online cancer forum change roles and that certain roles are predictors of prolonged commitment to the group. Chancellor et al. (2018) examined online weight loss forums and determined how support influences user behavior changes. MacLean et al. (2015) analyzed different phases of opioid addiction in an online forum focused on discussions around opioid use recovery.

Our work is different from prior work in that we analyze posts published in online substance use recovery forums with the aim to determine if and how emotional and informational support sought in published posts in substance use recovery forums elicit comments from members of the forums. This study received exempt status from the University of Pennsylvania Institutional Review Board.

3 Dataset

Our dataset consists of posts and meta-data from two active Reddit substance use recovery forums, */r/Leaves* and */r/OpiatesRecovery*, which have 147,000 members and 27,000 members, respectively, as of September 2020. */r/Leaves* is self-described as *"a support and recovery community for practical discussions about how to quit pot, weed, cannabis, edibles, BHO, shatter, or whatever THC-related product you're using, and support in staying stopped"*. */r/OpiatesRecovery* is self described as *"We are a group of people dedicated to helping each other kick the habit"*. We chose */r/Leaves* and */r/OpiatesRecovery* because these forums are the Reddit substance use recovery forums focused on marijuana and opioid use, respectively, with the most number of users.

Typically in these forums, a member writes a post (*title* and *selftext*) and other members respond to the post by either voting the post *up* or *down* or writing a comment. In this paper, we focus only on the comment responses to posts. Using Google's BigQuery[1], which is a data warehouse containing data from Reddit, we collected and processed all posts published in */r/Leaves* and */r/OpiatesRecovery* between December 2015 and August 2019 and collected the following data related to each post: the post-title, the user who published the post, the time the post was created, the comments the post received, and the number of comments the post received. Table 1 highlights the summary of our dataset.

Attribute	*/r/Leaves*	*/r/OpiatesRecovery*
Number of unique users	18,100	4,374
Number of posts	35,961	9,900
Number of comments	227,850	129,801

Table 1: Summary of the */r/Leaves* and */r/OpiatesRecovery* datasets

4 Social Support

Several studies have shown the importance of the expression of emotional and informational social supports in forums focused on discussions around health (Wang et al., 2012; Yang et al., 2017, 2019a). Using a similar method from previous work by Wang et al. (2012), we built two models to determine how much emotional and informational support, respectively, is sought in post-titles in our dataset. We had 3 annotators - who were health

---

[1]https://cloud.google.com/bigquery/

care professionals with graduate degrees and familiar with substance use recovery, to rate a sample of 1,000 post-titles from our dataset, on (i) how much informational support each post-title sought and (ii) how much emotional support each post-title sought; where informational support post-titles provide/seek advice or information and emotional support post-titles seek encouragement, understanding, or affirmation (Wang et al., 2012). Similar to prior work, (Wang et al., 2012), the annotators rated these post-titles using a 7-point Likert scale (1 meant "social support was not expressed in a post-title" and 7 meant "social support was expressed a lot in a post-title"). To measure the reliability of the annotators, we used intra-class correlation (ICC) (Bartko, 1966), which measures annotator reliability when each post-title is rated by different groups of annotators; the ICC for informational support sought and emotional support sought were 0.95 and 0.93, respectively. For each post-title, the annotator ratings were averaged, hence each post-title had a score that ranged between 1 and 7 which indicated how much informational and emotional support was sought.

4.1 Features

We extracted several language features from the annotated post-titles.

Using Linguistic Inquiry and Word Count (LIWC) (Pennebaker et al., 2015) - a dictionary comprising different psycho-linguistic categories, we selected the following LIWC categories relevant to informational and emotional support (Wang et al., 2012): "positive emotion", "negative emotion", "she/he", "you", "we", "i",impersonal pronoun", auxiliary" "verb", "past", "present", "future","religion", "death" "they", "cognitive mechanism", "biological processes", "time".

Similar to Wang et al. (2012), from each post-title, we extract the number of sentences, the number of words in each sentence, the number of sentences that contain negation words/phrases such as "not", and the number of sentences phrased as questions.

We also extracted the number of specific parts-of-speech and the number of strong subjectivity words such as "affirmation" and weak subjectivity words such as "abandoned" (Wilson et al., 2005; Wang et al., 2012).

Post-titles seeking advice or involving requests were identified and counted (Wang et al., 2012) by (i) selecting sentences that began with the word "you" and followed by a Modal verb such as "may" and (ii) selecting sentences that began with the word "please" and followed by a verb.

We collected names of medicines from the Food and Drug Administration website website [2]; also a comprehensive list of nicknames for drugs was compiled (Wang et al., 2012); we counted the number of drug names in each post-title.

We trained a model of 20 Latent Dirichlet Allocation (LDA) (Blei et al., 2003) topics from 45,000 randomly selected post-titles from our dataset. Two physicians, who are familiar with substance use recovery, manually assigned a label to each of the topics, as shown in Table 2.

4.2 Social Support Prediction Model

We built two Random Forest models that each output a numerical value that indicates how much emotional support and informational support is expressed in a post-title based on the annotations. We experimented with SVM, logistic regression, and Random Forest; Random Forest performed better. We randomly partitioned the annotated posts into a training set (80%), a validation set (10%), and a test set (10%). We used the validation set to evaluate the performance of the models; when the performance on the validation set was satisfactory, the models were then evaluated on the test set. Similar to Wang et al. (2012), Pearson's correlation was used to measure the correlation of the models with the annotated data.

These models correlated with the average annotator ratings with Pearson's correlation $r = 0.46$ and $r = 0.51$ for seeking emotional support and informational support, respectively. We then applied these models to the posts in our dataset. Table 3 shows the 5 most important features, as ranked by the Random forest model.

5 Does social support expressed in post-titles elicit comments?

A challenge in substance use recovery forums is that several support-seeking posts do not receive any comments, thereby leaving some posters potentially without adequate support. In this section, we aim to determine if emotional and informational support expressed in post-titles elicit comments in */r/Leaves* and */r/OpiatesRecovery*. For our analysis, we select posts by users with 5 or more published

Table 2: Summary of LDA topic themes and top 5 highly correlated words associated with each topic

LDA topic themes	Highly correlated words
Time sober	months, weeks, sober, clean, year
Wanting reasons to stop	stop, can't, high, anymore, friends
Feelings: anxious and depressed	feeling, depressed, tired, high, anxious
Time sober before relapse	days, sober, clean, hours, free
Withdrawal symptoms and addiction	withdrawal, drug, test,addiction,job
Cravings and relapse	night, strong, cravings, weekend, relapsed
Advice for quitting	quitting, advice, tips,support, benefits
Ready to quit	time, quit, finally, hard, stop
Making the decision to quit	made, make, life, things, friends
Feelings of quitting	anxiety, quitting, depression, deal,pains
mood and feelings	good, today, bad, high,start
Years of using	years, daily, heavy, user, habit
Reason for quitting	quitting, brain, back, motivation, fog
Impact of addiction	life, addiction, love, hate, relationship
Quitting	quit, ago, months,stop, haven't
Side effects	dreams, sleep, night, nightmares, insomnia
Struggling with relapse	day, end, relapse, struggling, thoughts
Time to start sobriety	day, today, start,journey, sobriety
Thinking of quitting	cold, turkey, thinking, cut, habit
Sharing stories	story, thought, wanted, share, addiction

Emotional Support	Informational Support
Thinking of quitting- (0.76)	Share stories - (0.69)
Word length - (0.033)	Thinking of quitting-(0.046)
Sharing stories - (0.032)	Word length - (0.044)
Noun - (0.021)	Noun (0.035)
Strong subjectivity - (0.016)	Strong subjectivity - (0.028)

Table 3: Top 5 most important features as ranked by the Random forest model

posts in our dataset i.e. 12,960 posts published by 1,285 users from */r/Leaves* and 4,055 posts published by 335 users from */r/OpiatesRecovery*. For each user, we calculate the average number of comments they received for all their posts. We also calculated the average extent of emotional and informational support scores for posts published by each user. We correlate the mean extent of emotional and informational support, respectively with the mean number of comments received per user.

Feature	Pearson r
Emotional Support Sought	0.17
Informational Support Sought	0.22

Table 4: Correlation between social support sought and number of comments: */r/Leaves*. $p < 0.001$. Number of users = 1,285

Feature	Pearson r
Emotional Support Sought	0.15
Informational Support Sought	- 0.13

Table 5: Correlation between social support sought and number of comments: */r/OpiatesRecovery*. $p < 0.001$. Number of users = 335

Results and Discussion: Tables 4 and 5 show the correlation between social support sought in post-titles and number of comments in */r/Leaves* and */r/OpiatesRecovery*, respectively. We observed that in */r/Leaves*, the average informational support sought by users in post-titles correlates more with the average number of comments received by these users compared to the average emotional support sought. Also, we observed that in */r/OpiatesRecovery*, the average emotional support sought had a positive correlation with the average number of comments received compared the average informational support sought which had a negative correlation with the average number of comments received.

These findings can benefit members of substance use recovery forums; for example, users seeking to elicit comments to their posts published on */r/Leaves* may use linguistic cues associated with higher informational support in their post-titles. Also, the findings from this work can benefit substance use recovery forum moderators; given that there is a negative correlation between the informational support sought in post-titles in */r/OpiatesRecovery*, this potentially means that some users seeking informational support in this forum are not receiving support. Hence moderators of the forum can come up with ways in which these informational support seeking posts receive comments; for example informational support seeking posts not receiving comments may be sent to moderators or users familiar with the support sought.

Limitations and Future Work:

In our analysis, we focused on two subreddits - */r/Leaves* and */r/OpiatesRecovery*, which are the forums focused on recovery from marijuana use and opiod use with the most number of members on Reddit. In the future, we would explore the relationship between social support expressed in posts and the responses (comments and votes) they receive, in other substance use recovery forums. While the results in this work indicate statistically significant correlations, in the future, we would look at the affect of author tenure and Reddit karma (reputation) - all of which could potentially contribute to the response rates of posts.

6   Conclusion

We built two models to measure the extent of informational and emotional social support expressed in post-titles in two substance use recovery. We used these models to show the social supports that elicit comments in these forums.

References

Tim Althoff, Cristian Danescu-Niculescu-Mizil, and Dan Jurafsky. 2014. How to ask for a favor: A case study on the success of altruistic requests. In *Eighth International AAAI Conference on Weblogs and Social Media*.

John J Bartko. 1966. The intraclass correlation coefficient as a measure of reliability. *Psychological reports*, 19(1):3–11.

David M Blei, Andrew Y Ng, and Michael I Jordan. 2003. Latent dirichlet allocation. *Journal of machine Learning research*, 3(Jan):993–1022.

Stevie Chancellor, Andrea Hu, and Munmun De Choudhury. 2018. Norms matter: contrasting social support around behavior change in online weight loss communities. In *Proceedings of the 2018 CHI Conference on Human Factors in Computing Systems*, page 666. ACM.

Maria Glenski and Tim Weninger. 2017. Predicting user-interactions on reddit. In *Proceedings of the 2017 IEEE/ACM International Conference on Advances in Social Networks Analysis and Mining 2017*, pages 609–612.

Jack Hessel, Lillian Lee, and David Mimno. 2017. Cats and captions vs. creators and the clock: Comparing multimodal content to context in predicting relative popularity. In *Proceedings of the 26th International Conference on World Wide Web*, pages 927–936. International World Wide Web Conferences Steering Committee.

Benjamin D Horne, Sibel Adali, and Sujoy Sikdar. 2017. Identifying the social signals that drive online discussions: A case study of reddit communities. In *2017 26th International Conference on Computer Communication and Networks (ICCCN)*, pages 1–9. IEEE.

Aaron Jaech, Victoria Zayats, Hao Fang, Mari Ostendorf, and Hannaneh Hajishirzi. 2015. Talking to the crowd: What do people react to in online discussions? *arXiv preprint arXiv:1507.02205*.

Lloyd D Johnston, Patrick M O'Malley, and Jerald G Bachman. 2003. Monitoring the future: National results on adolescent drug use: Overview of key findings. *Focus*, 1(2):213–234.

Diana MacLean, Sonal Gupta, Anna Lembke, Christopher Manning, and Jeffrey Heer. 2015. Forum77: An analysis of an online health forum dedicated to addiction recovery. In *Proceedings of the 18th ACM Conference on Computer Supported Cooperative Work & Social Computing*, pages 1511–1526. ACM.

James W Pennebaker, Ryan L Boyd, Kayla Jordan, and Kate Blackburn. 2015. The development and psychometric properties of liwc2015. Technical report.

Marya T Schulte and Yih-Ing Hser. 2013. Substance use and associated health conditions throughout the lifespan. *Public Health Reviews*, 35(2):3.

Trang Tran and Mari Ostendorf. 2016. Characterizing the language of online communities and its relation to community reception. *arXiv preprint arXiv:1609.04779*.

Yi-Chia Wang, Robert Kraut, and John M Levine. 2012. To stay or leave?: the relationship of emotional and informational support to commitment in online health support groups. In *Proceedings of the ACM 2012 conference on Computer Supported Cooperative Work*, pages 833–842. ACM.

Yi-Chia Wang, Robert E Kraut, and John M Levine. 2015. Eliciting and receiving online support: using computer-aided content analysis to examine the dynamics of online social support. *Journal of medical Internet research*, 17(4):e99.

Miaomiao Wen and Carolyn Penstein Rosé. 2012. Understanding participant behavior trajectories in online health support groups using automatic extraction methods. In *Proceedings of the 17th ACM international conference on Supporting group work*, pages 179–188. ACM.

Theresa Wilson, Janyce Wiebe, and Paul Hoffmann. 2005. Recognizing contextual polarity in phrase-level sentiment analysis. In *Proceedings of Human Language Technology Conference and Conference on Empirical Methods in Natural Language Processing*.

Diyi Yang, Robert Kraut, and John M Levine. 2017. Commitment of newcomers and old-timers to online health support communities. In *Proceedings of the 2017 CHI conference on human factors in computing systems*, pages 6363–6375. ACM.

Diyi Yang, Robert E Kraut, Tenbroeck Smith, Elijah Mayfield, and Dan Jurafsky. 2019a. Seekers, providers, welcomers, and storytellers: Modeling social roles in online health communities. In *Proceedings of the 2019 CHI Conference on Human Factors in Computing Systems*, page 344. ACM.

Diyi Yang, Zheng Yao, Joseph Seering, and Robert Kraut. 2019b. The channel matters: Self-disclosure, reciprocity and social support in online cancer support groups.

I miss you babe: Analyzing Emotion Dynamics
During COVID-19 Pandemic

Lynnette Hui Xian Ng[1]   **Roy Ka-Wei Lee[2]**   **Md Rabiul Awal[3]**

[1] Carnegie Mellon University
[2] Singapore University of Technology and Design
[3] University of Saskatchewan

`lynnetteng@cmu.edu, roy_lee@sutd.edu.sg, mda219@usask.ca`

Abstract

With the world on a lockdown due to the COVID-19 pandemic, this paper studies emotions expressed on Twitter. Using a combined strategy of time series analysis of emotions augmented by tweet topics, this study provides an insight into emotion transitions during the pandemic. After tweets are annotated with dominant emotions and topics, a time-series emotion analysis is used to identify disgust and anger as the most commonly identified emotions. Through longitudinal analysis of each user, we construct emotion transition graphs, observing key transitions between disgust and anger, and self-transitions within anger and disgust emotional states. Observing user patterns through clustering of user longitudinal analyses reveals emotional transitions fall into four main clusters: (1) erratic motion over short period of time, (2) disgust $\rightarrow$ anger, (3) optimism $\rightarrow$ joy. (4) erratic motion over a prolonged period. Finally, we propose a method for predicting users subsequent topic, and by consequence their emotions, through constructing an Emotion Topic Hidden Markov Model, augmenting emotion transition states with topic information. Results suggests that the predictions fare better than baselines, spurring directions of predicting emotional states based on Twitter posts.

1   Introduction

In August 2020, the COVID-19 pandemic raged throughout the world. Caused by the virus SARS-CoV-2 (Mehta et al., 2020), the pandemic, still ongoing during this study, has infected more than 26 million people and has taken over 800,000 lives. Globally, countries have taken unprecedented measures for virus containment, most notably, implementing cities lockdown and forcing citizens into isolation.

Despite limited face interactions, digitalization has provided a space for expression. Twitter users have expressed their yearning for loved ones, their lifestyles, the freedom of social activities and travels: *"[...] I miss you babe. I wish this shit is over and we will travel Himalay together!*. Others express frustration about missed opportunities and the stress of isolation: *#covid [..] will kill but #starvation WILL definitely kill*.

Previous studies of emotion analysis on Twitter largely focused on identifying emotions for general tweets (Sailunaz et al., 2018; Colnerič and Demsar, 2018; Subramaniam et al., 2017), and during the COVID-19 period (Mukherjee et al., 2020; Gupta et al., 2020). In analyzing emotion dynamics on Twitter, Naskar et al. (2019) modelled emotional states of Twitter users with a Hidden Markov Model, and further showed that Twitter users change their emotional state against their topics (Naskar et al., 2020).

Our study aims to characterize emotional states and transitions of Twitter users during the global COVID-19 lockdown. The study contributes to ongoing literature through the following research questions: (1) What are the emotion dynamics expressed amid the COVID-19 pandemic? That is, what are the topics discussed and the corresponding emotions? (2) What are the profiles of emotion transitions over time? (3) How might we effectively predict a user's subsequent tweet's emotion?

To investigate the above questions, we collected a Twitter dataset during the COVID-19 pandemic (Section 3) to study emotion dynamics, which is the interplay between topics discussed and emotions expressed in a tweet. We computationally annotated our collected tweets with emotions from an emotion classifier pre-trained on an labeled emotion dataset (Mohammad et al., 2018). To augment the emotion label, we learned topics of tweets using Latent Dirichlet Allocation (Mimno and Mimno, 2013). In Section 4, we study user emotion transitions by first constructing an aggregate emotion

Proceedings of the Fourth Workshop on Natural Language Processing and Computational Social Science, pages 41–49
Online, November 20, 2020. ©2020 Association for Computational Linguistics
https://doi.org/10.18653/v1/P17

transition graph across all users, representing emotions as nodes and edges as emotion transitions between user tweets. We then cluster users' emotion transition graphs and observe emotional transition patterns. In Section 5, we propose an Emotion Topic Hidden Markov Model (ET-HMM), adopting a Hidden Markov Model (Rabiner, 1989) on the users' emotion transition states augmented with topic information, and evaluate the model's prediction of the topic and emotion expressed in a user's subsequent tweet. Our findings, as discussed in Section 6, suggest that the ET-HMM outperform baselines, and are hopefully useful in monitoring emotional health through social media.

2 Related Work

Emotion analysis in text is a widely studied area, spanning the evolution of emotions, emotion models, emotion detection methods and construction of datasets, detailed in several surveys highlighting the methods and challenges (Sailunaz et al., 2018; Binali et al., 2010; Kao et al., 2009; Jain et al., 2017).

Twitter, a text-rich social media, is a valuable and popular data source for emotion analysis (Sailunaz and Alhajj, 2019; Colneriĉ and Demsar, 2018; Subramaniam et al., 2017). Previous studies have proposed methods to detect and analyze Twitter users' emotional responses towards an event (Jones et al., 2016) and understand users' mental health (Wang et al., 2016; Seabrook et al., 2018). Colneriĉ and Demsar (2018) investigated and compared classification methods to recognize eight expressed emotions: joy, sadness, trust, disgust, fear, anger, surprise, anticipation.

Besides classifying user emotions on Twitter, existing studies analyzed emotion dynamics and changes of user emotions over time. Naskar et al. (2020) investigated social dynamics of emotions in Twitter users' opinions, and attempted to change user emotions towards social issues over time. During the pandemic, Mukherjee et al. (2020) analysed emotion trends on Indian tweets and the influence of public emotions on individual emotions, while Gupta et al. (2020) performed emotion and topical analysis on over 63 million tweets. Naskar et al. (2019) proposed a Hidden Markov Model (HMM) to model emotional changes through a Twitter user's consecutive sequence of tweets.

This study contributes to ongoing emotion analysis research by characterizing Twitter users' emotion dynamics during the COVID-19 pandemic. More specifically, we provide a preliminary understanding of the transition of emotional and mental states as the global pandemic develops. To the best of our knowledge, this is the first study that examines emotional dynamics amid a pandemic event.

3 Data Collection

We adopt the Twitter dataset collected in (Awal et al., 2020). Specifically, we begin with a random sample of 5.4 million tweets from 10.1 million users taken from the 1% Twitter streaming API collected during a period of seven weeks beginning from March 22, 2020. The tweets were collected with the following hashtags: '#covid-19', '#COVID-19', '#COVID', '#corona', '#Coronavirus', '#coronavirus', '#CoronaVirus'. From these tweets, we selected for tweets that contained the English words related to "yearning" and their related word forms (i.e. miss, yearn, pine, long, wish, crave), so as to ensure that a substantial number of tweets express some emotions (i.e. do not classify as neutral), and a spectrum of emotions is expressed. In this first selection of data, we obtained 2.8 million tweets from 233,932 users.

Using the selected set of users, we extracted all their tweets during our collection period, to facilitate longitudinal user emotion dynamic studies. This process yielded us a total of 3,035,844 tweets from 233,932 unique users. We thus use this consolidated dataset for further analysis and experiments.

4 Characterizing Emotion Dynamics

4.1 Topic Discovery

To discover topics in the datasets, we apply the Mallet LDA topic modelling tool (Mimno and Mimno, 2013) to learn topic clusters and their corresponding keywords. Each topic is represented by a probability distribution over the entire vocabulary, and created a topic model with the number of topics derived through the elbow rule from model coherence scores.

In the initial selected set of tweets, the topic analysis revealed four dominant topics, signifying the entities Twitter users yearn for. These topic clusters are: (1) hope: hope, find, story; (2) transition to online: online, call, show, work; (3) life and death: life, die, religion, helpless, crisis; (4) activities and people missed: summer, friend, family, future.

Table 1: Distributions and sample keywords of topics

	Topic	Keywords	Tweets (%)
1	General	medium, news, social, response, government, order, fact, question	9
2	Vaccines and Testing	testing, human, vaccine, risk, treatment, drug, infection	9
3	Country specific	country, world, safe, good, home, spread, nation, end	10
4	Lockdown	lockdown, government, police, citizen, fight, regime, law	10
5	Call for leader	people, time, crisis, work, great, leader, support, action	9
6	High case numbers	death, case, positive, total, high, bad, rate	10
7	Elections	trump, call, election, free, mask, pandemic	10
8	Relationships	people, life, year, family, friend, good	12
9	Concern for healthcare workers	patient, doctor, hospital, health, care, worker, long, hour, medical, staff	11
10	Business and job reliefs	state, economy, business, job, global, pandemic, money, relief	12

As the tweets are short, we assume each tweet only contain one topic and we annotate the tweet with the most dominant topic, i.e., the topic with the highest percentage weightage. This topic information per tweet is used to augment the Emotion Topic Hidden Markov Model, drawing on the fact that tweet topics can significantly influence expressed emotions (Naskar et al., 2020). The final dataset yielded a topic cluster of 10 topics, presented in Table 1.

4.2 Emotion Profiling

Emotion Annotation. To perform emotion profiling, we first annotate all tweets with their emotions. We constructed an Emotion Annotation Model based on SemEval-2018 (Mohammad et al., 2018), which contains English tweets that have been manually annotated with 11 emotions: anger, anticipation, disgust, fear, joy, love, optimism, pessimism, sadness, surprise, trust and neutral.

For the Emotion Annotation Model, we express each tweet as a vector representation of GloVe embeddings (Pennington et al., 2014). Then we built a two-fold deep-learning classifier using Keras Tensorflow on the training dataset. The first fold consists of a 100-unit Bidirectional Long-Short-Term-Memory (LSTM) followed by a 200-filter unit Convolutional Neural Network (CNN). The second fold consisted of a 100-filter unit CNN combined with a 100-unit Bidirectional LSTM. The two folds are combined with an Attention layer, and a consistent 0.3 dropout rate is used in both folds. With this model, we obtained an accuracy of 84% on the test dataset provided. Each tweet is annotated with the corresponding emotions, and its dominant emotion is determined as the emotion class with the highest percentage weightage. The tweets that are deemed not to display any emotions are annotated as neutral. While the original annotations had 11 categories, our final emotion annotation contains only seven emotion categories as the rest do not surface as dominant emotions in the tweets. Figure 1 shows the distribution of tweets and its annotated emotions. We note that the tweets are mostly dominated by anger, which is a reasonable emotion during this trying times. We further note that fear is present but in very low proportions.

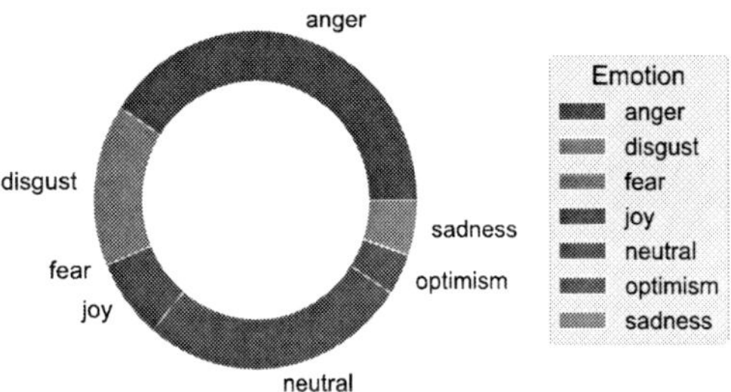

Figure 1: Distribution of tweets by emotions

Singular Emotion Dynamics. Emotion dynamics corresponding to a singular emotion is represented with the topic distribution across the seven emotional categories (Figure 2). Tweets expressing anger and disgust are discuss the spectrum of all 10 topics. Tweets exhibiting fear have a high pro-

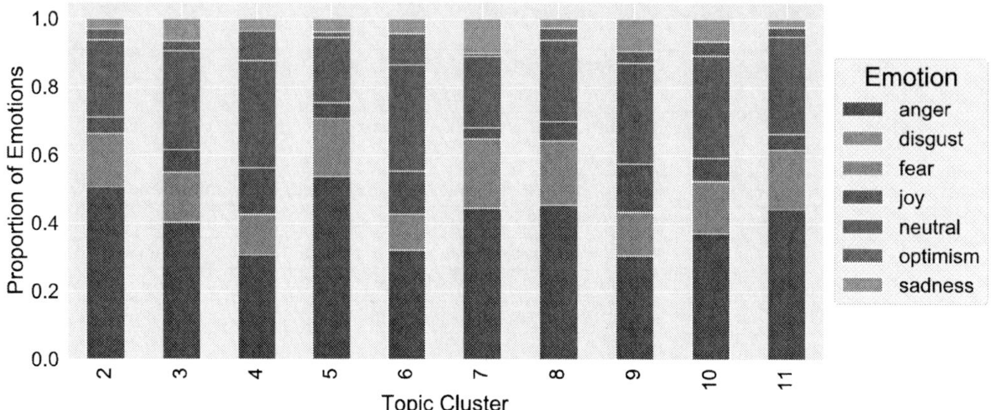

Figure 2: Emotion distribution across topics.

portion of discussion around topics 9 and 10 (concern for healthcare workers; business/ job reliefs). Anger is observed to be the dominating sentiment towards the lockdown (topic 4) and business/ job reliefs (topc 10). Relationship discussions dominate sad and joyful tweets, situating users emotional states when talking about loved ones.

Emotion Transitions across the Corpus. We begin our profiling of an aggregate of emotion transitions during the month of March by first constructing a longitudinal study of emotions per user. For each user, we construct an emotion transition graphs using a chronological trail of his collected tweets, representing emotions as nodes and emotion transitions between tweets as links. We ignore users that have a trail length of two or less, where the emotion trail is too short. The transition probability from emotion e_1 to the emotion e_2 indicates the probability that a Twitter user writes a tweet at time t of emotion e_1 and a tweet at the next time step, $t + 1$, with emotion e_2. To reduce graph complexity, we generated an undirected graph, that is, we aggregated transitions of disgust $\rightarrow$ anger and anger $\rightarrow$ disgust together. The summation of individual user graphs produces Figure 3, an aggregated emotion transition graph across the corpus.

In this corpus, the emotions that are expressed most frequently are: anger comprising of 33.3% (1.01 million) tweets, and disgust with 34.4% (1.04 million) tweets. The least frequent observed emotion is fear with only 11 tweets. Joy, optimism and sadness are observed around 15.3% of the time. During our analysis timeframe, the disgust-anger transition is most prominent with 913,867 tweets,

and the optimism-fear transition is the least frequent with 121 counts.

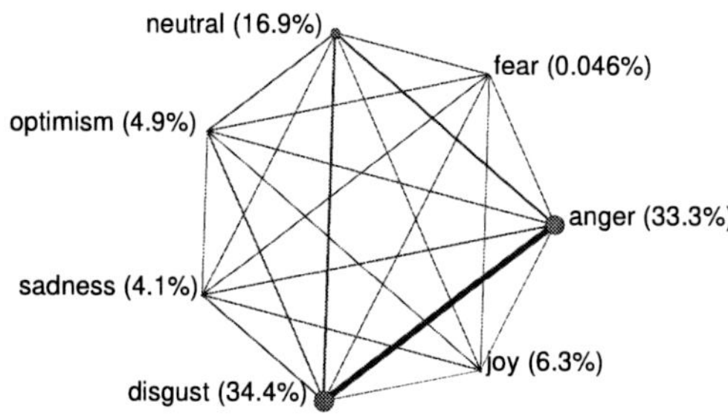

Figure 3: Aggregated Emotion Transition Graph. Width of links represent the frequency of transition, size of node show the number of tweets annotated with the emotions.

Patterns of "Mood Swings". We characterize profiles of user emotion transitions over time, observing patterns of "mood swings". Representing each user's sequence of emotion as a trail, we clustered all the trails together using a trail depth of 1 and a 60% similarity in the trail (Gullapalli and Carley, 2013), using the software ORA (Carley, 2014). A trail depth of 1 compares each emotion singularly and the similarity thresholds the length of trail overlap to be clustered together. With these parameters, the trail (disgust $\rightarrow$ anger $\rightarrow$ disgust $\rightarrow$ optimism $\rightarrow$ joy) is clustered together with (disgust $\rightarrow$ anger $\rightarrow$ disgust $\rightarrow$ anger $\rightarrow$ disgust) because 60%, or 3 out of 5, of the emotion transitions overlap.

Figure 4 displays the "mood swing" profiles in a chronological Emotion Clustering Chart. In this time-series representation, four main clusters are

44

observed: (1) erratic emotion transitions across several emotion states over a short period of time; (2) emotion transitions between disgust and anger; (3) emotion transitions between optimism and joy; (4) erratic emotion transitions across several emotion states across a prolonged period of time. Table 2 shows example tweets from three representative users from these clusters.

Longitudinal Emotion Dynamics. We reflect emotion dynamics corresponding to this longitudinal study of emotion transitions as dominant topics for each emotion transition (Table 3). Clusters 2 and 4 exhibit different profiles, where the former alternates between two emotions while the latter displays "mood swings", yet the topics discussed are the same. Where users exhibit "mood swings" over a short time period, the topics are very focused on the medical science of the virus, and users alternating between optimism and joy exudes hope for people (doctors, healthcare workers, government).

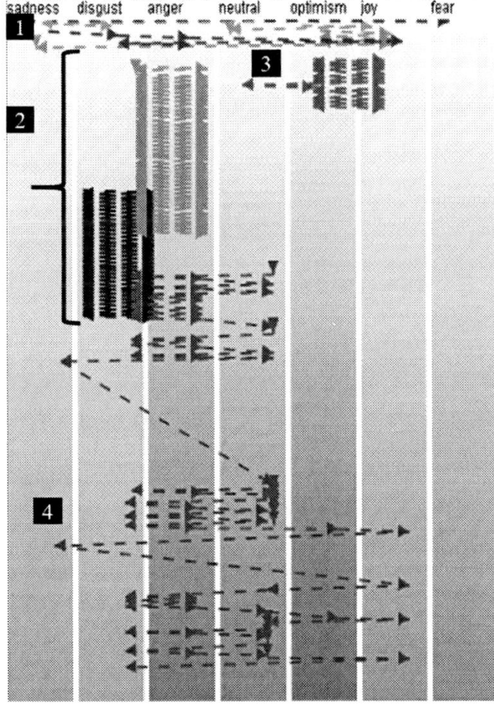

Figure 4: Emotion Clustering Chart in chronological order. Each trail is a group of users that exhibit similar longitudinal emotional profiles.

5 Predicting Emotion Dynamics

We describe the method and results in predicting emotion dynamics through a proposed Emotion Topic Hidden Markov Model (ET-HMM) framework. We evaluate our ET-HMM against Naive Bayesian and Support Vector Classifier models.

Emotion Topic Hidden Markov Model. We model user emotion state transitions using a probabilistic sequence model: the Markov Model (Rabiner, 1989). In the Markov model, the exhibition of the next emotional state is based on the current state, defined by the transition probabilities of moving from one state to another across neighbouring time periods. We augment the user transition markov model with discrete distributions of dominant topics as hidden states, constructing an Emotion Topic Hidden Markov Model (ET-HMM) [1], which reflects the importance of topics on emotions, to explore user feelings when they tweet on a particular topic.

Figure 5 shows the result of the ET-HMM constructed using the Pomegranate python library (Schreiber, 2018). We observe that the emotions anger and neutral has the highest initial probability, meaning when a random user first tweets, he is likely to post a tweet with these emotions during the pandemic. With the exception of fear, all emotions are equally as likely to be found at the last tweet of a trail. If a user is in an angry state, the probability of staying in the same state in subsequent tweets is higher than other emotional states.

Emotion Prediction with ET-HMM. We perform a predictive task using our ET-HMM model. Given a user's past emotion dynamics trail consisting of a sequence of topics and emotions, we attempt to predict his subsequent emotion dynamic. We construct an emotion dynamic trail for each user using the dominant topic and emotions for each tweet. We then remove the final tweet's emotion dynamics from the trail, to be used as the test data point for the sequence. Using the Viterbi algorithm, we predict the emotion dynamic of each user, given his emotion dynamic trail. We select the states that have the maximum probability of occurring given the trail of previous topics and emotions.

Baseline Emotion Prediction. We evaluate the performance of our ET-HMM framework by comparing against a multinomial Naive Bayesian (NB) classifier and a Support Vector Classifier (SVC). We constructed a 7 emotion x 10 topics = 70 dimension matrix, and filled its rows with the (topic, emotion) of each user at the particular time period.

---

[1] Code: https://gitlab.com/bottle$_s hop/wellness/ethmm$

Table 2: Emotion transition clusters with illustrations from three users.

Tweet text	Emotion
Example Tweets from *user_1* (Cluster 2: disgust → anger)	
Mental health issues raging in India among #COVIDIOTS Before and after #COVID-19	Disgust
He wants to starve Indians to die before #COVID-19 can kill them	Anger
Till 31st March - yes Stop ferrying back Indians from different countries to destroy our Stage 3 and make it Stage 1 again	Disgust
#covid MAY strike and Without testing and treatment, will kill but #starvation WILL definitely kill	Anger
Example Tweets from *user_2* (Cluster 3: optimism → joy)	
Thankful to be able to help in any possible way during these tough times. — Use Wysa to vent or just talk through negative thoughts. Let it help you cope with pandemic anxiety and lockdowns. It is anonymous, safe and free. #covid #mentalhealth	Joy
We know that uncertainty can be worrying but let's try to be patient and be hopeful, brighter days could be just around the corner! RT and share this with someone who needs to hear this! #corona #Covid-19 #hope #uncertainty #positivity	Optimism
Every cloud has a silver lining, doesn't it? Let's focus on the positive and stay hopeful! — RT and share it with someone who needs to see this! #silverlinings #covid #hope #positivity	Optimism
Example Tweets from *user_3* (Cluster 1, 4: erratic motions)	
@madus661 @LizClaman MyPOV: correct. But aren't there provisions in many privacy policies and legislation that enables anonymized aggregate data sharing without explicit opt in consent. #privacy vs #publichealth #coronavirus #covid19	Disgust
MyPOV; Tech putting its might in the war on #coronavirus @IBM helps bring #super-computers into the global fight against COVID-19 #covid19	Anger
MyPOV: rediscovering that piano. #shelterinplace #weekend #coronavirus #covid19	Joy
MyPOV: a kale salad, more leftover fried rice #ShelterInPlace #coronapocalypse #covid19 #coronavirus	Neutral
[...] as for response get set of the #postpandemic playbook. We will reveal more next week. Have been meeting with CEOs	Optimism

For both the NB and SVC, we used the matrix constructed at time t_{n-3} and t_{n-2} as a training set, representing the (topic, emotion) transition from time t_{n-3} and t_{n-2}, and performed predictions on the matrix at time step t_{n-1}. The predicted matrix is compared with the actual matrix of t_n.

Experiment Results. Table 4 shows the results of the emotion prediction experiment. The baselines are observed to performed poorly, achieving only 0.035 F1 scores for both Multinomial NB and SVC. ET-HMM is observed to outperformed the baselines, achieving 0.213 for F1 score. We postulate that the ET-HMM model's superior performance could be attributed to its consideration sequential information.

6 Discussion

In this study, we analyzed emotion dynamics in Twitter during the COVID-19 pandemic, characterizing topics, emotions and their transitions. In our dataset, we observe a sharp increase in the number of tweets collected from the week of March 22 to March 29. During this week, at least eight states in the US have issued stay-at-home orders, and many other countries begin movement restrictions, which might cause the great outpouring of yearning expressed on Twitter as people adjust to staying and working at home. Another week of note is April 19 to May 3, where countries like Spain, Italy and Malaysia extend stay-at-home orders due to persistent rise in cases. We postulate the decrease in the number of tweets may be due to adjustments to new routines and people have leveraged digital technologies to overcome the yearning for family

Table 3: Dominant topics per emotion transition

Erratic transitions (short time period)	Disgust → Anger	Optimism → Joy	Erratic transitions (long time period)
Topic 2 vaccine testing treatment drug	**Topic 7** trump elections free mask	**Topic 9** patient doctor hospital healthcare worker	**Topic 7** trump elections free mask
Topic 6 death case total rate	**Topic 9** patient doctor hospital healthcare worker	**Topic 1** medium news government fact	**Topic 9** patient doctor hospital healthcare worker

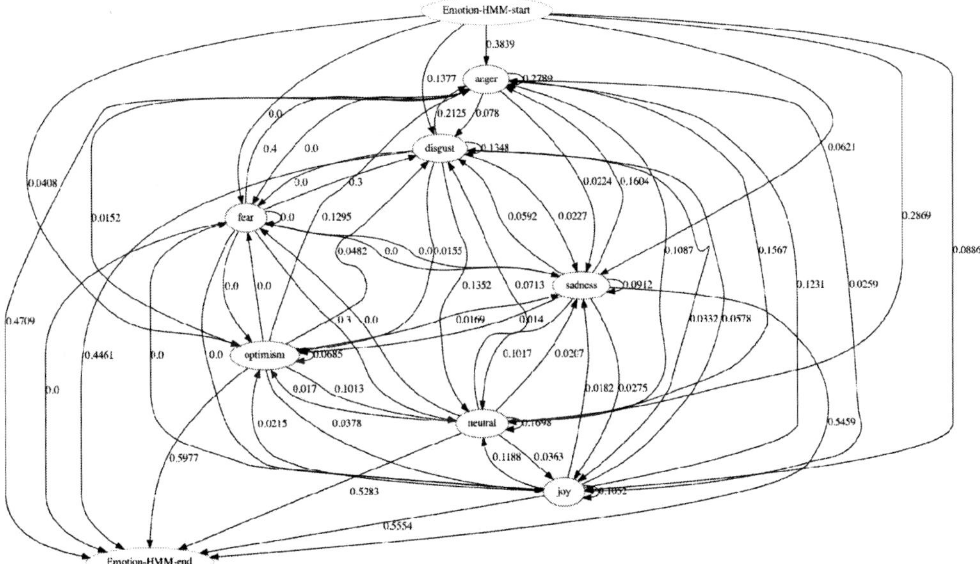

Figure 5: Hidden Markov Model of Emotions with Topics as Hidden States

Table 4: Emotion prediction experiment results.

Model	Prec.	Rec.	Micro-F1
Multinomial NB	0.031	0.048	0.035
SVC	0.032	0.047	0.035
ET-HMM	0.241	0.375	0.213

and friends.

Topic Discovery. From initial filtering of tweets based on word related to yearning, we observe that Twitter users find hope and love, yet feel helpless and turn to religion. Many users miss their loved family and friends and activities like summer, school and recreational play. This is not unusual in a lockdown situation.

The topic analysis in the final corpus reflects themes that users are concerned about during these emotional times (Table 1 and Figure 2). Users reflect worry for the medical progress of vaccines, compassion for healthcare workers at the frontlines of the crisis and worry about their economic situation (i.e. businesses and jobs). This pandemic coincides with the 2020 US elections, which is discussed extensively. Another key topic of discussion is the lockdown situation and personal relationships, because people are unable to see their loved ones face-to-face.

Emotion Dynamics. With emotion dynamics,

we observe that emotions are not strongly correlated with topics, where some topics are discussed more extensively when expressing certain emotions. The dominant topic distribution is different when considering singular emotions dynamics and longitudinal emotions dynamics.

Tweets exhibiting the emotion fear generally discuss topics 9 and 10 (concern for healthcare workers and business/ job reliefs). The topic of relationships dominates tweets with emotions of joy and sadness. These observations situate emotional states when talking about economic situation and loved ones, providing a preliminary characterization into the topics prevalent for each emotion.

Emotion Transitions. In a helpless pandemic situation, it is not uncommon for a person to express high amounts of disgust and anger, and oscillate between both states or remain in those states. Our results show that the (disgust $\rightarrow$ anger) transition and self-loops of (disgust $\rightarrow$ disgust) and (anger $\rightarrow$ anger) are observed significantly more than other emotion transition pair. Disgust-Anger falls into first category of Pluchik's colour wheel of emotions, which means they are most often felt and expressed together (Kołakowska et al., 2015). This emotion pair suggest contempt of the situation.

Our study of "mood swing" patterns indicate that emotion dynamic trails in Cluster 2 (disgust $\rightarrow$ anger) mostly tweet about the government's handling of the situation and social issues arising from lockdown like starvation and strike. Trails in Cluster 3 (optimism $\rightarrow$ joy) mostly tweet self-help and motivational tweets, while erratic trails typically present a twitter-log of the user's lives. It is interesting to note that many accounts have defined personas as inferred from their emotion dynamic trails, and a person's twitter-log reflects fluctuations of emotions, or "mood swings".

Predicting Emotion Dynamics. A random user is most likely to begin his emotion dynamic trail with an angry tweet, reflecting how people turn to social media to vent their frustration of movement control. With trails ending with all emotions except fear, we postulate that tweeting and the interaction from can diffuse anger and change users' emotions.

Our ET-HMM framework correctly classified 21% of the emotions of the test tweets respectively, outperforming baseline classifiers. A possible reason for ET-HMM superior performance could be the model's consideration of sequential information. ET-HMM is able to learn the sequential information from the transition of topic and emotion in users' tweets. Nevertheless, the current prediction task does not account for advance temporal properties between tweets, i.e. accounting where a prolonged time between tweets may affect the emotions expressed differently. Future research could utilize the sequential alignment of emotion trails and integrating additional factors like temporal or geographical information that may affect the emotion class.

Limitations. As with any study, there are several limitations of this work. In particular, the corpus presents a highly skewed data of users. 45% of users have less than 2 tweets, while less than 1% of users have over 5000 tweets. The corpus also presents a skewed representation of emotions, which makes characterising emotions difficult: disgust and anger tweets comprise of 67%, while only 0.0004% of tweets exhibit fear. Nonetheless, there are promising directions stemming from this work, such as harnessing time-series and user network information in emotion profiling and emotion dynamics prediction.

7 Bye, Iĺl miss you babe: Conclusion

In this paper, we characterised Twitter users' emotion dynamics during the COVID-19 pandemic in March 2020 by performing longitudinal user studies profiling topics discussed and the emotions exhibited. During this time period, disgust and anger are the most commonly expressed emotions, and that user emotion transitions tend to exhibit four main "mood swing" profiles. We construct an Emotion Topic Hidden Markov Model to reflect the importance of tweet content on emotional state, presenting a model that outperforms baselines. We hope our work sheds light on user emotions during a pandemic, and will inspire future directions in monitoring emotional states during isolation events, providing a means to identify high-risk individuals to offer emotional support through trying times.

For future work, we will consider tweet geographical location information in our analysis. For example, countries have different developments of the COVID-19 pandemic, and the varying health situation may elicit different emotions of Twitter users living in the country. Geolocation analysis may explain the changes in the users' emotional states at certain locations at certain times. We will also consider modeling emojis and other multimedia content in our topic and emotion analysis.

References

Md Rabiul Awal, Rui Cao, Sandra Mitrovic, and Roy Ka-Wei Lee. 2020. On analyzing antisocial behaviors amid covid-19 pandemic. *arXiv preprint arXiv:2007.10712*.

Haji Binali, Chen Wu, and Vidyasagar Potdar. 2010. Computational approaches for emotion detection in text. In *4th IEEE International Conference on Digital Ecosystems and Technologies*, pages 172–177. IEEE.

Kathleen M. Carley. 2014. *ORA: A Toolkit for Dynamic Network Analysis and Visualization*, pages 1219–1228. Springer New York, New York, NY.

Niko Colnerîc and Janez Demsar. 2018. Emotion recognition on twitter: Comparative study and training a unison model. *IEEE transactions on affective computing*.

Aparna Gullapalli and Kathleen M. Carley. 2013. Extracting ordinal temporal trail clusters in networks using symbolic time-series analysis. *Social Network Analysis and Mining*, 3(4):1179–1194.

Raj Kumar Gupta, Ajay Vishwanath, and Yinping Yang. 2020. Covid-19 twitter dataset with latent topics, sentiments and emotions attributes.

Vinay Kumar Jain, Shishir Kumar, and Steven Lawrence Fernandes. 2017. Extraction of emotions from multilingual text using intelligent text processing and computational linguistics. *Journal of computational science*, 21:316–326.

Nickolas M Jones, Sean P Wojcik, Josiah Sweeting, and Roxane Cohen Silver. 2016. Tweeting negative emotion: An investigation of twitter data in the aftermath of violence on college campuses. *Psychological methods*, 21(4):526.

Edward Chao-Chun Kao, Chun-Chieh Liu, Ting-Hao Yang, Chang-Tai Hsieh, and Von-Wun Soo. 2009. Towards text-based emotion detection a survey and possible improvements. In *2009 International Conference on Information Management and Engineering*, pages 70–74. IEEE.

Agata Kołakowska, Agnieszka Landowska, Mariusz Szwoch, Wioleta Szwoch, and Michał R Wróbel. 2015. Modeling emotions for affect-aware applications. *Information Systems Development and Applications*, pages 55–69.

Puja Mehta, Daniel F McAuley, Michael Brown, Emilie Sanchez, Rachel S Tattersall, and Jessica J Manson. 2020. Covid-19: consider cytokine storm syndromes and immunosuppression. *The Lancet*, 395(10229):1033–1034.

David Mimno and Maintainer David Mimno. 2013. Package 'mallet'. *A wrapper around the Java machine learning tool MALLET*.

Saif M. Mohammad, Felipe Bravo-Marquez, Mohammad Salameh, and Svetlana Kiritchenko. 2018. Semeval-2018 Task 1: Affect in tweets. In *Proceedings of International Workshop on Semantic Evaluation (SemEval-2018)*, New Orleans, LA, USA.

Rajdeep Mukherjee, Sriyash Poddar, Atharva Naik, and Soham Dasgupta. 2020. How have we reacted to the covid-19 pandemic? analyzing changing indian emotions through the lens of twitter.

Debashis Naskar, Eva Onaindia, Miguel Rebollo, and Subhashis Das. 2019. Modelling emotion dynamics on twitter via hidden markov model. In *Proceedings of the 21st International Conference on Information Integration and Web-based Applications & Services*, pages 245–249.

Debashis Naskar, Sanasam Ranbir Singh, Durgesh Kumar, Sukumar Nandi, and Eva Onaindia de la Rivaherrera. 2020. Emotion dynamics of public opinions on twitter. *ACM Transactions on Information Systems (TOIS)*, 38(2):1–24.

Jeffrey Pennington, Richard Socher, and Christopher D. Manning. 2014. Glove: Global vectors for word representation. In *Empirical Methods in Natural Language Processing (EMNLP)*, pages 1532–1543.

Lawrence R Rabiner. 1989. A tutorial on hidden markov models and selected applications in speech recognition. *Proceedings of the IEEE*, 77(2):257–286.

Kashfia Sailunaz and Reda Alhajj. 2019. Emotion and sentiment analysis from twitter text. *Journal of Computational Science*, 36:101003.

Kashfia Sailunaz, Manmeet Dhaliwal, Jon Rokne, and Reda Alhajj. 2018. Emotion detection from text and speech: a survey. *Social Network Analysis and Mining*, 8(1):28.

Jacob Schreiber. 2018. pomegranate: Fast and flexible probabilistic modeling in python. *Journal of Machine Learning Research*, 18(164):1–6.

Elizabeth M Seabrook, Margaret L Kern, Ben D Fulcher, and Nikki S Rickard. 2018. Predicting depression from language-based emotion dynamics: longitudinal analysis of facebook and twitter status updates. *Journal of medical Internet research*, 20(5):e168.

G Subramaniam, R Aswini, M Ranjitha, and Praveen Kumar Rajendran. 2017. Survey on user emotion analysis using twitter data. In *2017 International Conference on Energy, Communication, Data Analytics and Soft Computing (ICECDS)*, pages 998–1001. IEEE.

Wei Wang, Ivan Hernandez, Daniel A Newman, Jibo He, and Jiang Bian. 2016. Twitter analysis: Studying us weekly trends in work stress and emotion. *Applied Psychology*, 65(2):355–378.

Assessing population-level symptoms of anxiety, depression, and suicide risk in real time using NLP applied to social media data

Alex B. Fine, Patrick Crutchley, Jenny Blase, Joshua Carroll, & Glen Coppersmith
Qntfy

{alex.fine, patrick, jenny.blase, josh, glen}@qntfy.com

Abstract

Prevailing methods for assessing population-level mental health require costly collection of large samples of data through instruments such as surveys, and are thus slow to reflect current, rapidly changing social conditions. This constrains how easily population-level mental health data can be integrated into health and policy decision-making. Here, we demonstrate that natural language processing applied to publicly-available social media data can provide real-time estimates of psychological distress in the population (specifically, English-speaking Twitter users in the US). We examine population-level changes in linguistic correlates of mental health symptoms in response to the COVID-19 pandemic and to the killing of George Floyd. As a case study, we focus on social media data from healthcare providers, compared to a control sample. Our results provide a concrete demonstration of how the tools of computational social science can be applied to provide real-time or near-real-time insight into the impact of public events on mental health.

1 Introduction

Measurements of the mental health of large populations often become quickly outdated, given traditional techniques for data collection, analysis, and dissemination. For example, estimates of suicide rates in the United States are often delayed by two years (Hedegaard et al., 2018). More up-to-date information about population-level mental health could provide clinicians and other decision-makers with crucial warning signals of shifts in mental health or burgeoning public health crises. Continuous access to sound estimates of population-level mental health variables could also provide a mechanism for evaluating community-level interventions.

The dramatic social upheavals of 2020 provide a visceral illustration of how specific communities are psychologically affected by specific events. For example, the COVID-19 pandemic, which took root in the United States in February and March of 2020, in addition to threatening the health of a broad swath of the population, placed particularly heavy demands on healthcare providers charged with responding to a highly contagious and deadly novel virus, often under resource-constrained circumstances. Anecdotal reports made it clear that the surge in cases–coupled with factors such as under-funded clinics and lack of a coordinated federal response–was leading to acute psychological distress and burnout among healthcare providers such as nurses and physicians. In addition, the killing of George Floyd on May 25, 2020 elicited nationwide responses of grief and anger, and is widely believed to have surfaced latent psychological trauma in large swaths of the American and international population. In both instances, we saw that there was and is no scalable technique for collecting population-scale data to quantify changes in mental health over time, to ask which segments of the population are most severely affected by the situation, or to determine which psychological symptoms are changing in prevalence and therefore what interventions should be prioritized by the community.

Here, we focus on healthcare providers (HCPs) as a case study, and present a framework for monitoring signs of psychological distress in a continuous, scalable, and ethical fashion (Mikal et al.) using public social media data. We use models of anxiety, depression, and suicide risk, trained on a separate data source, to produce longitudinal es-

Proceedings of the Fourth Workshop on Natural Language Processing and Computational Social Science, pages 50–54
Online, November 20, 2020. ©2020 Association for Computational Linguistics
https://doi.org/10.18653/v1/P17

timates of the prevalence of symptoms associated with these conditions among HCPs and a comparison sample.

The model-derived estimates of symptom prevalence show relative changes in mental health aligned with the timing of events related to COVID-19 and the killing of George Floyd among HCPs in the US. For example, we were able to observe the particularly negative impact of the COVID-19 pandemic across the population. Furthermore, we find no evidence that rescinding stay-at-home orders reversed the deleterious effects of the pandemic on mental health, nor do we find evidence that either healthcare workers or the general population had returned to their respective pre-COVID levels of anxiety, depression, and suicide risk at the time of writing.

Moreover, we find evidence that the killing of George Floyd and subsequent civil unrest across the United States had a measurably deleterious effect on all aspects of mental health measured in both the HCP and control populations.

These findings constitute, we believe, a persuasive proof of concept for the use of transparently and ethically collected social media data in providing aggregated, real-time, population-level estimates of emotional and psychological distress, extending the capabilities of what is commonly known as infoveillance (Paul and Dredze, 2011; Eichstaedt et al., 2015; Paparrizos et al., 2016; Eysenbach, 2009). (For a review of different approaches to assessing population-level mental health, see Aoun et al. (2004)) We believe the data collection and modeling techniques reported here can inform and improve public and private efforts to promote population-level mental health.

2   Data

All analyses were performed using public social media data collected from Twitter between January 1 and June 1, 2020. Analyses are based on two groups: healthcare professionals and a community sample group. Healthcare professionals ($HCPs$, $n = 25,040$) are comprised of providers working directly with patients (e.g., nurses, doctors) and those in adjacent roles (e.g., epidemiologists and hospital administrators). Users were geo-located using self-stated location in the user profile, and only US-based users were included in the analysis. In order to determine which individuals in our sample were HCPs, we used techniques modeled on those reported by Beller et al. (2014), who automatically identify profession and other fine-grained social roles on the basis of self-disclosure. Here, we manually constructed a corpus of HCP professional labels (e.g., "physician", "doctor", "nurse", "RN") and searched for strings containing these labels in contexts demonstrated by Beller et al. to indicate that the author identifies with that role (e.g., "I'm a ___", "As a ___ I think"). This classification was then manually assessed by human annotators and found to have a 95% true positive rate. The control sample used in these analyses comprise a sample of the general population in the United States (henceforth *Community*, $n = 10,000$) that did not self-identify as HCPs, selected randomly from users for whom geographic data was available (either through a geotagging algorithm or disclosure of their location in their public profile). Users with fewer than 100 posts between the start of the year until the end of May were excluded from the analysis.

3   Methods

We estimate the impact of various national events in 2020 on population mental health. To do so, we compare measures of average anxiety, depression and suicide risk before and after each event. We will refer to the "Pre-Lockdown Baseline" as the time period from January 1-February 29. The national emergency declaration from the White House came on March 13, 2020, and many stay-at-home orders were put in place around that time. We define "Early Lockdown" as March 15 to March 31, as it signifies a time when people were adjusting to the changes induced by the lockdown including job loss, homeschooling, and working from home. We refer to the period of April 15 to April 30 as "Mid Lockdown".[1] States took a varied approach to lifting lockdown restrictions, and each followed their own timeline. We suspect the lifting of stay-at-home guidance may have impacted people's mental health, and obtained the state-specific dates on which those orders were lifted. On May 25, George Floyd was killed in police custody, setting off protests and unrest across the United States. We examine one week prior to and after his death (May 18-25; May 26-June 2).

We use classification models, trained on sepa-

---

[1]These time periods were specified before the analyses reported below. We did not experiment with multiple time windows.

rate data sets from the one described above, to score each Tweet in the sample with an estimate of the probability that Tweet was authored by a person experiencing anxiety or depression or who had attempted suicide. The labels used in the training were derived via self-stated diagnosis: a user was considered to be living with anxiety, depression, or suicidality if they explicitly reported that they had received a diagnosis of an anxiety disorder or depression or had previously attempted suicide, respectively. Examples of self-statements include disclosures such as, "As a person who has been diagnosed with general anxiety disorder, I can tell you...", "today marks one year since I tried to take my own life". Self-statements were found using manually constructed search terms and regular expressions; we then confirmed their plausibility and validity using human annotators with clinical training. Logistic regression with character n-gram features were trained on three separate samples (anxiety, depression, suicide) to distinguish users with a self-stated mental health diagnosis from control users reporting no such diagnoses. We employed the same models reported in our previous work, using the anxiety and depression models from Coppersmith et al. (2015) and the suicide model from Coppersmith et al. (2018). AUC scores for the anxiety, depression, and suicide models were .84, .72, and .73, respectively.

For each measure (anxiety, depression, suicide), we computed the mean of all messages per user per day. Each user is thus represented as the mean of their per-day estimates. This allows for matched-sample t-tests between time periods, and independent t-tests between groups within the same time period. User data was de-identified prior to being submitted to these models, and all statistical analysis was conducted over aggregated user data.

4   Results

Baseline scores for each mental health variable were higher (i.e., more severe) for HCPs than the Community population. This suggests that, prior to COVID-19 lockdowns, HCPs were experiencing anxiety, depression, and suicide risk at higher rates than the general population ($p < 0.001$; note that the figure below, for the sake of comparison, shows by-group z-scores so that this Pre-Lockdown difference is not apparent).

To get a sense of how each event affected each group relative to their Pre-Lockdown baseline, we calculated by-group Z-scores from this baseline. This is illustrated in Figure 1, along with the time periods under consideration.

First, note that every time period after lockdown exhibits higher scores for all mental health conditions we examined. Furthermore, the killing of George Floyd appears to have had a significant effect on mental health across all groups.

Longitudinal changes in depression for HCPs and Community do not differ reliably ($p > 0.1$). HCPs exhibit less change in their anxiety over time compared to Community (though HCPs are still at a higher base-rate of anxiety). Interestingly, HCPs show a larger change in suicide-related risk during Early Lockdown. This disappears in Mid Lockdown and gets closer to returning to baseline rates towards the end of May (note, again, that baseline rates for HCPs remain higher than for Community).

5   Discussion

Real-time information about the population's mental health is critically important, especially in times of crisis. Our work is relevant to government agencies or other organizations with the resources to craft population-scale public health interventions or policy recommendations. The current study provides a proof of concept of how publicly available social media data might be used to assess population-level mental health in a way that could support these organizations.

We hasten to emphasize that this work represents a proof of concept, and raises several questions for future research. First, the population of social media users does not perfectly mirror the general population, and it is plausible that those who do not engage in social media were affected differently by COVID and the killing of George Floyd. We can only speculate about how such a bias might influence our results. Second, we did not correct for population demographic rates in the creation of the community group, but did take care to capture a geographically diverse population.

Finally, in future work we plan to explore how the outputs of the models reported here can be continuously calibrated and refined using psychometrically validated clinical scales of constructs such as anxiety and depression. We take it as uncontroversial that using methods of the general kind employed here to measure phenomena as complex as

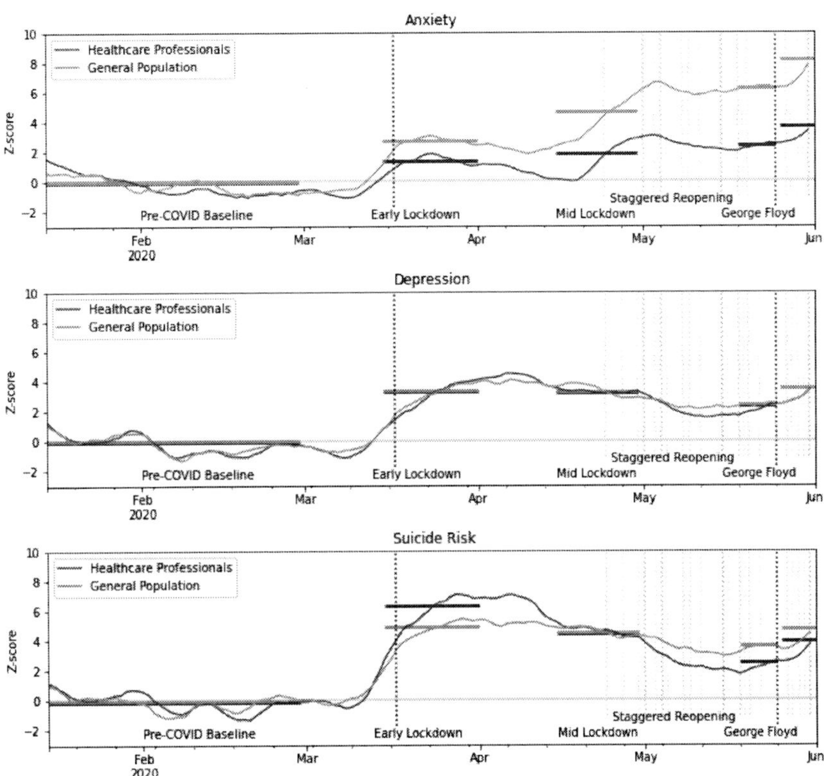

Figure 1: Changes in mental health compared to Pre-Lockdown baseline for HCPs and Community. Y-axis indicates Z-scores compared to each group's Pre-Lockdown baseline; a score of 0 means a return to Pre-Lockdown baseline levels. Time periods for comparison are indicated by thick horizontal bars at the mean for that group across the relevant time period. Significant events are indicated by vertical dotted lines. State reopenings are represented as faded dotted lines.

anxiety, depression, and suicide will demand extensive collaboration and iteration.

6 Conclusion

We have demonstrated the ability to assess population-level mental health constructs in real time, based on publicly available social media data. Quick access to this information could allow lawmakers, mental health practitioners, and others to determine what type of interventions are needed, and where, in the face of rapidly changing conditions. Harnessing this kind of information may be critical to our recovery from COVID-19, and in allowing skillful responses to future crises.

References

S. Aoun, D. Pennebaker, and C. Wood. 2004. Assessing population need for mental health care: A review of approaches and predictors. *Mental Health Serv. Res.*, 6:33–46.

Charley Beller, Rebecca Knowles, Craig Harman, Shane Bergsma, Margaret Mitchell, and Benjamin Van Durme. 2014. I'ma belieber: Social roles via self-identification and conceptual attributes. In *Proceedings of the 52nd Annual Meeting of the Association for Computational Linguistics (Volume 2: Short Papers)*, pages 181–186.

Glen Coppersmith, Mark Dredze, Craig Harman, and Kristy Hollingshead. 2015. From ADHD to SAD: Analyzing the language of mental health on Twitter through self-reported diagnoses. In *Proceedings of the Workshop on Computational Linguistics and Clinical Psychology: From Linguistic Signal to Clinical Reality*, Denver, Colorado, USA. North American Chapter of the Association for Computational Linguistics.

Glen Coppersmith, Ryan Leary, Patrick Crutchley, and Alex Fine. 2018. Natural language processing of social media as screening for suicide risk. *Biomedical informatics insights*, 10:1178222618792860.

Johannes C Eichstaedt, Hansen Andrew Schwartz, Margaret L Kern, Gregory Park, Darwin R Labarthe, Raina M Merchant, Sneha Jha, Megha Agrawal, Lukasz A Dziurzynski, Maarten Sap, et al. 2015. Psychological language on twitter predicts county-level heart disease mortality. *Psychological science*, 26(2):159–169.

Gunther Eysenbach. 2009. Infodemiology and infoveillance: framework for an emerging set of public health informatics methods to analyze search, communication and publication behavior on the internet. *Journal of medical Internet research*, 11(1):e11.

Holly Hedegaard, Sally C Curtin, and Margaret Warner. 2018. *Suicide rates in the United States continue to increase.* US Department of Health and Human Services, Centers for Disease Control and . . . .

J. Mikal, S. Hurst, and M. Conway. Ethical issues in using twitter for population-level depression monitoring: a qualitative study. *BMC Medical Ethics*, 17(22).

John Paparrizos, Ryen W. White, and Eric Horvitz. 2016. Screening for pancreatic adenocarcinoma using signals from web search logs: Feasibility study and results. *Journal of Oncology Practice*, 12(8):737–744. PMID: 27271506.

Michael J Paul and Mark Dredze. 2011. You are what you tweet: Analyzing twitter for public health. In *Fifth International AAAI Conference on Weblogs and Social Media*.

Viable Threat on News Reading: Generating Biased News Using Natural Language Models

Saurabh Gupta[1], Huy H. Nguyen[2,4], Junichi Yamagishi[2,4] and Isao Echizen[2,3,4]
[1] Indraprastha Institute of Information Technology - Delhi, Delhi, India
[2] National Institute of Informatics, Tokyo, Japan; [3] University of Tokyo, Japan
[4] The Graduate University for Advanced Studies, SOKENDAI, Kanagawa, Japan
`saurabhg@iiitd.ac.in`, {`nhhuy, jyamagis, iechizen`}`@nii.ac.jp`

Abstract

Recent advancements in natural language generation has raised serious concerns. High-performance language models are widely used for language generation tasks because they are able to produce fluent and meaningful sentences. These models are already being used to create fake news. They can also be exploited to generate biased news, which can then be used to attack news aggregators to change their reader's behavior and influence their bias. In this paper, we use a threat model to demonstrate that the publicly available language models can reliably generate biased news content based on an input original news. We also show that a large number of high-quality biased news articles can be generated using controllable text generation. A subjective evaluation with 80 participants demonstrated that the generated biased news is generally fluent, and a bias evaluation with 24 participants demonstrated that the bias (left or right) is usually evident in the generated articles and can be easily identified.

1 Introduction

Natural language generation is defined as the creation of understandable text using a language model (LM) trained on a large collection of texts. An (LM) is a probability distribution over a sequence of words. Given a set of training text sequences, we can train an LM to produce texts similar to the training data. Researchers have used deep learning algorithms to generate more fluent and semantically meaningful texts than those generated using conventional methods like n-grams (Lu et al., 2018). Such LMs are being used to generate image captions (Vinyals et al., 2015), perform machine translations (Bahdanau et al., 2015), paraphrase and summarize text (Zhang et al., 2017). High performance LMs can generate fake news, fake reviews, and fake comments

(Adelani et al., 2020; Zellers et al., 2019).

Recent studies have revealed various types of bias in top US news sources, which often report political news in a biased way, for example, attention can be drawn to particular events and entities while ignoring others (Ribeiro et al., 2018; Groseclose and Milyo, 2005; Kulshrestha et al., 2017). The selection of what to report about an entity (positive or negative) produces bias. There are two major political sides in the U.S.: *Democrats* on the left and *Republicans* on the right.

The news aggregating platforms like Google News and Yahoo News are the most viewed news websites in U.S. with 150 and 175 million unique visitors every month, respectively (Watson, 2019). They offer content relevant to a wide range of global audiences, and therefore, they have a responsibility to maintain the same sentiment and bias. However, they can utilize language models to generate biased content (news headlines and articles) to model the behavior of their readers. Exposure to biased news is very harmful as it can increase/flip the political bias of a reader (Bail et al., 2018). For example, (Wong, 2019) found that exposure to biased news can alter the political inclinations of people, and (Wanta and Hu, 1994) found that false representation of news from a news source can lead to broken trust between the reader and the news source.

Previous works on media bias mostly focused on detecting bias either by using cues from the social media presence of the news sources (Kulshrestha et al., 2017; An et al., 2012; Ribeiro et al., 2018), or by analyzing how bias is manifested within each news article (Chen et al., 2018). Chen et al. (2018) focused on flipping the bias of news headlines, which is a short one line text. Bail et al. (2018) showed that exposure to opposing views can increase political polarization. To the best of our knowledge, ours is the first attempt at gener-

Proceedings of the Fourth Workshop on Natural Language Processing and Computational Social Science, pages 55–65
Online, November 20, 2020. ©2020 Association for Computational Linguistics
https://doi.org/10.18653/v1/P17

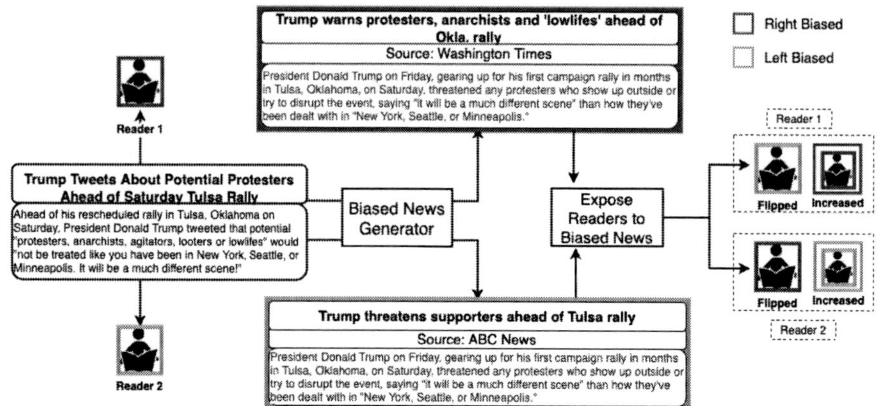

Figure 1: Proposed threat model. Original news is used as seed by the "Biased News Generator" (explained in Section 4) to generate left or right biased news. Readers are then exposed to the generated biased news to change their original bias (either flip or increase).

ating full length biased news articles using high performance language models.

Our Contribution. In this paper, we use a threat model (Figure 1) to demonstrate that publicly available language models can reliably generate biased news content based on original news. In an ideal scenario, a user consumes original news from an aggregator and develops a confirmation bias (Nickerson, 1998) about entities mentioned in the news. If the news complements their bias, they likely jump to the original source to continue reading (Swire et al., 2017). Our threat model, we assume that the attacker is able to access the original news and have control over what a user will see when visiting the aggregator's platform. In this scenario, the attacker can rework the original news, by either shifting its bias farther than it originally was (Levendusky, 2013), or by flipping its original bias (Bail et al., 2018). The attacker is also assumed to be able to access a large collection of news articles labeled with the bias (left or right) to use for training an LM. The attacker uses the original news as input to the LM for using as context to generate biased news. Finally, the attacker exposes readers to the generated biased news.

To generate biased news, we fine-tuned the GPT-2 language model (LM) (Radford et al., 2019) to create two different LMs, each trained on a specific type of biased news. We used an API built on a RoBERTa–based model (Liu et al., 2019) (explained in a later section) to classify the generated news as left or right biased. However, generating only the text for news is not enough.

Therefore, we then fine-tuned another generative model, known as GROVER (Zellers et al., 2019), which enables controllable generation of an entire news article – the body, title, news source, publication date, and author list. Finally, we performed a subjective evaluation with 80 participants - 32 native and 48 non-native English speakers. The results show that the news articles generated by the models (machine-generated news) had almost the same fluency as those written by people (human-written). The participants tended to randomly select human-written news when asked to choose between two options: an excerpt from machine-generated news, and one from human-written news. Then we choose 24 of the 80 participants to evaluate the bias in the machine-generated news articles. They were able identify a bias 92% of the times, and assigned a correct bias rating 62.91% of the time.

2 Related Work

In this section, we discuss related work on political bias datasets, bias analysis, bias generation and detection in news articles.

2.1 Political Bias Datasets

In the works that study bias, Arapakis et al. (2016) collected a dataset of 561 news articles, each being labeled with 14 qualitative aspects along with article's subjectivity. Another dataset, the multi-perspective question answering (MPQA) corpus (Wiebe et al., 2005), contains 692 news articles, each with a label of its subjectivity. These two corpora were carefully developed with labels at the article and sentence levels. However, the labeling technique is costly to scale, and the corpora are not large enough ($<$ 1000 samples), so Chen et al. (2018) developed a corpus of 2,781 events from the AllSides website to characterize and flip bias in news headlines. The corpus contains news headlines and articles presented by a left-leaning and a right-leaning news source paired together with an unbiased summary of the event. However, the labeling is news source specific, so there is no information about the bias at the article level. Moreover, the corpus is not large enough to be used to generate news articles. Therefore, for this study, we used the "All-The-News" dataset footnotehttps://www.kaggle.com/snapcrack/all-the-news.

2.2 Bias Analysis

Media bias has been under study for decades (Groseclose and Milyo, 2005; Fang et al., 2012; Arapakis et al., 2016), and various aspects of political bias have been studied from different perspectives. For example, Groseclose and Milyo (2005) quantified bias for a sample of 20 news sources in the U.S. on the basis of the number of citations used by think tanks and policy groups. Their work is among the first ones to provide clear evidence of bias in media. Lin et al. (2011) proposed categorizing bias on the basis of variables like mentions of political parties, legislators, and ideology. Another study, (Chen et al., 2018), focused on liberal and conservative bias, and using manual annotation, found that bias indicators usually include named entities. A more recent study explored the idea with right and left bias, and experimentally showed that named entities are indeed important, and that bias is more evident in longer texts, i.e., in full length news articles, rather than in shorter texts like sentences and paragraphs (Chen et al., 2018). We performed the same analyses to evaluate the reliability of our dataset.

2.3 Biased Headline Generation

Advances in natural language processing have led to rapid development of several language generation techniques. With the release of transformer based model architectures and text representations (Vaswani et al., 2017; Devlin et al., 2018), machines are now able to generate high quality text outputs (Radford et al., 2019), which may or may not preserve the context. To generate text that better preserves context, researchers have studied *controllable text generation*, i.e., how to rewrite a text so that it has certain attributes (Keskar et al., 2019; Zellers et al., 2019). Several of these studies demonstrated that the text style can be transferred by simply changing the relevant words in an unsupervised manner (Li et al., 2018; Adelani et al., 2020; Shen et al., 2017). Chen et al. (2018) demonstrated bias flipping in text, but only for the headlines of a news articles. To the best of our knowledge, ours is the first study on generating full-length biased news articles.

2.4 Identification of Bias in News Articles

There have been several attempts in the past to identify bias as left or right at the article level (Zhao et al.; Baly et al., 2018; Wang, 2019), and at the source level (Ribeiro et al., 2018; Kulshrestha et al., 2017; An et al., 2012). The classification of a media source as left leaning or right leaning is flawed if one starts to look at each article to identify its bias. We are more interested in the text and style of bias in news articles, and therefore, we focused on bias at the article level. At article level, Zhao et al.; Baly et al. (2018) used a smaller dataset and shallow models to classify bias at an article level using three labels. Using recent advancements in the field of natural language processing, Wang (2019) created a state-of-the-art regression model to quantify bias in news articles by using RoBERTa-based model (Liu et al., 2019) and trained it on several datasets like the Adfontes-Media's list of articles and webhose.io[1], and so on for generalizability. We used the RoBERTa-based model to generate automatic bias ratings and evaluate bias in generated text.

3 Dataset and Discriminativeness Ratio

3.1 All The News Dataset and Automatic Bias Ratings

The dataset we used is a collection of 139,668 full length news articles curated using the Internet Archive[2] from 15 major news sources in the U.S. and is available on the Kaggle website under the name of "All the news" data[3]. For each source, the Internet Archive was used to grab the past year-and-a-half of either homepage headlines or RSS feeds and their links were parsed through

---

[1]http://webhose.io/

[2]https://archive.org

[3]https://www.kaggle.com/snapcrack/all-the-news

a scraper. The data obtained were not the product of scraping an entire site, but rather of scraping the more prominently placed articles. For example, CNN's articles from 5 June 2016 were what appeared on the homepage of CNN at the time of data collection. Similarly, Vox's articles from that time were everything that appeared in the Vox RSS reader, and so on. Therefore, we had a news article with its headline, publication source, publication date, and full-length body.

The collection of news articles did not have its bias ratings at the article level. We used a RoBERTa-based regression model made available to us upon requesting to "The Bipartisan Press"[4] to create bias ratings. "The Bipartisan Press" annotated the data using Adfontes Media's methodology (Otero, 2019), which involves an initial screening and training to hire experts to annotate news articles with their bias on a scale of -42 to +42. A negative sign indicates a left-leaning bias and a positive sign indicates a right-leaning bias. We used the regression model to calculate the bias in each news article and treated these bias ratings as the ground truth. We further used the same model to evaluate the bias of the generated news articles. Table 1 lists some statistics about the "All the news" dataset.

Number of news articles	139,668
Number of unique news sources	15
Average number of sentences in each news article	49
Number of left biased news articles	90,664
Number of right biased news articles	49,004

Table 1: "All the news" dataset statistics.

3.2 Discriminativeness Ratio

Bias can be found in a text if it expresses sentiment towards a specific entity (a person, a place, or a policy). Chen et al. (2018) proposed a *discriminativeness ratio* to capture the fundamental difference between biased and sentimental text based on word frequency. The ratio is given as:

$$\frac{occ(w, D_t)}{occ(w, D_{t'})}$$

where $occ(w, D)$ is the frequency of w in text D and t and t' are types of text. In biased text, t and t' correspond to *right* and *left*, while in sentimental text they represent *positive* and *negative* sentiments, respectively. Usage of the discriminativeness ratio results in type-unrelated words having values close to 1, as they appear almost equally in both types of text. On the other hand, words that appear often in one type and rarely in the other will have higher (type t) and lower values (type t') values, respectively.

Sentimental Text		Biased Text	
Word	**Ratio**	**Word**	**Ratio**
excellent	220.22	The Atlantic	73.0
gem	183.99	Aleppo	64.5
wonderful	183.66	Ivanka Trump	61.0
mushrooms	1.01	aired	1.0
breadsticks	1.01	suspicion	1.0
dresser	0.99	recuse	1.0
unfortunately	<0.01	Trump	<0.01
terrible	<0.01	Truther - Breitbart	<0.01
rude	<0.01	Netanyahu	<0.01

Table 2: Three words with highest and lowest discriminativeness ratio, and words with ratio very close to one.

Table 2 lists the words having the highest and the words having the lowest discriminativeness ratio for sentimental text and biased text. We show the results for sentimental text to simplify the explanation. The top three words in the sentimental text are positive, the bottom three are negative, and sentiment-unrelated words have a value close to one. In the biased text, the three type-unrelated words (ratio of 1.0) included both positive ("aired" and "recused") and negative ("suspicion") sentiment words. This is because both left- and right-biased texts use sentiment words to support and oppose entities. In addition, the top three and the bottom three biased-text words are named entities, indicating that articles with either bias tend to criticize or support different named entities, using the same words to convey sentiments. In line with this, a bias analysis by Yano et al. (2010) revealed that named entities are often bias indicators.

4 Biased News Generation

The most important parts of the proposed method for generating biased news is the GPT-2 text gen-

---

[4]https://www.thebipartisanpress.com/political-bias-api-and-integrations/

eration model (Radford et al., 2019) and the controllable text generation model (Zellers et al., 2019). As shown in Figure 2, we used a two step approach to generate biased news: generation and validation. In the generation step, an attacker provides an original news article **x** as the seed input to a generation models. The models then generate a modified article **x'** based on x. In the validation step, the generated articles are classified on the basis of bias. The attacker is assumed to have access to such a classifier and uses it to segregate left- and right- biased news. The details of our proposed method are discussed below.

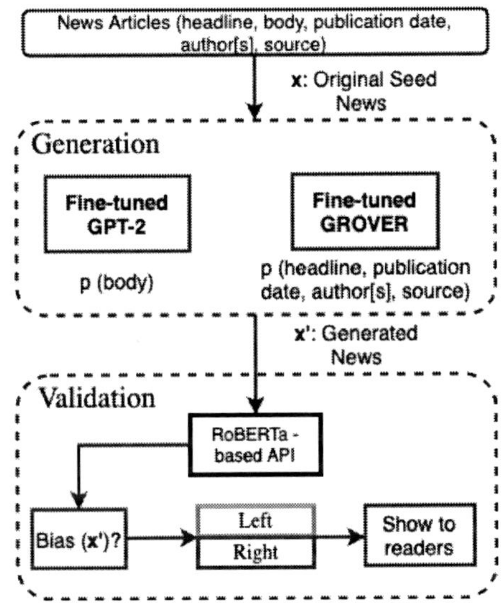

Figure 2: Biased News Generation Procedure.

4.1 GPT-2 Model

The task of a language model is to learn the probability distribution of a text corpus to enable the next word to be predicted on the basis of contextual words. Given a sequence of words, $w = (w_1, w_2, ..., w_T)$, the probability of the sequence is given as:

$$P(w) = \prod_{i=1}^{T} P(w_t | w_1, w_2, ..., w_{t-1}) \quad (1)$$

Probability P(w) is calculated by learning the conditional probability of each word given a fixed number of k-context words. Many neural network architectures have been used to estimate P(w) including a feed-forward neural network (Bengio

et al., 2003), a recurrent neural network (Mikolov et al., 2010; Sundermeyer et al., 2012), and the transformer architectures (Radford et al., 2018). A GPT-2 model (Radford et al., 2019) based on a transformer architecture has been shown to have a lower perplexity for language modeling datasets, and to generate high quality fluent texts. Therefore, we used a GPT-2 model and fine tuned it on a dataset of left- and right- biased news.

In the fine-tuning, the model was first initialized using pre-trained weights instead of random initial weights. Fine-tuning is faster than training an LM with a large number of parameters from scratch. It has been shown that fine-tuning using labeled data after initializing the model with pre-trained parameters improves the accuracy of downstream tasks (Devlin et al., 2018). Therefore, we fine tuned the GPT-2 LM using left- biased and right- biased news.

Using techniques from Zhang et al. (2015), we divided the news articles from each set into training and test sets. We used a reliable implementation of the GPT-2 model available on Github[5] to fine-tune the pre-trained model on the "All the news" dataset. We used the default values for all hyperparameters. The number of training samples for left- and right- biased media were unbalanced, but since we trained a separate model for each, we had enough data for fine-tuning two good models. We fine tuned two 117M GPT-2 models, one for each type of bias. We used 85,664 and 44,004 news articles, respectively, to train the two models and 5000 each to test them for perplexity. The perplexity on the test set for the two models trained was 17.43 and 18.30, respectively, which is quite good (i.e., value less than 20 is what we look for (Radford et al., 2019)).

Finally, we generated 5000 samples for each bias type. We loaded the corresponding model and used prompts from the original articles to generate biased ones. Table 3 shows a sample for each type of bias. The generated articles are fluent and meaningful. The generated news is "fake" and reports incorrect factual information. For example, in the first sample, the original news has entities like {U.S. farm industry, White House} while the generated one completely changed them to {U.S. Economy, San Jose}.

---

[5] https://github.com/huggingface/transformers

Right Biased
Seed Text: President Donald Trump said he would seek to keep his tough immigration enforcement policies from harming the U. S. farm industry and its largely immigrant workforce, according to farmers and officials who met with him. At a roundtable on farm labor at the White House last month, Trump said he did not want to create labor problems for farmers and would look into improving a program that brings in temporary agricultural workers on legal visas.
*President Donald Trump said he would seek to keep his tough immigration enforcement policies from harming the U. S. economy, and that the 25 countries with "green cards" had jobs to farm industry and its largely immigrant workforce according to farmers and officials who met with him last week in San Jose. (**Bias: 5.0**)*

Left Biased
Seed Text: Hillary Clinton and her team got in on the challenge, too, offering a special message to voters to "Don't Stand Still, Vote Today. ". Her video features cameos from former President Bill Clinton along with Huma Abedin and Jon Bon Jovi. The original video had no soundtrack, so Slim Jxmmi of Rae Sremmurd added in their track "Black Beatles" to the Clinton version. Pretty hip.
*Hillary Clinton and her team got in on the challenge too offering a special message to voters to Dont Stand Still Vote Today and Trump's campaign just couldn't do anything better. Her video features cameos from former President Bill Clinton along with Huma Abedin and Jon Bon Jovi. The clip was posted on YouTube in reaction to Trump's comments, which BuzzFeed News reported. (**Bias: -13.0**)*

Table 3: Example biased news generated using fine-tuned GPT-2 LM. For the sake of brevity, only the first three sentences of original and generated articles are presented (Grusky et al., 2018). Generated text is shown in *italics*.

Right Biased
Headline: Shaun King is Really Mad About President Trump
Domain: Breitbart , **Date**: June 01, 2017 , **Author[s]**: Jack Montgomery
*You know what is really sad? Yet another hate-filled, blame-the-victim tweet from the self-identified Brooklyn blogger and occasional Obama apologist. Wednesday night Shaun King got really fired up on social media, arguing that President Trump "took out" Chance the Rapper on Twitter — "another white, wealthy liberal take, no questions asked." At the behest of an enraged social media following he promptly added, in his screen name, "How dare you christian white men call me racist?" (**Bias: 14.21**)*

Left Biased
Headline: Trump ditches press pool to play golf
Domain: CNN , **Date**: December 31, 2016 , **Author[s]**: Eugene Scott
*(CNN) — President-elect Donald Trump rode a golf cart through the course at his golf course in New Jersey on Saturday before visiting New York City to watch his son Eric Donald Trump give a New Year's Day address. The trip marked the first time Trump has left his Trump Tower residence since he won the November election. Since the election, Trump has visited his golf courses at least once a week. He played golf Friday in New Jersey and Florida and last week in Bedminster, New Jersey. (**Bias: -11.01**)*

Table 4: Example biased news generated using fine-tuned GROVER LM. For the sake of brevity, only the first three sentences of original and generated articles are presented (Grusky et al., 2018). Generated text is shown in *italics*.

4.2 GROVER model

The news articles generated by the GPT-2 model contain unstructured text, beginning with a ⟨*start*⟩ token and ending with an ⟨*end*⟩ token. The ⟨*end*⟩ token is particularly important as it in-dicates when to stop generating. However, in addition to unstructured running text, i.e., the body text, a news article has additional elements, including the publication domain, the publication date,the authors, and the headline. Generating a realistic and controlled news article requires producing all of these components. Therefore, a news article can be modeled as a joint distribution:

$$P(domain, date, authors, headline, body) \quad (2)$$

Zellers et al. (2019) used the language modeling framework from equation 1 in a way that enables flexible decomposition of equation 2. GROVER starts with a set of fields $\mathbb{F}$ as context, with each field containing specific start and end tokens. To generate a target field τ, we append the field specific $\langle start - \tau \rangle$ to the given context tokens to sample from the model until the $\langle end - \tau \rangle$ token is reached. For biased news generation, we fix the body of the article as the target field τ and use the other fields (domain, date, authors, headline) as context. We load pre-trained model weights to fine tunethe GROVER LM to generate biased news.

We used the same training-test distribution as for the GPT-2 model. We defined context $\mathbb{F}$ as the set $\{headline, date, author[s], domain\}$ and target τ as the body of the article to be generated using F as context. Note that, GROVER does not need seed phrases for generation. Instead, it uses headline, date, author[s], and domain for generating the body. Table 4 shows a sample for each type of bias. The generated articles are fluent and appear consistent as they are presented with a domain, date, headline and author[s] names.

Figure 3 shows the bias distributions for all the 5000 generated articles, reflecting the bias of each source. As can be clearly seen, the distributions are shifted towards the extremes for both the left- and right- biased samples, shown by the bumps being closer to the left extreme (-20) or the right extreme (+20).

4.3 Subjective Evaluation

To subjectively evaluate our proposed method, we asked a pool of native and non-native English speakers (annotators) to evaluate the generated biased news articles on the basis of fluency and the bias of the text. We explicitly instructed them to ignore factuality because we wanted to evaluate and validate the quality and bias of the generated articles, not their correctness.

For evaluating quality, we considered two categories of articles: human-written ones from news sources, and machine-generated ones produced by the GPT-2 or GROVER models. The participants were asked to identify whether an excerpt was taken from a human-written, or a machine-generated article. They were shown two options to choose from, one from each class, human-written and machine-generated. Each annotator was shown ten pairs of excerpts (one human-written and one machine-generated) and asked to identify, which was the human-written one. The average selection rate was used as the metric. Fur-

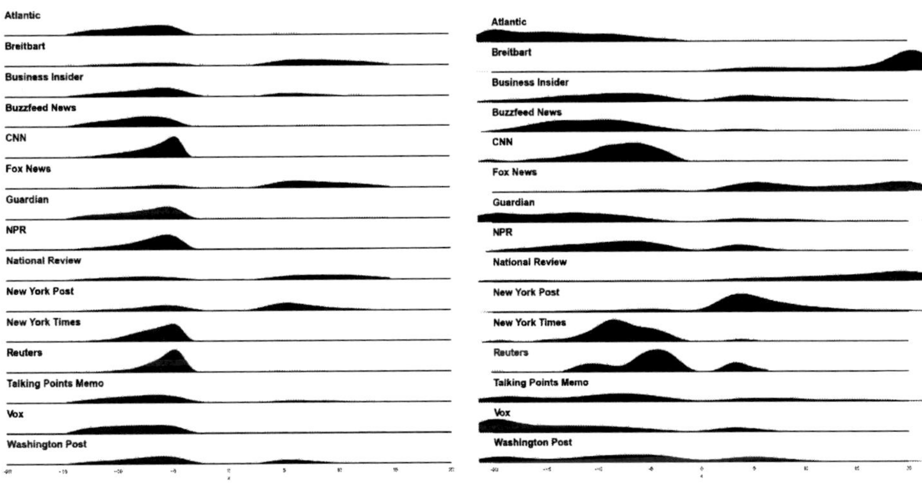

(a) Bias Distribution in Human Written News

(b) Bias Distribution in Machine Generated News

Figure 3: Difference in bias ratings between human-written and machine generated news (using human-written news as seed for each generation). The machine-generated news is more extreme (biased) due to being generated by fine tuned models.

ther, to facilitate the evaluation, the excerpts were shortened to only three or four sentences. The evaluations were performed on a web interface with the two types of excerpts chosen randomly from two pools of samples.

Of the 80 participants, 32 were native speakers and the rest 48 were non-native speakers. As shown in Table 5, the non-native English speakers tended to mark the machine-generated excerpts as human-written ones. Since the outputs from the GPT-2 and GROVER models were very similar, the ratio of participants who failed to identify the human-written news correctly was about the same for the GPT-2- and GROVER- generated samples. The lowest ratio (43%) was for native speakers and the GROVER samples, and the highest ratio (50%) was for non-native speakers and the GPT-2 samples. Most of the values are closer to 0.50, which indicates that the participants tended to make a random selection among the two categories of articles.

Model	Native	Non Native	Overall
GPT-2	0.46 (16)	0.50 (23)	0.49 (39)
GROVER	0.43 (16)	0.48 (25)	0.46 (41)

Table 5: Ratio of number of participants who marked machine-generated excerpt as human-written. Number of participants is shown in parentheses.

For evaluating bias, we selected 24 of the 80 participants, each having at least a college degree or who were enrolled in college at the time of annotation. We trained them to understand the media bias using various resources[6]. Since the training was not rigorous, we made the problem simpler by treating bias as a binary variable having two values, i.e., *left* and *right*. For cases in which the participant was not sure, we asked them to mark the question with *can't say*. Each participant was shown ten excerpts at random from the generated text and they were asked to mark their bias rating. As in the quality evaluation, only three or four sentences were shown for the sake of simplicity.

The participants were able to identify a clear bias 92% of the times. They marked the option of *can't say* only 8% of the time. To determine the percentage of times the participants were able to identify the bias correctly, we needed to define "correctly", which is subjective. We judged that a bias rating was correct if the participant's choice

(left or right) matched that of the automatic bias evaluation . We used the API built on a RoBERTa-based model to automatically generate bias ratings for the sample excerpts shown to the participants. We found that the participants were able to identify the bias correctly 63% of the time. The percentage might have been higher with more training and a better understanding of bias.

5 Discussion

Our use of the API made available to us by "The Bipartsan Press" to evaluate bias is a major limitation of this study. Evaluating text for bias is a very complex problem. The API was built on a RoBERTa based model trained on a dataset curated by Adfontes Media. The dataset was annotated by 20 expert annotators with at least a college degree after an extensive screening and training process[7]. Hiring and training such annotators is expensive, and relying on non-expert annotators to calculate media bias in generated news is not promising. Since our findings conforms to the results reported by relevant literature on media bias, it is safe to assume that the results obtained using the RoBERTa-based model (with a 4% error rate) are reliable in terms of segregating left-biased media from right-biased media.

6 Conclusion and Future Work

We have presented a threat model and discussed how news aggregators (attackers) can manipulate readers' opinions by flipping or increasing their bias. We described two language models generating biased news: the high-performance GPT-2 LM and the GROVER LM for controllable text generation. We used a large news article dataset to fine tune them. We used a RoBERTa-based regression model to create automatic bias ratings and to evaluate bias in generated news. Subjective evaluation of generated news articles by 80 participants suggests that they made random selections between the machine-generated and human-written news excerpts, indicating that the machine-generated news is fluent and looks similar to human-written news. Out of the 80 participants, 24 were chosen for a bias evaluation. The participants were able to see a clear bias most of the times, and marked correct bias 63% of the times.

---

[6]https://www.coursera.org/learn/media

[7]https://www.adfontesmedia.com/how-ad-fontes-ranks-news-sources/?v=402f03a963ba

For future work, techniques for a more granular control on text generation can be explored, where one can adversarially inject bias to generate twisted versions of news stories. Techniques to introduce bias during machine translation of a news article from one language to another can be explored and evaluated by comparing the generated news after translation with the news generated by non-native speakers while converting news from other languages. Apart from named entities and sentence length, there are more intrinsic patterns representing presence of bias in text. Exploration studies to find such patterns can also be done in future to better understand bias distribution in text. Another future direction can be to quantify the impact of delivering biased news to real-world users using some social media platform.

Acknowledgments

This research was partly supported by JST CREST Grant JPMJCR18A6 and JSPS KAKENHI Grant JP16H06302 and JP18H04120, Japan.

References

David Ifeoluwa Adelani, Haotian Mai, Fuming Fang, Huy H Nguyen, Junichi Yamagishi, and Isao Echizen. 2020. Generating sentiment-preserving fake online reviews using neural language models and their human-and machine-based detection. In *International Conference on Advanced Information Networking and Applications*, pages 1341–1354. Springer.

Jisun An, Meeyoung Cha, Krishna Gummadi, Jon Crowcroft, and Daniele Quercia. 2012. Visualizing media bias through twitter. In *Sixth International AAAI Conference on Weblogs and Social Media*.

Ioannis Arapakis, Filipa Peleja, Barla Berkant, and Joao Magalhaes. 2016. Linguistic benchmarks of online news article quality. In *Proceedings of the 54th Annual Meeting of the Association for Computational Linguistics (Volume 1: Long Papers)*, pages 1893–1902.

Dzmitry Bahdanau, Kyunghyun Cho, and Yoshua Bengio. 2015. Neural machine translation by jointly learning to align and translate. *CoRR*, abs/1409.0473.

Christopher A Bail, Lisa P Argyle, Taylor W Brown, John P Bumpus, Haohan Chen, MB Fallin Hunzaker, Jaemin Lee, Marcus Mann, Friedolin Merhout, and Alexander Volfovsky. 2018. Exposure to opposing views on social media can increase political polarization. *Proceedings of the National Academy of Sciences*, 115(37):9216–9221.

Ramy Baly, Georgi Karadzhov, Dimitar Alexandrov, James Glass, and Preslav Nakov. 2018. Predicting factuality of reporting and bias of news media sources. *arXiv preprint arXiv:1810.01765*.

Yoshua Bengio, Réjean Ducharme, Pascal Vincent, and Christian Jauvin. 2003. A neural probabilistic language model. *Journal of machine learning research*, 3(Feb):1137–1155.

Wei-Fan Chen, Henning Wachsmuth, Khalid Al Khatib, and Benno Stein. 2018. Learning to flip the bias of news headlines. In *Proceedings of the 11th International Conference on Natural Language Generation*, pages 79–88.

Jacob Devlin, Ming-Wei Chang, Kenton Lee, and Kristina Toutanova. 2018. Bert: Pre-training of deep bidirectional transformers for language understanding. *arXiv preprint arXiv:1810.04805*.

Yi Fang, Luo Si, Naveen Somasundaram, and Zhengtao Yu. 2012. Mining contrastive opinions on political texts using cross-perspective topic model. In *Proceedings of the fifth ACM international conference on Web search and data mining*, pages 63–72.

Sebastian Gehrmann, Hendrik Strobelt, and Alexander M Rush. 2019. Gltr: Statistical detection and visualization of generated text. *arXiv preprint arXiv:1906.04043*.

Tim Groseclose and Jeffrey Milyo. 2005. A measure of media bias. *The Quarterly Journal of Economics*, 120(4):1191–1237.

Max Grusky, Mor Naaman, and Yoav Artzi. 2018. Newsroom: A dataset of 1.3 million summaries with diverse extractive strategies. *arXiv preprint arXiv:1804.11283*.

Nitish Shirish Keskar, Bryan McCann, Lav R Varshney, Caiming Xiong, and Richard Socher. 2019. Ctrl: A conditional transformer language model for controllable generation. *arXiv preprint arXiv:1909.05858*.

Juhi Kulshrestha, Motahhare Eslami, Johnnatan Messias, Muhammad Bilal Zafar, Saptarshi Ghosh, Krishna P Gummadi, and Karrie Karahalios. 2017. Quantifying search bias: Investigating sources of bias for political searches in social media. In *Proceedings of the 2017 ACM Conference on Computer Supported Cooperative Work and Social Computing*, pages 417–432.

Matthew S Levendusky. 2013. Why do partisan media polarize viewers? *American Journal of Political Science*, 57(3):611–623.

Juncen Li, Robin Jia, He He, and Percy Liang. 2018. Delete, retrieve, generate: A simple approach to sentiment and style transfer. *arXiv preprint arXiv:1804.06437*.

Yu-Ru Lin, James P Bagrow, and David Lazer. 2011. More voices than ever? quantifying media bias in networks. In *Fifth International AAAI Conference on Weblogs and Social Media*.

Yinhan Liu, Myle Ott, Naman Goyal, Jingfei Du, Mandar Joshi, Danqi Chen, Omer Levy, Mike Lewis, Luke Zettlemoyer, and Veselin Stoyanov. 2019. Roberta: A robustly optimized BERT pretraining approach. *CoRR*, abs/1907.11692.

Sidi Lu, Yaoming Zhu, Weinan Zhang, Jun Wang, and Yong Yu. 2018. Neural text generation: Past, present and beyond. *arXiv preprint arXiv:1803.07133*.

Tomáš Mikolov, Martin Karafiát, Lukáš Burget, Jan Černocký, and Sanjeev Khudanpur. 2010. Recurrent neural network based language model. In *Eleventh annual conference of the international speech communication association*.

Raymond S Nickerson. 1998. Confirmation bias: A ubiquitous phenomenon in many guises. *Review of general psychology*, 2(2):175–220.

Vanessa L Otero. 2019. Display and analysis system for media content. US Patent App. 16/204,795.

Alec Radford, Karthik Narasimhan, Tim Salimans, and Ilya Sutskever. 2018. Improving language understanding by generative pre-training. *URL https://s3-us-west-2. amazonaws. com/openai-assets/researchcovers/languageunsupervised/language understanding paper. pdf*.

Alec Radford, Jeffrey Wu, Rewon Child, David Luan, Dario Amodei, and Ilya Sutskever. 2019. Language models are unsupervised multitask learners. *OpenAI Blog*, 1(8):9.

Filipe N Ribeiro, Lucas Henrique, Fabricio Benevenuto, Abhijnan Chakraborty, Juhi Kulshrestha, Mahmoudreza Babaei, and Krishna P Gummadi. 2018. Media bias monitor: Quantifying biases of social media news outlets at large-scale. In *Twelfth International AAAI Conference on Web and Social Media*.

Tianxiao Shen, Tao Lei, Regina Barzilay, and Tommi Jaakkola. 2017. Style transfer from non-parallel text by cross-alignment. In *Advances in neural information processing systems*, pages 6830–6841.

Irene Solaiman, Miles Brundage, Jack Clark, Amanda Askell, Ariel Herbert-Voss, Jeff Wu, Alec Radford, and Jasmine Wang. 2019. Release strategies and the social impacts of language models. *arXiv preprint arXiv:1908.09203*.

Martin Sundermeyer, Ralf Schlüter, and Hermann Ney. 2012. Lstm neural networks for language modeling. In *Thirteenth annual conference of the international speech communication association*.

Briony Swire, Ullrich KH Ecker, and Stephan Lewandowsky. 2017. The role of familiarity in correcting inaccurate information. *Journal of experimental psychology: learning, memory, and cognition*, 43(12):1948.

Ashish Vaswani, Noam Shazeer, Niki Parmar, Jakob Uszkoreit, Llion Jones, Aidan N Gomez, Łukasz Kaiser, and Illia Polosukhin. 2017. Attention is all you need. In *Advances in neural information processing systems*, pages 5998–6008.

Oriol Vinyals, Alexander Toshev, Samy Bengio, and Dumitru Erhan. 2015. Show and tell: A neural image caption generator. In *Proceedings of the IEEE conference on computer vision and pattern recognition*, pages 3156–3164.

Winston Wang. 2019. Calculating political bias and fighting partisanship with ai.

Wayne Wanta and Yu-Wei Hu. 1994. The effects of credibility, reliance, and exposure on media agenda-setting: A path analysis model. *Journalism Quarterly*, 71(1):90–98.

Amy Watson. 2019. Leading news websites in the u.s. 2018, by unique visitors.

Janyce Wiebe, Theresa Wilson, and Claire Cardie. 2005. Annotating expressions of opinions and emotions in language. *Language resources and evaluation*, 39(2-3):165–210.

Julia Carrie Wong. 2019. The cambridge analytica scandal changed the world—but it didn't change facebook. *The Guardian*, 18.

Tae Yano, Philip Resnik, and Noah A Smith. 2010. Shedding (a thousand points of) light on biased language. In *Proceedings of the NAACL HLT 2010 Workshop on Creating Speech and Language Data with Amazon's Mechanical Turk*, pages 152–158. Association for Computational Linguistics.

Rowan Zellers, Ari Holtzman, Hannah Rashkin, Yonatan Bisk, Ali Farhadi, Franziska Roesner, and Yejin Choi. 2019. Defending against neural fake news. In *Advances in Neural Information Processing Systems*, pages 9054–9065.

Chi Zhang, Shagan Sah, Thang Nguyen, Dheeraj Peri, Alexander Loui, Carl Salvaggio, and Raymond Ptucha. 2017. Semantic sentence embeddings for paraphrasing and text summarization. In *2017 IEEE Global Conference on Signal and Information Processing (GlobalSIP)*, pages 705–709. IEEE.

Xiang Zhang, Junbo Zhao, and Yann LeCun. 2015. Character-level convolutional networks for text classification. In *Advances in neural information processing systems*, pages 649–657.

Jason Zhao, Abraham Ryzhik, and Nathaniel Lee. Deepnews. ai: Detecting political bias.

A Supplemental Material

A.1 Granularity Analysis

Sometimes biased text segments can be identified just by looking into the title (i.e. only one sentence), as we go along the bias may or may not increase. Intuitively, as we increase the length of text tested for presence of bias, the bias should also increase.

We have taken equal number of samples, i.e. 5,000, from both sides of bias. To test this hypothesis, we divided the news into 4 parts: sentence-1, which is just the title; sentence-3, first three sentences of news article (Grusky et al., 2018)(Lede-3); sentence-10, first 10 sentences of the news article (Chen et al., 2018); and finally full-length, which represents the complete news. Figure 4 shows that bias ratings increase as we increase the length of news being tested for bias.

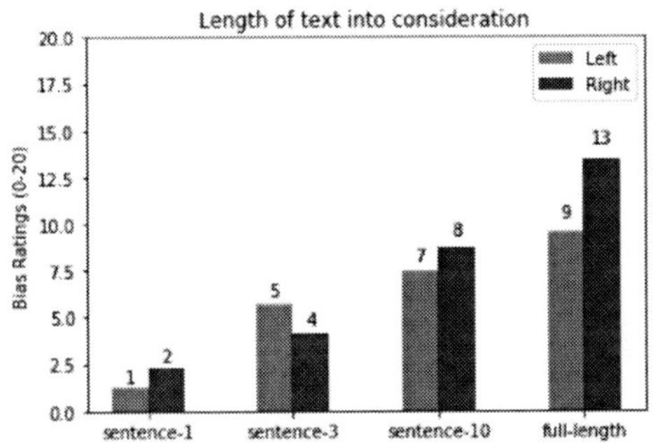

Figure 4: Granularity Analysis. The bias ratings increase as we increase the length of text to test for bias infestation.

A.2 Automatic Detection

We evaluated three automatic detection models, GLTR (Gehrmann et al., 2019), GROVER (Zellers et al., 2019), and GPT-2 PD (Solaiman et al., 2019) using 80 samples (news excerpts) each from human written, GPT-2 generated, and GROVER generated news. GLTR gives different probabilities of words being in top10, top100, and so on, and the other models give a probability score. We have used regression models as fusion functions while predicting with combined models. Table 6 shows detection results.

Detector	GPT-2 Generated	GROVER Generated	Overall
GLTR (A)	0.37	0.43	0.41
GPT-2 PD (B)	0.22	0.33	0.29
GROVER (C)	0.35	0.28	0.32
A + B	0.21	0.38	0.30
A + C	0.30	0.24	0.27
B + C	0.30	0.31	0.30
A + B + C	0.21	0.24	0.23

Table 6: Equal error rate in differentiating between human written and machine generated news. We have used three approaches independently as well as a combination of them. "+" indicates score fusion.

Unsupervised Anomaly Detection in Parole Hearings using Language Models

Graham Todd
Stanford University
gdrtodd@stanford.edu

Catalin Voss
Stanford University
catalin@stanford.edu

Jenny Hong
Stanford University
jyunhong@stanford.edu

Abstract

Each year, thousands of roughly 150-page parole hearing transcripts in California go unread because legal experts lack the time to review them. Yet, reviewing transcripts is the only means of public oversight in the parole process. To assist reviewers, we present a simple unsupervised technique for using language models (LMs) to identify procedural anomalies in long-form legal text. Our technique highlights unusual passages that suggest further review could be necessary. We utilize a *contrastive perplexity score* to identify passages, defined as the scaled difference between its perplexities from two LMs, one fine-tuned on the target (parole) domain, and another pre-trained on out-of-domain text to normalize for grammatical or syntactic anomalies. We present quantitative analysis of the results and note that our method has identified some important cases for review. We are also excited about potential applications in unsupervised anomaly detection, and present a brief analysis of results for detecting fake TripAdvisor reviews.

1 Introduction

California houses America's largest "lifer" population, with 25% of its 115,000 prisoners serving life sentences. Each year, the Board of Parole Hearings (BPH) conducts thousands of parole hearings to decide whether to grant prisoners early release. As California has enacted legislation to reduce its prison population, the number of hearings is scheduled to double this year and continue to rise for the foreseeable future. While each hearing is transcribed into about 150 pages of dialogue and sent to the BPH and governor's office for review, capacity constraints mean that, in practice, only grants of parole are reviewed. Legal scholars who painstakingly analyzed small subsets of transcripts have found that parole decisions are sometimes made

```
PRESIDING COMMISSIONER: Let me ask you a
question, Mr.   [REDACT].  Are you angry?
INMATE [REDACT]: No.
PRESIDING COMMISSIONER: You seem kind of
like you're a smart ass.  I don't mean
to say that rudely, but are you a smart
ass?
```

Figure 1: Example of a semantic anomaly

in an arbitrary and capricious manner (Bell, 2019), but they lack the resources for ongoing review.

To help alleviate these capacity constraints and allow for greater review of parole denials, we propose an automatic anomaly detection system that allows reviewers to focus their attention on the most anomalous portions of text in each hearing.[1] The lack of gold anomaly labels precludes the use of many supervised anomaly detection techniques, so instead we propose using language models trained on the parole transcripts to perform unsupervised anomaly detection.

Defining an "anomaly" in this context is challenging. There are many ways in which a piece of text might be unusual without constituting grounds for additional review. We distinguish primarily between *non-semantic*, *semantic*, and *procedural* anomalies. We define a *non-semantic* anomaly as an irregularity in the linguistic structure of a piece of text (for instance, a sentence fragment). A *semantic* anomaly, by contrast, is one caused by the meaning of the text. In the context of a parole hearing, a conversation that deviates substantially from the typical topics of discussion would constitute a semantic anomaly. Finally, a *procedural anomaly* is an irregularity that indicates the hearing differed substantively from the prescribed guidelines. Often, a procedural anomaly will also be a semantic

---

[1] Our project raises ethical questions about the use of technology in criminal justice review procedures. We provide a statement about the ethical implications of our work in Appendix A.

Proceedings of the Fourth Workshop on Natural Language Processing and Computational Social Science, pages 66–71
Online, November 20, 2020. ©2020 Association for Computational Linguistics
https://doi.org/10.18653/v1/P17

anomaly. Figure 1 represents such a case, as it both includes language atypical for a parole hearing and, more generally, indicates a breakdown in communication between the commissioner and the parole candidate. We note that there are also, of course, legal anomalies that do not manifest as atypical language.

A language model (LM) provides an organic way to identify unusual text through its perplexity score. We hypothesize that many procedural anomalies can be identified by examining statistical anomalies in the texts of transcripts, which would seemingly allow for their detection by an LM. However, most instances of unusual text found by a naive LM are *non-semantic*, consisting of typos, ungrammatical sentences, etc. To solve this problem, we instead use a pair of language models. We define our anomaly metric, the *contrastive perplexity score*, as the scaled difference between the perplexity of one LM, which has been fine-tuned on the target domain, and the perplexity of another LM, which has only been pre-trained on out-of-domain text. Non-semantic anomalies will have high perplexity under both LMs (and thus low *contrastive perplexity*), so the second LM acts as a "normalizer" for non-semantic content. We present our results on a human-annotated subset of the parole data. Our method recalls 71% of human-labeled *procedural* anomalies while only asking experts to review 50% of the text of each transcript. We also show that our method can be extended to other domains where a large labeled corpus of anomalous text is unavailable, namely the task of opinion spam detection in TripAdvisor reviews.

2   Related Work

Anomaly detection (AD) techniques cover a range of problem settings. Schölkopf et al. (1999); Hodge and Austin (2004); Chandola et al. (2009); Sakurada and Yairi (2014); Ruff et al. (2018); Schlegl et al. (2017) present general techniques for out-of-sample anomaly detection, with an increasing interest in deep unsupervised AD.

Text is a challenging regime for AD because of the importance of domain-dependence: what is shocking in one case might be mundane in another. Few, if any, universal features for AD exist. General approaches for text AD include non-negative matrix factorization (Kannan et al., 2017) and the use of "selectional preferences" (Dasigi and Hovy, 2014). One notable approach, studied in the dis-

course coherence literature, is to focus on local abnormalities in topics. Li and Jurafsky (2017) and Lin et al. (2011) present deep models for identifying incoherent passages of text, but discourse coherence studies much shorter text than parole hearings. To address longer text, our approach, like that of Guthrie et al. (2008), splits each document into segments ranked by anomaly score.

Our strategy of using LMs for AD has precedents, but primarily much simpler LMs, and for AD contexts that require more supervision than is available in the parole hearing setting. Rieck and Laskov (2006, 2007) and Aktolga et al. (2011) use n-gram LMs to identify anomalous sections and documents in a corpus of American bills presented before Congress. Axelrod et al. (2011) and Xu et al. (2019) also explore using a "baseline" LM for translation and discourse coherence, respectively.

3   Approach

Our model uses GPT-2, a transformer-based LM pre-trained on WebText, a corpus scraped from the internet (Radford et al., 2019; Vaswani et al., 2017). The following three observations motivate our approach to identifying anomalous text: (1) The perplexity of a *fine-tuned* LM on a target domain yields a score that measures both genre-specific semantic anomalies and general language anomalies (e.g. ungrammatical inputs, misspellings, incoherence). (2) The perplexity of an LM only *pre-trained* on many domains represents solely general language anomalies. (3) Putting the two together, the difference in perplexity between a fine-tuned language model and a pre-trained language model gives a "semantic anomaly score" of a piece of text.

We define the *contrastive perplexity* LM anomaly score to be the scaled difference in perplexities observed from two models. One model, the *fine-tuned LM*, is fit to a target corpus of text, without any supervision on which passages are anomalies. The other model, the *normalizer LM*, is the out-of-the-box GPT-2 model (Radford et al., 2019; Vaswani et al., 2017).

$$\text{LM anom.} = \text{pplx}_{\text{fine-tuned}} - \beta \cdot \text{pplx}_{\text{normalizer}}.$$

For a mundane piece of text, both $\text{pplx}_{\text{fine-tuned}}$ and $\text{pplx}_{\text{norm.}}$ are low. For a non-semantic anomaly, both are high. In both cases, contrastive perplexity is low. However, for a semantic anomaly, we expect $\text{pplx}_{\text{fine-tuned}}$ to be high, because of its sensitivity to the text's context domain, and

$\text{pplx}_{\text{norm}}$ to be low, because the text may not otherwise be unusual in general English, leading to high contrastive perplexity.

Because the fine-tuned LM achieves a lower perplexity, we use β to re-scale the perplexity output of the normalizer and ensure the models operate at the same scale. While β can be tuned as a hyperparameter, a reasonable and balanced choice is the ratio between the mean perplexities achieved by the fine-tuned model and the normalizer model on a validation dataset.

$$\beta = \frac{\sum_{x \in \text{val}} \text{pplx}_{\text{fine-tuned}}(x)}{\sum_{x \in \text{val}} \text{pplx}_{\text{normalizer}}(x)}$$

3.1 Anomaly Aggregation

We can use our LM anomaly score to identify the top k chunks of anomalous text for a given set of documents directly. In a completely unsupervised setting, with no labels as to which documents (or chunks) are anomalies, there is no way to associate the absolute contrastive perplexity scores with the predictive target. However, if given a *clean dataset* (i.e. a validation set that is labeled and known not to contain anomalies) we can instead anchor the scores to the clean dataset and detect anomalies by performing an out-of-distribution test.

4 Experimental Setup

4.1 Baselines

We compare our model to a number of unsupervised baseline models.

Within AD, most existing algorithms are unsuitable for our task (e.g. due to the need for supervision, incompatibility with long-form text). The most straightforward baseline is simply the fine-tuned GPT-2 model alone. We also compare our work to an unsupervised topic-modeling baseline that should also be agnostic to non-semantic anomalies, like Misra et al. (2008). We fit a latent Dirichlet allocation (LDA) model (Blei et al., 2003) to our train-corpus, then compute the mean representation and covariance matrix over topics, over a held-out portion of data. At prediction time, we compute the LDA representation for some text $f(x)$ and use its Mahalanobis distance from the mean representation as our anomaly score: $\sqrt{(f(x) - \mu_T)^T \Sigma_T^{-1}(f(x) - \mu_T)}$, where μ_T and Σ_T are the sample mean and covariance over the topic mixture embeddings, respectively.

4.2 Parole Hearings

Our analysis is performed over the complete[2] set of parole hearing transcripts in California between January 2007 and July 2018, which totals 30,734 transcripts. Each document is a transcript of an hours-long conversation between the parole board and a candidate (other parties are occasionally also present), which ends in a decision from the parole board. Transcribed, each hearing is roughly 27,000 tokens long.

We train our model on a train corpus of 27,577 transcripts, each split into non-overlapping chunks of 1024 tokens. We fit β on a validation corpus of 1,963 transcripts, with chunksize 256. The training chunksize was selected to maximize efficiency of the underlying GPT-2 model, while the smaller validation chunksize better matches the scale at which we expect to observe linguistic anomalies. We collected a held-out test corpus of anomalies over 315 transcripts by asking undergraduate and law students to label instances of anomalous language. Out of 82,959 chunks, students found 179 anomalies. An experienced parole attorney checked the anomalies and confirmed 68. Student reviewers were asked to identify *semantic* anomalies and the expert was asked to determine which of those were also *procedural* anomalies. While we believe that this offers a viable estimate of the true set of procedural anomalies, this leaves out anomalies that are not manifested by irregular language. To evaluate our model's recall, we investigate the tradeoff between the share of the expert's "true anomalies" we recover, and the number of chunks human reviewers must read. We asked the parole attorney to review our model's predictions at a fixed threshold. We compute the mean reciprocal rank (MRR) (?), rather than precision, because a single anomaly suffices to flag a whole transcript for review: only the rank of the highest scoring anomaly affects reviewer time. Details are given in Appendix B.

4.3 Hotel Reviews

Our second experiment is performed over the Deceptive Opinion Spam dataset (Ott et al., 2011, 2013). The dataset consists of 1,600 short human-generated reviews of 20 hotels in the Chicago area. 800 of these reviews were scraped from TripAdvisor and are marked "authentic"; the remaining 800 reviews are marked "anomalous" and were gen-

---

[2]The Dept. of Corrections withheld a a few hundred transcripts from that period, citing "confidential information."

Model	k=20	k=50
LDA Baseline	0.103	0.426
Fine-tuned LM	0.235	0.573
Contrastive Perplex.	0.279	0.676

Table 1: True anomaly recall achieved by reviewing the top-k chunks for each document. The average document has 105 chunks in this sample.

erated by Mechanical Turk workers. In order to fine-tune GPT-2, we use a collection of TripAdvisor reviews collected by (Wang et al., 2010).[3] We only include the 171,016 reviews that were shorter than 1024 tokens and longer than 30 tokens. Additionally, we hold out 10,000 reviews to fit μ and Σ for the LDA baseline.

4.4 Model & Training

We use the GPT-2 base model for all of our experiments, trained for 48 hours using the Adam optimizer with an initial learning rate of 10^{-5} and linear decay.

5 Results & Analysis

5.1 Parole Hearings

Our fine-tuned and normalizer model achieve mean perplexities of 9.22 and 22.99 ($\beta = 0.40$), respectively, on the validation set with fixed chunksize 256. Figure 2 describes the tradeoff between recall and the percentage the transcript human reviewers must read for our model and baselines as we vary the model. Contrastive perplexity outperforms all baselines, but overall recall is low. We also observe that the LM anomaly score produced by our model is not well-conserved across documents. Rather than using a global threshold for our model, we can instead ask reviewers to always use top k predictions for each document. Table 1 shows recall for different values of k.

We evaluate our model's precision at the threshold that yields an average of 55 chunks per document (corresponding to about 52% of average transcript length) and recall of 0.68, marked on the plot. At this threshold, our model achieves an MRR of 0.227. Student annotators achieve 0.264 precision (note that, because the ratings from the students were not ranked, it is not possible to compute their MRR). The low human precision underscores the

<hr>

[3] We ensured that there is no overlap in between the reviews used for fine-tuning and the Deceptive Opinion Spam dataset.

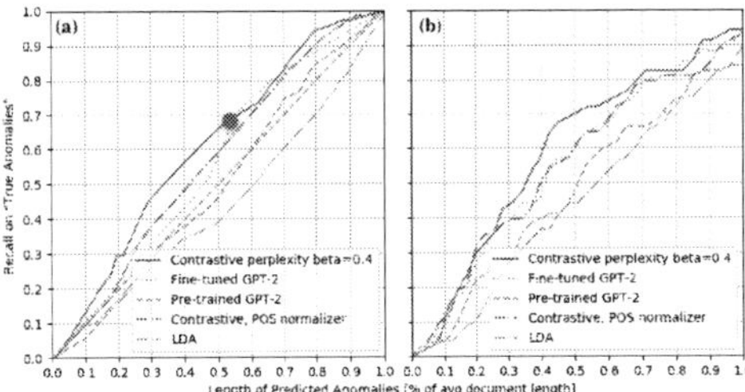

Figure 2: Recall on true anomalies vs. the amount of reading required of the reviewer; (a) by varying the threshold, (b) by fixing k chunks per document.

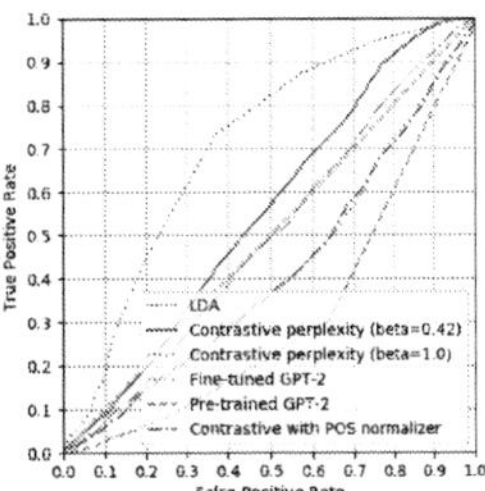

Figure 3: ROC curve for unsupervised fake review prediction on TripAdvisor dataset. The un-tuned $\beta = 0.42$ is outperformed by $\beta = 1$.

intrinsic difficulty of the task and the level of disagreement between human annotators over what constitutes an anomaly.

5.2 Hotel Reviews

Our fine-tuned and normalizer model achieve mean perplexities of 22.62 and 53.60 ($\beta = 0.42$) on the validation set of "real" TripAdvisor reviews. Figure 3 shows the ROC curve of our model compared to baselines, using our unsupervised LM anomaly measure as a "fake review classifier" on the Deceptive Opinion Spam dataset. Our model achieves an F1 of 0.537 at the optimal threshold. With manually tuned $\beta = 1.0$, we achieve 0.679. While below the 0.898 F1 achieved by the best fully supervised models (Ott et al., 2011), this indicates that our model is a promising unsupervised predictor.

6 Discussion & Conclusion

We present a novel contrastive perplexity-based approach for unsupervised anomaly detection. We define semantic and non-semantic anomalies, and present evidence that our model can distinguish between them better than other unsupervised baselines. Detecting procedural anomalies in legal cases is easier with structured data, but that data is often not readily available. Our approach seeks to support legal decision makers in identifying anomalous cases for review when structured records are unavailable.

Our experiments on an unexplored dataset of 30,734 parole hearing transcripts have identified troubling cases for review. However, our quantitative evaluations also show the difficulty of defining a semantic anomaly consistently. Our results on detecting fake hotel reviews indicate that our approach becomes more powerful when anomaly-free documents are available to perform an out-of-distribution test.

In future work, we seek to use conditional LMs to bridge the gap between our unsupervised method and settings in which some structured data is available.

References

Elif Aktolga, Irene Ros, and Yannick Assogba. 2011. Detecting outlier sections in us congressional legislation. In *Proceedings of the 34th International ACM SIGIR Conference on Research and Development in Information Retrieval*, SIGIR '11, pages 235–244, New York, NY, USA. ACM.

Amittai Axelrod, Xiaodong He, and Jianfeng Gao. 2011. Domain adaptation via pseudo in-domain data selection. In *Proceedings of the Conference on Empirical Methods in Natural Language Processing*, EMNLP '11, pages 355–362, Stroudsburg, PA, USA. Association for Computational Linguistics.

Kristen Bell. 2019. A stone of hope: Legal and empirical analysis of california juvenile lifer parole decisions. *Harv. CR-CLL Rev.*, 54:455.

David M. Blei, Andrew Y. Ng, and Michael I. Jordan. 2003. Latent dirichlet allocation. *J. Mach. Learn. Res.*, 3:993–1022.

Varun Chandola, Arindam Banerjee, and Vipin Kumar. 2009. Anomaly detection: A survey. *ACM Comput. Surv.*, 41(3):15:1–15:58.

Pradeep Dasigi and Eduard Hovy. 2014. Modeling newswire events using neural networks for anomaly detection. In *Proceedings of COLING 2014, the 25th International Conference on Computational Linguistics: Technical Papers*, pages 1414–1422, Dublin, Ireland. Dublin City University and Association for Computational Linguistics.

David Guthrie, Louise Guthrie, and Yorick Wilks. 2008. An unsupervised probabilistic approach for the detection of outliers in corpora. In *LREC 2008*.

Victoria Hodge and Jim Austin. 2004. A survey of outlier detection methodologies. *Artificial Intelligence Review*, 22(2):85–126.

Ramakrishnan Kannan, Hyenkyun Woo, Charu C. Aggarwal, and Haesun Park. 2017. Outlier detection for text data : An extended version.

Jiwei Li and Dan Jurafsky. 2017. Neural net models of open-domain discourse coherence. In *Proceedings of the 2017 Conference on Empirical Methods in Natural Language Processing*, pages 198–209, Copenhagen, Denmark. Association for Computational Linguistics.

Ziheng Lin, Hwee Tou Ng, and Min-Yen Kan. 2011. Automatically evaluating text coherence using discourse relations. In *Proceedings of the 49th Annual Meeting of the Association for Computational Linguistics: Human Language Technologies - Volume 1*, HLT '11, pages 997–1006, Stroudsburg, PA, USA. Association for Computational Linguistics.

Hemant Misra, Olivier Cappé, and François Yvon. 2008. Using LDA to detect semantically incoherent documents. In *CoNLL 2008: Proceedings of the Twelfth Conference on Computational Natural Language Learning*, pages 41–48, Manchester, England. Coling 2008 Organizing Committee.

Myle Ott, Claire Cardie, and Jeffrey T. Hancock. 2013. Negative deceptive opinion spam. In *Proceedings of the 2013 Conference of the North American Chapter of the Association for Computational Linguistics: Human Language Technologies*, pages 497–501, Atlanta, Georgia. Association for Computational Linguistics.

Myle Ott, Yejin Choi, Claire Cardie, and Jeffrey T. Hancock. 2011. Finding deceptive opinion spam by any stretch of the imagination. In *Proceedings of the 49th Annual Meeting of the Association for Computational Linguistics: Human Language Technologies*, pages 309–319, Portland, Oregon, USA. Association for Computational Linguistics.

Alec Radford, Jeffrey Wu, Rewon Child, David Luan, Dario Amodei, and Ilya Sutskever. 2019. Language models are unsupervised multitask learners.

Konrad Rieck and Pavel Laskov. 2006. Detecting unknown network attacks using language models. In *Detection of Intrusions and Malware & Vulnerability Assessment*, pages 74–90, Berlin, Heidelberg. Springer Berlin Heidelberg.

Konrad Rieck and Pavel Laskov. 2007. Language models for detection of unknown attacks in network traffic. *Journal in Computer Virology*, 2(4):243–256.

Lukas Ruff, Robert Vandermeulen, Nico Goernitz, Lucas Deecke, Shoaib Ahmed Siddiqui, Alexander Binder, Emmanuel Müller, and Marius Kloft. 2018. Deep one-class classification. In *Proceedings of the*

35th International Conference on Machine Learning, volume 80 of *Proceedings of Machine Learning Research*, pages 4393–4402, Stockholmsmässan, Stockholm Sweden. PMLR.

Mayu Sakurada and Takehisa Yairi. 2014. Anomaly detection using autoencoders with nonlinear dimensionality reduction. In *Proceedings of the MLSDA 2014 2Nd Workshop on Machine Learning for Sensory Data Analysis*, MLSDA'14, pages 4:4–4:11, New York, NY, USA. ACM.

Thomas Schlegl, Philipp Seeböck, Sebastian M. Waldstein, Ursula Schmidt-Erfurth, and Georg Langs. 2017. Unsupervised anomaly detection with generative adversarial networks to guide marker discovery.

Bernhard Schölkopf, Robert Williamson, Alex Smola, John Shawe-Taylor, and John Platt. 1999. Support vector method for novelty detection. In *Proceedings of the 12th International Conference on Neural Information Processing Systems*, NIPS'99, pages 582–588, Cambridge, MA, USA. MIT Press.

Ashish Vaswani, Noam Shazeer, Niki Parmar, Jakob Uszkoreit, Llion Jones, Aidan N Gomez, Łukasz Kaiser, and Illia Polosukhin. 2017. Attention is all you need. In *Advances in neural information processing systems*, pages 5998–6008.

Hongning Wang, Yue Lu, and Chengxiang Zhai. 2010. Latent aspect rating analysis on review text data: A rating regression approach. In *Proceedings of the 16th ACM SIGKDD International Conference on Knowledge Discovery and Data Mining*, KDD '10, pages 783–792, New York, NY, USA. ACM.

Peng Xu, Hamidreza Saghir, Jin Sung Kang, Teng Long, Avishek Joey Bose, Yanshuai Cao, and Jackie Chi Kit Cheung. 2019. A cross-domain transferable neural coherence model.

Identifying Worry in Twitter: Beyond Emotion Analysis

Reyha Verma   Christian von der Weth   Jithin Vachery   Mohan Kankanhalli
School of Computing
National University of Singapore, Singapore
`{reyha,chris,jithin,mohan}@comp.nus.edu.sg`

Abstract

Identifying the worries of individuals and societies plays a crucial role in providing social support and enhancing policy decision-making. Due to the popularity of social media platforms such as Twitter, users share worries about personal issues (e.g., health, finances, relationships) and broader issues (e.g., changes in society, environmental concerns, terrorism) freely. In this paper, we explore and evaluate a wide range of machine learning models to predict worry on Twitter. While this task has been closely associated with emotion prediction, we argue and show that identifying worry needs to be addressed as a separate task given the unique challenges associated with it. We conduct a user study to provide evidence that social media posts express two basic kinds of worry – normative and pathological – as stated in psychology literature. In addition, we show that existing emotion detection techniques underperform, especially while capturing normative worry. Finally, we discuss the current limitations of our approach and propose future applications of the worry identification system.

1   Introduction

Knowing what an individual or society at large, worry about – e.g., unemployment, health issues, ageing, the rise of AI – is an indicator of people's well-being. Capturing information like the possible source and nature (e.g., type, intensity) of people's worry is used by many governmental agencies[1,2,3] to guide their policy decisions. This can range from minor decisions such as initiation of information campaigns (e.g., to counter false information being spread during the COVID-19 pandemic) to major policy changes like introduction and amendment of laws (e.g., increase of minimum wage, mandatory health insurance, data privacy and fake news). Many private companies (e.g., Toyota) listen to the worries of their customers using techniques like "Voice-of-Customer" (Griffin and Hauser, 1993) as part of their Quality Function Deployment (QFD) process (Toma and Naruo, 2017).

Measuring worry, however, is quite challenging. Traditional approaches rely on time-consuming and costly user surveys and polls (e.g., on a large scale, the World Happiness Report (Helliwell et al., 2020), the Global Risk Report (WEF, 2020)). These surveys, although very well-structured, suffer from some severe limitations. Firstly, being resource-consuming, (large) surveys are generally conducted periodically (e.g., 1-2 times a year). This, in turn, creates knowledge gaps as it is hardly possible to track short-term trends following significant events (e.g., pandemic outbreak, natural disasters, terrorist attacks). Secondly, most of the surveys tend to have a narrow scope with a specific, pre-defined purpose. For example, surveys conducted by the public housing agency are most likely to be limited to the worries of the residents of those societies. Lastly, surveys involving sensitive subjects (e.g., racism, immigration, LGBT rights, abortion, religion, politics) tend to suffer from non-response bias of the participants who might divulge their true opinions – even if they are ensured anonymity – in order to adhere to political correctness.

In contrast, social media provides a platform for individuals to freely and continuously express their thoughts, feelings and experiences as well as to share information with other members of the society. Content on platforms like Twitter is generally public and can be easily collected on a large scale, thereby, making social media mining a promising approach to observe and analyze people's worries. Social media, however, comes with its own set

---

[1]https://www.reach.gov.sg/participate/public-consultation

[2]https://innovate.mygov.in/dpi-public-consultation/

[3]https://www.hpb.gov.sg/community/national-population-health-survey

Proceedings of the Fourth Workshop on Natural Language Processing and Computational Social Science, pages 72–82
Online, November 20, 2020. ©2020 Association for Computational Linguistics
https://doi.org/10.18653/v1/P17

Figure 1: Emotion prediction on tweets with worry.

of challenges in form of self-censorship bias and the presence of scripted bots. Besides this, unlike well-structured surveys that often have structured questions (single or multiple-choice, rating and ranking), social media content is quite unstructured. Sophisticated analytics, most of them using state-of-the-art machine learning algorithms, are often required to extract meaningful and in-depth insights from such unstructured data.

Many works have been proposed to capture people's well-being using social media; see Section 2. In most of these works, worry is associated with notions such as anxiety, fear and nervousness. However, as per psychology literature, worry is primarily considered to be a thought process concerned with future events that often has adverse and uncertain outcomes (Borkovec et al., 1983). Since people are confronted with or affected by events with uncertain outcomes in their day-to-day life, most of them are worried to some extent. Only when the extent of these worries becomes uncontrollable and excessive, this normative process becomes pathological and results in anxiety or depression (Brown, 1997; Watkins, 2008). With the increase in people's worries, their emotional responses tend to get stronger, typically expressed as fear. Thus, while fear implies worry, not all worries necessarily result in fear (Levy and Guttman, 1985). Therefore, we argue that the existing approaches used to evaluate people's mental or emotional states (fear, anxiety, depression, etc.) are not sufficient to accurately capture the notion of worry due to these arguably subtle but important differences. Figure 1 (using ParallelDots[4] API) shows evidence that an emotion classifier is unable to predict worry in tweets classified as sad and happy.

To validate our hypothesis, we first compare people's perception of worry and emotions using the same underlying data. We use crowdsourcing to re-annotate a well-established Twitter dataset curated for emotion prediction for our new target task of identifying worry. We analyze this dataset

[4]https://www.paralleldots.com/emotion-analysis

to establish that emotion is not an adequate predictor of worry. Secondly, using the re-annotated dataset, we train different machine learning models – feature-based, word embedding-based and contextual embedding-based – to refine further the subtleties that result in differences between emotion and worry. Next, we perform an in-depth analysis of different kinds of worry – normative and pathological – by conducting a user study. Lastly, we perform error analysis to highlight current shortcomings as well as challenges while discussing the future work leading to more effective worry prediction.

2 Related Work

Psychology literature defines worry to be a future-oriented thought process typically concerned with a problem whose potentially negative outcome is uncertain (Borkovec et al., 1983). Most people deal with some degree of worry on a daily basis in the form of normative or non-pathological worry (Eysenck, 1995). However, excessive, pervasive and uncontrollable worry becomes pathological in the form of generalized anxiety disorder (Brown, 1997). Besides this difference in intensity of worry, psychology also categorizes worry into various life domains (e.g., health, social relations, environment) as well as the object of worry (e.g., self, close friends/relatives, society and the world) (Boehnke et al., 1998; Schwartz et al., 2000; Schwartz and Melech, 2000).

As social media has become one of the most popular services online, users on these platforms indulge in widespread sharing of thoughts, opinions and feelings, as well as, events that constitute their everyday lives like check-ins, relationships, and more (Schwartz et al., 2013). Several studies have shown that the language, linguistic style and behavior derived from social media posts often reflect users' personal characteristics (Kosinski et al., 2013; Schwartz et al., 2016). Consequently, many methods have been proposed to use social media content to predict users' personality traits and well-being. Most works such as (Azucar et al., 2018; Farnadi et al., 2016; Skowron et al., 2016; Hughes et al., 2012), aim to predict the personality of social media users using the Big 5 personality traits: OCEAN (openness, conscientiousness, extraversion, agreeableness, and neuroticism). While personality traits help in understanding how often a user might worry, they do not allow us to predict whether a particular post expresses worry.

Existing efforts towards evaluating users' well-being related to worry have focused on emotion prediction (Canales, Lea and Martínez-Barco, Patricio, 2014), depression (Guntuku et al., 2017; Choudhury et al., 2013), anxiety and stress (Coppersmith et al., 2014), suicidal thoughts (De Choudhury et al., 2016) – that is, on pathological causes affecting users' well-being. However, worrying is not necessarily pathological and only becomes so when it grows excessive and uncontrollable (Brown, 1997). Similarly, since "daily worries" are part of most people's lives, not all worries trigger a (strong) emotional response. Worry, as a thought process concerned with future events that have uncertain and potentially (very) negative outcomes, is most closely related to fear and anxiety. In fact, many existing works predicting emotions in users' social media posts (Lamb et al., 2013; Harb and Becker, 2018; Wang et al., 2012) associate fear with worry. Since worry does not necessarily imply fear, emotions alone are not a good predictor for worry, as they are skewed towards strong feelings of worry that more likely yield an emotional response.

3 Datasets and Experimental Setup

In this section, we firstly describe our dataset for the task of identifying worry in tweets, then briefly discuss the methodology of data pre-processing and finally outline the set of machine learning models used for evaluation.

3.1 Worry Datasets

For identifying worry in tweets, we leverage on the existing dataset made available to by the SemEval-2018 Task 1: Affect in Tweets (Mohammad et al., 2018), containing 12,634 tweets. This dataset contains four subsets – one for each emotion (joy, fear, anger and sadness). Each of these tweets contains an integer intensity score ranging from 0 to 3 representing no, low, moderate and high intensity respectively. However, there are 1,544 overlapping tweets that are present in more than one subset (e.g., a tweet in "fear" subset with intensity 3 is also present in "joy" subset with intensity 0). We remove these overlapping tweets for the ease of annotation.

Before finalizing the annotation procedure, we conducted three pilot studies with 1,000 tweets per study. We used Amazon Mechanical Turk[5] as the crowdsourcing platform for all the studies. There were 50 annotation tasks each comprising of 20 tweets that were labeled by 5 different native English annotators. Each annotation task included a detailed set of instructions containing examples of different kinds of worries (such as explicit and implicit).

The first pilot study had a 5-point Likert scale with classes: "definitely yes", "probably yes", "not sure", "definitely not" and "probably not" where 'yes' and 'no' referred to the presence and absence of worry respectively. We found that 79.4% of the 1,000 total tweets had no consensus among the workers and, therefore, had to be rejected. Since the task of worry identification is highly subjective, classes containing words 'definitely' and 'probably' added a notion of worry intensity, making it difficult for the workers to be confident of their annotations. Therefore, for our second study, we switched over to the 3-point Likert scale with classes: "worry", "non-worry" and "not sure". The rejection rate drastically reduced to 30.15% as workers became more confident of their assessment. However, on a closer inspection, we found that some annotations to be unsatisfactory due to lack of quality control.

We performed the third pilot study with a 3-point Likert scale with classes: "worry", "non-worry" and "not sure" and a quality control mechanism in the form of test tweets. For quality control, 3 out of every 20 tweets were test tweets manually created by the authors that unquestionably expressed worry or no worry as a result of which the rejection rates further fell down to 16.4%. Finally, we used the last pilot study to label the remaining 11,090 tweets. After discarding tweets labeled as "not sure", we got a total of 10,191 tweets which are contained in our worry Twitter (**WT**) dataset. The rejection rate for the final dataset is 15.14% and the inter-rater agreement is 0.258 ('fair agreement' as per Fleiss Kappa (Landis and Koch, 1977)) Details are given in Table 1.

---

[5]https://www.mturk.com/

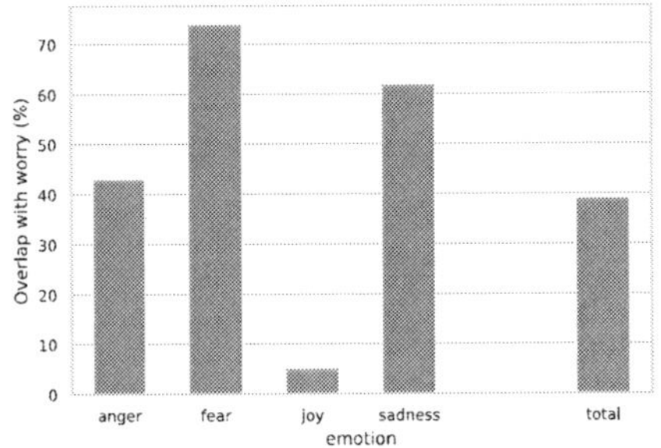

Figure 2: Overlaps of emotion and worry labels.

To compare worry with emotion (cf. 4.2), we create an additional **WT-Short** dataset removing 4,165 tweets with intensity 0 out of the total 10,191 annotated tweets. The original **WT** dataset is used to evaluate our worry classifier whereas the **WT-Short** dataset is used primarily to analyze the differences between worry and emotion.

Dataset	Non-Worry	Worry	Total
WT	6,836	3,355	10,191
WT-Short	3,666	2,360	6,026

Table 1: Details of used datasets.

Having a single **WT-Short** dataset annotated with both worry and emotions allows us to compare the two concepts. Figure 2 shows the overlap between the tweets labeled with worry for each of the four emotions. While, not unexpectedly, the overlap between fear and worry is the highest and the overlap between joy and worry is the lowest, there is no clear connection of other emotions - sadness, anger - with worry.

3.2 Data Pre-processing

We use the Ekphrasis tool (Baziotis et al., 2017) as the pre-processor for our dataset. Ekphrasis recognizes Twitter mark-up, emoticons, emojis, dates, currencies and words with emphasis using an exhaustive list of regular expressions. Using Ekphrasis, we perform Twitter-specific tokenization followed by spell correction and word normalization. For traditional feature-based models, we remove the stop-words and lemmatize the tweets as an additional step.

3.3 Model Description

To carry out the experiments, we explore three different machine learning approaches for worry detection: a traditional approach using feature-based models, deep learning approaches based on non-contextual (word-based) embeddings and deep learning approaches based on contextual embeddings.

For traditional approaches, we use (1) Multinomial Naïve Bayes (MNB), and (2) Support Vector Machine (SVM) implementations available in scikit-learn (Pedregosa et al., 2012). For deep learning approaches using the word-based embeddings, we use (1) Hierarchical Attention Network (HAN) (Yang et al., 2016), which utilizes hierarchical nature of the text along with the attention mechanism, and (2) CNN for sentence classification (CNN-static) (Kim, 2014) which consists of max pooling and convolution. Since emojis are quite frequently used in tweets and convey important information, we combine the GloVe vectors (Pennington et al., 2014) trained on $840B^6$ tokens with 300-dimensional emoji2vec embeddings (Eisner et al., 2016) to ensure that our emojis are also well-represented while training. For deep learning approaches based on contextual embeddings, we use (1) RoBERTa: A Robustly Optimized BERT Pretraining Approach (Liu et al., 2019) and XL-Net: Generalized Autoregressive Pretraining for Language Understanding (Yang et al., 2019) made available by HuggingFace.[7] We, then, fine-tune these models for our classification task.

For training the models in experiments mentioned in Section 4, we split the dataset into 80-10-10(%) for train-dev-test respectively. We repeat each experiment five times and average the results. For optimizing our network, we use Adam (Kingma and Ba, 2015) with a mini-batch of size 32. We use TensorFlow (Abadi et al., 2016) for implementing all our deep learning models. Details on the hyper-parameter values and the modifications made to the architectures are mentioned in the Appendix.

4 Experiments and Results

This section covers four parts: the evaluation of our worry classifier, the effect of emotion on worry prediction, analysis of different kinds of worry using a user study and an error analysis discussing the core challenges towards further improving this task.

---

[6]https://nlp.stanford.edu/projects/glove/
[7]https://huggingface.co/transformers/

4.1 Worry Prediction

For this experiment, we train six different models, as discussed in Section 3.3, using both **WT** and **WT-Short** dataset. Table 6 shows the results on the test set using different metrics. Note, we use the Matthew Correlation Coefficient (MCC) as an additional metric because our dataset is highly imbalanced.

Model	Precision	Recall	F1-score	Accuracy	MCC
MNB	0.84	0.08	0.14	0.68	0.19
SVM	0.59	0.46	0.52	0.71	0.32
CNN-static	0.59	0.62	0.60	0.73	0.39
HAN	0.62	0.52	0.57	0.74	0.38
RoBERTa-GRU	0.69	0.55	**0.61**	0.76	0.45
XLNet-GRU	0.73	0.50	0.59	0.75	0.44
Model	Precision	Recall	F1-score	Accuracy	MCC
MNB	0.79	0.31	0.45	0.68	0.34
SVM	0.67	0.63	0.65	0.72	0.42
CNN-static	0.66	0.78	0.72	0.74	0.41
HAN	0.68	0.74	0.71	0.75	0.43
RoBERTa-GRU	0.66	0.86	**0.75**	0.76	0.5
XLNet-GRU	0.68	0.79	0.73	0.74	0.45

Table 2: Performance of worry classifiers on the **WT** dataset (top) and the **WT-Short** dataset (bottom)

We see that for **WT** dataset, the deep learning models achieve a much higher F1-score as compared to the traditional models. Among different deep learning models, RoBERTa that uses a byte-level BPE (Byte-Pair Encoding) token on top of the BERT (Bidirectional Encoder Representations from Transformers) model outperforms others (F1-score: 61%). Though the score is only slightly higher than the other models, given the nature of the task, these results are not surprising as worry identification requires in-depth contextual knowledge. On careful analysis of the false positives and false negatives, we observe that these tweets are more ambiguous and subjective, making them more difficult to classify. We detail these challenging cases in Section 4.4

The six additional classifiers that are trained using the **WT-Short** dataset to compare worry and emotion as specified in Section 4.2. This dataset contains tweets with emotion intensity equal to or greater than one making it possible for us to perform comparative analysis. It is because the **WT-Short** dataset is more balanced as compared to the **WT** dataset that we find a clear difference between the results obtained, as shown in Table 6.

4.2 Worry with/vs. Emotion Prediction

To analyze the relationship between worry and emotion, we perform two additional series of experiments. Firstly, we evaluate if emotion and sentiment improve the task of identifying worry. As worry is often assumed to be related to negative future events (Borkovec et al., 1983), we additionally use sentiment labels. The main objective of analyzing sentiment is to understand if polarity, particularly negative polarity, plays any role in aiding worry detection task.

In order to do this, we train three classifiers – SVM, CNN-static and RoBERTa-GRU – the best performing models in their respective categories (cf. Table 6). For each of these three classifiers, we train four combinations with the following inputs: (1) worry (W) (2) worry and sentiment (W+S) (3) worry and emotion (W+E) (4) worry, emotion and sentiment (W+E+S) to be able to perform an in-depth analysis. To obtain the sentiment labels, we use VADER (Hutto and Gilbert, 2014), a sentiment analyzer optimized for social media content such as tweets. For deep learning models, sentiment and emotion annotations are added as input layers before the dense output layer. For traditional models, input features are simply concatenated together.

Model	Input	Precision	Recall	F1-score	Accuracy	MCC
SVM	W	0.67	0.63	0.65	0.72	0.42
	W+S	0.69	0.66	0.68	0.71	0.41
	W+E	0.70	0.67	0.69	0.75	0.48
	W+E+S	0.69	0.67	0.68	0.74	0.47
CNN-static	W	0.66	0.78	0.72	0.74	0.41
	W+S	0.64	0.73	0.68	0.72	0.46
	W+E.	0.67	0.84	0.74	0.75	0.47
	W+E+S	0.68	0.75	0.72	0.74	0.52
RoBERTa-GRU	W	0.66	0.86	0.75	0.76	0.50
	W+S	0.66	0.76	0.71	0.74	0.50
	W+E	0.72	0.78	0.75	0.79	0.50
	W+E+S	0.71	0.75	0.73	0.77	0.47

Table 3: Performance of the worry classifiers and joint classifiers on the **WT-Short** dataset. Here, W = worry, W+S = worry and sentiment, W+E = worry and emotion, W+E+S = worry, emotion and sentiment.

Table 3 shows the results over the **WT-Short** dataset. We observe that for all the four different combinations, RoBERTa-GRU performs better than the rest. Although emotion does not improve worry prediction to a great extent, there is a slight increase in the scores obtained. For RoBERTa-GRU, the accuracy after adding the emotion inputs (W+E) improves from 76% to 79%. Note, this does not indicate emotion is an equally good predictor of worry. The F1-score for both W+S and W+E+S decreases, thereby suggesting a negative impact of sentiment on the results.

Secondly, we evaluate how well an emotion classifier can serve as a predictor of worry. For example, if a tweet is classified as "fear" or "sadness", how good is the prediction with respect to worry.

For this experiment, we first perform a logistic regression analysis using emotion labels as inputs to predict worry. The coefficients for fear, anger, sadness and joy are 0.445, 0.035, 0.429 and -1.55 respectively. As expected, fear and joy have the highest and the lowest coefficients respectively. Next, we move on to text modeling and train an emotion classifier using **WT-Short** dataset as shown in Table 4. We use the best model for emotion classification (RoBERTa-GRU) to evaluate the results for all possible combinations of the four emotions. Figure 3 shows the corresponding F1-scores for the worry classification task ranked from best to worst. Each combination represents one class, and each class consists of one or more emotions combined together to predict worry.

Model	Fear	Anger	Sadness	Joy
SVM	0.73	0.77	0.68	0.71
CNN-static	0.78	0.80	0.73	0.92
RoBERTa-GRU	0.80	0.85	0.76	0.94

Table 4: F1-scores of emotion classifiers trained on **WT-Short** dataset.

As intuitively expected, the best emotion combinations contain "fear", although "fear" on its own performs quite low. Given the relationship between worry and emotions, it is not surprising that emotion classification can serve as a predictor for worry, although subpar to our worry classifier. However, we also argue that the results in Figure 3 represent a best-case scenario since we built upon a dataset created for emotion classification. In the following sections, we show that worry is often only implied in a neutral, "emotionless" manner, making an emotion classifier generally unsuitable for worry prediction.

4.3 User Study

We evaluate the ability of our classifiers to clearly distinguish between pathological and normative worry by conducting an empirical study using a non-emotion dataset. The reason for selecting a non-emotion dataset is to obtain sufficient tweets containing normative worry as emotion datasets are usually dominated by tweets with pathological worry. To compare worry with emotion, we consider the combination of three negative emotions – i.e. "fear", "sadness" and "anger" – as worry and the positive emotion "joy" as non-worry throughout this section. It is because these combinations are found to be the best and the worst predictors of

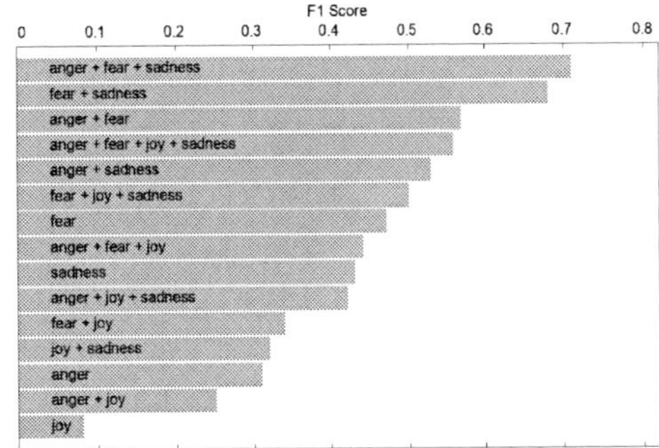

Figure 3: F1 scores of different emotion classifiers for the prediction of worry.

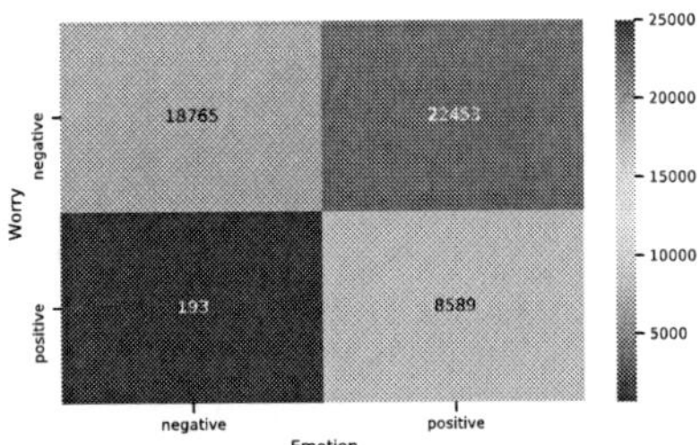

Figure 4: Worry vs. Emotion using **Sentiment140** dataset.

worry respectively (cf. Figure 3). In this section, we will first describe the setup for our study and then discuss the results obtained.

4.3.1 Experimental Setup

For setting up this experiment, we use the **Sentiment140** dataset provided by Go et al. (2009). This dataset is a corpus for sentiment analysis that contains 1.6 million tweets annotated with polarity 0 (negative) and 1 (positive). Out of the 1.6 million tweets, we randomly sample 50k tweets containing an equal number of tweets with positive and negative sentiment. Using the classifiers discussed in Section 4, we predict emotion and worry for these 50k tweets. Figure 4 shows the overall distribution. We then annotate 500 tweets - 193 worry tweets with negative emotion and 307 worry tweets with positive emotion (randomly sampled out of approximately 8k tweets). We follow the same annotation process, as the one discussed in Section 3.1 and obtain worry labels to validate our worry predictions.

4.3.2 Normative vs. Pathological Worry

Next, we examine the annotated dataset for normative and pathological worries. Table 5 shows different normative and pathological tweets. Normative tweets are the worry tweets correctly predicted by our worry classifier but incorrectly predicted by our emotion classifier. The pathological tweets, on the other hand, are the worry tweets correctly predicted by both our worry and emotion classifier.

Pathological tweets like *"im pissed!!as in very very pissed!!"* or *"have my phone interview for DCU today.... soooooooooooooooo nervous!!!"* are the tweets where users explicitly mention they are experiencing a negative emotion and/or are often associated with high emotional intensity. These are mostly correctly predicted as worry by both worry and emotion classifier. This is, however, not true for normative worries. While evaluating normative worries, we find there are two different kinds of tweets.

Mixed Emotions. The most frequent scenario is where a tweet expresses mixed emotions, that is, both positive and negative emotions simultaneously. For example, *"Home alone again......YAY!!!! BUT STILL HAVE TO DO MORE CHORES.....UGH."*. The first half of this sentence conveys happiness, while the second half expresses sadness. The emotion classifier, being unable to capture the underlying worry, predicts this to be joy (non-worry). The emotion classifier usually performs poorly on such tweets. To correctly classify worry tweets with mixed emotions, it is imperative to train the model on dataset that is specifically curated for the task of worry detection.

Low or Zero Emotional Intensity. Social media users use different writing styles to express themselves. For example, *"Wow only got 3 hrs of sleep!! Bad Bad bad!!!! got a huge headache!!!"* represents an extremely intense tweet with high intensity of negative emotion, making it easier for our emotion classifier to classify it as worry. However, tweets having an extremely low or zero emotional intensity such as *"I really wish my life was a little more exciting"* are most likely to not get captured by the emotion classifier. It is because of these subtle differences in the nature of the task of emotion detection and worry detection that we argue the need to study worry detection as a separate problem.

When using emotion classifier as a predictor of worry, the chances of missing out on capturing worry, especially normative worry, in tweets is quite high due to above-mentioned differences. This shows that the task of worry classification can be considerably improved when studied separately.

4.4 Error Analysis and Discussion

The results in Section 4.1 show that identifying worry is a non-trivial task. In this section, we perform a qualitative error analysis by looking at all false positives and false negatives in order to identify the common causes of incorrect classifications.

Expressed vs. Implied Worry. The most prominent case where a tweet is labeled with worry but is not correctly classified is when worry is not explicitly expressed but only implied. For example, consider the tweet *"My parents just had a car accident."* On a purely syntactic level, this tweet does not express a worry. However, knowing that car accidents are generally associated with adverse outcomes such as injury (or death) and financial burden – and also granting the writer empathy – it is very likely that the writer is indeed worried. That worry which is only implied but not (strongly) expressed is particularly common for everyday worries such as issues at home or work that are not severe enough to cause a strong (emotional) response that would more likely reflect in the tweet. This distinction between expressed and implied worry is an instance of a fundamental challenge for NLP: the difference between what a text states and the full message conveyed by the text in the context of shared and common knowledge (e.g., traffic accidents often result in serious injuries). While methods to incorporate external knowledge for text classification have been proposed (Wang et al., 2017; Chen et al., 2019), they work on concept hierarchies (e.g., accident *is-a* misfortune *is-a* event) and it is not apparent how they can sufficiently capture the notion of worry.

Emotions "Hiding" Worry. In contrast to psychological literature that states that any fear implies a worry (Levy and Guttman, 1985), our dataset contains many tweets labeled as "fear" but not as "worry" (similar for "sadness" and "anger"). When inspecting those tweets, we observed that in many cases, the emotion was very obvious like in *"I..I can't! I'm scared! Bees terrify me"* or *"I can never find the exact #emoji that I'm after at the exact moment that I need it #panic"*, both labeled with "fear" but not with "worry". Our explanation is that

Type	Tweets
Normative	I really wish my life was a little more exciting
	Awesome day again, shame the good weather will be gone by the weekend
	sick and in good spirits. its only a sore throat.
	Traffic on a beautiful day where the hell is everyone going
	Sooo happy to be home but it's bittersweet because my wife, son and dog aren't here
	Home alone again......YAY!!!! BUT STILL HAVE TO DO MORE CHORES.....UGH
	Rain is cool until it starts leaking into your house, ruining stuff.
	I'm also suddenly not feeling well. That's fun.
	Its been a slow day at home, one of my kids is sick. This little picture cheered me up URL
	It's beautiful outside! But I'm stuck inside doing homework
Pathological	im pissed!!as in very very pissed!!
	Goddammit..I'm in trouble
	have my phone interview for DCU today.... soooooooooooooooo nervous!!!!
	Oh my god my head hurts so damn bad! I wanna sleep!
	WOOOOAAAWWW I'M A HORRIBLE STUDENT!!!! AND THE SINGLE WORST PROCRASTINATOR IN THE WHOLE WIDE WORLD!!!!!!!
	Wow only got 3 hrs of sleep!! Bad Bad bad!!!! got a huge headache!!!
	Im kinda nervous for this orientation
	Feeling terrible. Why isn't the day over yet?
	Still not asleep. Ahhh Wtf?!
	MY MOM NEVER CAME HOME AND CALLED REALY EARLY BUT I WAS ASLEEP AND NOW SHE WONT ANSWER THE PHONE AND SHE IS NOT AT WORK I AM SCARED!

Table 5: Normative and Pathological worry tweets obtained using **Sentiment140** dataset.

a strong and explicit expression of emotion, particularly fear, may distract from the underlying cause such as worry. Furthermore, while these tweets have negative sentiment, they do no express or imply an uncertain outcome of a future event, making them less likely to be associated with worry by a reader. This subjectivity is a fundamental issue and may only be addressed adequately in the context of a specific application scenario.

Informal Writing and Stylistic Devices. Lastly, as for most NLP tasks over social media content such as tweets, our worry classifier suffers not only from the informal writing style but also from the often used stylistic devices. Despite careful preprocessing of the tweets, typos, non-standard abbreviations, Internet slang, expressive lengthenings, etc. – e.g., *"I start work tmrw yall, I'm neeervous lol"* – negatively affect the learning and prediction process. Stylistic devices such as sarcasm, irony or humor make it very difficult, even for humans, to assess whether a worry (or emotion or sentiment) is sincere. *"I absolutely love having an anxiety attack halfway through a family meal"* and *"I want my diamonds as bright as my future"* are two examples for this. Existing works towards, e.g., sarcasm detection (Bamman and Smith, 2015; Rajadesingan et al., 2015) or irony detection (Reyes

et al., 2013) might help in the long run to further improve the identification of worry in tweets.

5 Conclusion and Future Work

Worry about a personal issue such as health or finance, or a broader external issue such as environmental pollution, technology change or social structure is commonly expressed on Twitter now-a-days. Most of the existing works utilizing social media for measuring well-being associate worry with emotions. Taking cues from the psychology literature that clearly differentiates pathological (uncontrollable with high emotion intensity) and normative (everyday with low/zero emotion intensity) worry, we argue as to why emotion classifier is unable to capture normative worry, thereby, establishing the need to treat worry detection as a separate task.

We started out by exploring the effectiveness of a worry classifier by comparing different state-of-the-art text classification models with/vs. emotion. We then conducted an empirical user study to further strengthen our hypothesis where we discussed the differences between pathological and normative worry in detail. Our results support our argument – that emotion classification can, at best, only be sufficient to predict pathological worries as they yield strong emotional responses. This topic is, however, less explored despite the immense potential in applications such as identifying day-to-day worries like excessive traffic on a certain route or stressful work environment.

This paper lays down an initial ground for future work in this direction but is far from perfect. We highlight the current limitations of this task by performing a qualitative error analysis. One of the main challenges is that worry is often only implied and requires access to shared or common knowledge. Utilizing such knowledge will be an important next step to improve the identification of worry. Looking at the bigger picture, we envision to implement a real-time, automated worry classification system capable of capturing both pathological and normative worries at different levels – local, national and global – to aid policy and decision making processes of organizations all around the world.

Acknowledgments

The authors gratefully acknowledge the research grant (R-252-000-A47-133) provided by Lloyd's Register Foundation Institute for the Public Understanding of Risk. This research is also supported by the National Research Foundation, Singapore under its Strategic Capability Research Centres Funding Initiative. Any opinions, findings and conclusions or recommendations expressed in this material are those of the author(s) and do not reflect the views of the funding agencies.

References

Martín Abadi, Ashish Agarwal, Paul Barham, Eugene Brevdo, Zhifeng Chen, Craig Citro, Gregory S. Corrado, Andy Davis, Jeffrey Dean, Matthieu Devin, Sanjay Ghemawat, Ian J. Goodfellow, Andrew Harp, Geoffrey Irving, Michael Isard, Yangqing Jia, Rafal Józefowicz, Lukasz Kaiser, Manjunath Kudlur, Josh Levenberg, Dan Mané, Rajat Monga, Sherry Moore, Derek Gordon Murray, Chris Olah, Mike Schuster, Jonathon Shlens, Benoit Steiner, Ilya Sutskever, Kunal Talwar, Paul A. Tucker, Vincent Vanhoucke, Vijay Vasudevan, Fernanda B. Viégas, Oriol Vinyals, Pete Warden, Martin Wattenberg, Martin Wicke, Yuan Yu, and Xiaoqiang Zheng. 2016. Tensorflow: Large-scale machine learning on heterogeneous distributed systems. *CoRR*, abs/1603.04467.

Danny Azucar, Davide Marengo, and Michele Settanni. 2018. Predicting the Big 5 Personality Traits from Digital Footprints on Social Media: A Meta-Analysis. *Personality and Individual Differences*, 124:150–159.

David Bamman and Noah Smith. 2015. Contextualized Sarcasm Detection on Twitter. In *International AAAI Conference on Web and Social Media*.

Christos Baziotis, Nikos Pelekis, and Christos Doulkeridis. 2017. Datastories at semeval-2017 task 4: Deep lstm with attention for message-level and topic-based sentiment analysis. In *Proceedings of the 11th International Workshop on Semantic Evaluation (SemEval-2017)*, pages 747–754, Vancouver, Canada. Association for Computational Linguistics.

Klaus Boehnke, Shalom Schwartz, Claudia Stromberg, and Lilach Sagiv. 1998. The Structure and Dynamics of Worry: Theory, Measurement, and Cross-National Replications. *Journal of Personality*, 66(5):745–782.

T.D. Borkovec, Elwood Robinson, Thomas Pruzinsky, and James A. DePree. 1983. Preliminary Exploration of Worry: Some Characteristics and Processes. *Behaviour Research and Therapy*, 21(1):9–16.

Timothy A Brown. 1997. The Nature of Generalized Anxiety Disorder and Pathological Worry: Current Evidence and Conceptual Models. *The Canadian Journal of Psychiatry*, 42(8):817–825. PMID: 9356769.

Canales, Lea and Martínez-Barco, Patricio. 2014. Emotion detection from text: A survey. In *Proceedings of the Workshop on Natural Language Processing in the 5th Information Systems Research Working Days (JISIC)*, pages 37–43. Association for Computational Linguistics.

Jindong Chen, Yizhou Hu, Jingping Liu, Yanghua Xiao, and Haiyun Jiang. 2019. Deep Short Text Classification with Knowledge Powered Attention. In *The Thirty-Third AAAI Conference on Artificial Intelligence, AAAI 2019*, pages 6252–6259. AAAI Press.

Munmun De Choudhury, Michael Gamon, Scott Counts, and Eric Horvitz. 2013. Predicting Depression via Social Media. In *International AAAI Conference on Web and Social Media (ICWSM)*. The AAAI Press.

Glen Coppersmith, Mark Dredze, and Craig Harman. 2014. Quantifying Mental Health Signals in Twitter. In *Proceedings of the Workshop on Computational Linguistics and Clinical Psychology: From Linguistic Signal to Clinical Reality*, pages 51–60. Association for Computational Linguistics.

Munmun De Choudhury, Emre Kiciman, Mark Dredze, Glen Coppersmith, and Mrinal Kumar. 2016. Discovering Shifts to Suicidal Ideation from Mental Health Content in Social Media. In *Proceedings of the 2016 CHI Conference on Human Factors in Computing Systems*, CHI '16, page 2098–2110, New

York, NY, USA. Association for Computing Machinery.

Ben Eisner, Tim Rocktäschel, Isabelle Augenstein, Matko Bošnjak, and Sebastian Riedel. 2016. emoji2vec: Learning Emoji Representations from their Description. In *Proceedings of The Fourth International Workshop on Natural Language Processing for Social Media*, pages 48–54. Association for Computational Linguistics.

Michael W. Eysenck. 1995. Worrying: Perspectives on Theory, Assessment and Treatment. Edited by G. C. L. Davey and F. Tallis. (Pp. 311; £24.95.) Wiley: Chichester. 1994. *Psychological Medicine*, 25(2):431–432.

Golnoosh Farnadi, Geetha Sitaraman, Shanu Sushmita, Fabio Celli, Michal Kosinski, David Stillwell, Sergio Davalos, Marie-Francine Moens, and Martine Cock. 2016. Computational Personality Recognition in Social Media. *User Modeling and User-Adapted Interaction*, 26(2–3):109–142.

Alec Go, Richa Bhayani, and Lei Huang. 2009. Twitter sentiment classification using distant supervision. *Processing*, pages 1–6.

Abbie Griffin and John R. Hauser. 1993. The voice of the customer. *Marketing Science*, 12(1):1–27.

Sharath Chandra Guntuku, David B Yaden, Margaret L Kern, Lyle H Ungar, and Johannes C Eichstaedt. 2017. Detecting Depression and Mental Illness on Social Media: An Integrative Review. *Current Opinion in Behavioral Sciences*, 18:43–49. Big data in the behavioural sciences.

Jonathas G. D. Harb and Karin Becker. 2018. Emotion Analysis of Reaction to Terrorism on Twitter. In *Proceedings of the SBC Brazilian Symposium on Databases*, pages 97–108. Association for Computational Linguistics.

John Helliwell, Richard Layard, and Jeffrey Sachs. 2020. World Happiness Report 2020, New York: Sustainable Development Solutions Network.

David John Hughes, Moss Rowe, Mark Batey, and Andrew Lee. 2012. A tale of Two Sites: Twitter vs. Facebook and the Personality Predictors of Social Media Usage. *Computers in Human Behavior*, 28(2):561–569.

Clayton J. Hutto and Eric Gilbert. 2014. VADER: A parsimonious rule-based model for sentiment analysis of social media text. In *Proceedings of the Eighth International Conference on Weblogs and Social Media, ICWSM 2014, Ann Arbor, Michigan, USA, June 1-4, 2014*. The AAAI Press.

Yoon Kim. 2014. Convolutional Neural Networks for Sentence Classification. In *Proceedings of the 2014 Conference on Empirical Methods in Natural Language Processing (EMNLP)*, pages 1746–1751. Association for Computational Linguistics.

Diederik P. Kingma and Jimmy Ba. 2015. Adam: A method for stochastic optimization. In *3rd International Conference on Learning Representations, ICLR 2015, San Diego, CA, USA, May 7-9, 2015, Conference Track Proceedings*.

Michal Kosinski, David Stillwell, and Thore Graepel. 2013. Private Traits and Attributes are Predictable from Digital Records of Human Behavior. *Proceedings of the National Academy of Sciences*, 110(15):5802–5805.

Alex Lamb, Michael J. Paul, and Mark Dredze. 2013. Separating Fact from Fear: Tracking Flu Infections on Twitter. In *Proceedings of the 2013 Conference of the North American Chapter of the Association for Computational Linguistics: Human Language Technologies*, pages 789–795. Association for Computational Linguistics.

J. Richard Landis and Gary G. Koch. 1977. The measurement of observer agreement for categorical data. *Biometrics*, 33(1):159–174.

Shlomit Levy and Louis Guttman. 1985. Worry, Fear, and Concern Differentiated. *Issues in Mental Health Nursing*, 7(1-4):251–264.

Yinhan Liu, Myle Ott, Naman Goyal, Jingfei Du, Mandar Joshi, Danqi Chen, Omer Levy, Mike Lewis, Luke Zettlemoyer, and Veselin Stoyanov. 2019. Roberta: A robustly optimized BERT pretraining approach. *CoRR*, abs/1907.11692.

Saif Mohammad, Felipe Bravo-Marquez, Mohammad Salameh, and Svetlana Kiritchenko. 2018. SemEval-2018 Task 1: Affect in Tweets. In *Proceedings of The 12th International Workshop on Semantic Evaluation*, pages 1–17. Association for Computational Linguistics.

Fabian Pedregosa, Gaël Varoquaux, Alexandre Gramfort, Vincent Michel, Bertrand Thirion, Olivier Grisel, Mathieu Blondel, Peter Prettenhofer, Ron Weiss, Vincent Dubourg, Jake VanderPlas, Alexandre Passos, David Cournapeau, Matthieu Brucher, Matthieu Perrot, and Edouard Duchesnay. 2012. Scikit-learn: Machine learning in python. *CoRR*, abs/1201.0490.

Jeffrey Pennington, Richard Socher, and Christopher D. Manning. 2014. Glove: Global vectors for word representation. In *Proceedings of the 2014 Conference on Empirical Methods in Natural Language Processing (EMNLP)*, pages 1532–1543. Association for Computational Linguistics.

Ashwin Rajadesingan, Reza Zafarani, and Huan Liu. 2015. Sarcasm detection on twitter: A behavioral modeling approach. In *Proceedings of the Eighth ACM International Conference on Web Search and Data Mining*, WSDM '15, page 97–106, New York, NY, USA. Association for Computing Machinery.

Antonio Reyes, Paolo Rosso, and Tony Veale. 2013. A multidimensional approach for detecting irony in twitter. *Lang. Resour. Eval.*, 47(1):239–268.

H. Schwartz, Maarten Sap, Margaret Kern, Johannes Eichstaedt, Adam Kapelner, MEGHA AGRAWAL, EDUARDO BLANCO, LUKASZ DZIURZYNSKI, GREGORY PARK, David Stillwell, MICHAL KOSINSKI, Martin Seligman, and Lyle Ungar. 2016. Predicting individual well-being through the language of social media. pages 516–527.

H. Andrew Schwartz, Johannes C. Eichstaedt, Margaret L. Kern, Lukasz Dziurzynski, Stephanie M. Ramones, Megha Agrawal, Achal Shah, Michal Kosinski, David Stillwell, Martin E. P. Seligman, and Lyle H. Ungar. 2013. Personality, Gender, and Age in the Language of Social Media: The Open-Vocabulary Approach. *PLoS ONE*, 8(9).

Shalom H Schwartz and Gila Melech. 2000. National differences in micro and macro worry: Social, economic, and cultural explanations. *Culture and subjective well-being*, pages 219–256.

Shalom H. Schwartz, Lilach Sagiv, and Klaus Boehnke. 2000. Worries and Values. *Journal of Personality*, 68(2):309–346.

Marcin Skowron, Marko Tkalčič, Bruce Ferwerda, and Markus Schedl. 2016. Fusing Social Media Cues: Personality Prediction from Twitter and Instagram. In *Proceedings of the 25th International Conference Companion on World Wide Web*, WWW '16 Companion, page 107–108, Republic and Canton of Geneva, CHE. International World Wide Web Conferences Steering Committee.

Sorin-George Toma and Shinji Naruo. 2017. Total quality management and business excellence: The best practices at toyota motor corporation. *Amfiteatru Economic Journal*, 19(45):566–580.

Jin Wang, Zhongyuan Wang, Dawei Zhang, and Jun Yan. 2017. Combining Knowledge with Deep Convolutional Neural Networks for Short Text Classification. In *Proceedings of the 26th International Joint Conference on Artificial Intelligence*, IJCAI'17, page 2915–2921. AAAI Press.

Wenbo Wang, Lu Chen, Krishnaprasad Thirunarayan, and Amit P.Sheth. 2012. Harnessing Twitter "Big Data" for Automatic Emotion Identification. In *2012 International Conference on Privacy, Security, Risk and Trust and 2012 International Conference on Social Computing*, pages 587–592. Association for Computational Linguistics.

E. Watkins. 2008. Constructive and unconstructive repetitive thought. *Psychological Bulletin*, 134:163 – 206.

World Economic Forum WEF. 2020. The Global Risks Report 2020.

Zhilin Yang, Zihang Dai, Yiming Yang, Jaime G. Carbonell, Ruslan Salakhutdinov, and Quoc V. Le. 2019. Xlnet: Generalized autoregressive pretraining for language understanding. *CoRR*, abs/1906.08237.

Zichao Yang, Diyi Yang, Chris Dyer, Xiaodong He, Alex Smola, and Eduard Hovy. 2016. Hierarchical attention networks for document classification. In *Proceedings of the 2016 Conference of the North American Chapter of the Association for Computational Linguistics: Human Language Technologies*, pages 1480–1489. Association for Computational Linguistics.

A Appendices

A.1 Details of Hyper-parameters

Model	Hyper-parameter	Value
SVM	kernel	linear
	decision function shape	ovo (one-vs-one)
	regularization parameter (C)	2
CNN-static	hidden dimension	100
	number of filters	10
	max sequence length	300
	filter size	(3,8)
	dropout probability	(0.3, 0.5)
HAN	max words per sentence	15
	word encoding dimension	200
	sentence encoding dimension	200
	max sequence length	300
RoBERTa	dropout probability	0.2
	attention dropout probability	0.2
	hidden dimension	64
	max sequence length	300
XLNet	dropout probability	0.2
	attention dropout probability	0.2
	hidden dimension	64
	max sequence length	300

Table 6: Details of hyper-parameters

A.2 Used vs. Original Architecture

1. For CNN-static, 10 filters were used instead of original 100, 2 filter sizes instead of 3, 100 hidden dimensions instead of 50, max pooling instead of global pooling.

2. For RoBERTa and XLNet, pre-trained embeddings followed by two stacked Bidirectional GRU layers and a dense layer.

Text Zoning and Classification for Job Advertisements in German, French and English

Ann-Sophie Gnehm
Institute of Sociology
University of Zurich
gnehm@soziologie.uzh.ch

Simon Clematide
Department of Computational Linguistics
University of Zurich
simon.clematide@uzh.ch

Abstract

We present experiments to structure job ads into text zones and classify them into professions, industries and management functions, thereby facilitating social science analyses on labor marked demand. Our main contribution are empirical findings on the benefits of contextualized embeddings and the potential of multi-task models for this purpose. With contextualized in-domain embeddings in BiLSTM-CRF models, we reach an accuracy of 91% for token-level text zoning and outperform previous approaches. A multi-tasking BERT model performs well for our classification tasks. We further compare transfer approaches for our multilingual data.

1 Introduction

Text mining on job advertisements has become important to analyze labor market demand, since job ads provide unique job-level data on employers' staff needs (Atalay et al., 2020; Das et al., 2020; Calanca et al., 2019; Dawson et al., 2019). Our proposed techniques will be useful to study how job tasks and skill demand have developed in Switzerland in different labor market segments over the last decades. We present preparatory work for precise skill and task extraction: First, we structure job ads into text zones, that is, text parts dedicated to particular topics. Second, we classify job ads into professions, industries and management function. By replacing human annotation with scalable NLP, more fine-grained analyses on big data will be feasible.

Job ads contain information on topics such as the company, the job, or required qualifications. For an accurate extraction of skills and tasks, we need to identify the corresponding text zones, as many key terms are ambiguous, for instance 'dynamic' might refer to a personality trait or to a dynamic CRM system. Information on different topics can be densely packed in sentences, thus it seems most reasonable to formalize text zoning for job ads as token-level sequence labeling. In addition to this structuring of job ads, we need automatic classifications of job ads to enable detailed analysis, most importantly into professions, but also into industries and management functions.

For Swiss data in German, French, English and Italian we need multilingual approaches. Most (labeled) data however is in German. To avoid sparse data problems for minority languages, we thus experiment with transfer approaches.

The empirical experiments presented a) investigate the benefit of contextualized embeddings for text zoning, b) compare multilingual modeling with machine translation based approaches, and c) explore the potential of multi-task models for sequence labeling and text classification.

2 Related Work

Gnehm (2018) achieved an accuracy of 89.8% for the text zoning task at hand, namely token-level sequence labeling of job ads into eight zones with BiLSTMs, task-specific word embeddings and ensembling.[1] Hermes and Schandock (2017) segment on paragraph level, distinguish four classes, and reach accuracy of 97% with KNN in a multi-label classification. Grüger and Schneider (2019) extract HTML lists for IT job ads. Distinguishing between four list classes, they reach accuracy of 95% with LinearSVC. These two less fine-grained approaches are not directly comparable to ours.

Classification of professions is often provided by companies, and their methods and performance are not reported (Burke et al., 2020; Das et al., 2020; Calanca et al., 2019). Atalay et al. (2020) use embedding similarity measures to match jobs to 110 classes, and reach an accuracy of 53%.

---

[1] See Appendix A.3 for zone definitions and examples.

Proceedings of the Fourth Workshop on Natural Language Processing and Computational Social Science, pages 83–93
Online, November 20, 2020. ©2020 Association for Computational Linguistics
https://doi.org/10.18653/v1/P17

3 Experimental Data

We use two job ad data sets, differing in size and data collection method. Both have each advantages for experiments here and for future analyses.

The **Swiss Job Market Monitor (SJMM)**[2] corpus consists of 80,000 job ads in German, French, English and Italian, from yearly samples representative for the Swiss job market, back to 1950. High-quality human annotations of profession, industry, and management function are available for all job ads. Text zones are annotated on German job ads until 2014. The SJMM provides us hence with labeled data for supervised machine learning experiments, and will allow analyses of how job tasks and skills developed over the last decades.

The **Online Ads (OA)** corpus contains 9 million ads in German, French, English and Italian from job portals and company websites in Switzerland crawled since 2012 by a private company. This big data set seems valuable for building in-domain embeddings for our experiments, and makes fine-grained analyses feasible for future research.

Text zoning in the SJMM is operationalized as introduced in Gnehm (2018). Eight zones are distinguished based on their content, and the text is segmented on token level.[3] Token level seems most appropriate, as information on different zones can be densely packed in single sentences. Not every ad contains information on every zone (e.g. not every job ad specifies personality traits of the ideal candidate) and zone distribution is strongly skewed: The job description (z6) comprises with more than 30% the largest share of tokens, whereas the least frequent zone, reason of the vacancy (z2), comprises 0.5% of tokens. Tokens show high zone ambiguity, with more than 90% of tokens showing up in more than one zone.

In text zoning experiments, we use the data split of Gnehm (2018), for comparability: Aiming for a model optimized for future application, dev and test set (*test set A*) are restricted to each 10% (n=650) of the most recent available data (2010-2014), the remaining 80% and all data further back to 1970 (n=22,700) serve as training data. In pure text classification experiments, we can use all multilingual SJMM data from the time span of interest (1990-2018, n=34,600), and take 80% for train, and 10% for dev and test set each (*test set B*).[4]

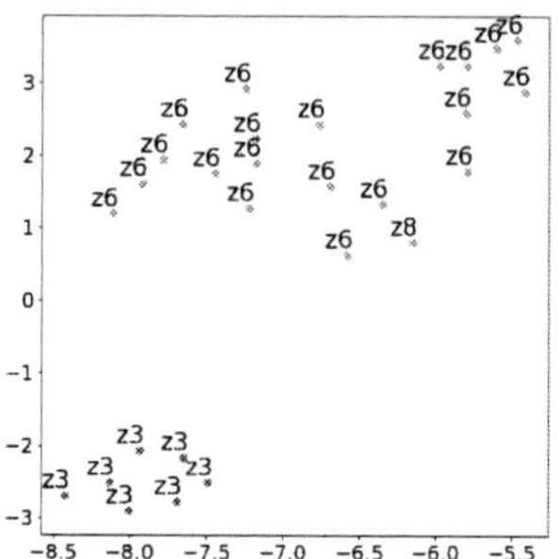

Figure 1: UMAP plot of FLAIRSJMM vectors for the term 'Ansprechpartner' *(contact person)* in test set A, appearing in zones job task (z6), wanted personality (z8) and residual (z3)

4 Experiments

4.1 Text Representation

We experiment with different text embeddings: **Static type-level** fastText (FT) embeddings provide a single vector for all occurrences of a word (Bojanowski et al., 2017). **Contextualized** embeddings allow to represent different word senses by capturing the semantics of surrounding text. We contrast BERT **sub-word** embeddings (Devlin et al., 2019) with **character-based** FLAIR embeddings (Akbik et al., 2018).

Given the large amount of in-domain texts, we train FLAIR embeddings on both of our corpora (FLAIRSJMM, FLAIROA).[5] We systematically compare the effect of these **in-domain** vs. **general domain** embeddings mentioned above.

Qualitative evidence for the usefulness of contextualized in-domain embeddings for text zoning is provided in Figure 1 with a UMAP (McInnes et al., 2018) vector visualization of the semantic space. The term 'Ansprechpartner' *(contact person)* in the zone for job description (z6) depicts that part of the job is to serve as contact person, probably for clients or co-workers, and the same term in the zone for the wanted personality (z8) hints furthermore that this person should be approachable or trustworthy. *Contact person* in the residual text (z3) however, simply refers to a contact information for the application procedure. The separation of the respective vectors in the semantic space in Figure 1 shows that such zone specific meanings can be recognized with our contextualized in-domain embeddings.

---

[2] Available under forsbase.unil.ch (Buchmann et al., 2019)
[3] Definitions and examples are shown in Appendix A.3.
[4] See Appendix A.1 for distribution over languages.
[5] Training hyper-parameters and preprocessing for all experiments can be found in the Appendix A.2.

Embeddings	Accuracy	Ens.
Gnehm (2018)$_d$	0.893 ± 0.001	0.898
FT$_g$	0.891	
FLAIR$_g$	0.902	
FLAIROA$_d$	0.907	
FLAIRSJMM$_d$	0.908 ± 0.001	0.909
FLAIRSJMM$_d$+FLAIROA$_d$	0.908	
FLAIRSJMM$_d$+FT$_g$	$\mathbf{0.909 \pm 0.001}$	**0.910**
BERT$_g$ first	0.880	
BERT$_g$ mean-pooling	0.881	
BERT$_g$ fine-tuned first	0.896	
BERT$_g$ fine-tuned mean-pooling	0.892	

Table 1: Accuracy of text zoning on test set A for different in-domain$_d$ and general$_g$ embeddings. The results with standard deviation report averages of 3 runs (of 5 runs for baseline by Gnehm (2018)) and column Ens. reports their majority vote ensemble (Rokach, 2010).

4.2 Text Zoning and Joint Classification

In this section, we first assess different text representations for our **text zoning** task, and evaluate the benefits of contextualized embeddings compared to previous work (Gnehm, 2018). We then explore the potential of **joint classification**, that is, including the classification of job ads into professions, industries and management functions in the sequence labeling text zoning task. Such a multi-tasking model would be most convenient in practical application. We assume furthermore that all these tasks are somewhat related and simultaneous learning could be beneficial.

For all these experiments we use the sequence labeling architecture proposed by Huang et al. (2015), a bidirectional LSTM with a CRF layer, implemented in the flair NLP library (Akbik et al., 2018). Model selection is based on dev set accuracy, and we evaluate on test set. For selected models we repeat the experiment three times and report mean performance and standard deviation (Reimers and Gurevych, 2017).

Text Zoning: For the first series of experiments, results in Table 1 show that models featuring contextualized FLAIR embeddings outperform all others in token-level sequence labeling of text zones. The best setting combines in-domain FLAIR embeddings with general domain FT word embeddings, reaching an ensemble accuracy of 0.91 and improving the baseline of Gnehm (2018) by more than 1 percentage point.[6]

This corresponds to earlier findings for PoS tagging and NER by Akbik et al. (2018). They hypothesize that type-level embeddings capture se-

mantics that is complementary to the character-level features of FLAIR.

Interestingly, FLAIROA embeddings built from the much larger online corpus are less useful than FLAIRSJMM, which is probably due to the fact that the SJMM text zoning data consist for the most part of job ads in print media.

The lower performance of the pretrained German BERT might be explained by sub-tokenization issues. The many compound nouns and abbreviations of our special domain seem to cause problems for building meaningful entities to calculate embeddings over.[7] Using the mean of all sub-token embeddings for a token does not resolve this, but an improvement can be observed if we fine-tune the embeddings to the task.[8]

We tried ensemble combinations of models with different input embeddings (not shown), and of models with three runs (see Table 1) The best ensembles reach accuracy of 0.91, indicating limited variance between models. The lack of performance increase is convenient, as running a single classifier is easier than applying ensembles.

Joint classification: In this second series of experiments, we investigate if it is beneficial to combine the sequence labeling text zoning task with the classification of industry (11 classes), profession (34 classes) and management function (2 classes) in a single model. To answer this question, we add three special class tokens and their labels at the end of each job ad text. We focus on the best FLAIRSJMM+FT embeddings for text zoning, and assess adding model capacity (layers, hidden states). To direct the model towards learning predictions for the three special tokens, we experimentally increase their class weights $w \in \{10, 50, 100\}$ in the loss function. For technical reasons, this is only applicable on models without CRF layer, hence we also assess the effect of CRF.

Different joint models in Table 2 show relatively stable results for text zoning, industry and management function classification, whereas for the more fine-grained profession classification, accuracy depends on the model specifics. Dropping CRF affects accuracy for industry, profession and management function strongly. This shows the interdependence of the three variables represented as neighboring tokens.

---

[6]See Appendix A.4 for per-class results.

[7]Subtokenizaton produces fragmented results for compound nouns ('Anforderung', '##spro', '##fil', *required profile*) and diploma abbreviations ('N', '##DS').

[8]A scalar layer mix (Liu et al., 2019a) does not help.

Model	Zoning	Ind.	Prof.	Mgmt.
FLAIRSJMM+FT, 1 hidden layer, hidden size 256	**0.910**	0.813	0.653	**0.952**
-CRF	0.909	0.634	0.530	0.864
+ size (512), special weights (*50) (-CRF)	0.902	0.831	0.696	0.914
+ size (512), special weights (*100) (-CRF)	0.898	**0.834**	0.695	0.918
+ layer (2), size (512), special weights (*50) (-CRF)	0.904	0.832	**0.717**	0.922
+ layer (2), size (512), special weights (*100) (-CRF)	0.901	**0.834**	0.706	0.923

Table 2: Accuracy of joint prediction sequence taggers for zoning (8 classes), profession (34 classes), industry (11 classes) and management function (2 classes) on test set A. Only a subset of all tested combinations is shown.

Large class weights $w \in \{50, 100\}$ compensate for this performance drop and tune the model to the fine-grained classification tasks. More capacity in the form of larger hidden sizes and additional layers is useful, although the second layer helps only in combination with other factors.[9] By adding model capacity and weighted loss of 50 for the classification tasks, we find the model that performs best regarding profession classification, with relatively good results for all other tasks.

Embeddings	Prof.	Ind.	Mgmt.
FLAIRSJMM+FT sT	0.765		
FLAIRSJMM+FT mT	0.756	0.806	**.931**
BERT sT	**0.778**	**0.819**	0.920
	± 0.005	± 0.007	± 0.001
BERT mT	0.773	0.818	0.928
	± 0.004	± 0.003	± 0.003

Table 3: Accuracy for profession (34 classes), industry (11 classes) and management function (2 classes) in single (sT) and multi-task (mT) classification on test set B

4.3 Text Classification

Results in Section 4.2 suggest that simultaneous learning of profession, industry and management function classification might be beneficial, but not enough model capacity is devoted to these tasks when including them into sequence labeling. Therefore, we experiment in the following with multi-tasking text classification for these three tasks. In **monolingual experiments**, we assess different multi-tasking models for classification of profession, industry and management function, and benchmark them with respective single task models. At last, we conduct **multilingual experiments** for profession classification. The SJMM data set is multilingual, but most labeled data (75%) is available for German. Hence we test different transfer approaches to avoid sparse data problems.

With the text classification implementation by Flair (Akbik et al., 2018), we obtain document level representations for job ads by feeding FLAIR or FT embeddings into an RNN. For BERT embeddings, we take the topmost layer of the transformer model and fine-tune embeddings during training. Document embeddings are extracted from the '[CLS]' token. In both cases, actual class labels are calculated by a linear layer on top.

Monolingual Experiments: We compare single vs. multi-tasking classification models using the best embeddings from previous experiments.[10] In multi-tasking, we simultaneously predict profession (34 classes), industry (11 classes) and management function (2 classes). We feed each job ad once for each task into the data, adding each time a special token that specifies the task to learn.

With text classifiers and BERT embeddings, we reach an accuracy of 0.778 for professions (see Table 3. Although test sets A and B are not directly comparable, this surpasses sequence labeling results. For the other, somewhat less important variables, accuracy here is slightly lower.[11] BERT outperforms in multi- and single task classification our domain-specific contextualized embeddings, probably because BERT embeddings get fine-tuned to the task during training. Multi-tasking does not seriously alter profession classification, and the multi-tasking BERT reaches similar accuracy for industry and management function as single-task classifiers. It is thus reasonable to a go for the BERT multi-tasking classifier.

A detailed error analysis for professions further strengthens trust in the model. First, prediction probabilities and errors are strongly correlated: While for p $\geq$ 0.9 error rate is only 12%, with p $\leq$ 0.5 error rate is 75%. Thus, probabilities

---

[9]See ablation study in Table 11 in Appendix.

[10]FLAIRSJMM+FT and BERT performed best in classification of 11 professions. And, classification worked better on the whole job ad text than just on the job description (z6).

[11]A multi-tasking BERT model trained on data split A reaches an accuracy of 0.835, 0.731, and 0.921 for profession, industries and management function.

are useful for error detection. Second, a human post-evaluation of a random sample of 20 errors with p $\geq$ 0.9 showed that only 10% of these errors are considered hard errors. In 90% of the cases, several class labels can be seen as correct options, and the model prediction is appropriate. This underlines that our model copes well with a sometimes ambiguous classification task.

Multilingual Experiments: On a classification task for 11 professions, we compare two approaches.[12] First, we use machine translation (MT) (DeepL) to translate French and English job ads to German, and apply a classifier trained for German. We test in this approach further, if familiarizing the classification model during training with partially awkward wording ('Translationese') helps, by including automatic translations in our train (and dev) set.[13] Second, we train multilingual classifiers on our German, French and English data with general-domain, multilingual FLAIR and BERT embeddings.

In the MT approach, accuracy decreases strongly, for French around 10, for English even up to 20 percentage points (see Table 4). One reason for the stronger effect in English is that class distribution differs from German.[14] Adding translated ads indeed helps, and raises accuracy by 9 points for English (BERT) and French (FLAIRSJMM+FT). Why French results vary more with FLAIRSJMM+FT and English results more with BERT needs further investigation.

Best performing are multilingual BERT for French (0.744), and BERT with Translationese for English (0.693). Multilingual models are a convenient solution, because no MT is needed for their application. For the MT approach, including translated ads in training seems necessary, especially if class distributions differ between languages. Either way, due to being fine-tuned to the task, BERT outperforms our domain-specific FLAIR embeddings.[15]

5 Conclusion

Contextualized embeddings facilitate precise information extraction. Our best single text zoning

---

[12]For the sake of sound evaluation, we choose here a broader classification scheme, and restrict experiments to French and English (the amount of ads in Italian is too small).

[13]Adding 4,100 (500) ads from French, 2,900 (350) from English to the original 20,700 (2,600) from German.

[14]See Table 13 in Appendix.

[15]The multilingual BERT without fine-tuning reaches accuracies below 0.3 for the 3 languages.

	Test set originally in:		
Approach	**DE**	**FR**	**EN**
MT & Model for DE:			
FLAIRSMM+FT	0.798	0.672	0.625
incl. Translationese		0.718	0.639
BERT	**0.811**	0.715	0.603
incl. Translationese		0.724	**0.693**
Multilingual Model:			
BERT	0.803	**0.744**	0.679
FLAIR	0.654	0.542	0.499

Table 4: Accuracy for profession (11 classes) for MT vs. multilingual approach on test set B

models with stacked in-domain FLAIR and general domain word embeddings outperform the baseline of Gnehm (2018) and reduce the relative error rate by 12%. The combination of sequence labeling for text zoning and text classification for professions, industries and management function in a single multi-task model did not lead to entirely satisfying results. But, we found a multi-tasking BERT text classifier that performs well and provides a convenient solution for structuring our corpus into professions, industries, and management function. Error analysis for profession classification raised trust in this model. The model's classification probabilities provide valuable information for post-validation and subsequent analyses.

Multilingual experiments showed that our classifiers are affected by MT. Utilizing translated material in training, or alternatively multilingual models, are potential strategies, but the question of the best transfer approaches for our multilingual data needs further investigation.

The most promising approach for future work seems to be the training of our own domain-specific BERT embeddings, both for optimizing classification and for intended subsequent skill and task extraction. This way, we can also exploit the large amount of data in the OA corpus. Another direction worthy to explore is multi-tasking, be it by including more variables, or by experimenting with more sophisticated approaches (Clark et al., 2019; Liu et al., 2019b).

Acknowledgments

We thank Dong Nguyen and the anonymous reviewers for their careful reading of this article and their helpful comments and suggestions, and Helen Buchs for her efforts in post-evaluation. This work is supported by the Swiss National Science Foundation under grant number 407740_187333.

References

Alan Akbik, Duncan Blythe, and Roland Vollgraf. 2018. Contextual String Embeddings for Sequence Labeling. In *Proceedings of the 27th International Conference on Computational Linguistics*, pages 1638–1649, Santa Fe, New Mexico, USA.

Enghin Atalay, Phai Phongthiengtham, Sebastian Sotelo, and Daniel Tannenbaum. 2020. The Evolution of Work in the United States. *American Economic Journal: Applied Economics*, 12(2):1–34.

Piotr Bojanowski, Edouard Grave, Armand Joulin, and Tomas Mikolov. 2017. Enriching Word Vectors with Subword Information. *Transactions of the Association for Computational Linguistics*, 5:135–146.

Marlis Buchmann, Helen Buchs, Felix Busch, Ann-Sophie Gnehm, Urs Klarer, Jan Müller, Marianne Müller, Stefan Sacchi, Alexander Salvisbert, and Anna von Ow. 2019. *Stellenmarkt-Monitor Schweiz 1950 – 2018.* Soziologisches Institut der Universität Zürich.

Mary Burke, Alicia Sasser Modestino, Shahriar Sadighi, Rachel Sederberg, and Bledi Taska. 2020. No Longer Qualified? Changes in the Supply and Demand for Skills within Occupations. Federal Reserve Bank of Boston Research Department Working Papers, Federal Reserve Bank of Boston. Series: Federal Reserve Bank of Boston Research Department Working Papers.

Federica Calanca, Luiza Sayfullina, Lara Minkus, Claudia Wagner, and Eric Malmi. 2019. Responsible team players wanted: an analysis of soft skill requirements in job advertisements. *EPJ Data Science*, 8(1):1–20. Number: 1 Publisher: SpringerOpen.

Kevin Clark, Minh-Thang Luong, Urvashi Khandelwal, Christopher D. Manning, and Quoc V. Le. 2019. BAM! Born-Again Multi-Task Networks for Natural Language Understanding. In *Proceedings of the 57th Annual Meeting of the Association for Computational Linguistics*, pages 5931–5937, Florence, Italy.

Subhro Das, Sebastian Steffen, Prabhat Reddy, Erik Brynjolfsson, and Martin Fleming. 2020. Forecasting Task-Shares and Characterizing Occupational Change across Industry Sectors. In *Harvard CRCS Workshop on AI for Social Good*.

N. Dawson, Marian-Andrei Rizoiu, Benjamin Johnston, and Mary-Anne Williams. 2019. Adaptively selecting occupations to detect skill shortages from online job ads. *2019 IEEE International Conference on Big Data (Big Data)*.

Jacob Devlin, Ming-Wei Chang, Kenton Lee, and Kristina Toutanova. 2019. BERT: Pre-training of Deep Bidirectional Transformers for Language Understanding. In *Proceedings of the 2019 Conference of the North American Chapter of the Association for Computational Linguistics: Human Language Technologies, Volume 1 (Long and Short Papers)*, pages 4171–4186, Minneapolis, Minnesota. Association for Computational Linguistics.

Ann-Sophie Gnehm. 2018. Text Zoning for Job Advertisements with Bidirectional LSTMs. *Proceedings of the 3rd Swiss Text Analytics Conference - SwissText 2018, CEUR Workshop Proceedings*, 2226:66–74.

Joscha Grüger and Georg Schneider. 2019. Automated Analysis of Job Requirements for Computer Scientists in Online Job Advertisements:. In *Proceedings of the 15th International Conference on Web Information Systems and Technologies*, pages 226–233, Vienna, Austria. SCITEPRESS - Science and Technology Publications.

Juergen Hermes and Manuel Schandock. 2017. *Stellenanzeigenanalyse in der Qualifikationsentwicklungsforschung: Die Nutzung maschineller Lernverfahren zur Klassifikation von Textabschnitten.* Bundesinstitut fuer Berufsbildung, Bonn.

Zhiheng Huang, Wei Xu, and Kai Yu. 2015. Bidirectional LSTM-CRF models for sequence tagging. *arXiv preprint arXiv:1508.01991*.

Nelson F. Liu, Matt Gardner, Yonatan Belinkov, Matthew E. Peters, and Noah A. Smith. 2019a. Linguistic Knowledge and Transferability of Contextual Representations. In *Proceedings of the 2019 Conference of the North*, pages 1073–1094, Minneapolis, Minnesota. Association for Computational Linguistics.

Xiaodong Liu, Pengcheng He, Weizhu Chen, and Jianfeng Gao. 2019b. Multi-Task Deep Neural Networks for Natural Language Understanding. In *Proceedings of the 57th Annual Meeting of the Association for Computational Linguistics*, pages 4487–4496, Florence, Italy. Association for Computational Linguistics.

Leland McInnes, John Healy, and James Melville. 2018. UMAP: Uniform Manifold Approximation and Projection for Dimension Reduction. *arXiv:1802.03426 [cs, stat]*. ArXiv: 1802.03426.

Nils Reimers and Iryna Gurevych. 2017. Reporting Score Distributions Makes a Difference: Performance Study of LSTM-networks for Sequence Tagging. In *Proceedings of the 2017 Conference on Empirical Methods in Natural Language Processing*, pages 338–348, Copenhagen, Denmark. Association for Computational Linguistics.

Lior Rokach. 2010. Ensemble-based classifiers. *Artificial Intelligence Review*, 33(1):1–39.

A Appendices

A.1 Data splits

	German
train set (1970-2014)	22,698
dev set (2010-2014)	672
test set A (2010-2014)	626

Table 5: Number of German SJMM job ads in data split A. Dev and test set restricted to years 2010-14

	German	French	English
train set	20,717	4,126	2,846
dev set	2,581	518	355
test set B	2,598	515	355

Table 6: Number of job ads in data split B for German, French and English, SJMM job ads from 1990-2018

A.2 Preprocessing & Training Parameters

Training parameters are set according to recommendations in the Flair library (Akbik et al., 2018) unless reported differently here.

Text representations: For FLAIRSJMM and FLAIROA we train forward and backward language models with LSTMs with one layer and 2048 hidden states on the SJMM (67MB) and the OA (4GB) corpus.

Preprocessing is kept simple: We map digits to 0, white space to single blanks, and replace web and e-mail addresses with special tokens (replaced-dns, replaced-email, replaced-url). We build our own domain-specific character dictionary, setting the rarest 0.0001% of characters to unknown.

We optimize with SGD, clip gradients at 0.25 and set dropout probability to 0.25. Sequence length is set to 250 and batch size to 100. We train our language models with a learning rate of 20 for 2 weeks, reaching perplexity of 1.73 (forward model), and 1.74 (backward model) for FLAIRSJMM and 1.45 and 1.46 on validation sets for forward and backward models of FLAIROA.

General-domain FLAIR embeddings are provided by Akbik et al. (2018), for German we use embeddings that are pretrained on a mixed corpus (Web, Wikipedia, Subtitles) and in the multilingual setting embedddings that are pretrained on JW300 corpus. For German BERT embeddings, we use the model trained by Deepset.ai with 12 layers, 768 hidden states, 12 heads and 110M parameters, for multilingual BERT embeddings

a model with the same configurations, trained on cased text in 104 languages.

FT are German FastText embeddings without character feature provided in the Flair library.

Sequence labeling: We optimize with SGD, clipping gradients at 5. Minibatch size is 32 and training starts with learning rate of 0.1 and is annealed with factor 0.5 after 5 periods with no loss decrease. We stop training after 150 epochs, or as soon as the learning rate ≤ 0.0001. We use variational dropout ($p = 0.5$) and word dropout ($p = 0.05$) for regularization.

Text classification: For all models with FLAIR embeddings (FLAIRSJMM, FLAIRSJMM+FT, multilingual FLAIR), training parameters are as described above for sequence labeling. Classifier with German or multilingual BERT embeddings are optimized with Adam over 5 epochs, with a learning rate of 3.00E-05, in minibatches of 16.

A.3 Text Zoning: Definitions and Examples

For/z1 our/z1 attractive/z1 product/z1 portfolio/z1 we/z3 are/z3 looking/z3 for/z3 an/z6 interior/z6 designer/z6 ./z6 You/z3 offer/z3 :/z3 -/z7 solid/z7 vocational/z7 training/z7 and/z7 experience/z7 ,/z7 -/z8 creativity/z8 and/z8 versatility/z8 ,/z8 -/z8 ideally/z8 you/z8 are/z8 between/z8 25/z8 and/z8 40/z8 years/z8 old/z8 ./z8 We/z3 offer/z3 :/z3 -/z6 a/z6 high/z6 degree/z6 of/z6 autonomy/z6 ,z6 -/z6 a/z6 large/z6 studio/z6 ,/z6 -/z6 an/z6 interesting/z6 and/z6 stimulating/z6 permanent/z6 position/z6 ./z6 Please/z3 send/z3 your/z3 application/z3 to/z3 POC/z3 ,/z3 ADDR/z3 ,/z3 Foto/z1 Hobby/z1 Inc./z1

Table 7: Example of job ad with text zoning annotation (Gnehm, 2018), translated from German to English

zone	definition	example
z1	company description	'ein erfolgreiches Unternehmen der Baubranche' *'a successful company in the construction industry'*
z2	reason of vacancy	'für unsere neu eröffnete Filiale' *'for our newly opened branch'*
z3	administration & residual text	'Ihre Bewerbung senden Sie an' *'Please send your application to'*
z4	job agency description	'Ihr Partner für die Vermittlung von Dauerstellen' *'your competent partner for permanent position placements'*
z5	material incentives	'ansprechendes Salär' *'attractive salary'*
z6	job description	'für den Kundenempfang' *'for the customer reception'*
z7	required hard skills	'eine Ausbildung und Berufserfahrung als Sozialarbeiter' *'a degree and experience in social work'*
z8	required personality (soft skills)	'Sie sind diskret und belastbar' *'you are diplomatic and able to work under pressure'*

Table 8: Definitions and example of text zones (Gnehm, 2018), translations from German to English added to shortened examples

A.4 Detailed Results

zone	Frequency abs.	rel.	precision	recall	F1
z1	22672	17.2%	0.898	0.921	0.909
z2	639	0.5%	0.863	0.757	0.807
z3	33186	25.2%	0.941	0.908	0.924
z4	964	0.7%	0.806	0.667	0.730
z5	2199	1.7%	0.870	0.752	0.807
z6	42610	32.4%	0.907	0.925	0.916
z7	16767	12.7%	0.917	0.925	0.921
z8	12515	9.5%	0.865	0.872	0.868

Table 9: Per zone frequencies, precision, recall and F1-values for best text zoning model FLAIRSJMM+FT on test set A, reaching accuracy of 0.91

prediction / truth	z1	z2	z3	z4	z5	z6	z7	z8
z1	92.1%	0.1%	1.8%	0.2%	0.3%	5.2%	0.1%	0.3%
	20878	29	406	56	59	1170	16	58
z2	6.4%	75.7%	7.4%	0.0%	0.0%	10.5%	0.0%	0.0%
	41	484	47	0	0	67	0	0
z3	2.0%	0.0%	90.8%	0.3%	0.1%	3.5%	1.9%	1.3%
	654	6	30147	97	38	1161	638	445
z4	23.2%	0.0%	8.4%	66.7%	0.0%	1.6%	0.0%	0.1%
	224	0	81	643	0	15	0	1
z5	3.7%	0.0%	3.4%	0.0%	75.2%	17.2%	0.1%	0.5%
	81	0	75	0	1653	378	2	10
z6	3.1%	0.1%	1.3%	0.0%	0.3%	92.5%	0.9%	1.8%
	1319	38	559	2	113	39433	388	758
z7	0.1%	0.0%	2.4%	0.0%	0.1%	2.3%	92.5%	2.6%
	15	0	399	0	15	392	15509	437
z8	0.3%	0.0%	2.6%	0.0%	0.2%	6.8%	2.9%	87.2%
	39	4	331	0	22	853	359	10907

Table 10: Confusion matrix for best zoning sequence model FLAIRSJMM+FT on test set A, reaching accuracy of 0.91, cells show row percentages and frequencies

Model	Zoning	Ind.	Prof.	Mgmt.
FLAIRSJMM, 1 hidden layer, hidden size 256	0.909	0.786	0.601	0.915
- CRF	0.909	0.634	0.530	0.864
+ size (512)	0.909	0.800	0.653	0.915
+ layer (2)	0.907	0.736	0.602	**0.926**
+ special weights (*10) (-CRF)	0.907	0.802	0.673	**0.926**
+ special weights (*50) (-CRF)	0.900	**0.808**	**0.695**	0.925
+ FT	**0.910**	0.813	0.653	0.925

Table 11: Accuracy of joint prediction sequence taggers for zoning (8 classes), profession (34 classes), industry (11 classes) and Mgmt. position (2 classes) on test set A

	Frequency		FLAIRSJMM+FT		BERT	
			mT	sT	mT	sT
Industry	abs.	rel.	F1	F1	F1	F1
unidentifiable	89	5.9%	0.515		0.545	0.558
Agriculture, private households	54	3.6%	0.855		0.851	0.816
Chemical, Food, Textile Industry	212	14.2%	0.713		0.739	0.733
MEM industries	260	17.4%	0.753		0.762	0.761
Construction	170	11.4%	0.763		0.785	0.777
Trade, Trasnsportation	503	33.6%	0.791		0.816	0.818
Hospitality, entertainment, pers. services	211	14.1%	0.786		0.830	0.834
Finance, Insurance	178	11.9%	0.898		0.896	0.916
Company services	228	15.2%	0.716		0.703	0.722
Public administration	240	16.0%	0.882		0.880	0.880
Education, Science, Health	453	30.3%	0.942		0.939	0.941
Profession						
Agricultural, forestry, fishery workers	27	0.9%	0.926	0.926	0.933	0.930
Food & luxury goods production workers	14	0.5%	0.923	0.929	0.922	0.858
Metal &machinery workers	85	2.8%	0.759	0.776	0.736	0.764
Electronics, watch making, automotive workers	73	2.4%	0.761	0.757	0.789	0.785
Wood, paper production workers	29	0.9%	0.772	0.759	0.803	0.782
Chemical, plastic production workers	13	0.4%	0.560	0.462	0.522	0.612
Textile production, printing, storage workers	39	1.3%	0.713	0.769	0.640	0.656
Engineers	111	3.6%	0.745	0.690	0.733	0.716
Technicians	72	2.3%	0.504	0.472	0.579	0.572
Technical drafting workers	18	0.6%	0.773	0.944	0.753	0.755
Technical workers	46	1.5%	0.315	0.333	0.286	0.338
Machine operators	9	0.3%	0.737	0.778	0.700	0.804
IT professionals	96	3.1%	0.804	0.812	0.830	0.818
Construction workers	130	4.2%	0.827	0.863	0.833	0.846
Commerce, Sales professions	373	12.2%	0.814	0.851	0.827	0.829
Marketing and tourism professionals	47	1.5%	0.450	0.383	0.564	0.530
Fiduciaries	43	1.4%	0.521	0.558	0.615	0.569
Transportation professions	54	1.8%	0.804	0.778	0.777	0.815
Post, Telecommunication workers	21	0.7%	0.581	0.476	0.628	0.677
Hospitality, housekeeping workers	145	4.7%	0.884	0.897	0.912	0.918
Cleaning, hygiene and personal care workers	90	2.9%	0.789	0.835	0.835	0.855
Entrepreneurs, directors, senior officials	190	6.2%	0.606	0.579	0.620	0.627
Merchants, administrative professions	316	10.3%	0.773	0.792	0.792	0.785
Banking, Insurance professions	88	2.9%	0.700	0.782	0.768	0.762
Security workers	17	0.6%	0.774	0.824	0.911	0.911
Legal professions	25	0.8%	0.816	0.833	0.852	0.801
Media professionals	21	0.7%	0.700	0.667	0.713	0.756
Artists	4	0.1%	0.667	0.750	0.736	0.814
Welfare, care, counseling professions	60	2.0%	0.810	0.850	0.795	0.802
Educational professions	100	3.3%	0.822	0.810	0.863	0.848
Humanities, social and natural science	20	0.7%	0.514	0.400	0.518	0.508
Medical, pharmaceutical professions	57	1.9%	0.891	0.945	0.906	0.931
Therapy and nursing professions	145	4.7%	0.907	0.924	0.902	0.923
unclassifiable workers	20	0.7%	0.176	0.250	0.242	0.319
management function						
no	2121	81.6%	0.958		0.956	0.952
yes	477	18.4%	0.799		0.809	0.759

Table 12: Class frequencies and F1-values for multi-(mT) and single task (sT) classifiers on test set B, for SJMM+FT and BERT. For BERT we report mean values over 3 training runs.

Professional Class	DE			FR			EN		
	abs. Freq.	rel. Freq.	F1	abs. Freq.	rel. Freq.	F1	abs. Freq.	rel. Freq.	F1
Industry & Transport	360	13.6%	0.809	75	14.6%	0.784	8	2.3%	0.182
Construction	205	7.7%	0.848	13	2.5%	0.696	0	0.0%	
Technology & Science	245	9.3%	0.748	43	8.3%	0.674	51	14.4%	0.730
IT	143	5.4%	0.872	25	4.9%	0.750	63	17.7%	0.806
Trade & Sales	195	7.4%	0.836	73	14.2%	0.787	19	5.4%	0.595
Office & Administration	120	4.5%	0.747	43	8.3%	0.605	29	8.2%	0.613
Financial & Fiduciary Services	409	15.5%	0.817	52	10.1%	0.796	64	18.0%	0.773
Management & Organisation	248	9.4%	0.591	42	8.2%	0.444	86	24.2%	0.625
Hospitality & Personal Services	209	7.9%	0.875	44	8.5%	0.830	4	1.1%	0.750
Health	243	9.2%	0.934	45	8.7%	0.932	6	1.7%	0.727
Teaching & Public Services	269	10.2%	0.868	60	11.7%	0.748	25	7.0%	0.604

Table 13: Class frequencies and F1-values for profession classification (11 classes) of best performing approach for German (German BERT), French (multilingual BERT), and English (Machine Translation & German BERT with Translationese), on test set B

Is Wikipedia succeeding in reducing gender bias?
Assessing changes in gender bias in Wikipedia using word embeddings

K.G. Schmahl[1], T.J. Viering[1], S. Makrodimitris[1], A. Naseri Jahfari[1], D. M. J. Tax[1] and M. Loog[12]
[1]Delft University of Technology, [2]University of Copenhagen
katjaschmahl@hotmail.com, {t.j.viering, s.makrodimitris, a.naserijahfari, d.m.j.tax, m.loog}@tudelft.nl

Abstract

Large text corpora used for creating word embeddings (vectors which represent word meanings) often contain stereotypical gender biases. As a result, such unwanted biases will typically also be present in word embeddings derived from such corpora and downstream applications in the field of natural language processing (NLP). To minimize the effect of gender bias in these settings, more insight is needed when it comes to where and how biases manifest themselves in the text corpora employed. This paper contributes by showing how gender bias in word embeddings from Wikipedia has developed over time. Quantifying the gender bias over time shows that art related words have become more female biased. Family and science words have stereotypical biases towards respectively female and male words. These biases seem to have decreased since 2006, but these changes are not more extreme than those seen in random sets of words. Career related words are more strongly associated with male than with female, this difference has only become smaller in recently written articles. These developments provide additional understanding of what can be done to make Wikipedia more gender neutral and how important time of writing can be when considering biases in word embeddings trained from Wikipedia or from other text corpora.

1 Introduction

Word embeddings are vectors that represent the meaning of words and their relation. They are the cornerstone of many NLP techniques. For example, word embeddings can be used to search in documents, to analyze sentiment and to classify documents [Mikolov et al., 2013a, Nalisnick et al., 2016, Parikh et al., 2018, Jang et al., 2019]. These embeddings are typically created using unsupervised learning from a large corpus of text [Krishna and Sharada, 2019].

Large corpora of text used for training word embeddings may contain stereotypical biases. Word embeddings can then inherit these biases [Mikolov et al., 2013a, Caliskan et al., 2017, Jones et al., 2020]. For example, stereotypical words such as 'marriage' can be more strongly associated with female words than male words. In fact, changes in word embedding can be useful for detecting minor changes in the meaning of words at small time scales [Kutuzov et al., 2018].

Biases in word embeddings may, in turn, have unwanted consequences in applications. Bolukbasi et al. [2016] show that when embeddings are used to improve search results, biased embeddings can lead to biased results. As an example, scientific research with male names may be ranked higher if male names have a stronger association with the scientific search words [Bolukbasi et al., 2016].

Another example of a downstream application with unwanted gender bias consequences is machine translation. When translating a sentence from a language with a gender neutral pronoun to English, a sentence about a nurse may be translated with a female pronoun while a sentence with the word engineer may be translated with a male pronoun [Prates et al., 2019]. Such stereotypical translations can be avoided by using a more gender neutral embedding [Font and Costa-Jussa, 2019].

Bolukbasi et al. [2016] have already proposed a method for debiasing word embeddings. However, it has been hypothesized that debiasing covers up biases instead of removing them [Gonen and Goldberg, 2019]. Stereotypical words remain clustered in the debiased embeddings and thus there is still a risk for algorithmic discrimination [Gonen and Goldberg, 2019]. A more robust debiasing procedure is yet to be proposed.

Gender bias, as measured in word embeddings trained on books, has been shown to decrease over time up to the year 2000 [Jones et al., 2020, Garg et al., 2018]. Whether the decreasing trend has con-

Proceedings of the Fourth Workshop on Natural Language Processing and Computational Social Science, pages 94–103
Online, November 20, 2020. ©2020 Association for Computational Linguistics
https://doi.org/10.18653/v1/P17

tinued in more recent years has not been tested. If bias has continued to decrease, a straightforward way to obtain less biased word embeddings would be to train word embeddings on more recent corpora of text. To investigate this issue, we will measure gender bias in one of the largest openly available text corpora: Wikipedia.

Wagner et al. [2015] already showed the presence of gender bias in Wikipedia. The editors of Wikipedia have actively tried to reduce this bias since 2013 [Wikipedia contributors, 2020a]. Our research can be used to evaluate the effectiveness of these efforts, and may inspire new strategies to reduce bias further. Towards that end, we will answer the question: 'How does gender bias in word embeddings from Wikipedia develop over the years 2006-2020?'.

Contributions: 1. We extend the work of Jones et al. [2020] and Garg et al. [2018] by looking at more recent years and applying their methods to the corpus of Wikipedia.

2. Our work provides insight in how gender bias has developed in Wikipedia using four categories. So far, most research into this is static. Our research shows to what extent the efforts of Wikipedia editors were successful, while also providing possible improvements on their current strategy.

3. We illustrate that year of retrieval is important for gender bias in the word embeddings from Wikipedia. If gender neutrality w.r.t. a domain is important, our results suggest what year to use.

2 Gender Bias in Wikipedia

In 2011, a big survey on the demographics of Wikipedia editors showed that less than 15% of Wikipedia editors are female [Collier and Bear, 2012]. This led to further investigations into the impact on content of Wikipedia considering different dimensions of gender bias. Two important dimensions of gender bias as researched by Wagner et al. [2015] are coverage bias and lexical bias.

Coverage bias means that notable women are not covered as well as notable men. For example, a smaller percentage of notable women have their own Wikipedia page or these pages may be less extensive. Wagner et al. [2015] looked at three data sets of notable people and found no coverage bias.

However, later research by Wagner et al. [2016] did show a small glass ceiling effect. Google search trends were used to assess the notability of people covered on Wikipedia. Women on Wikipedia

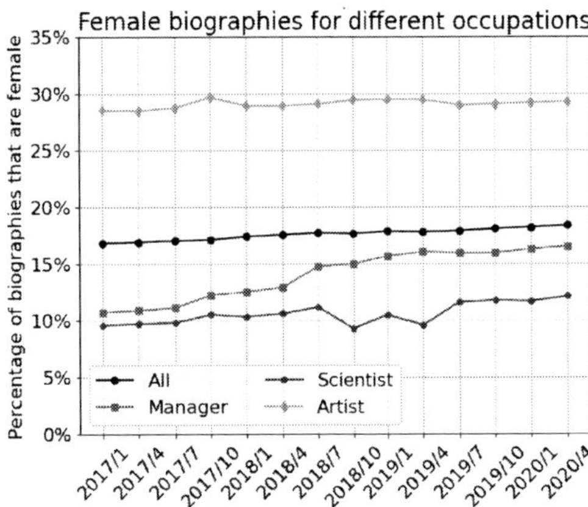

Figure 1: The percentage of biographies of women on Wikipedia for different occupations since 2017. Data from Envel Le Hir [2017-2020].

were found to be more notable than men on average, which suggests that women have to be more notable to be covered on Wikipedia. The efforts of Wikipedia editors have mostly focused on this coverage bias, specifically by making lists of missing notable women and creating articles for these women [Wikipedia contributors, 2020b]. In terms of gender associations in word embeddings, this may have caused words that are commonly used in these biographies to have become more female associated.

Lexical bias relates to the words used on pages written about women and men. Wagner et al. [2016] found two significant differences. Words related to family and relationships are more present in female articles compared to male articles. An article about a divorced person is 4.4 times more likely to be about a woman. The second difference is a stronger emphasis on gender. Articles about women contain more words that are gender-specific, such as 'female' or 'woman'. This can cause biases in the word embeddings. When biographies about women for example contain phrases as 'female scientist', whereas men are referred to as 'scientist', the word scientist would be more closely associated to female, despite there being both male and female scientists.

Besides this, there has also been research to the development of the gender proportion in the Wikipedia biographies. This has been recorded since 2014 and since 2017 this has also been measured by occupation (see Figure 1) [Konieczny and Klein, 2018].

The biggest change can be seen for the occupation 'manager', for which the percentage of female biographies increased with more than 5% in the last 3 years. However, this is still below average. The occupation artist has a female percentage far above average with almost 30%. Furthermore, the overall fraction of female biographies has increased steadily towards around 18% [Envel Le Hir, 2017-2020]. Thus matters are improving, but women are generally still less represented in Wikipedia.

3   Word Embedding Association Test

As proposed by Caliskan et al. [2017], we use the Word Embedding Association Test (WEAT) to quantify gender bias. This test uses four categories that are considered stereotypical towards gender: Arts, Science, Family and Career [Caliskan et al., 2017]. These categories have shown significant bias towards male or female words in embeddings from Google News corpora [Mikolov et al., 2013a], Google Books [Jones et al., 2020], as well as a 'Common Crawl' corpus [Caliskan et al., 2017]. Each category C has a set of eight words and there are two sets (M and F) of target words relating to male and female respectively (Table 7 in the Appendix). These words are based on an implicit association test also used in psychology [Caliskan et al., 2017].

The WEAT score is computed as follows: the association between a pair of words with vectors v_1 and v_2 is measured by the cosine similarity:

$$s(v_1, v_2) = \frac{v_1^T v_2}{\|v_1\|\|v_2\|}. \tag{1}$$

Let v_c denote a word from category C, v_m a male-specific word (e.g. "he" or "his") and v_f a female-specific word (e.g. "she" or "her"). First, the gender bias per word is calculated using equation 2.

$$b(v_c) = \frac{1}{|M|} \sum_{v_m \in M} s(v_c, v_m) - \frac{1}{|F|} \sum_{v_f \in F} s(v_c, v_f). \tag{2}$$

Here, a negative value indicates the category word is female biased and a positive value indicates a male bias. This score is averaged over all words in the category C to get the bias score $b(C)$,

$$b(C) = \frac{1}{|C|} \sum_{v_c \in C} b(v_c). \tag{3}$$

We chose to use WEAT since it is a popular way to measure bias in word embeddings and it allows us to compare our results to those of Jones et al. [2020]. This test will show whether these words contain differences in association with male and female, but how these differences relate to negative consequences in different applications is not precisely known. The results should be interpreted in this general sense, as it shows the existence of bias, but not how problematic the gender bias is.

4   Experimental Setup

All code and the models used for the experiments are made publicly available [1].

Data and preprocessing. We obtained full copies of all articles on Wikipedia in 2006, 2008 to 2010 and 2014 to 2020 from dumps.wikimedia.org and archive.org. To make a comparison between full Wikipedia backups and newly added articles, we created a second corpus by taking all articles for which the ID was not present on Wikipedia two years before. For example, to create a corpus for 2020, we removed all articles that were added before 2019. All articles were converted to tokens using the build-in functionality from the gensim library [Řehůřek and Sojka, 2010]. This tool removes all articles shorter than 50 words, next to all markup, comments and punctuation.

Training of word embeddings. The word2vec model was used to train word embeddings [Mikolov et al., 2013a]. This model uses Continuous-bag-of-words to obtain word vectors that represent the word semantics as well as possible [Mikolov et al., 2013a]. Vectors that are closer together in the vector space represent words that co-occur more often. We mostly used the default settings for word2vec as provided by gensim [Řehůřek and Sojka, 2010]. However, we did not remove the 5% most common words, because this would also remove the words 'he' and 'she'. To ensure that the training had sufficiently converged, we calculated the bias after training for one, ten and twenty iterations (epochs), besides the standard of five.

Quality of embeddings. We used the Word-Sim353 benchmark to assess the quality of word embeddings [Finkelstein et al., 2001]. This evaluation looks at the similarity of 353 word pairs and evaluates the correlation between the results of the embeddings and the true similarity as defined by

---

[1] https://gitlab.com/kschmahl/
wikipedia-gender-bias-over-time

humans. We used this as a sanity check to assess whether the word embeddings reasonably embed true word semantics. These correlation scores can be found in Table 8 in the Appendix, they are all between .63 and .66. This is comparable to the correlations between .60 and .67 that were found using word2vec by Jatnika et al. [2019], which is already better than the model trained by Google they used as comparison [Mikolov et al., 2013b]. As may be expected with a smaller corpus, the scores for the data set of new articles are slightly lower (between .59 and .64), but still reasonable.

Significance of change in WEAT score. We performed a linear regression on the WEAT score versus time. We measured whether the change in WEAT score is significant by performing a t-test to compute whether the slope is significantly different from zero. To reduce the amount of false discoveries from multiple testing, we use a Benjamini-Hochberg correction with a False Discovery Rate (FDR) of 5% [Benjamini and Hochberg, 1995].

Significance against random words. A significant change in WEAT scores may not tell the whole story. It could be the case that, for some reason, all word vectors in the vocabulary become more similar to male or female words. To exclude this possibility, we also computed WEAT scores of random words, using a method proposed in the code from Jones et al. [2020]. We performed a regression on these WEAT scores for many different groups of random words to obtain a histogram of slopes. This histogram of slopes indicates the distribution of slopes for random words. We can then inspect how likely it is for a word category (such as Arts) to have the observed slope, and to see whether the slope is significantly different from slopes of random words. To this end, we used a sample of 1000 random word sets and counted how many of these slopes are at least as extreme as the observed one to determine a permutation p-value for the category word set. On these p-values we did another Benjamini-Hochberg correction with the same FDR of 5%.

Deviation of gender bias within a category. The WEAT score used to quantify the gender bias is a mean over several words in a category. It could be the case that one of the words of a word category influences the mean more than others (e.g. as an outlier). This could indicate either that a word in a word category is inappropriate, thus indicating a

problem with the WEAT test. Alternatively, it can indicate where Wikipedia editors should focus their efforts on changing the language in the articles to reduce the measured gender bias. To investigate this, we also compute the deviation from the means of the different categories for 2008, 2014 and 2020. This will show if there are categories with words with large deviations. In case of large deviations, we look at the individual word scores to investigate which words have the largest influence on the bias.

Number of articles per category. A further explanation of why gender bias has changed over time could be provided by looking at the categories of the articles on Wikipedia. We therefore counted the amount of articles which contained at least one of the words of the word categories for these three available time points.

5   Results

Gender bias scores over time. The gender biases for Wikipedia over time are shown in Figure 2a for the different word categories. The box plots indicate the distribution of WEAT scores for random words, which changes little over time and whose mean seems close to zero, indicating that random words are almost unbiased on average. Career, Arts and Family seem to have strong biases since they fall outside the box plots, while biases in Science seem milder, as its WEAT score is comparable to those of random sets of words.

Table 1 lists the p-values for whether a slope is significantly different from zero, corrected using the Benjamini-Hochberg method. Career has a strong association with male words that has not significantly changed over time. The category Science had a male bias in 2006, but this bias slowly changed over time, and is currently associated slightly more strongly with female words. This could be because the words in this category have been used in the same context as female words as opposed to male words more often since 2014. The words in the Family category have a significantly decreasing female bias, but in 2020 they are still strongly associated with female words. The Arts category is stereotypically female-associated and these words are becoming more biased towards female words, with a statistically significant slope.

Evaluation using only newly added articles. The gender bias over time for the articles added in the two years before the time point is shown in

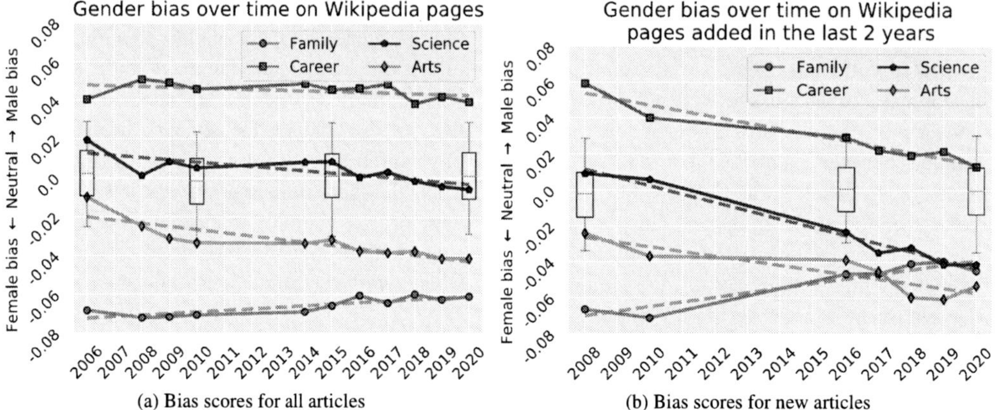

Figure 2: The biases of word categories over time for Wikipedia from 2006 to 2020. Positive means the words are more associated with male, negative scores correspond to word sets more associated with female. Box plots show the distribution of biases for random word sets to put the amount of bias in perspective, the whiskers show the 5th and 95th percentiles. The years without box plots have a similar distribution and are hidden to improve clarity.

Figure 2b and the p-values for the slope tests in Table 1. It can be seen that the developments are similar, but steeper than when looking at all articles. The slope of the bias of all four categories is significantly different from zero in those articles. This suggests that new articles are especially less biased than older articles for the categories Career and Family. Arts and Science are more biased in recently added articles, so new articles do not seem to be better in all aspects of gender bias.

	p-value	
	All articles	New articles
Career	.207	$< .001$
Science	.007	$< .001$
Family	.001	$< .001$
Arts	.001	.010

Table 1: The corrected *p*-values of t-test for the slope of the WEAT score over time. Considered significant $\leq .05$, values are corrected with a FDR of 5%.

WEAT scores of random words. The histograms of the slopes found from random word sets are given in Figure 3. The mean slope is $4.8 \cdot 10^{-5}$, with a standard deviation of $6.3 \cdot 10^{-4}$. We conclude that the whole vocabulary of Wikipedia has on average not become a lot more male or female biased over time. This is confirmed by the fact that the box plots in Figure 2a do not shift over time.

The slope for random words has a larger vari-ance when looking at only the new articles. Random word sets have a mean slope of $2.3 \cdot 10^{-4}$ with a standard deviation of $1.0 \cdot 10^{-3}$ in the word embeddings from recent articles. This shows that the larger slopes seen in the category words for recent articles might be partly caused by larger changes seen in all word embeddings (see Figure 3b). Results of new articles are therefore less reliable, also due to a smaller corpus and less time points.

The p-values can be found in Table 2. Arts (.024) is the only category where the change is also significant compared to changes in random words for the complete Wikipedia corpus. All categories change significantly when considering only newly-added articles. The lower significance in comparison to random words means that despite the existence of slopes significantly different from 0, there may still be reason to doubt the effectiveness of the effort from Wikipedia. It also calls into question whether changes in bias in Table 1 were really significant.

Effect of number of word2vec iterations. We ran the training procedure of the word embeddings and computed the bias for each word category for one, five, ten and twenty iterations. The results are given in Table 3. Between one and five iterations the gender bias slope changes quite a bit. For example, the slope of Science changes from about $-3.1 \cdot 10^{-3}$ to $-1.1 \cdot 10^{-3}$ and the p-value of Arts varies between 0.05 and 0.01. However, most differences between five and ten iterations are smaller, including the slope values for Arts.

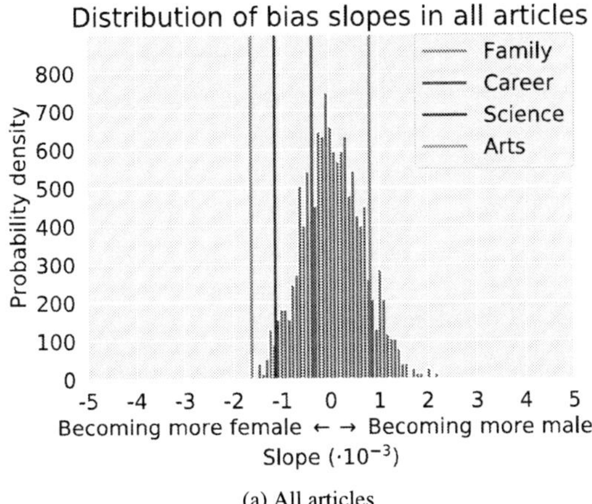

(a) All articles

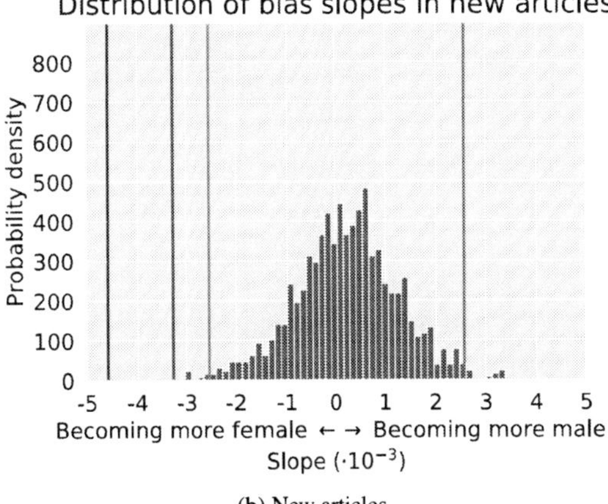

(b) New articles

Figure 3: Probability density of the slopes of random word sets from the vocabulary.

	p-value	
	All articles	New articles
Career	.633	.024
Science	.115	$< .008$
Family	.255	.024
Arts	.024	.052

Table 2: The corrected *p*-values for the test of the slope of the WEAT score for categories as compared to the slopes of random words. Values $\leq .05$ are considered significant, they were corrected using a FDR of 5%. The p-value of $< .008$ is due to the finite amount of permutations (1000).

		1 epoch	5 epochs	10 epochs
C	slope ($\cdot 10^{-3}$)	-1.8	-0.37	-0.29
	p-value	.019	.554	.627
F	slope ($\cdot 10^{-3}$)	1.4	0.81	0.65
	p-value	.065	.191	.282
S	slope ($\cdot 10^{-3}$)	-3.1	-1.1	-1.3
	p-value	$< .001$	.072	.047
A	slope ($\cdot 10^{-3}$)	-1.5	-1.6	-1.3
	p-value	.054	.009	.045

Table 3: The bias scores of the categories Career (C), Family (F), Science (S) and Arts (A) from models trained with a different amount of iterations. The p-value is the computed probability comparing the category words to random words. Twenty epochs are not included since these models have much lower quality.

#Iterations	1	5	10	20
All articles	.63	.64	.64	.57
New articles	.57	.61	.62	.62

Table 4: Quality versus epochs, where quality is the average Pearson correlations of WordSim353.

The quality of the word embeddings also changed little after 5 iterations (see Table 4). This validates our choice of using the default value of 5 iterations. To further investigate if the slope and p-values were converged, we also tried 20 iterations. The resulting word embeddings had significantly lower quality scores (0.57 on average), with models trained on the most data (in more recent years) achieving scores as low as 0.52. We believe that this might be due to overtraining and therefore chose not to use these embeddings for measuring bias. We note that the number of iterations can influence the measured biases and should be varied to make certain the values have converged while models do not become overfitted.

Deviation within a word category. The means and standard deviations for the categories at three time points are given in Table 5. Family has a higher variance than the other categories. To understand why, we looked at the bias of each word in this category in 2020, see Table 6. The words 'wedding', 'marriage' and 'children' have a very strong female bias, whereas 'home', 'cousins' and 'family' are only slightly more female associated.

		F	C	S	A
2008	mean	−0.07	0.05	≈ 0.00	−0.03
	std	0.04	0.03	0.02	0.03
2014	mean	−0.07	0.05	0.01	−0.04
	std	0.04	0.02	0.03	0.02
2020	mean	−0.06	0.04	−0.01	−0.04
	std	0.04	0.02	0.02	0.02

Table 5: Means and variance within categories.

home	parents	children	family
−0.02	−0.07	−0.12	−0.02
cousins	marriage	wedding	relatives
≈ 0.00	−0.10	−0.10	−0.04

Table 6: Bias per word for the Family words in 2020.

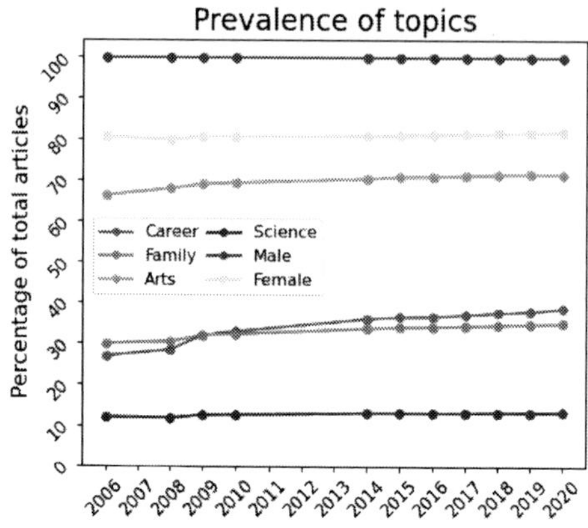

Figure 4: The percentage of articles in Wikipedia that contain at least one of the category words.

Number of articles per category. The percentage of articles which contained at least one of the words of the sets is given in Figure 4. Observe that the proportions have changed little over time, so this does not provide an explanation for the changes in bias over time. All periods thus have similar contribution to the category bias. Male words are present in more of the articles than female words.

6 Discussion and Future Work

Since societal gender bias is decreasing [Garg et al., 2018], we expected that using text written more recently would result in less gender biased word embeddings. We have shown that stereotypical gender bias in the categories Family and Science is indeed decreasing, but these changes are not significant in comparison to random word sets. Words related to Career did not seem to change since 2006. Bias in Arts has significantly increased, also in comparison to random words. Further research, maybe on a longer time period, is necessary to conclude what causes these changes and how significant the changes are.

The vast majority of biographies in Wikipedia are about men [Envel Le Hir, 2017-2020]. This discrepancy has decreased a little since 2017. This is confirmed by the fact that a lot more articles contain words from our male set than from our female set. However, we do not observe that random words are more associated with male words. This could also be seen in the fact that Science words are more female associated in 2020, despite less than 15% of the scientists with biographies being female. A possible reason for this is that articles about women contain more gender-specific words [Wagner et al., 2016], for example: 'female scientist'. The expected gender goes without saying, whereas the minority gender is explicitly specified [Pratto et al., 2007]. This causes words to become more female-associated than expected from the ratio of biographies. Wikipedia may inform its contributors about this skew in female biographies in the hope that this bias will be reduced.

To reduce gender bias in Family further, our results suggest that a focus on equal representation in the topics of marriage and children would be most beneficial. It is unclear why the Arts category is becoming more and more female biased.

When word embeddings are used in downstream tasks such as classification, our research shows it is important to consider the time of retrieval of a corpus. For example, if one wants to have a gender neutral word embedding related to Science, one may best use the corpus of 2018. Such effects may also occur in other corpora. More research is needed to further understand the quality of word embeddings as measured by performance in downstream tasks and unwanted biases in such tasks.

New articles are not gender neutral either. They have similar developments, but more strongly and also significant in comparison to random words. We could not completely determine if new articles are the cause for changes in gender bias, since we did not consider changes in existing articles. Little statistics are known relating to gender bias of Wikipedia. This makes it difficult to place our results in a wider context. Since our work indicates biases are currently increasing further for some categories, current strategies to reduce bias may need to be changed. To further improve the editing strategies of Wikipedia, more automated measures of biases may provide necessary insights.

Compared to the historical embeddings (1800-2000) from the study of Jones et al. [2020], we find several differences but also agreements. In contrast, we find that Art related words are becoming more biased towards female. The bias of Family is decreasing in their study as well, however, they find less steep slopes. The decrease they found in the Career category was not found as clearly in our results, this may also be due to the shorter time span. It is hard to say where the differences stem from: perhaps due to different societal changes or because of a different platform?

One limitation of this research is the fact that no backups of Wikipedia were available between 2010 and 2014. Moreover, we did not look at what text was written exactly when. This information could provide more insight in the developments of gender bias. The current version of Wikipedia still contains text written in 2001, and thus biases in the full corpus of Wikipedia may not represent development of societal biases precisely. The analysis on only new articles may give a better estimate in that respect. However, due to the unreliability of using page ids, this still does not give a perfect representation.

The WEAT-score is not a perfect measure of gender bias of its underlying content. One of the problems is interpretability: where do the biases come from? To that end, Wikipedia's content should also be looked at in more detail. We tried to make this connection using word counts over all Wikipedia pages, but a more elaborate analysis is necessary to complement our analysis. Another option is to use the technique of Brunet et al. [2019] to find the most bias influencing articles. This will give further clues how to make Wikipedia more gender neutral.

Hamilton et al. [2016] discovered laws of semantic shift by looking at word embeddings over large time spans. These laws could explain some of our observed changes in gender bias. The most relevant law is the law of conformity: frequent words change embedding location more slowly. This might be taken to imply that the Arts category, whose words are most used on Wikipedia (see Figure 4), would change bias the least. However, the opposite is the case, as Arts has one of the steepest slopes. Sadly, we cannot compare our rates of change to those found by Hamilton et. al. since we cannot find the raw rates of change per year in their work. This could be used to place changes of WEAT-scores over time in context. We note, however, that the slopes of the categories are already (crudely) placed in context when they are compared against the slopes of random words. Here a further correction could be made with word frequencies to take the law of conformity into account. On the other hand, since our work focuses on a much shorter time scale, we can assume that such changes are negligible, especially for the WEAT words which are generally frequently used and therefore less likely to have major changes in meaning within 20 years.

Word embeddings were shown to be surprisingly unstable over restart with different random initialisation [Wendlandt et al., 2018]. In that work, stability was defined as the fraction of the 10 nearest neighbours of each word that are the same before and after the restart. Thus, this is a measure of local stability. The WEAT score is determined, however, over larger distances of word embeddings. Thus, local instability does not directly imply that WEAT scores would also be unstable. To mitigate this potential instability, we initialized each model with the same seed. While a more elaborate investigation of the stability of WEAT to multiple random restarts is out of the scope of this work, we think it is an important point to investigate in order to verify that our results and those of Jones et al. [2020] and Garg et al. [2018] are robust.

We considered the four default word sets as provided by the WEAT test, to allow comparison to Jones et al. [2020]. Remarkably, these word sets include two male names: Einstein and Shakespeare. Einstein is on average about 0.04 above the category mean of Science, and Shakespeare approximately 0.03 above the mean of Arts, influencing the category means positively, making them more male-biased. It is expected that the names Einstein and Shakespeare co-occur more with male words such as 'he' or 'him'. However, this may not be representative of the rest of Science or Arts words in general, and thus may overestimate male bias in these subjects. We realize that Einstein and Shakespeare were and still are very influential in the fields of science and arts respectively. However, if our goal is that articles about more important individuals (which might be read by more people) have higher impact on the bias calculation we could weigh articles based on notability [Wagner et al., 2016] at the embedding learning stage. To further understand the (perhaps unwanted) effects of using these two words, we believe that more research in the choice of words of WEAT is necessary.

7 Conclusion

In this paper, we used word embeddings to estimate changes in gender bias in Wikipedia articles over time. We found evidence that gender bias is decreasing for Science and Family, while increasing for Arts. Biases in the male associated category Career seems constant. Further analysis of these results provides insights that can potentially lead to new practices to reduce gender bias in Wikipedia even more in the future.

Acknowledgments

We would like to thank the anonymous reviewers for their useful suggestions and comments. We would also like to thank Thijs Raymakers for his help coming up with the research plan.

References

Tomas Mikolov, Kai Chen, Greg Corrado, and Jeffrey Dean. Efficient estimation of word representations in vector space. *arXiv preprint arXiv:1301.3781*, 2013a.

Eric Nalisnick, Bhaskar Mitra, Nick Craswell, and Rich Caruana. Improving document ranking with dual word embeddings. In *Proceedings of the 25th International Conference Companion on World Wide Web*, pages 83–84, 04 2016. doi: 10.1145/2872518.2889361.

Yash Parikh, Abhinivesh Palusa, Shravankumar Kasthuri, Rupa Mehta, and Dipti Rana. Efficient word2vec vectors for sentiment analysis to improve commercial movie success. In *Advanced Computational and Communication Paradigms*, pages 269–279. Springer, 2018.

Beakcheol Jang, Inhwan Kim, and Jong Wook Kim. Word2vec convolutional neural networks for classification of news articles and tweets. *PloS one*, 14(8), 2019.

P Preethi Krishna and A Sharada. Word embeddings-skip gram model. In *International Conference on Intelligent Computing and Communication Technologies*, pages 133–139. Springer, 2019.

Aylin Caliskan, Joanna J Bryson, and Arvind Narayanan. Semantics derived automatically from language corpora contain human-like biases. *Science*, 356(6334):183–186, 2017.

Jason J Jones, Mohammad Ruhul Amin, Jessica Kim, and Steven Skiena. Stereotypical gender associations in language have decreased over time. *Sociological Science*, 7:1–35, 2020.

Andrey Kutuzov, Lilja Øvrelid, Terrence Szymanski, and Erik Velldal. Diachronic word embeddings and semantic shifts: a survey, 2018.

Tolga Bolukbasi, Kai-Wei Chang, James Zou, Venkatesh Saligrama, and Adam Kalai. Quantifying and reducing stereotypes in word embeddings. *arXiv preprint arXiv:1606.06121*, 2016.

Marcelo OR Prates, Pedro H Avelar, and Luís C Lamb. Assessing gender bias in machine translation: a case study with google translate. *Neural Computing and Applications*, pages 1–19, 2019.

Joel Escudé Font and Marta R Costa-Jussa. Equalizing gender biases in neural machine translation with word embeddings techniques. *arXiv preprint arXiv:1901.03116*, 2019.

Hila Gonen and Yoav Goldberg. Lipstick on a pig: Debiasing methods cover up systematic gender biases in word embeddings but do not remove them. In *Proceedings of the 2019 Conference of the North American Chapter of the Association for Computational Linguistics: Human Language Technologies, Volume 1*, pages 609–614, 2019.

Nikhil Garg, Londa Schiebinger, Dan Jurafsky, and James Zou. Word embeddings quantify 100 years of gender and ethnic stereotypes. *Proceedings of the National Academy of Sciences*, 115(16):E3635–E3644, 2018.

Claudia Wagner, David Garcia, Mohsen Jadidi, and Markus Strohmaier. It's a man's wikipedia? assessing gender inequality in an online encyclopedia. In *Ninth international AAAI conference on web and social media*, 2015.

Wikipedia contributors. Gender bias on wikipedia — Wikipedia, the free encyclopedia. https://en.wikipedia.org/w/index.php?title=Gender_bias_on_Wikipedia&oldid=952307164, 2020a. [Online; accessed 30-April-2020].

Envel Le Hir. Denelezh — gender gap in wikimedia projects. https://www.denelezh.org/, 2017-2020. [Online; accessed 25-May-2020].

Benjamin Collier and Julia Bear. Conflict, criticism, or confidence: An empirical examination of the gender gap in wikipedia contributions. In *Proceedings of the ACM 2012 Conference on Computer Supported Cooperative Work*, CSCW '12, page 383–392, New York, NY, USA, 2012. Association for Computing Machinery. doi: 10.1145/2145204.2145265.

Claudia Wagner, Eduardo Graells-Garrido, David Garcia, and Filippo Menczer. Women through the glass ceiling: gender asymmetries in wikipedia. *EPJ Data Science*, 5(1):5, 2016.

Wikipedia contributors. Wikipedia:wikiproject women in red — Wikipedia, the free encyclopedia, 2020b. URL https://en.wikipedia.org/w/index.php?title=Wikipedia:WikiProject_Women_in_Red&oldid=962959922. [Online; accessed 17-June-2020].

Piotr Konieczny and Maximilian Klein. Gender gap through time and space: A journey through wikipedia biographies via the wikidata human gender indicator. *New Media & Society*, 20(12):4608–4633, 2018.

Radim Řehůřek and Petr Sojka. Software Framework for Topic Modelling with Large Corpora. In *Proceedings of the LREC 2010 Workshop on New Challenges for NLP Frameworks*, pages 45–50, Valletta, Malta, May 2010. ELRA.

Lev Finkelstein, Evgeniy Gabrilovich, Yossi Matias, Ehud Rivlin, Zach Solan, Gadi Wolfman, and Eytan Ruppin. Placing search in context: The concept revisited. In *Proceedings of the 10th International Conference on World Wide Web*, WWW '01, page 406–414, New York, NY, USA, 2001. Association for Computing Machinery. doi: 10.1145/371920. 372094.

Derry Jatnika, Moch Arif Bijaksana, and Arie Ardiyanti Suryani. Word2vec model analysis for semantic similarities in english words. *Procedia Computer Science*, 157:160–167, 2019.

Tomas Mikolov, Quoc V Le, and Ilya Sutskever. Exploiting similarities among languages for machine translation. *arXiv preprint arXiv:1309.4168*, 2013b.

Yoav Benjamini and Yosef Hochberg. Controlling the false discovery rate: a practical and powerful approach to multiple testing. *Journal of the Royal statistical society: series B (Methodological)*, 57(1): 289–300, 1995.

Felicia Pratto, Josephine D Korchmaros, and Peter Hegarty. When race and gender go without saying. *Social Cognition*, 25(2):221–247, 2007.

Marc-Etienne Brunet, Colleen Alkalay-Houlihan, Ashton Anderson, and Richard Zemel. Understanding the origins of bias in word embeddings. In *International Conference on Machine Learning*, pages 803–811, 2019.

William L Hamilton, Jure Leskovec, and Dan Jurafsky. Diachronic word embeddings reveal statistical laws of semantic change. *arXiv preprint arXiv:1605.09096*, 2016.

Laura Wendlandt, Jonathan K Kummerfeld, and Rada Mihalcea. Factors influencing the surprising instability of word embeddings. *arXiv preprint arXiv:1804.09692*, 2018.

A WEAT Categories

Table 7: The category and target words used to quantify biases in WEAT.

Topic	Words
Male	he, his, man, male, boy, son, brother, father, uncle, gentleman
Female	she, her, woman, female, girl, daughter, sister, mother, aunt, lady
Career (C)	executive, management, professional, corporation, salary, office, business, career
Family (F)	home, parents, children, family, cousins, marriage, wedding, relatives
Arts (A)	poetry, art, dance, literature, novel, symphony, drama, sculpture, shakespeare
Science (S)	science, technology, physics, chemistry, einstein, nasa, experiment, astronomy

B Quality per year (5 epochs)

Table 8: The Pearson correlation of the WordSim353 quality test for the word embeddings trained from Wikipedia.

	All articles	New articles
2006	.65	
2008	.64	.62
2009	.64	
2010	.64	.63
2014	.63	
2015	.64	
2016	.63	.61
2017	.63	.61
2018	.63	.62
2019	.63	.61
2020	.63	.60

Effects of Anonymity on Comment Persuasiveness in Wikipedia Articles for Deletion Discussions

Yimin Xiao   **Lu Xiao**
School of Information Studies, Syracuse University
yxiao39@syr.edu, lxiao04@syr.edu

Abstract

It has been shown that anonymity affects various aspects of online communications such as message credibility, the trust among communicators, and the participants' accountability and reputation. Anonymity influences social interactions in online communities in these many ways, which can lead to influences on opinion change and the persuasiveness of a message. Prior studies also suggest that the effect of anonymity can vary in different online communication contexts and online communities. In this study, we focus on Wikipedia Articles for Deletion (AfD) discussions as an example of online collaborative communities to study the relationship between anonymity and persuasiveness in this context. We find that in Wikipedia AfD discussions, more identifiable users tend to be more persuasive. The higher persuasiveness can be related to multiple aspects, including linguistic features of the comments, the user's motivation to participate, persuasive skills the user learns over time, and the user's identity and credibility established in the community through participation.

1 Introduction

In communication, people can be motivated to achieve anonymity or identifiability based on multiple reasons, and the desire for being anonymous or identified depends on the specific communication context (Marx, 1999). Anonymity is "the degree to which a communicator perceives the message source is unknown and unspecified" (Anonymous, 1998, p.387). It is a continuum from fully identifiable to fully unidentifiable (Marx, 1999). Anonymity can be constructed by the absence of identity information or by providing a fake identity through the use of pseudonyms (Anonymous, 1998). The online space affords people with multiple ways to remain anonymous: visual anonymity by the lack of physical cues, disassociation of online identity from real-life identity, and the lack of identifiability that can link users to their real identity (Morio and Buchholz, 2009).

The anonymity that people construct can be categorized as physical anonymity where there is no visual or physical presence of the source and discursive anonymity where a message does not disclose personal information that can be traced to a certain source (Anonymous, 1998). In addition, it can be classified as self- and other-anonymity depending on whether the anonymity is perceived by the message source or the message receiver. A message receiver perceives different levels of source anonymity with different amount of identification knowledge available, interaction history with the message source, the receiver's perception of their own anonymity, and the communication context (Rains and Scott, 2007).

Previous studies suggest that in certain online communication contexts, anonymous messages can hurt trust and lower credibility, accountability, and social appreciation (e.g., Haines et al., 2006; Kang, 2017). These communication factors can in turn affect message persuasiveness (e.g., Burgoon et al., 1990; Xiao and Khazaei, 2019). However, prior studies have not directly established an empirical relationship between anonymity and perceived persuasiveness in online communication.

The effects of anonymity on communication and participation behaviors are found to vary in different communication contexts (Kang, 2017; Moore, 2018; Morio and Buchholz, 2009; Rains and Scott, 2007). One prior study shows that anonymity can motivate users to participate in online communication as it potentially opens up freedom for people to express unpopular or

Proceedings of the Fourth Workshop on Natural Language Processing and Computational Social Science, pages 104–115
Online, November 20, 2020. ©2020 Association for Computational Linguistics
https://doi.org/10.18653/v1/P17

undesired opinions, but the anonymous participants are less persuasive (Haines et al., 2006). However, the study was conducted in an experiment setting so that there was no sense of community among the participants. While some online communications are embedded in similar contexts (e.g., Reddit), others are not (e.g., Wikipedia). It is yet to be explored whether anonymity has a similar effect on participation and persuasiveness in these different communication contexts.

Addressing these literature gaps, we focus on Wikipedia Article for Deletion (AfD) discussions as an example of online collaborative communities. We analyze how anonymity of a participant is related to their communication behavior and persuasiveness in this particular type of communication context. The rest of the paper is organized as follows. Section 2 reviews previous work related to the effects anonymity has on communication behaviors in different communication contexts and online persuasion. Section 3 introduces this paper's methodology, data sources, and the data analysis processes. Section 4 details the data analysis results. We discuss the implications of the findings in section 5 and concludes in section 6.

2   Related work

2.1   Anonymity in online communications: its effects

Anonymity plays important roles in affecting interactions in online support groups (Kang, 2017), online group decision support systems (Tsikerdekis, 2013), electronic meeting systems (Rains, 2007), and other computer-mediated communication (Anonymous, 1998). In general, anonymity can be a way to boost participation (Haines et al., 2006), protect privacy (Morio and Buchholz, 2009), prevent people from getting harassed or lose reputation in their real life (Forte et al., 2017), and give people the freedom to speak what they truly want to say (Haines et al., 2006; Moore, 2018) and challenge existing power structures (Champion et al., 2019). Anonymous feedback can be more positively reacted to compared to those given by "a peer or an authority" (Nguyen et al., 2017, p.1024). However, the freedom of speech associated with anonymity can be abused as well (Choi et al., 2016; Singh et al., 2017). Thus, the anonymous condition may need to

be removed in certain online communications in order to reduce the number of unacceptable and antisocial comments (Kilner and Hoadley, 2005).

In online discussions and collective decision-making, anonymity helps to create opportunities for "strategic and deceptive communication" because the audience cannot decide the real intention and any bias of the speaker (Moore, 2018, p.182). Anonymity may also help to facilitate information flow, encourage information seeking and self-help (Anonymous, 1998), and give rise to more diverse opinions in the process (Haines et al., 2006). On the other hand, anonymous communication can hurt trust among the participants (Scott et al., 2011), reduce a message's credibility (Kang, 2017), and slightly reduce the possibility that an individual participant conforms to the group opinion (Tsikerdekis, 2013). Anonymous (1998) argues that identifiability, the opposite of anonymity, can help to build the source's accountability and reputation which are important factors of a message's persuasiveness (Burgoon et al., 1990; Gamson, 1966). In fact, in a series of experiments with scenarios of different anonymity, Haines et al. (2006) find that an anonymous communication setting gives rise to participation as users can freely express reticent opinions without being identified; but at the same time, anonymous comments can be less persuasive. The authors speculate that the lack of social status cues and the deindividualization of the users give the other participants the impression that the multiple anonymous messages were a repetitive argument made by a single person (Haines et al., 2006).

2.2   Anonymity in online communications: the effects of the contexts

The effects that anonymity has on communication behaviors can vary with the degrees and types of anonymity, the audience of the communication (Kang, 2017; Moore, 2018), and the culture of the community within which the communication is taking place (Morio and Buchholz, 2009). For example, in cultures where affiliation to the group is emphasized and rewards are given to the group not individuals (Haines et al., 2006), anonymous situations are preferred (Morio and Buchholz, 2009), whereas in cultures that emphasize autonomy and personal award, such tendency is reversed (Morio and Buchholz, 2009).

There has also been research on anonymity in specific online communities or communication contexts. In New York Times online comments, anonymous commentators receive less recommendations than the non-anonymous ones (Pierson, 2015). A Reddit study finds that the perceived anonymity by the user themselves can affect their use of "throwaway" accounts (Leavitt, 2015). These accounts establish a temporary identity. The choice of using "throwaway" accounts in the Reddit discussions also correlates with the user's gender (Leavitt, 2015). In the context of Wikipedia, the level of a Wikipedia editor's perceived anonymity and the actual anonymity state are found to decrease an individual's likelihood of conforming to the group decision, though the influence is small and may be subject to factors other than anonymity in the communication (Tsikerdekis, 2013). A forensic qualitative analysis of Tor-based anonymous users on Wikipedia finds both positive behaviors and contributions that violate community policies (Champion et al., 2019).

Prior studies suggest that the contexts of online communication mediate the effects of anonymity (Paskuda and Lewkowicz, 2015). Paskuda (2016) conducts a comparative study to understand how anonymity affects user participation in YouTube, Hack News, and Quora. The researcher (2016) finds that the integration of the YouTube comment system with Google+ limits users to post anonymous comments, and there are more interactions, more polite comments, and more rude comments after this integration. In Quora, when users answer questions anonymously, the length of the answer correlates with the number of upvotes it receives (Paskuda, 2016). Hacker News site publishes technology related news articles and claims to have a strong community aspect (Paskuda, 2016). The researcher finds that anonymity on Hacker News site does not have a statistically significant influence on social appreciation and participation, but identity factors have positive influence on them. These identity factors are defined specifically in the context of Hacker News and include the use of pseudonym and disclosed information (e.g., mentioning an email address, a website, or a Twitter profile) in a user's self-description. They are considered potential indicators of a real and stable identity on the site.

2.3 Online persuasion

There are three main directions in researching persuasion in the context of computer-mediated human-human interactions. One line focuses on developing annotated corpora for online persuasion studies, e.g., corpora that annotate the persuasive attempts and tactics in the participants' comments (Anand et al., 2011; Young et al., 2011). Another line of research investigates factors that could affect persuasion, such as the participants' gender (Guadagno and Cialdini, 2002) and prior experiences (Cooke et al., 2002; Gershoff et al., 2003; Lydon et al., 1988), and the group setting (Price et al., 2006). The third line focuses on the development of computational techniques to predict the online users' persuasive power in various scenarios, e.g., in identifying influential people in online communities (e.g., Biran et al., 2012; Quercia et al., 2011), in detecting which online reviews are more helpful than the others (Li and Zhan, 2011), and in examining what made some fund requests in the crowdfund sites successful (Hsieh et al., 2013; Mitra and Gilbert, 2014).

The existing research body primarily focuses on the language and content analysis of the comments in the online discussions. These studies (e.g., Tan et al., 2016; Xiao, 2018; Xiao and Khazaei, 2019) suggest that there are linguistic indicators of an online comment's persuasion power, such as the use of function words, the emotional tones, the use of words that reflect one's thinking styles (e.g., logical/analytical thinking or informal reasoning), and the length of the comment. The use of persuasion strategies in online discussion content is also examined (Hidey et al., 2017). These studies make inconsistent findings in different discussion contexts, e.g., Wikipedia's Article for Deletion (AfD) discussions and Reddit "Change My View" (CMV) discussions. For example, while the length of a CMV comment is a strong indicator of the comment's persuasion power, it is not an indicator for AfD comments' persuasion power. The contextual factors of a discussion are also explored limitedly, such as the interaction dynamics among participants (Jo et al., 2018), the commenter's credibility (Xiao and Khazaei, 2019), and the susceptibility of users facing the persuasion attempts (Mensah et al., 2019).

3 Methodology

Our literature review suggests that anonymity affects various aspects of online communication. We also identify related findings to the focal interest of this study – the effects of a participant's anonymity on the perceived persuasiveness of one's messages in online discussions. For instance, as mentioned earlier, messages made in an anonymous setting are found to be less persuasive (Haines et al., 2006). Prior research also shows that the communication context mediates this influence (e.g., Paskuda, 2016). We speculate that in online discussions, anonymity's influence on one's perceived persuasiveness is also mediated by the discussion context. Yet, to our best knowledge, this has not been explored. Additionally, while prior research has shown that a message's persuasiveness is reflected from the language use (Tan et al., 2016; Xiao and Khazaei, 2019), it is unknown to us whether and how one's anonymity is related to the individual's language use in online communications. Furthermore, the effects of anonymity on the message's persuasiveness are explained by their influences on accountability and credibility (Burgoon et al., 1990; Gamson, 1966; Kang, 2017; Scott et al., 2011). It is however not clear to us whether anonymity motivates people to participate more in online discussions thus more motivated to make persuasion attempts towards others.

In this study, we examine anonymity in Wikipedia's Article for Deletion (AfD) discussions. We operationalize anonymity as the amount of personal information a Wikipedian discloses in the community. We aim to understand how the choice of being anonymous or identifiable in Wikipedia plays a role in how a user constructs their comments and in turn their persuasiveness perceived by others. In this section, we detail our study to explore these issues.

3.1 Data collection

Wikipedia is an online community in which members strive for offering an online encyclopedia through open online collaboration. Wikipedia advocates the creation of a user account to establish a stable identity, build up credibility and reputation, and protect user privacy to facilitate their collaborative work within the community (Wikipedia, n.d.). To ensure the quality of its articles, Wikipedia has established four mechanisms to examine and delete articles that are not appropriate to be included: Speedy Deletion, Proposed Deletion, BLP Deletion, and Deletion Discussion. In this study, we examine the anonymity aspect in the Deletion Discussions. Such a discussion occurs if it is unclear to the community whether the focal article should be deleted. Named as the Article for Deletion (AfD), this discussion often lasts about a couple of weeks during which any user can offer their opinion (e.g., to keep the article) and provide the corresponding rationale, i.e., the justification of their opinion. Wikipedia's AfD policy requires that the final decision about the article be made based on the rationales. In Wikipedia, these AfD discussions are organized according to the date the discussions were started. An example AfD discussion page can be found by following this link: https://en.wikipedia.org/wiki/Wikipedia:Articles_f or_deletion/Log/2017_May_20.

We leverage the Wikipedia AfD dataset collected by Mayfield and Black (2019). The dataset includes 1,967,769 AfD comments in English and other related information, e.g., the AfD discussion a comment belongs to, the commenter information, etc. There are 179,864 AfD participants included in this dataset.

3.2 Measuring message's persuasiveness of a certain user

With the AfD discussion data, we first label each comment as persuasive or non-persuasive adapting the annotation mechanism by Xiao (2018). Specifically, an AfD comment is a user's suggestion about what to do with the focal article along with their justifications, e.g., to keep it in Wikipedia and why, to delete it from Wikipedia and why, etc. We only consider two opinions in the comment: keep and delete, as labeled in the original dataset (Mayfield and Black, 2019), and the same two possible outcomes of an AfD discussion: keep and delete. Then, comments that have the same opinions as the discussion outcome are considered persuasive, and the comments that have the opposing views as the discussion outcome are considered non-persuasive. Some discussions have more persuasive messages than non-persuasive ones. In such cases, it is possible that a labelled persuasive message contributes to the final decision not because of its persuasive rationale but because of persuasive power accumulated through multiple persuasive comments. We therefore remove comments from these discussions to better identify individual persuasive comments. Our subset data accounts for 5% of the original dataset.

Following is an example persuasive comment and an example non-persuasive comment:

Persuasive "Delete for now. The fact that it's in a copyright database is meaningless: episodes change names in planning stages. Also bogus is the argument that it'll just be recreated - that's why we have a CSD for previously-deleted material. Salting the earth is also possible. Per Aldux, the article can be recreated when there's actually material. –"

Non-persuasive "let's be careful here. How do we know he's not notable? I'd like to hear some confirmation by someone familiar with the Malayalam language or at least someone very familiar with the litterature of India. Here's a source that mentions him. Now of course I have absolutely no way of knowing whether that site is just rewriting from Wikipedia content so that does not say much. Still I think a bit of research is needed before we go ahead and throw this away."

We measure an individual's persuasiveness using the subset data by the percentage of this person's persuasive comments within all the comments the individual made. This process results in data of 10,746 users with an average of 0.3776 persuasive score.

3.3 Measuring a user's level of anonymity

Marx (1999) measures identifiability through seven dimensions of identity knowledge including name, location, pseudonyms that can or cannot be linked to other identity knowledge, behavior patterns, social categorizations, and certain eligibility or non-eligibility symbols. A message source can achieve different levels of anonymity when some of their identity knowledge is absent (Anonymous, 1998), e.g. when people withhold their personal information (gender, name, email, location, etc.) in online communication (Qian and Scott, 2007). Inspired by these works, we use the amount of one's personal and identity information that is openly available in the Wikipedia environment to measure the individual's anonymity in this online community. We first use the presence of the individual's gender information to measure the user's anonymity level, as users can

easily disclose this information on their user page in structured and accessible ways (e.g., by listing themselves as a member of the Male Wikipedian group, stating that "I am a male", or using 'he' to describe themselves). Previous studies have developed models to predict gender information based on usernames (e.g., Knowles et al., 2016). However, for a more accurate measurement of a user's choice to disclose their personal information, we rely on existing dataset to obtain user's gender information. The dataset from Mayfield and Black (2019) includes gender information of some participants. We verify and make that information more complete based on the publicly available "Female Wikipedians" [1] and "Male Wikipedians"[2] lists from Wikipedia (as of November 2019). Through this process, we identify 3,069 users with gender information and 7,677 users without.

To validate using the presence of gender information to measure one's level of anonymity in Wikipedia community, we compare the amount of personal information disclosed on the participants' user page between these two groups (i.e., provision of the gender information vs. not). As our analysis focuses on the degree to which a Wikipedian wishes to appear identifiable in the community, rather than how their anonymity is perceived by other community members, we consider it appropriate to leverage the information on the user page, which is provided by the user themselves, to measure anonymity. User page texts from Wikimedia Downloads[3] (as of March 2020) are obtained. We pre-process the texts by removing stop words and other HTML formatting strings. Then, we calculate a Shannon Entropy score for each user page text using formulas (1) and (2), where i is the individual word in the text. This entropy score offers a way to measure the amount of information contained in a text content.

$$entropy = -\Sigma(p_i * log_2 p_i) \qquad (1)$$
$$p_i = text.count(i) / len(text) \qquad (2)$$

Finally, using a Named Entity Recognition algorithm in SpaCy (Honnibal and Montani, 2017), we identify the words that are related to several identity categories including nationality, political or religious groups, organizations, locations, products, languages, and dates. We measure the amount of identity information in each category by

---

[1] https://en.wikipedia.org/wiki/Category:Female_Wikipedians
[2] https://en.wikipedia.org/wiki/Category:Male_Wikipedians
[3] https://dumps.wikimedia.org/backup-index.html

calculating the normalized frequencies of the words in the category.

Our comparison of the amount of personal identity information in the user page texts is conducted through Mann-Whitney U tests. As shown by the average values in table 1 below, compared to those who do not reveal their gender, users who disclose their gender also disclose statistically more personal and identity information on their user pages. The statistical significance is based on a Bonferroni corrected α value 0.0015, because of the 33 comparisons made between the two groups in this study. The effect sizes of the Mann-Whitney U tests are all between 0.5 and 0.8, indicating a medium sized comparison between the two groups (Cohen, 1988). The only category that does not show statistically significant difference is the category of language, i.e., language names such as English, Japanese, and Chinese. The insignificance of this category is likely resulted by the fact that the majority of the texts (99% of a random sample of 1,000 users from our dataset) do not contain any language names, leaving the two groups of users being similar with each other.

Feature	Users with gender informa-tion	Users without gender informa-tion	Effect size
User Page text length	308.04	173.23	0.6537
Entropy	4.25	3.12	0.6402
Named entity - nationality, political, religious groups	0.11	0.06	0.5244
Named entity – organization	0.32	0.26	0.5847
Named entity – location	0.25	0.14	0.5514
Named entity – product	0.04	0.02	0.5098
Named entity – language	Not significant		
Named entity – date	0.27	0.14	0.5634

Table 1: Amount of personal information disclosed on user pages by users with and without gender information in Wikipedia

Based on the result, we group all 10,746 participants into two categories: the group of low anonymity that includes those with gender information and more personal and identity information (3,069 users, 15,906 comments), and the group of high anonymity that consists of participants whose gender information is not available in Wikipedia and who have also provided less personal and identity information (7,677 users, 25,094 comments). Figure 1 and figure 2 are example profiles of users of low and high anonymity respectively.

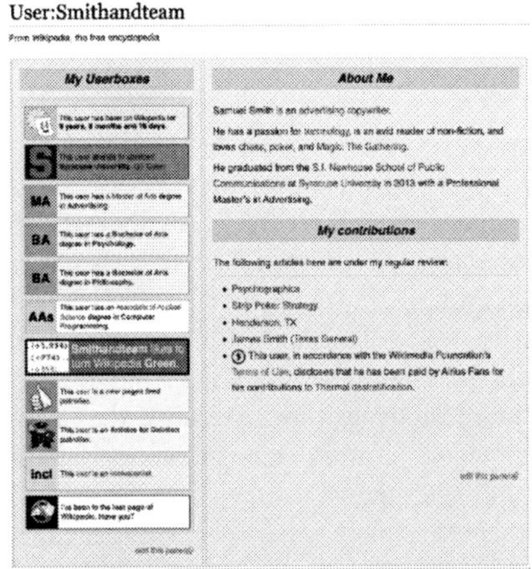

Figure 1: Example profile of a user of low anonymity classified based on section 3.3

User:Kaligelos

From Wikipedia, the free encyclopedia

Figure 2: Example profile of a user of high anonymity classified based on section 3.3

3.4   Data analysis

With this data, we examine whether one's level of anonymity affects one's persuasiveness through a Mann-Whitney U test.

Additionally, we analyze whether one's level of anonymity affects one's language use in the discussions. We measure the use of linguistic attributes and the presence of various cognitive, social, and affective categories by the word choice using Linguistic Inquiry & Word Count (LIWC) 2015 (Pennebaker et al., 2015). We also measure the use of transitional phrase[4] and hedging and boosting words and phrases[5]. We use Mann-Whitney U tests to compare the linguistic features of the two groups of users.

---

[4] http://www.studygs.net/wrtstr6.htm

[5] https://github.com/jumayel06/Tension-Analysis

Furthermore, we apply Spearman's correlation test to examine whether one's persuasiveness correlates with one's participation behavior in AfD discussions, which is reflected from the number of comments they made in AfD, their total edit counts in Wikipedia, and the length of their membership in the Wikipedia community. We also apply Mann Whitney U tests to examine whether a user's level of anonymity correlates with their participation behaviors in the AfD discussions. Wikipedia AfD discussions allow people to provide their opinions on what to do with the articles being discussed. The policy that requires the final decision about the article be made based on the participants' rationales emphasizes the importance of the participants offering rationales to defend their opinions and to convince the others. We assume that people's participation behavior in these discussions reflects how strongly they are motivated to help control the quality of Wikipedia. In other words, if one participates in these discussions more, the person is more motivated. We speculate that a stronger motivation may make one put more efforts in their reasonings, therefore their rationales may be perceived as more persuasive. We also expect that how anonymous a user wants to remain in the community influences how they participate in AfD discussions.

4   Results

4.1   Anonymity and persuasiveness

The results of the Mann-Whitney U test indicate that users of low anonymity (average = 0.42) have statistically higher persuasive scores than the other group (average = 0.36, effect size = 0.54, corrected α = 0.0015). In other words, in Wikipedia AfD discussions the participants who are more identifiable tend to be more persuasive. This is consistent with a prior study that finds comments made in anonymous experiment settings are less persuasive because of the absence of a commenter's status cues and the presence of more diverse comments (Haines et al., 2006).

4.2   Anonymity and linguistic features

We report the average of each language use aspect of the two groups of users and the effect size of Mann-Whitenet U tests in table 2 (corrected α value 0.0015). The LIWC *clout* category measures languag that reflects confidence, social status, or leadership, and the *authentic* category refers to an honest or authentic way of speaking (LIWC, n.d.).

Feature	Group 1 - Low anony-mity	Group 2 - High anony-mity	Effect Size
LIWC - word count	47.9	47.5	0.521
LIWC - tone	Not significant		
LIWC - positive emotion	Not significant		
LIWC - negative emotion	1.40	1.20	0.544
LIWC - clout	40.9	43.1	0.467
LIWC – word per sentence	16.8	16.1	0.525
LIWC - authentic	26.8	26.5	0.518
LIWC - analytical	70.0	71.4	0.470
LIWC - cognitive process	12.9	12.23	0.525
Average booster word counts	.0088	.0082	0.529
Average hedging word counts	0.017	0.016	0.527
Average transitional phrase counts	.0053	.0050	0.532

Table 2: Linguistic feature comparison between users of low and high anonymity in Wikipedia AfD

From this analysis, we find that users of low anonymity tend to be more authentic in their communication, write longer comments and longer sentences, and covey more negative emotion. Their comments are also more likely to relate to their cognitive or thinking process, contain more booster words or phrases to strengthen their argument, and utilize more transitional phrases to organize their argument. These findings conform to previous studies on the linguistic features of a comment's persuasiveness in online discussions (Tan et al., 2016; Xiao, 2018; Xiao and Khazaei, 2019). On the other hand, we also observe less clout, less analytical words, and more hedging words in their communication, though it has been found in a previous study that more persuasive Wikipedia AfD comments have more analytical words (Xiao,

2018). These findings suggest that in Wikipedia AfD discussions, anonymity affects one's persuasiveness through several aspects including but not limited to linguistic features. Specifically, as one is more identifiable, one may invest more intellectual and cognitive effort in the discussions (e.g., longer comments and sentences) – this is expected because of our tendency in impression management (Goffman, 1978). Additionally, the fact that they are more identifiable makes their arguments perceived as being more credible when they are more open to show their negative emotions and uncertainty.

4.3 Anonymity, participation, and comment features

The results shown in table 3 confirm a positive correlation between all three participation behaviors and persuasiveness. This result conforms to our speculation that users who participate more tend to put more efforts to constructing persuasive messages.

Feature	Persuasiveness
Voting comment count in the dataset	r = 0.251, p < 0.01
Total edit count in Wikipedia	r = 0.284, p < 0.01
Length of Wikipedia membership	r = 0.128, p < 0,01

Table 3: Community participation behavior and message persuasiveness in Wikipedia

We also find that users of low anonymity have statistically more comments in our dataset and make more Wikipedia edits in general, though there is no significant difference in the length of their Wikipedia membership. The average of user's participation statistics and the effect size of the Mann-Whitney U tests are given in table 4 below (adjusted α value after Bonferroni correction 0.0015). The result implies that users of low anonymity in Wikipedia are more motivated to actively participate in the collaborative work in the community.

In summary, our analysis on anonymity, participation, and comment features shows that more identifiable Wikipedia users participate more in the community. As longer and higher amount of contribution to the community is associated with higher persuasiveness, we speculate that this group of Wikipedians are more motivated to construct persuasive messages. Alternatively, as found by Luu et al. (2019) that debaters improve their persuasive skills over time, these Wikipedians may have acquired the skills to be persuasive in the community through their long participation.

Feature	Group 1 – Low anony-mity	Group 2 - High anony-mity	Effect size
Comment count in the dataset	5.18	3.27	0.576
Total edit count in Wikipedia	29,885	12,110	0.703
Length of Wikipedia member-ship	Not significant		

Table 4: Community participation behavior comparison between users of high and low anonymity in Wikipedia

5 Discussion

Our results show that in Wikipedia discussions, persuasive comments, i.e., those express congruent views with the final decision, are made more often by identifiable users. These users also participate more actively in the discussions. This is inconsistent with the findings of Haines et al.'s (2006) experiments in which anonymous participants were found to be more actively participating in the online discussion but less persuasive.

In Wikipedia discussions, participants share a common identity as Wikipedians in the community and conduct collaborative work (Baytiyeh and Pfaffman, 2010). Motivated to be associated with the community, the members' active participation helps them establish and maintain their identities with the community. In addition, Wikipedia encourages non-anonymous participation (Wikipedia, n.d.). Apart from the fact that more disclosed personal information makes one more identifiable in the community, one's participation in various Wikipedia activities is connected to the collective goal of the community and reflects one's identity in Wikipedia. The higher participation level makes an additional contribution to establishing their identity, credibility, and reputation within the community and decreases perceived anonymity of the message receiver. Wikipedians may also learn to be more persuasivenss through their long-term participation in the community.

Our findings on the influences of anonymity on persuasiveness are potentially limited because our way of extracting personal information based on a Wikipedian's user page text features and named entity recognition may not reflect user anonymity accurately. The classification of high and low anonymity therefore needs to be validated more rigorously. Additionally, we are not able to measure how a user's identifiability is perceived by other communicators and how the perceived anonymity affects perceived persuasiveness. When measuring persuasinvess, we only consider data from discussions that have more non-persuasive comments than persuasive ones for higher accuracy. This choice leaves users and their anonymity choice and persuasivenss in the alterative situation unaccounted for, which is worth exploring in future work.

Nevertheless, our study provides empirical evidence that anonymity is related to a comment's persuasiveness through linguistic and behavioral features. Our finding in the Wikipedia context suggests that it is a successful practice in terms of establishing credibility and reputation in Wikipedia by requiring one to create and use their user accounts in Wikipedia activities. It would be interesting to examine whether this applies to other online communities where peer-to-peer collaborations are the norms, and how these communities constrast with those without extensive collaborative work.

Our future work includes establishing a more direct relationship between anonymity and user credibility and accountability to understand the mechanisms behind anonymity's influence on persuasiveness. For example, a prototype design of asynchronous online deliberation uses the feature of voting for participants to measure the constructiveness of a message and ensure the accountability of anonymous participation (Kaplan et al., 2013). A similar mechanism can be implemented to study whether or not accountability measured in this way differs between anonymous and identified messages. Similarly, the methods used by Wagenknecht et al. (2018) can also be used to understand the mechanisms through which anonymity affects persuasiveness. We would also like to explore in more details how being anonymous or having an established identity in online communities affects a user's motivation to participate in the community. Lastly, in some online communities such as Quora, a user can switch between revealing their identities and showing as anonymous when asking questions and offering answers. It will help us gain a more comprehensive understanding of users' online behavior and their perspectives regarding online identities by exploring their motivations and communication strategies in choosing these communication situations and compare their language use in the two cases.

6 Conclusion

In this study, we analyze whether or not a user's anonymity level affects their comment persuasiveness in the Wikipedia Article for Deletion (AfD) discussions. We collect user and comment data of the discussions and annotate them for anonymity and persuasiveness. In this specific context, we measure anonymity by the amount of personal information disclosed in their user page using named entity recognition and other linguistic features. Message persuasiveness is measured by the degree to which a message can lead to an agreed group decision on the focal Wikipedia article. We also analyze the relationship between anonymity and the linguistic features of a user's comment and the user's participation in the community to understand how anonymity is related to persuasiveness.

Our findings conform to what has been suggested in previous research: a user's message persuasiveness is related to his or her anonymity status or level of identifiability in the community. In Wikipedia AfD discussions, users of lower anonymity are are more persuasive and participate more in the community. Our finding suggests that the higher persuasiveness can be related to multiple aspects, including linguistic features of their comments, the user's motivation to participate, the persuasive skills acquired over time, and the user's identity and credibility established in the community through prolonged participation. The results shed light on how anonymity affects communication behavior and communication results in an online collaborative community. We also suggest multiple perspectives for further research including closer examinations of the relation between anonymity and accountability or credibility, anonymity and participation in online communities, and comparative studies on other types of online communities.

References

Pranav Anand, Joseph King, Jordan Boyd-Graber, Earl Wagner, Craig Martell, Doug Oard, and Philip Resnik. 2011. Believe me—we can do this! Annotating persuasive acts in blog text. In *The AAAI 2011 workshop on Computational Models of Natural Argument*, San Francisco, CA.

Anonymous. 1998. To Reveal or Not to Reveal: A Theoretical Model of Anonymous Communication. *Communication Theory* 8, 4, 381–407. https://doi.org/10.1111/j.1468-2885.1998.tb00226.x

Hoda Baytiyeh and Jay Pfaffman. 2010. Volunteers in Wikipedia: Why the Community Matters. *Journal of Educational Technology & Society.* 13, 2, 128–140.

Or Biran, Sara Rosenthal, Jacob Andreas, Kathleen McKeown, and Owen Rambow. 2012. Detecting influencers in written online conversations. In *Proceedings of the Second Workshop on Language in Social Media*, Association for Computational Linguistics, Montréal, Canada, 37–45. https://www.aclweb.org/anthology/W12-2105

Judee K. Burgoon, Thomas Birk, and Michael Pfau. 1990. Nonverbal Behaviors, Persuasion, and Credibility. *Human Communication Research.* 17, 1, 140–169. https://doi.org/10.1111/j.1468-2958.1990.tb00229.x

Kaylea Champion, Nora McDonald, Stephanie Bankes, Joseph Zhang, Rachel Greenstadt, Andrea Forte, and Benjamin Mako Hill. 2019. A Forensic Qualitative Analysis of Contributions to Wikipedia from Anonymity Seeking Users. *Proceedings of the ACM on Human-Computer Interaction*, 3(CSCW), 1–26. https://doi.org/10.1145/3359155

Jae Young Choi, Gyoo Gun Lim, and Mi Na Woo. 2016. A Study on the Anonymity Perceptions Impacting on Posting Malicious Messages in Online Communities. In *PACIS 2016 Proceedings*, 266.

Jacob Cohen. 1988. Statistical Power Analysis for the Behavioral Sciences. New York: Routledge, https://doi.org/10.4324/9780203771587

Alan D. J. Cooke, Harish Sujan, Mita Sujan, and Barton A. Weitz. 2002. Marketing the unfamiliar: The role of context and item-specific information in electronic agent recommendations. *Journal Marketing Research.* 39, 4, 488–497. https://doi.org/10.1509/jmkr.39.4.488.19121

Andrea Forte, Nazanin Andalibi, and Rachel Greenstadt. 2017. Privacy, Anonymity, and Perceived Risk in Open Collaboration: A Study of Tor Users and Wikipedians. In *Proceedings of the 2017 ACM Conference on Computer Supported Cooperative Work and Social Computing*, ACM, Portland Oregon USA, 1800–1811. https://doi.org/10.1145/2998181.2998273

William A. Gamson. 1966. Reputation and Resources in Community Politics. *American Journal of Sociology.* 72, 2, 121–131.

Andrew D. Gershoff, Ashesh Mukherjee, and Anirban Mukhopadhyay. 2003. Consumer acceptance of online agent advice: Extremity and positivity effects. *Journal of Consumer Psychology.* 13, 1–2, 161–170.

Erving Goffman. 1978. *The presentation of self in everyday life.* London: Harmondsworth.

Rosanna E. Guadagno and Robert B. Cialdini. 2002. Online persuasion: An examination of gender differences in computer-mediated interpersonal influence. *Group Dynamics: Theory, Research, and Practice.* 6, 1, 38–51. https://doi.org/10.1037/1089-2699.6.1.38

Russell Haines, Lan Cao, and Douglas Haines. 2006. Participation and Persuasion via Computer-Mediated Communication: Anonymous versus Identified Comments. *ICIS 2006 Proc.* 50.

Christopher Hidey, Elena Musi, Alyssa Hwang, Smaranda Muresan, and Kathy McKeown. 2017. Analyzing the semantic types of claims and premises in an online persuasive forum. In *Proceedings of the 4th Workshop on Argument Mining*, Association for Computational Linguistics, Copenhagen, Denmark, 11–21. https://doi.org/10.18653/v1/W17-5102

M. Honnibal and I. Montani. 2017. Spacy 2: Natural language understanding with bloom embeddings, convolutional neural networks and incremental parsing. *To appear.*

Gary Hsieh, Youyang Hou, Ian Chen, and Khai N. Truong. 2013. "Welcome!": social and psychological predictors of volunteer socializers in online communities. In *Proceedings of the 2013 conference on Computer supported cooperative work - CSCW '13*, ACM Press, San Antonio, Texas, USA, 827–838. https://doi.org/10.1145/2441776.2441870

Yohan Jo, Shivani Poddar, Byungsoo Jeon, Qinlan Shen, Carolyn P. Rose, and Graham Neubig. 2018. Attentive Interaction Model: Modeling Changes in View in Argumentation. *ArXiv180400065 Cs.* Retrieved May 25, 2020 from http://arxiv.org/abs/1804.00065

Katie K. Kang. 2017. Anonymity and Interaction in an Online Breast Cancer Social Support Group. *Communication Studies.* 68, 4, 403–421. https://doi.org/10.1080/10510974.2017.1340902

Michael Kaplan, Gilly Leshed, and Toren Kutnick. 2013. Public spheres: ideas taking shape. In *Proceedings of the 2013 conference on Computer supported cooperative work companion - CSCW '13*, ACM Press, San Antonio, Texas, USA, 161. https://doi.org/10.1145/2441955.2441996

Peter G. Kilner and Christopher M. Hoadley. 2005. Anonymity options and professional participation in an online community of practice. In *Proceedings of the 2005 conference on Computer support for collaborative learning learning 2005: the next 10 years! - CSCL '05*, Association for Computational Linguistics, Taipei, Taiwan, 272–280. https://doi.org/10.3115/1149293.1149328

Rebecca Knowles, Josh Carroll, and Mark Dredze. 2016. Demographer: Extremely Simple Name Demographics. *Proceedings of the First Workshop on NLP and Computational Social Science*, 108–113. https://doi.org/10.18653/v1/W16-5614

Alex Leavitt. 2015. "This is a Throwaway Account": Temporary Technical Identities and Perceptions of Anonymity in a Massive Online Community. In *Proceedings of the 18th ACM Conference on Computer Supported Cooperative Work & Social Computing - CSCW '15*, ACM Press, Vancouver, BC, Canada, 317–327. https://doi.org/10.1145/2675133.2675175

Jin Li and Lingjing Zhan. 2011. Online Persuasion: How the written word drives WOM: Evidence from consumer-generated product reviews. *Journal of Advertising Research.* 51, 1, 239–257. https://doi.org/10.2501/JAR-51-1-239-257

LIWC. n.d. LIWC: Linguistic Inquiry and Word Count. Retrieved online from http://liwc.wpengine.com/

Kelvin Luu, Chenhao Tan, and Noah A. Smith. 2019. Measuring Online Debaters' Persuasive Skill from Text over Time. *Transactions of the Association for Computational Linguistics,* 7, 537-550. https://doi.org/10.1162/tacl_a_00281

John E. Lydon, David W. Jamieson, and Mark P. Zanna. 1988. Interpersonal Similarity and the Social and Intellectual Dimensions of First Impressions. *Social. Cognition.* 6, 4, 269–286. https://doi.org/10.1521/soco.1988.6.4.269

Gary T. Marx. 1999. What's in a Name? Some Reflections on the Sociology of Anonymity. *The Information Society.* 15, 2, 99–112. https://doi.org/10.1080/019722499128565

Elijah Mayfield and Alan W. Black. 2019. Analyzing Wikipedia Deletion Debates with a Group Decision-Making Forecast Model. *Proceedings of ACM on Human-Computer Interaction.* 3, CSCW, 1–26. https://doi.org/10.1145/3359308

Humphrey Mensah, Lu Xiao, and Sucheta Soundarajan. 2019. Characterizing susceptible users on Reddit's ChangeMyView. In *Proceedings of the 10th International Conference on Social Media and Society - SMSociety '19*, ACM Press, Toronto, ON, Canada, 102–107. https://doi.org/10.1145/3328529.3328550

Tanushree Mitra and Eric Gilbert. 2014. The language that gets people to give: phrases that predict success on kickstarter. In *Proceedings of the 17th ACM conference on Computer supported cooperative work & social computing - CSCW '14*, ACM Press, Baltimore, Maryland, USA, 49–61. https://doi.org/10.1145/2531602.2531656

Alfred Moore. 2018. Anonymity, Pseudonymity, and Deliberation: Why Not Everything Should Be Connected: Anonymity, Pseudonymity & Deliberation. *The Journal of Political Philosophy.* 26, 2, 169–192. https://doi.org/10.1111/jopp.12149

Hiroaki Morio and Christopher Buchholz. 2009. How anonymous are you online? Examining online social behaviors from a cross-cultural perspective. *AI & Society.* 23, 2, 297–307. https://doi.org/10.1007/s00146-007-0143-0

Thi Thao Duyen T. Nguyen, Thomas Garncarz, Felicia Ng, Laura A. Dabbish, and Steven P. Dow. 2017. Fruitful Feedback: Positive Affective Language and Source Anonymity Improve Critique Reception and Work Outcomes. In *Proceedings of the 2017 ACM Conference on Computer Supported Cooperative Work and Social Computing*, ACM, Portland Oregon USA, 1024–1034. https://doi.org/10.1145/2998181.2998319

Malte Paskuda. 2016. *The influence of anonymity on participation in online communities.* Doctoral Dissertation. University of Technology of Troyes, Troyes, France.

Malte Paskuda and Myriam Lewkowicz. 2015. Anonymous Quorans are still Quorans, just anonymous. In *Proceedings of the 7th International Conference on Communities and Technologies - C&T '15*, ACM Press, Limerick, Ireland, 9–18. https://doi.org/10.1145/2768545.2768551

James W Pennebaker, Ryan L Boyd, Kayla Jordan, and Kate Blackburn. 2015. *The Development and Psychometric Properties of LIWC2015.* Austin, TX: University of Texas at Austin.

Emma Pierson. 2015. Outnumbered but Well-Spoken: Female Commenters in the New York Times. In *Proceedings of the 18th ACM Conference on Computer Supported Cooperative Work & Social Computing - CSCW '15*, ACM Press, Vancouver, BC, Canada, 1201–1213. https://doi.org/10.1145/2675133.2675134

Vincent Price, Lilach Nir, and Joseph N. Cappella. 2006. Normative and informational influences in online political discussions. *Communication. Theory* 16, 1, 47–74. https://doi.org/10.1111/j.1468-2885.2006.00005.x

Hua Qian and Craig R. Scott. 2007. Anonymity and Self-Disclosure on Weblogs. *Journal of Computer-Mediated Communication.* 12, 4, 1428–1451. https://doi.org/10.1111/j.1083-6101.2007.00380.x

Daniele Quercia, Jonathan Ellis, Licia Capra, and Jon Crowcroft. 2011. In the mood for being influential on Twitter. In *2011 IEEE Third International Conference on Privacy, Security, Risk and Trust and 2011 IEEE Third International Conference on Social Computing*, IEEE, Boston, MA, USA, 307–314.

Stephen A. Rains. 2007. The Impact of Anonymity on Perceptions of Source Credibility and Influence in Computer-Mediated Group Communication: A Test of Two Competing Hypotheses. *Communication Research.* 34, 1, 100–125. https://doi.org/10.1177/0093650206296084

Stephen A. Rains and Craig R. Scott. 2007. To Identify or Not to Identify: A Theoretical Model of Receiver Responses to Anonymous Communication. *Communication Theory* 17, 1, 61–91. https://doi.org/10.1111/j.1468-2885.2007.00288.x

Craig R. Scott, Stephen A. Rains, and Muge Haseki. 2011. Anonymous Communication Unmasking Findings Across Fields. *Annals of the International Communication Association.* 35, 1, 299–340. https://doi.org/10.1080/23808985.2011.11679120

Vivek K. Singh, Marie L. Radford, Qianjia Huang, and Susan Furrer. 2017. "They basically like destroyed the school one day": On Newer App Features and Cyberbullying in Schools. In *Proceedings of the 2017 ACM Conference on Computer Supported Cooperative Work and Social Computing*, ACM, Portland, Oregon, USA, 1210–1216. https://doi.org/10.1145/2998181.2998279

Chenhao Tan, Vlad Niculae, Cristian Danescu-Niculescu-Mizil, and Lillian Lee. 2016. Winning arguments: Interaction dynamics and persuasion strategies in good-faith online discussions. *Proceedings of the 25th International Conference on World Wide Web - WWW 16*, 613–624. https://doi.org/10.1145/2872427.2883081

Michail Tsikerdekis. 2013. The effects of perceived anonymity and anonymity states on conformity and groupthink in online communities: A Wikipedia study. *Journal of the American Society for Information Science and Technology.* 64, 5, 1001–1015. https://doi.org/10.1002/asi.22795

Wikipedia. n.d. Wikipedia: Why create an account? Retrieved online from https://en.wikipedia.org/wiki/Wikipedia:Why_create_an_account%3F

Lu Xiao. 2018. A message's persuasive features in Wikipedia's Article for Deletion discussions. In *Proceedings of the 9th International Conference on Social Media and Society - SMSociety '18*, ACM Press, Copenhagen, Denmark, 345–349. https://doi.org/10.1145/3217804.3217942

Lu Xiao and Taraneh Khazaei. 2019. Changing others' beliefs online: Online comments' persuasiveness. In *Proceedings of the 10th International Conference on Social Media and Society - SMSociety '19*, ACM Press, Toronto, ON, Canada, 92–101. https://doi.org/10.1145/3328529.3328549

Joel Young, Craig Martell, Pranav Anand, Pedro Ortiz, and Henry Tucker Gilbert IV. 2011. A Microtext Corpus for Persuasion Detection in Dialog. In *Workshops at the Twenty-Fifth AAAI Conference on Artificial Intelligence.*

Thomas Wagenknecht, Timm Teubner, and Christof Weinhardt. 2018. A Janus-faced matter—The role of user anonymity for communication persuasiveness in online discussions. *Information & Management* 55, 8, 1024–1037. https://doi.org/10.1016/j.im.2018.05.007

Uncertainty over Uncertainty: Investigating the Assumptions, Annotations, and Text Measurements of Economic Policy Uncertainty

Katherine A. Keith[*]
University of Massachusetts Amherst
`kkeith@@cs.umass.edu`

Christoph Teichmann
Bloomberg
`cteichmann1@bloomberg.net`

Brendan O'Connor
University of Massachusetts Amherst
`brenocon@@cs.umass.edu`

Edgar Meij
Bloomberg
`emeij@bloomberg.net`

Abstract

Methods and applications are inextricably linked in science, and in particular in the domain of text-as-data. In this paper, we examine one such text-as-data application, an established economic index that measures *economic policy uncertainty* from keyword occurrences in news. This index, which is shown to correlate with firm investment, employment, and excess market returns, has had substantive impact in both the private sector and academia. Yet, as we revisit and extend the original authors' annotations and text measurements we find interesting text-as-data methodological research questions: (1) Are annotator disagreements a reflection of ambiguity in language? (2) Do alternative text measurements correlate with one another and with measures of external predictive validity? We find for this application (1) some annotator disagreements of *economic policy uncertainty* can be attributed to ambiguity in language, and (2) switching measurements from keyword-matching to supervised machine learning classifiers results in low correlation, a concerning implication for the validity of the index.

1 Introduction

The relatively novel research domain of *text-as-data*, which uses computational methods to automatically analyze large collections of text, is a rapidly growing subfield of computational social science with applications in political science (Grimmer and Stewart, 2013), sociology (Evans and Aceves, 2016), and economics (Gentzkow et al., 2019). In economics, textual data such as news editorials (Tetlock, 2007), central bank communications (Lucca and Trebbi, 2009), financial earnings calls (Keith and Stent, 2019), company disclosures (Hoberg and Phillips, 2016), and newspa-

pers (Thorsrud, 2020) have recently been used as new, alternative data sources.

In one such economic text-as-data application, Baker et al. (2016) aim to construct an *economic policy uncertainty* (EPU) index whereby they quantify the aggregate level that policy is influencing economic uncertainty (see Table 1 for examples). They operationalize this as the proportion of newspaper articles that match keywords related to the economy, policy, and uncertainty.

The index has had impact both on the private sector and academia.[1] In the private sector, financial companies such as Bloomberg, Haver, FRED, and Reuters carry the index and sell financial professionals access to it. Academics show economic policy uncertainty has strong relationships with other economic indicators: Gulen and Ion (2016) find a negative relationship between the index and firm-level capital investment, and Brogaard and Detzel (2015) find that the index can positively forecast excess market returns.

The EPU index of Baker et al. has substantive impact and is a real-world demonstration of finding economic signal in textual data. Yet, as the subfield of text-as-data grows, so too does the need for rigorous methodological analysis of how well the chosen natural language processing methods operationalize the social science construct at hand. Thus, in this paper we seek to re-examine Baker et al.'s linguistic, annotation, and measurement assumptions. Regarding measurement, although keyword look-ups yield high-precision results and are interpretable, they can also be brittle and may suffer from low recall. Baker et al. did not explore alternative text measurements based on, for example, word embeddings or supervised machine learning classifiers.

---

[*]This work was done during an internship at Bloomberg.

[1]As of October 7, 2020, Google Scholar reports Baker et al. (2016) to have over 4400 citations.

Proceedings of the Fourth Workshop on Natural Language Processing and Computational Social Science, pages 116–131
Online, November 20, 2020. ©2020 Association for Computational Linguistics
https://doi.org/10.18653/v1/P17

No.	Example
1	Demand for new clothing is uncertain because several states may implement large hikes in their sales tax rates.
2	The outlook for the H1B visa program remains highly uncertain. As a result, some high-tech firms fear that shortages of qualified workers will cramp their expansion plans.
3	The looming political fight over whether to extend the Bush-era tax cuts makes it extremely difficult to forecast federal income tax collections in 2011.
4	Uncertainty about prospects for war in Iraq has encouraged a build-up of petroleum inventories and pushed oil prices higher.
5	Some economists claim that uncertainties due to government industrial policy in the 1930s prolonged and deepened the Great Depression.
6	It remains unclear whether the government will implement new incentives for small business hiring.

Table 1: Positive examples of *policy-related economic uncertainty*. We label spans of text as indicating policy, economy, uncertainty, or a causal relationship. Examples were selected from hand-labeled positive examples and the coding guide provided by Baker et al. (2016).

In exploring Baker et al.'s construction of EPU, we identify and disentangle multiple sources of uncertainty. First, there is the *real underlying uncertainty* about economic outcomes due to government policy that the index attempts to measure. Second, there is *semantic uncertainty* that can be expressed in the language of newspaper articles. Third, there is *annotator uncertainty* about whether a document should be labeled as EPU or not. Finally, there is *modeling uncertainty* in which text classifiers are uncertain about the decision boundary between positive and negative classes.

In this paper, we revisit and extend Baker et al.'s human annotation process (§3) and computational pipeline that obtains EPU measurement from text (§4). In doing so, we draw on concepts from quantitative social science's *measurement modeling*, mapping observable data to theoretical constructs, which emphasizes the importance of *validity* (is it right?) and *reliability* (can it be repeated?) (Loevinger, 1957; Messick, 1987; Quinn et al., 2010; Jacobs and Wallach, 2019).

Overall, this paper contributes the following:

- We examine the assumptions Baker et al. use to operationalize *economic policy uncertainty* via keyword-matching of newspaper articles. We demonstrate that using keywords collapses some rich linguistic phenomena such as *semantic uncertainty* (§2.1).

- We also examine the *causal* assumptions of Baker et al. through the lens of *structural causal models* (Pearl, 2009) and argue that readers' *perceptions* of economic policy uncertainty may be important to capture (§2.2).

- We conduct an annotation experiment by re-annotating documents from Baker et al.. We find

preliminary evidence that disagreements in annotation could be attributed to inherent ambiguity in the language that expresses EPU (§3).

- Finally, we replicate and extend Baker et al.'s data pipeline with numerous *measurement sensitivity* extensions: filtering to US-only news, keyword-matching versus supervised document classifiers, and prevalence estimation approaches. We demonstrate that a measure of *external predictive validity*, i.e., correlations with a stock-market volatility index (*VIX*), is particularly sensitive to these decisions (§4).

2 Assumptions of Measuring *Economic Policy Uncertainty* from News

The goal of Baker et al. (2016) is to measure the *theoretical construct* of *policy-related economic uncertainty* (EPU) for particular times and geographic regions. Baker et al. assume they can use information from newspaper articles as a *proxy* for EPU, an assumption we explore in great detail in Section 2.2, and they define EPU very broadly in their coding guidelines: "Is the article about policy-related aspects of economic uncertainty, even if only to a limited extent?"[2] For an article to be annotated as positive, there must be a stated causal link between *policy* and *economic consequences* and either the former or the latter must be *uncertain*.[3] Grounds for labeling a document as a positive include "uncertainty regarding the economic effects of policy actions" (or inactions), and "uncertainty

---

[2] `http://policyuncertainty.com/media/ Coding_Guide.pdf`

[3] "If the article discusses economic uncertainty in one part and policy in another part but never discusses policy in connection to economic uncertainty, then do not code it as about economic policy uncertainty."

	KeyOrg	KeyExp
Economy	economic, economy	+ growth, economies, financial, recession, slowdown
Uncertainty	uncertain, uncertainty	+ unclear, unsure, uncertainties, turmoil, confusion, worries
Policy	regulation, deficit, legislation, congress, white house, federal reserve, the fed, regulations, regulatory, deficits, congressional, legislative, legislature	

Table 2: Original keywords used in Baker et al.'s monthly United States index (KeyOrg). Expanded keywords include all words from KeyOrg plus the five nearest neighbors from pre-trained GloVe embeddings for the economy and uncertainty categories (KeyExp).

over who makes or will make policy decisions that have economic consequences." In Table 1, we provide examples of text spans that successfully encode EPU given these guidelines. For instance, the first example indicates that a government policy (increase in state sales tax) is causing uncertainty in the economy (demand for new clothing). Baker et al. *operationalize* this theoretical construct of EPU as keyword-matching of newspaper documents: for each document, if the document has at least one word in each of the economy, uncertainty, and policy keyword categories (see Table 2 in the Appendix) then it is considered a positive document. Counts of positive documents are summed and then normalized by the total number of documents published by each news outlet.

2.1 Semantic Uncertainty

While the keywords Baker et al. (2016) select ("uncertain" or "uncertainty") are the most overt ways to express uncertainty via language, they do not capture the full extent of how humans express uncertainty. For instance, Example No. 6 in Table 1 would be counted as a negative by Baker et al. despite indicating semantic uncertainty via the phrase "it remains unclear." These keyword assumptions are a threat to *content validity*, "the extent to which a measurement model captures everything we might want it to" (Jacobs and Wallach, 2019).

We look to definitions from linguistics to potentially expand the operationalization of uncertainty; we refer the reader to Szarvas et al. (2012) for all subsequent definitions and quotes. In particular, *uncertainty* is defined as a phenomenon that represents a lack of information. With respect to truth-conditional semantics, *semantic uncertainty* refers to propositions "for which no truth value can be attributed given the speaker's mental state." *Discourse-level uncertainty* indicates "the speaker intentionally omits some information

from the statement, making it vague, ambiguous, or misleading" and in the context of Baker et al. could result from journalists' linguistic choices to express ambiguity in economic policy uncertainty. For instance, in the first example in Table 3, the lexical cues "suggest" and "might" indicate to the reader that the journalist writing the article is unclear about the intention of Alan Greenspan. In contrast, *epistemic modality* "encodes how much certainty or evidence a speaker has for the proposition expressed by his utterance," (e.g., "Congresswoman X: 'We *may* delay passing the tariff bill.'") and *doxastic modality* refers to the beliefs of the speaker ("I *believe* that Congress will . . ."). In the second example in Table 3, the entity "he" seems to be uncertain about the fate of the economy because he "shakes his head in bewilderment," which demonstrates that uncertainty can also be conveyed through world knowledge and inference.

Collapsing all these types of *semantic uncertainty* to the keywords "uncertainty" and "uncertain" has major implications: (a) the relationship between the uncertainty journalists express and what readers infer impacts the causal assumptions (§2.2) and annotation decisions (§3) of this task, and (b) Baker et al.'s keywords are most likely low-recall which could affect empirical measurement results (§4). We see fruitful future work in improving *content validity* and recall via automatic uncertainty and modality analysis from natural language processing, e.g. McShane et al. (2004); Ganter and Strube (2009); Saurí and Pustejovsky (2009); Farkas et al. (2010); Szarvas et al. (2012).

2.2 Causal Assumptions

Using the paradigm of *structural causal models* (Pearl, 2009), we re-examine the causal assumptions of Baker et al.. In Figure 1, for a single timestep,[4] U^* represents the real, aggregate level of

---

[4]Baker et al. (2016) aggregate by day, month, quarter, or year.

Example	Docid
The stock market had soared on Mr. Greenspan's suggestion that global financial problems posed as great a threat to the United States as inflation did, **suggesting** that a rate cut to stimulate the economy **might be on the horizon**	1047100
But ask him whether the Mexican stock market will rise or plunge tomorrow and **he shakes his head in bewilderment.**	1043578

Table 3: Selected examples extracted from the New York Times Annotated Corpus (*NYT-AC*) that convey semantic uncertainty about the economy. Bolding is our own. Docids are from the *NYT-AC* metadata.

economic policy uncertainty in the world which is unobserved. If one could obtain a measurement of U^*, then one could analyze the causal relationship between U^* and other macroeconomic variables, M. Presumably, newspaper reporting, X, is affected by U^* and $x = f_X(u^*)$ where f_X is a non-parametric function that represents a causal process. In our setting, f_X represents the process of media production: for example, the ability of journalists to collect information from sources; or editorial decisions on what topics will be published. The major assumption of Baker et al. is that they can obtain a measure of U^* via a *proxy* measure from newspaper text, U, where $u = f_U(x)$. By simple composition, $u = f_U(f_X(u^*))$. Yet, aside from examining the political bias of media, Baker et al. largely ignore f_X and how the media production process could influence EPU measurements.

However, an alternative causal path from U^* to M goes through H^*, the macro-level human perception of real EPU. In this case, U^* is irrelevant as long as people are *perceiving* policy-related economic uncertainty to be changing, they could potentially make real economic decisions (e.g. hiring or purchases) that could affect the greater macro-economy, M.

It is unclear how to design a causal intervention in which one manipulates the real EPU, $do(U^*)$, in order to estimate its effect on X and M. However, one could design an ideal causal experiment to intervene on newspaper text, $do(X)$; one could artificially change the level of EPU coverage in synthetic articles, show these to participants, and measure the resulting difference in participants' economic decisions. If H^* to M is the causal path of interest,[5] then it is extremely important

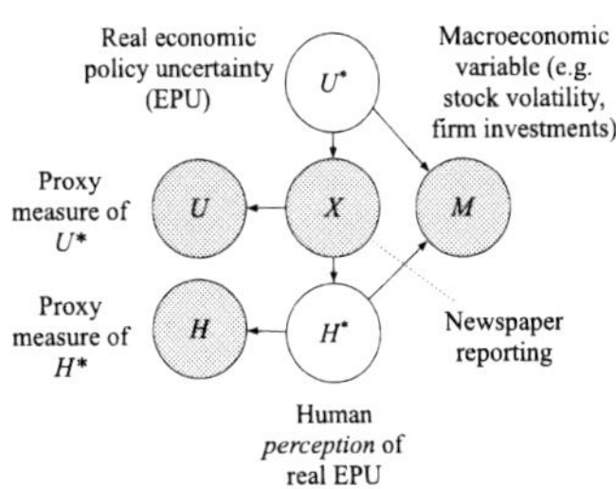

Figure 1: Structural causal model of the *economic policy uncertainty* measurements in which variables are nodes and directed edges denote causal dependence. Unlike Baker et al. (2016) who claim to measure U, we posit that measuring H is important. Shaded nodes are observed variables and unshaded nodes are latent.

to measure and model human *perception* of EPU, an assumption we explore in terms of annotation decisions in Section 3.

3 Annotator Uncertainty

Reliable human annotation is essential for both building supervised classifiers and assessing the internal validity of text-as-data methods. In order to validate their EPU index, Baker et al. sample documents from each month, obtain binary labels on the documents from annotators, and then construct a "human-generated" index which they report has a 0.86 correlation with their keyword-based index (aggregated quarterly). Yet, in our analysis of Baker et al.'s annotations (denoted below as *BBD*), we find only 16% of documents have more than one annotator and of these, the agreement rates are moderate: 0.80 pairwise agreement and 0.60 Krippendorff's α chance-adjusted agreement (Artstein and Poesio, 2008). See Line 2 of Table 4 for additional descriptive statistics of these annotations. The original authors did not address whether this disagreement is a result of annotator bias, error in annotations, or true ambiguity in the text.

In contrast to the popular paradigm that one should aim for high inner-annotator agreement rates (Krippendorff, 2018), recent research has shown "disagreement between annotators provides a useful signal for phenomena such as ambiguity in the text" (Dumitrache et al., 2018). Additionally, recent research in natural language processing

---

[5] There is some evidence from the original authors that human perception is important: In the EPU index released to the public, one of three underlying components is a disagreement of economic forecasters as a proxy for uncertainty. See `http://policyuncertainty.com/methodology.html`.

Subset	Ann. Source	Num. Docs	Num. Anns.	Prop. Pos. Anns.	Prop. Docs. Agr.	Pairwise Agree	Krip.-α
All	BBD	13797	16060	0.42	–	–	–
2+ Anns.	BBD	2150	4413	0.43	0.80	0.80	0.60
Sample A (Unan.)	BBD	19	41	0.29	1.00	1.00	1.00
	Ours	19	96	0.29	0.37	0.68	0.21
Sample B (Non-unan.)	BBD	18	40	0.50	0.00	0.07	-0.80
	Ours	18	97	0.54	0.28	0.65	0.27

Table 4: **Rows 1-2:** Descriptive statistics for *BBD*, Baker et al. (2016)'s annotated dataset, and the subset of these documents that have more than two annotations each (2+ Anns.). **Rows 3-6:** Sample A with *unanimous* (unan.) agreement in *BBD* labels and Sample B with *non-unanimous* (non-unan.) *BBD* labels. For these samples, we gather additional annotations. **Columns:** Annotation (ann.) source, number of documents (num. docs), number of annotations (num. anns.), proportion of positive annotations (prop. positive anns.), proportion of documents for which all annotator labels are in unanimous agreement (prop. docs. agr.), pairwise agreement in labels, and Krippendorff's α (Krip.-α).

Sample	PXA	Total pairs
A	0.70	206
B	0.50	218

Table 5: Pairwise cross-agreement (PXA) rates between *BBD* and our annotations.

(Paun et al., 2018; Pavlick and Kwiatkowski, 2019) and computer vision (Sharmanska et al., 2016) has leveraged annotator uncertainty to improve modeling. Thus, for our setting, we ask the following research question:

RQ1: Is there inherent ambiguity in the language that expresses *economic policy uncertainty*? If so, are annotator disagreements a reflection of this ambiguity?

The following evidence lends to our hypothesis that there *is* inherent ambiguity in whether documents encode EPU: (1) the original coding guide of Baker et al. had 17 pages of "hard calls" that describe difficult or ambiguous documents, (2) there was a moderate amount of annotator disagreement in *BBD* (Table 4), (3) we qualitatively analyze examples with disagreement and reason about what makes the inferences of these documents difficult (§3.2, and Tables 11 and 10 in the Appendix), and (4) we run an experiment in which we gather additional annotations and show that our annotations have more disagreement with documents that have non-unanimous labels in *BBD* (§3.1).

3.1 Our annotation experiment

The ideal assessment of inherent annotator uncertainty would be to gather a large number of annotations for many documents and then analyze the posterior distribution over labels.[6] We perform a similar, small-scale experiment in which we recruit 10 annotators, a mix of professional analysts and PhD students, who annotate 37 documents for a total of 193 annotations.[7] We sampled documents from the pool of *BBD* documents that had more than one annotator and the *BBD* labels were unanimous (Sample A) and non-unanimous (Sample B). We re-annotated these samples in order to provide insight into the nature of these unanimous and non-unanimous labels. See Figure 4 in the Appendix for our full annotation instructions.

Pairwise cross-agreement. In order to quantitatively compare two annotation rounds (ours vs. Baker et al.'s), we provide a new metric, *pairwise cross-agreement* (PXA). Formally, for each document of interest, $d \in \mathcal{D}$, let the $\mathcal{A}_d$ and $\mathcal{B}_d$ be the set of annotations on that document from each of the two rounds respectively. Let P_d be the set of all pairs, $(a \in \mathcal{A}_d, b \in \mathcal{B}_d)$ from combining one annotation from each of the two rounds. Then,

$$\text{PXA} = \frac{\sum_{d \in \mathcal{D}} \sum_{(a,b) \in P_d} \mathbb{1}(a = b)}{\sum_{d \in \mathcal{D}} |P_d|}. \quad (1)$$

Results. The results of our experiment (Tables 4 and 5) provide evidence supporting our hypothesis that there is inherent ambiguity in documents about EPU that contributes to annotator disagreement. In Table 5, PXA is higher in Sample A (0.70), in which *BBD* annotators had unanimous

---

[6]For instance, Pavlick and Kwiatkowski (2019) analyze disagreement in natural language inference by gathering 50 annotations per document and find the label distributions are often bi-modal, indicating meaningful disagreement.

[7]We originally sampled 40 documents but after annotation had to discard some that were duplicates or had errors from HTML extraction.

agreement, compared to Sample B (0.50) in which *BBD* annotators had non-unanimous labels. Since our annotations agreed with Sample A more, this could indicate these documents inherently have more agreement. The pairwise agreement between our annotations on Sample A and B are roughly the same (Table 4) but the proportion of documents that had unanimous agreement among our five annotators per document was slightly more in Sample A versus Sample B (0.37 vs. 0.28). Limitations of our experiment include that our sample size is relatively small and our annotation instructions are different and significantly shorter than Baker et al..

3.2 Qualitative Document Analysis

Our qualitative analysis suggests that readers' *perceptions* of EPU differ meaningfully and it is difficult to measure EPU with a simple document-level binary label. In Tables 10 and 11 in the Appendix, we present documents with the highest levels of agreement from Sample A and disagreement from Sample B. Annotators are likely to disagree on the label of the document when need real world knowledge to infer whether a policy is contributing to economic uncertainty. For instance, in Table 11 Example 1, the reader has to infer that the author of an op-ed would only write an op-ed about a policy if it was uncertain, but the uncertainty is never explicitly stated in text. In other instances, the causal link between policy and economic uncertainty is unclear. In Table 11 Example 4, economic downturn is mentioned as well as turnover in the administration but these are never explicitly linked; yet, some annotators may have read "questions about what lies ahead" as uncertainty that also encompasses economic uncertainty. Although there has been a rise of common sense reasoning research in natural language processing (e.g. Bhagavatula et al. (2020); Huang et al. (2019); Sap et al. (2019)), we suspect current state-of-the-art NLP systems would be unable to accurately resolve the inferences stated above. Furthermore, if there is inherent ambiguity in the language that expresses EPU, and, as we argue in Section 2.2, human perception is important, then we may desire to build models that can *identify* ambiguous documents and account for the uncertainty from ambiguity of language into measurement predictions, e.g. Paun et al. (2018). We leave this for future work.

Split	Model	Prec.	Recall	F1	Acc.
Train	KeyOrg	0.63	0.67	0.65	0.65
	LogReg-BOW	0.86	0.90	0.88	0.88
Test	KeyOrg	0.61	0.69	0.64	0.70
	LogReg-BOW	0.69	0.72	0.71	0.76

Table 6: Document-level classification statistics. Training is *BBD* documents 1985-2007 (N=1844) with annotations from a single annotator and testing is all *BBD* annotated documents 2007-2012 (N=687). For testing, the majority class is used and ties are randomly broken.

4 Measurement

For text-as-data applications, substantive results are contingent on how researchers operationalize measurement of the (latent) theoretical construct of interest via observed text data. Using Baker et al.'s original causal assumptions (Section 2.2), we formally define the *measurement* of interest as:

$$U = g(X), \qquad (2)$$

where g is the measurement function that maps text, X, to economic policy uncertainty, U.[8] For text-as-data practitioners, we emphasize that there is a "garden of forking paths" (Gelman and Loken, 2014) of how g can be operationalized, for instance, in the representation of text (bag-of-words vs. embeddings), document classification function (deterministic keyword matching vs. supervised machine learning classifiers), and ways of aggregating individual document predictions (mean of predictions vs. prevalence-aware aggregation).

RQ2: What happens when we change g to equally or more valid measurement functions? In particular, we are interested in *sensitivity*: for two measurements, g_1 and g_2, does U_1 correlate well with U_2; and *external predictive validity*: for each measurement, g_i, does U_i correlate well with the VIX, a stock-market volatility index based on S&P 500 options prices?

Baker et al. also use the VIX as a measure of external validity, and like Baker et al. we note that the VIX is a good proxy for *economic uncertainty*, but does not necessarily capture *policy* uncertainty. As Baker et al. mention, "differences in the topical scope between the VIX and the EPU index are an important source of distinct variation in the two measures." In the future, we could compare our

---

[8]Egami et al. (2018) call this g function the *codebook* function and describe how it can generically map text to any lower-dimensional representation.

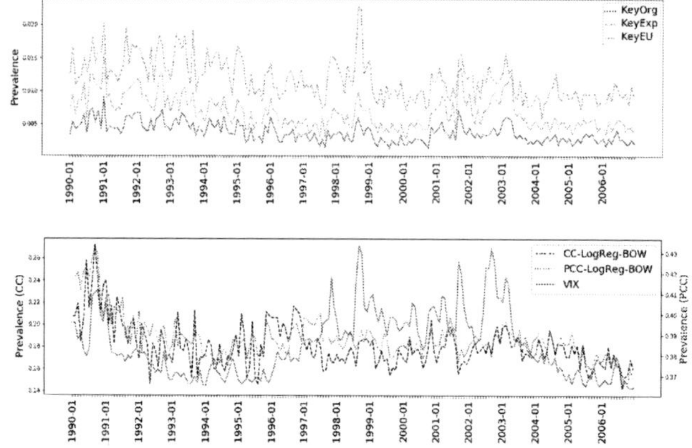
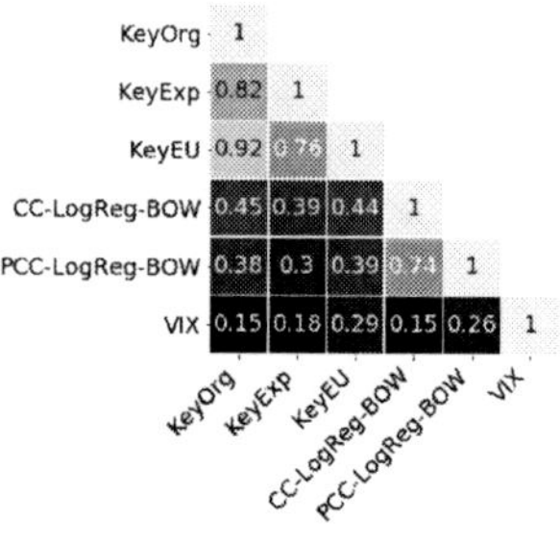

Figure 2: EPU Index, prevalence of documents exhibiting *economic policy uncertainty*, at inference time on the *NYT-AC* for all keyword methods (top) and document classifier methods (bottom) as well as the VIX. Note, for the bottom figure, the scale of the y-axis differs for CC versus PCC.

Figure 3: Pearson correlation between all text measurement models and the VIX.

measures to the other two external validity measures of Baker et al.: mentions of *uncertain* in the Federal Reserve's Beige Books and large daily moves in the S&P stock index.

Data and pre-processing. Although Baker et al. use 10 newspapers to construct their US-based index, we instead use the New York Times Annotated Corpus (*NYT-AC*) (Sandhaus, 2008) because the text data is cleaned, easily accessible, and results on the corpus are reproducible. This collection includes over 1.8 million articles written and published by the New York Times between January 1, 1987 and June 19, 2007. Baker et al. assume that using newspapers based in the United States is sufficient to find a signal of US-based EPU. To test this assumption, we apply a simple heuristic to the dateline of *NYT-AC* articles and remove articles that mention non-US cities. However, we find relatively little variation in results via this heuristic (see Appendix, Figure 7).

4.1 Keyword matching

Matching keyword lists, also known as *lexicons* or *dictionaries*, is a straightforward method to retrieve and/or classify documents of interest, and has the advantage of being interpretable. However, relying on a small set of keywords can create issues with recall and generalization. On *NYT-AC*, we apply the original keyword matching method of Baker et al. (2016) who label a document as positive if it matches any of 2 *economy* keywords, AND any of 2 *uncertainty* keywords, AND any of 13 *policy* keywords, (**KeyOrg**). We also compare a method with

the same economy and uncertainty matching criteria without *policy* keyword matching (**KeyEU**); and a method for which we expand the economic and uncertainty keywords via word embeddings (**KeyExp**). See Table 2 in the Appendix for the full list of keywords.

KeyExp. Although Baker et al. use human auditors to find *policy* keywords that minimize the false positive and false negative rates, they do not expand or optimize for *economy* or *uncertainty* keywords. Thus, we expand these keyword lists via GloVe word embeddings[9] (Pennington et al., 2014), and find the five nearest neighbors via cosine distance.[10] This is a simple keyword expansion technique. In future work, one could look to the literature on *lexicon induction* to improve creating lexicons that represent the semantic concepts of interest (Taboada et al., 2011; Pryzant et al., 2018; Hamilton et al., 2016; Rao and Ravichandran, 2009). Alternatively, one could also create a probabilistic classifier over pre-selected lexicons to soften the predictions, or use other uncertainty lexicons or even automatic uncertainty cue detectors.

4.2 Document classifiers

Probabilistic supervised machine learning classifiers are optimized to minimize the training loss

---

[9] We used the 200-dimensional, 6B token corpus from Wikipedia and Common Crawl `http://nlp.stanford.edu/data/glove.6B.zip`

[10] We manually remove clear obvious negative keywords: *policy* from the economic keyword bank and *prospects* and *remain* from the uncertainty keyword banks.

between the predicted and true classes, and typically have better precision and recall trade-offs compared to keyword matching methods. We use 1844 documents and labels from *BBD* from 1985-2007 as training data and 687 documents from 2007-2012 as a held-out test set. We train a simple logistic regression classifier using `sklearn`[11] (Pedregosa et al., 2011) with a bag-of-words representation of text (**LogReg-BOW**). We tokenize and prune the vocabulary to retain words that appear in at least 5 documents, resulting in a vocabulary size of 15,968. We tune the L2-penalty via five-fold cross-validation. We also try alternative (non-BOW) text representations but these did not result in improved performance (Appendix, § D). Note that the labeled documents in *BBD* are a biased sample as the authors select documents to annotate that match the *economy* and *uncertainty* keyword banks and do not select documents at random.

4.3 Prevalence estimation

Measuring economic policy uncertainty is an instance of *prevalence estimation*, the task of estimating the proportion of items in each given class. Previous work has shown that simple aggregation methods over individual class labels can be biased if there is a shift in the distribution from training to testing or if the task is difficult (Keith and O'Connor, 2018). We compare aggregating via **classify and count (CC)**, taking the mean over binary labels, and **probabilistic classify and count (PCC)**, taking the mean over classifiers' inferred probabilities. See the Appendix §D.3 for additional prevalence estimation experiments.

4.4 Results

Addressing RQ2, our experimental results show that changes in measurement can result in substantial differences in the corresponding index. Table 6 presents individual classification results on the training and test sets of *BBD*, and Figures 2 and 3 show inference of the models on *NYT-AC*. In Figure 2, we note that the overall prevalences are substantially different: KeyExp has higher prevalence than KeyOrg as expected with more keywords but the supervised methods infer prevalences near 0.2 (CC) and 0.4 (PCC) which indicates they may be biased towards the training prevalence. LogReg-BOW achieves both better individual classification predictive performance and combined with a probabilistic classify and count (PCC) prevalence esti-

	Pearson's r
KeyOrg-10 vs. KeyOrg-NYT	0.68
KeyOrg-10 vs. VIX	0.57
KeyOrg-NYT vs. VIX	0.15

Table 7: We use the official EPU index from Baker et al. which applies keyword-matching (KeyOrg) on newspapers from 10 major outlets (10). For the years 1990-2006, we correlate this index with the same keyword-matching method on only the New York Times Annotated Corpus (NYT) and with the VIX.

mation method achieves better correlation with the VIX (0.26 vs. KeyOrg's 0.15). The better predictive performance and correlation with VIX suggests PCC-LogReg-BOW represents a reasonable measurement of *economic policy uncertainty*. Given this, the low correlation between PCC-LogReg-BOW and KeyOrg (0.38) raises concerning questions about KeyOrg's validity.

4.5 Limitations

We use the *NYT-AC* as a "sandbox" for our experiments because of proprietary restrictions that limit us from acquiring the full text of all 10 news outlets used by Baker et al. To understand the limitations of using only a single news outlet, we compare the "official" aggregated index of Baker et al.[12] with KeyOrg applied to only the *NYT-AC*. Table 7 shows a 0.68 correlation between the official EPU index (KeyOrg-10) and the same keyword-matching method on only the NYT-AC (KeyOrg-NYT). Yet, KeyOrg-10 has a much higher correlation with the VIX, 0.57, compared to KeyOrg-NYT's correlation of 0.15. See Figure 8 in the Appendix for a graph of these different indexes. We hypothesize applying PCC-LogReg-BOW to the texts of the all 10 newspapers used by Baker et al. would result in improved external predictive validity, but we leave an empirical confirmation of this to future work. In practice, while keyword look-ups have lower recall than supervised methods they have the advantage of being interpretable and can use counts from document retrieval systems instead of full texts.

5 Related work

There have been only a few other attempts to construct alternative, non-keyword measurements of *economic policy uncertainty*. Azqueta-Gavaldón (2017) apply topic models and manually map the

---

[11]Version 0.22.1 `https://scikit-learn.org/`

[12]From "News_Based_Policy_Uncert_Index" column of `http://policyuncertainty.com/media/US_Policy_Uncertainty_Data.xlsx`

topics to Baker et al.'s EPU categories and find their method tightly correlates (0.94) with the original index. In an unpublished manuscript, Nyman and Ormerod (2020) expand the *uncertainty* keywords of Baker et al. via nearest neighbor embeddings and find Granger causality between their expanded keyword list and the original EPU index. In contrast, we are the first to take a fully supervised learning approach to measuring EPU and analyze the original annotations of Baker et al..

Measurement of economic variables from text. Other work has examined measuring economic variables from text data (see Gentzkow et al. (2019) for a survey). For example, topic models have been applied to central bank communications (Hansen et al., 2018) and newspaper articles (Thorsrud, 2020; Bybee et al., 2020) while other work identifies negated uncertainty markers (e.g. "there is *no* uncertainty") in the Federal Reserve's Beige Books (Saltzman and Yung, 2018) and extracts sentiment from central bank communications (Apel and Grimaldi, 2012). Boudoukh et al. (2019) use off-the-shelf supervised document classifiers to demonstrate that the information in news can predict stock prices.

Text-as-data methods. Traditional ways of analyzing textual data include *content analysis* where human annotators read and hand-code documents for particular phenomena (Krippendorff, 2018). In the last decade, many researchers have adapted machine learning and NLP methods to the needs of social scientists (Card, 2019; O'Connor et al., 2011). NLP technologies such as lexicons, topic models (Roberts et al., 2014; Blei et al., 2003), supervised classifiers, word embeddings (Mikolov et al., 2013; Pennington et al., 2014), and large-scale pre-trained language model representations (Devlin et al., 2019) have been applied to textual data to extract relevant signals. More recent work attempts to extend text-as-data methods to incorporate principles from causal inference (Pryzant et al., 2018; Wood-Doughty et al., 2018; Veitch et al., 2020; Roberts et al., 2020; Keith et al., 2020).

6 Future directions

In the future, estimating the sensitivity of causal estimates to the different measurement approaches presented in this paper could potentially have substantive impact. Using a Bayesian modeling approach to annotator uncertainty (Paun et al., 2018), investigating better calibration, which has been shown to improve prevalence estimation (Card and Smith, 2018), or estimating *model uncertainty* could improve measurement. One could also shift from document-level predictions of EPU to paragraph, sentence, or span-level predictions. Annotating discourse structure and selecting discourse fragments, e.g. Prasad et al. (2004), could potentially increase annotator agreement. These sub-document extraction models could also potentially provide human-interpretable contextualization of movements in an EPU index.

7 Conclusion

There is great promise for text-as-data methods and applications; however, we echo the cautionary advice of Grimmer and Stewart (2013) that automatic methods require extensive "problem-specific validation." Our paper's investigation of Baker et al. provides a number of general insights for text-as-data practioners along these lines. First, *content validity:* when dealing with text data, one needs to think carefully about the kinds of linguistic information one is trying to measure. For instance, mapping *economic policy uncertainty* to a document-level binary label collapses all types of semantic uncertainty, many of which cannot be identified via keywords alone. Second, one needs to examine *social perception* assumptions. Is one trying to *prescribe* an annotation schema, or, as we argue in this paper, are people's perceptions about the concept as important as the concept itself, especially in the face of ambiguity in language? Third, *sensitivity of measurements:* text-as-data practitioners can strengthen their substantive conclusions if multiple measurement approaches give similar results. For *economic policy uncertainty*, this paper demonstrates that switching from keywords to aggregating the outputs of a document classifier are not tightly correlated, a concerning implication for the validity of this index.

Acknowledgements

The authors thank Bloomberg's AI Engineering team, especially Diego Ceccarelli, Miles Osborne and Anju Kambadur, as well as Su Lin Blodgett for helpful feedback and directions. Additional thanks to the anonymous reviewers from the 2020 Natural Language Processing and Computational Social Science Workshop for their insights. Katherine Keith acknowledges support from Bloomberg's Data Science Ph.D. Fellowship.

References

Mikael Apel and Marianna Grimaldi. 2012. The information content of central bank minutes. *Riksbank Research Paper Series*.

Sanjeev Arora, Yingyu Liang, and Tengyu Ma. 2017. A simple but tough-to-beat baseline for sentence embeddings. In *ICLR*.

Ron Artstein and Massimo Poesio. 2008. Inter-coder agreement for computational linguistics. *Computational Linguistics*, 34(4):555–596.

Andrés Azqueta-Gavaldón. 2017. Developing news-based economic policy uncertainty index with unsupervised machine learning. *Economics Letters*, 158:47–50.

Scott R Baker, Nicholas Bloom, and Steven J Davis. 2016. Measuring economic policy uncertainty. *The Quarterly Journal of Economics*, 131(4):1593–1636.

Iz Beltagy, Matthew E Peters, and Arman Cohan. 2020. Longformer: The long-document transformer. *arXiv preprint arXiv:2004.05150*.

Chandra Bhagavatula, Ronan Le Bras, Chaitanya Malaviya, Keisuke Sakaguchi, Ari Holtzman, Hannah Rashkin, Doug Downey, Wen-tau Yih, and Yejin Choi. 2020. Abductive commonsense reasoning. In *ICLR*.

David M Blei, Andrew Y Ng, and Michael I Jordan. 2003. Latent dirichlet allocation. *Journal of machine Learning research*, 3(Jan):993–1022.

Jacob Boudoukh, Ronen Feldman, Shimon Kogan, and Matthew Richardson. 2019. Information, trading, and volatility: Evidence from firm-specific news. *The Review of Financial Studies*, 32(3):992–1033.

Jonathan Brogaard and Andrew Detzel. 2015. The asset-pricing implications of government economic policy uncertainty. *Management Science*, 61(1):3–18.

Leland Bybee, Bryan T Kelly, Asaf Manela, and Dacheng Xiu. 2020. The structure of economic news. Technical report, National Bureau of Economic Research.

Dallas Card. 2019. *Accelerating Text-as-Data Research in Computational Social Science*. Ph.D. thesis, Carnegie Mellon University.

Dallas Card and Noah A Smith. 2018. The importance of calibration for estimating proportions from annotations. In *Proceedings of the 2018 Conference of the North American Chapter of the Association for Computational Linguistics: Human Language Technologies, Volume 1 (Long Papers)*, pages 1636–1646.

Jacob Devlin, Ming-Wei Chang, Kenton Lee, and Kristina Toutanova. 2019. Bert: Pre-training of deep bidirectional transformers for language understanding. In *NAACL-HLT*.

Anca Dumitrache, Lora Aroyo, and Chris Welty. 2018. Crowdsourcing ground truth for medical relation extraction. *ACM Transactions on Interactive Intelligent Systems*, 8(2):1–20.

Naoki Egami, Christian J Fong, Justin Grimmer, Margaret E Roberts, and Brandon M Stewart. 2018. How to make causal inferences using texts. *arXiv preprint arXiv:1802.02163*.

James A Evans and Pedro Aceves. 2016. Machine translation: Mining text for social theory. *Annual Review of Sociology*, 42:21–50.

Richárd Farkas, Veronika Vincze, György Móra, János Csirik, and György Szarvas. 2010. The CoNLL-2010 shared task: learning to detect hedges and their scope in natural language text. In *Proceedings of the fourteenth conference on computational natural language learning–Shared task*, pages 1–12.

Viola Ganter and Michael Strube. 2009. Finding hedges by chasing weasels: Hedge detection using wikipedia tags and shallow linguistic features. In *Proceedings of the ACL-IJCNLP 2009 Conference Short Papers*, pages 173–176.

Andrew Gelman and Eric Loken. 2014. The statistical crisis in science: data-dependent analysis–a "garden of forking paths". *American scientist*, 102(6):460–466.

Matthew Gentzkow, Bryan Kelly, and Matt Taddy. 2019. Text as data. *Journal of Economic Literature*, 57(3):535–74.

Justin Grimmer and Brandon M Stewart. 2013. Text as data: The promise and pitfalls of automatic content analysis methods for political texts. *Political analysis*, 21(3):267–297.

Huseyin Gulen and Mihai Ion. 2016. Policy uncertainty and corporate investment. *The Review of Financial Studies*, 29(3):523–564.

William L Hamilton, Kevin Clark, Jure Leskovec, and Dan Jurafsky. 2016. Inducing domain-specific sentiment lexicons from unlabeled corpora. In *Proceedings of the Conference on Empirical Methods in Natural Language Processing. Conference on Empirical Methods in Natural Language Processing*, volume 2016, page 595. NIH Public Access.

Stephen Hansen, Michael McMahon, and Andrea Prat. 2018. Transparency and deliberation within the FOMC: a computational linguistics approach. *The Quarterly Journal of Economics*, 133(2):801–870.

Gerard Hoberg and Gordon Phillips. 2016. Text-based network industries and endogenous product differentiation. *Journal of Political Economy*, 124(5):1423–1465.

Lifu Huang, Ronan Le Bras, Chandra Bhagavatula, and Yejin Choi. 2019. Cosmos QA: Machine reading comprehension with contextual commonsense reasoning. In *Proceedings of the 2019 Conference on Empirical Methods in Natural Language Processing and the 9th International Joint Conference on Natural Language Processing (EMNLP-IJCNLP)*, pages 2391–2401.

Mohit Iyyer, Varun Manjunatha, Jordan Boyd-Graber, and Hal Daumé III. 2015. Deep unordered composition rivals syntactic methods for text classification. In *Proceedings of the 53rd annual meeting of the association for computational linguistics and the 7th international joint conference on natural language processing (volume 1: Long papers)*, pages 1681–1691.

Abigail Z Jacobs and Hanna Wallach. 2019. Measurement and fairness. *arXiv preprint arXiv:1912.05511*.

Katherine Keith, David Jensen, and Brendan O'Connor. 2020. Text and Causal Inference: A review of using text to remove confounding from causal estimates. In *Proceedings of the 58th Annual Meeting of the Association for Computational Linguistics*, Online. Association for Computational Linguistics.

Katherine Keith and Brendan O'Connor. 2018. Uncertainty-aware generative models for inferring document class prevalence. In *Proceedings of the 2018 Conference on Empirical Methods in Natural Language Processing*, pages 4575–4585.

Katherine Keith and Amanda Stent. 2019. Modeling financial analysts' decision making via the pragmatics and semantics of earnings calls. In *Proceedings of the 57th Annual Meeting of the Association for Computational Linguistics*, pages 493–503.

Klaus Krippendorff. 2018. *Content analysis: An introduction to its methodology*. Sage publications.

Yinhan Liu, Myle Ott, Naman Goyal, Jingfei Du, Mandar Joshi, Danqi Chen, Omer Levy, Mike Lewis, Luke Zettlemoyer, and Veselin Stoyanov. 2019. Roberta: A robustly optimized BERT pretraining approach. *arXiv preprint arXiv:1907.11692*.

Jane Loevinger. 1957. Objective tests as instruments of psychological theory. *Psychological reports*, 3(3):635–694.

David O Lucca and Francesco Trebbi. 2009. Measuring central bank communication: an automated approach with application to fomc statements. Technical report, National Bureau of Economic Research.

Marjorie McShane, Sergei Nirenburg, and Ron Zacharski. 2004. Mood and modality: out of theory and into the fray. *Natural Language Engineering*, 10(1):57–89.

Samuel Messick. 1987. Validity. *ETS Research Report Series*, 1987(2):i–208.

Tomas Mikolov, Ilya Sutskever, Kai Chen, Greg S Corrado, and Jeff Dean. 2013. Distributed representations of words and phrases and their compositionality. In *Advances in neural information processing systems*, pages 3111–3119.

Rickard Nyman and Paul Ormerod. 2020. Text as data: a machine learning-based approach to measuring uncertainty. *arXiv preprint arXiv:2006.06457*.

Brendan O'Connor, David Bamman, and Noah A Smith. 2011. Computational text analysis for social science: Model assumptions and complexity. In *Second Workshop on Comptuational Social Science and the Wisdom of Crowds (NIPS 2011)*.

Silviu Paun, Bob Carpenter, Jon Chamberlain, Dirk Hovy, Udo Kruschwitz, and Massimo Poesio. 2018. Comparing Bayesian models of annotation. *Transactions of the Association for Computational Linguistics*, 6:571–585.

Ellie Pavlick and Tom Kwiatkowski. 2019. Inherent disagreements in human textual inferences. *Transactions of the Association for Computational Linguistics*, 7:677–694.

Judea Pearl. 2009. *Causality*. Cambridge university press.

Fabian Pedregosa, Gaël Varoquaux, Alexandre Gramfort, Vincent Michel, Bertrand Thirion, Olivier Grisel, Mathieu Blondel, Peter Prettenhofer, Ron Weiss, Vincent Dubourg, et al. 2011. Scikit-learn: Machine learning in python. *the Journal of machine Learning research*, 12:2825–2830.

Jeffrey Pennington, Richard Socher, and Christopher D Manning. 2014. Glove: Global vectors for word representation. In *Proceedings of the 2014 conference on empirical methods in natural language processing (EMNLP)*, pages 1532–1543.

Rashmi Prasad, Eleni Miltsakaki, Aravind Joshi, and Bonnie Webber. 2004. Annotation and Data Mining of the Penn Discourse Treebank. In *In Proceedings of the ACL Workshop on Discourse Annotation*.

Reid Pryzant, Kelly Shen, Dan Jurafsky, and Stefan Wagner. 2018. Deconfounded lexicon induction for interpretable social science. In *Proceedings of the 2018 Conference of the North American Chapter of the Association for Computational Linguistics: Human Language Technologies, Volume 1 (Long Papers)*, pages 1615–1625.

Kevin M Quinn, Burt L Monroe, Michael Colaresi, Michael H Crespin, and Dragomir R Radev. 2010. How to analyze political attention with minimal assumptions and costs. *American Journal of Political Science*, 54(1):209–228.

Delip Rao and Deepak Ravichandran. 2009. Semi-supervised polarity lexicon induction. In *Proceedings of the 12th Conference of the European Chapter of the ACL (EACL 2009)*, pages 675–682.

Margaret E. Roberts, Brandon M. Stewart, and Richard A. Nielsen. 2020. Adjusting for confounding with text matching. *American Journal of Political Science*.

Margaret E Roberts, Brandon M Stewart, Dustin Tingley, Christopher Lucas, Jetson Leder-Luis, Shana Kushner Gadarian, Bethany Albertson, and David G Rand. 2014. Structural topic models for open-ended survey responses. *American Journal of Political Science*, 58(4):1064–1082.

Bennett Saltzman and Julieta Yung. 2018. A machine learning approach to identifying different types of uncertainty. *Economics Letters*, 171:58–62.

Evan Sandhaus. 2008. The new york times annotated corpus. *Linguistic Data Consortium, Philadelphia*, 6(12):e26752.

Maarten Sap, Hannah Rashkin, Derek Chen, Ronan LeBras, and Yejin Choi. 2019. SocialIQA: Commonsense reasoning about social interactions. *EMNLP*.

Roser Saurí and James Pustejovsky. 2009. Factbank: a corpus annotated with event factuality. *Language resources and evaluation*, 43(3):227.

Viktoriia Sharmanska, Daniel Hernández-Lobato, Jose Miguel Hernandez-Lobato, and Novi Quadrianto. 2016. Ambiguity helps: Classification with disagreements in crowdsourced annotations. In *Proceedings of the IEEE Conference on Computer Vision and Pattern Recognition*, pages 2194–2202.

György Szarvas, Veronika Vincze, Richárd Farkas, György Móra, and Iryna Gurevych. 2012. Cross-genre and cross-domain detection of semantic uncertainty. *Computational Linguistics*, 38(2):335–367.

Maite Taboada, Julian Brooke, Milan Tofiloski, Kimberly Voll, and Manfred Stede. 2011. Lexicon-based methods for sentiment analysis. *Computational linguistics*, 37(2):267–307.

Paul C Tetlock. 2007. Giving content to investor sentiment: The role of media in the stock market. *The Journal of finance*, 62(3):1139–1168.

Leif Anders Thorsrud. 2020. Words are the new numbers: A newsy coincident index of the business cycle. *Journal of Business & Economic Statistics*, 38(2):393–409.

Victor Veitch, Dhanya Sridhar, and David Blei. 2020. Adapting text embeddings for causal inference. In *Conference on Uncertainty in Artificial Intelligence*, pages 919–928. PMLR.

Zach Wood-Doughty, Ilya Shpitser, and Mark Dredze. 2018. Challenges of using text classifiers for causal inference. In *Proceedings of the Conference on Empirical Methods in Natural Language Processing. Conference on Empirical Methods in Natural Language Processing*, volume 2018, page 4586. NIH Public Access.

Appendix

A Datasets

Here we provide more information on the data used in annotation and measurement experiments.

- *BBD.* From Baker et al. (2016), we combine the authors' annotations with the full text data they provided.[13] These documents and annotations are sampled from ten major newspapers in the United States.[14] We also study and refer to their *Code Guide* when analyzing examples for this paper.[15] See Lines 1-2 of Table 4 for descriptive statistics of this dataset.

- *NYT-AC.* We use the *New York Times Annotated Corpus* as a sandbox for our experiments (Sandhaus, 2008).[16] This corpus includes over 1.8 million articles written and published by the New York Times between January 1, 1987 and June 19, 2007.

- *VIX.* The VIX is an index of market expectations of the next 30 days' U.S. stock market volatility, derived from S&P 500 options prices. Like Baker et al., we take a monthly average over the daily VIX measures, obtained from a standard proprietary database.

B Annotation notes

We provide additional descriptive statistics of Baker et al. (2016)'s original annotations in Tables 8 and 9. The annotation instructions for our experiment (§3.1) are provided in Figure 4. In our annotation experiment, the mean annotator confidence levels are 3.81 for Sample A and 3.85 for Sample B.

C Qualitative examples

Figures 10 and 11 provide examples with high annotator agreement and disgreement respectively.

---

[13] http://policyuncertainty.com/AUDIT_ANALYSIS.zip and http://policyuncertainty.com/media/All%20Audit%20Hard%20Copies.rar

[14] LA Times, USA Today, Chicago Tribune, Washington Post, Boston Globe, Wall Street Journal, New York Times, Miami Herald, Dallas Morning News, San Francisco Chronicle

[15] http://policyuncertainty.com/media/Coding_Guide.pdf

[16] https://catalog.ldc.upenn.edu/LDC2008T19

Annotator	Mean pos.	Std	N
A	0.300	0.46	50
B	0.619	0.49	278
C	0.431	0.50	297
D	0.445	0.50	449
E	0.551	0.50	472
F	0.330	0.47	790
G	0.402	0.49	1168
H	0.389	0.49	1185
I	0.350	0.48	1265
J	0.398	0.49	1443
K	0.455	0.50	1606
L	0.397	0.49	1740
M	0.405	0.49	2320
N	0.443	0.50	2997

Table 8: Descriptive statistics for the original annotations of Baker et al. (2016). Annotator names have been anonymized to letters. For each annotator, we report the mean number of positive annotations (mean pos.), the standard deviation of positive annotations (std), and the total number of annotations by that annotator (N).

Num. Annotators	Num. Docs
1	11647
2	2053
3	83
4	12
5	2

Table 9: For Baker et al.'s original dataset, the number of documents that have a particular number of annotators. Here, 16% of documents have only a single annotator.

D Measurement: Additional Experiments

In this section, we provide additional measurement experiments. Also note there is a very small overlap between our training time documents and inference time NYT-AC documents. There are 375 documents at training time from NYT between the years of 1990 and 2006. However, the total number of inference documents is 1,501,131 so this is less than 0.025% of documents.

D.1 Filtering to US-Only News

Initial qualitative analysis reveals that many documents, and in particular articles with high annotator disagreement, are focused on events outside the

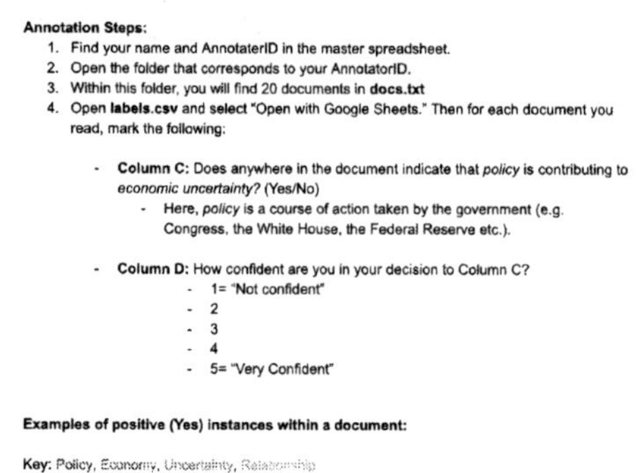

Figure 4: Annotation instructions for our experiment.

United States. An unstated assumption of Baker et al. (2016) is that US-based news sources will primarily report US-based news and thus US-based economic policy uncertainty. We test this assumption empirically.

To remove non-US news, we use a simple heuristic that gives almost perfect precision. *NYT-AC* has metadata about the dateline of an article, for example "KUWAIT, Sunday, March 30," "SAN ANTONIO, March 29," or "BAGHDAD, Iraq, March 29." We (1) use the *GeoNames* Gazateer[17] and filter to cities that have greater than 15,000 inhabitants;[18] (2) separate these city names into US and non-US cities such that ties go to US. For example, *Athens* would not be removed because the town of Athens, Georgia is in the United State; (3) write a rule-based text parser that extracts the span of text that is in all capitals, (4) if the city name is in non-US cities, we discard the document.

Per month, on average, we remove 449 documents that were about non-US news. See Figure 6 for a comparison of all NYT articles, articles with the dateline, and US-only articles based on our heuristic.

Figure 7 displays correlation results for all models with the US-Only document filter. Applying the US-Only filter only slightly improves correlation of all models with the VIX (0.01-0.04 correlation). From these results, it seems that Baker et al.'s assumption is valid. However, we also acknowledge that our heuristic is high-precision, low recall and

---

[17] http://www.geonames.org/
[18] https://datahub.io/core/world-cities

	Example selection	Our analysis	Label Mean, Docid
1	…Several recent news reports have questioned the stamina of Wells Fargo's real estate portfolio in the event of a recession that extends to California. The analysis had driven the bank's stock sharply down. ….	Stock market newsletter digest. Economics policy is not mentioned as uncertain	0.0, MIHB_11_1990_8
2	…Just eight days before the threatened imposition of punitive U.S. tariffs on Japanese luxury cars, Japanese automakers are signaling a strong desire to compromise with Washington in the bitter dispute over automotive trade. …	Report on international trade dispute. "threatened" directly expresses uncertainty, "tariffs" are economic policy	0.8, DMNB_6_1995_8

Table 10: Hand-selected examples with strong annotator agreement. Docids correspond to those provided in Baker et al. (2016)'s dataset. Label mean is the mean over our experiment's five annotations per document.

	Example selection	Our analysis	Label Mean, Docid
1	…I am a true believer that mobile broadband will help my company and hundreds of other businesses in South Florida work more efficiently, better serve consumers and hire more employees. On a related matter, policymakers in Washington, D.C. are making decisions on whether to allow AT&T to pay approximately $39 billion for its wireless rival T-Mobile. This is a deal of vital importance to our community ….	An op-ed arguing that a merger should be allowed to go forward. Arguing for a certain outcome implies uncertainty of the outcome, but uncertainty is never explicitly stated.	0.4, MIHB_5_2011_3
2	…angst over rising interest rates triggered a nasty sell-off in the stock market Friday …The markets also fret that the Federal Reserve Board will move to curb that inflation threat …	Reports on downturn in stock market. Annotators must decide: is there uncertainty about FED actions or strong expectation of disfavoured actions.	0.4, LA_8_1997_9
3	…If Cuba's fledgling recovery is to continue, Mr. Castro must legalize small- and medium-sized businesses, boost wages and gradually introduce free markets, U.S. officials say. …Cuban officials have a very different view and blame the long-time U.S. ban on trade with the island for much of their economic woes….	Reports on state of affairs in Cuba. States assumption that US or Cuban policy will eventually lead to economic problems. Uncertainty is only implied and no concrete policies are mentioned	0.6, DMNB_12_1999_2
4	…Two military coups and several attempts, race riots and poverty have made the Kingdom in the Sky a place of turmoil in the past years. Economic problems and the repeal of apartheid in South Africa, Lesotho's overpowering neighbor on all sides, raise even more questions about what lies ahead. Sympathetic foreign powers have donated millions to Lesotho. …	Describes situation in Lesotho. Mentions economic downturn, large turnover in administrations and race riots. Not stated that turnover/riots lead to uncertainty over economic policy, but could be reasonably inferred as part reason for downturn.	0.4, MIHB_7_1991_15

Table 11: Hand-selected examples with strong annotator disagreement. Docids correspond to those provided in Baker et al. (2016)'s dataset. Label mean is the mean over our experiment's five annotations per document.

in the future, one could possibly use a country-level document classifier instead.

D.2 Predicting after EU filter

As we acknowledge in the main text, the training set is biased because documents were sampled only if they matched the *economy* and *uncertainty* keyword banks. To make a fair comparison at inference time, we looked at the predictions of our document classifiers on the subset of documents in *NYT-AC* that also matched these *economy* and *uncertainty* keyword banks (KeyEU). In Figure 5, we see that the subset of these models had lower correlation with the VIX.

Split	Model	Prec.	Recall	F1	Acc.
Train	LogReg-BERT	0.79	0.77	0.78	0.79
Test	LogReg-BERT	0.61	0.59	0.60	0.68

Table 12: Performance results on the training and test sets for the *LongFormer* representation with logistic regression (LogReg-BERT). The results in this table are comparable to Table 6.

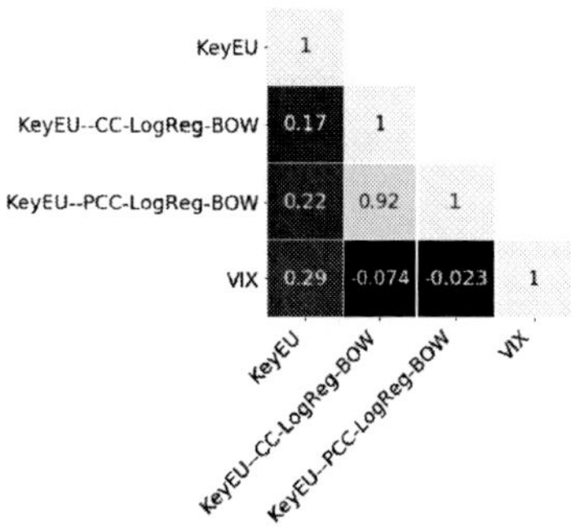

Figure 5: Estimate PCC and CC only within the set of documents that pass the EU filter.

D.3 Additional prevalence estimation experiments

As an alternative to classify and count (CC) and probabilistic classify and count (PCC) prevalence estimation methods, we also experiment with the *Implicit Likelihood (ImpLik)* prevalence estimation method of Keith and O'Connor (2018). This method gives the predictions of a discriminative classifier a generative re-interpretation and backs out an implicit individual-level likelihood function which can take into account bias in the training prevalence. We use the authors' `freq-e` software package.[19] Figure 7 shows a high correlation between *ImpLik* and *PCC*, 0.83 correlation; however, *ImpLik* had much lower correlation with the VIX (0.1). Note, the mean prevalences from *ImpLik* are much lower than PCC or CC with a mean monthly prevalence across 1990-2006 of 0.02. Thus, the method seems to be correcting for a more realistic prevalence but the true prevalence values may be too low to pick-up relevant signal via this method.

D.4 BERT representations

Finally, we acknowledge that a bag-of-words representation in the document classifier is dissatisfying to capture long-range semantic dependencies and the contextual nature of language that has motivated recent research in contextual, distributed representations of text. Thus, we use the frozen representations of a large, pre-trained language model that has been optimized for long documents, the *LongFormer* (Beltagy et al., 2020). This is a model that optimizes a RoBERTa model (Liu et al., 2019) for long documents. We use the `huggingface` implementation of the Long-Former[20] and use the 768-dimensional "pooled output"[21] as our document representation. We then use the same `sklearn` logistic regression training as the BOW models.

Comparing Table 12 to Table 6, we see that this representation has decreased performance compared to LogReg-BOW. We speculate that this decrease in performance may originate in having to truncate documents to 4096 tokens due to the constraints of the model architecture. With more computational resources, we would fine-tune the pre-trained weights instead of leaving them frozen. Future work could also consider obtaining alternative representations of text via weighted averaging of embeddings (Arora et al., 2017), deep averaging networks (Iyyer et al., 2015), or pooling BERT embeddings of all paragraphs in a document.

___

[19]`https://github.com/slanglab/freq-e`. For the label prior we used the training prevalence of 0.48.

[20]`https://huggingface.co/transformers/model_doc/longformer.html`

[21]This is the hidden state of the last layer of the first token of the sequence which is then passed through a linear layer and Tanh activation function. The linear layer weights are trained from the next sentence prediction objective during pre-training.

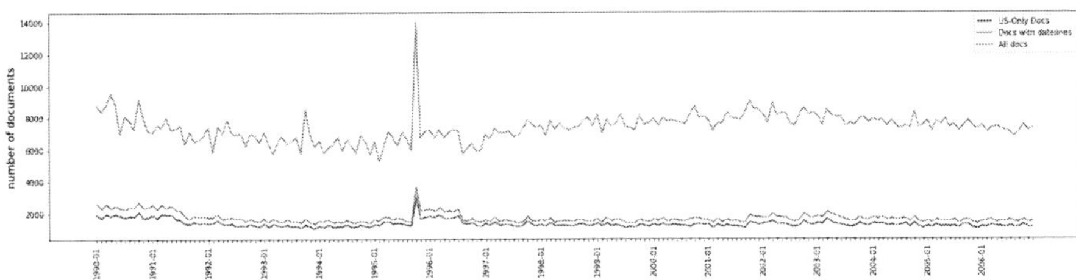

Figure 6: NYT total documents (red), documents with datelines (green) and documents for which the dateline does not have a non-US city (blue). We checked and confirmed and the spike in 1995-10 is an artifact of the corpus.

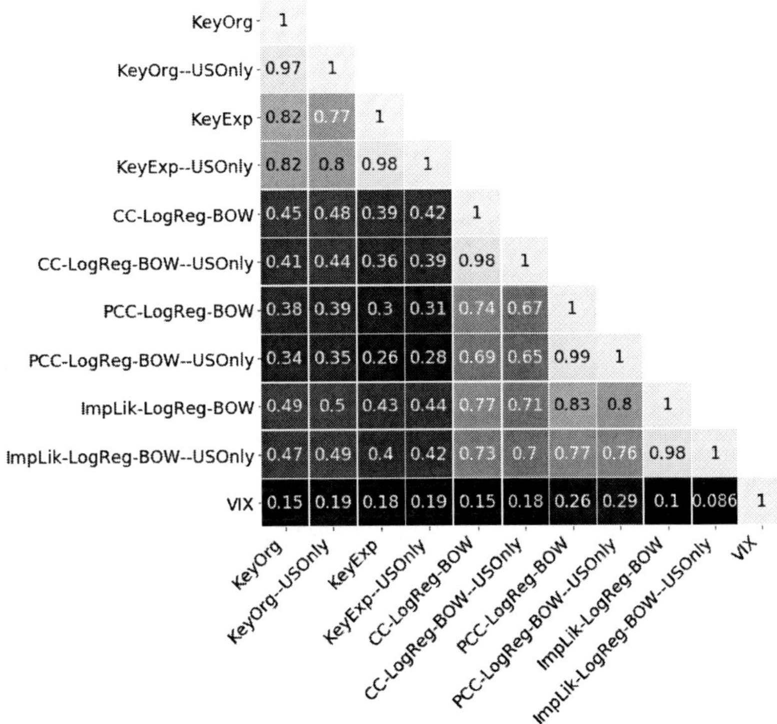

Figure 7: Correlations between all models. The addition of *–USOnly* to a model name means we apply the model only on the subset of documents that have passed our USOnly heuristic. *ImpLik* is the implicit likeihood prevalence estimation method of Keith and O'Connor (2018).

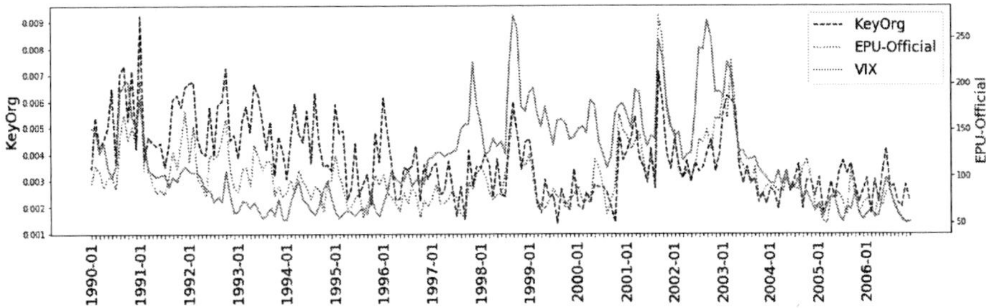

Figure 8: Official EPU versus the original keywords on the *NYT-AC* (KeyOrg).

131

Recalibrating classifiers for interpretable abusive content detection

Bertie Vidgen
The Alan Turing Institute

Sam Staton
University of Oxford

Scott A. Hale
University of Oxford

Ohad Kammar
University of Edinburgh

Helen Margetts
The Alan Turing Institute

Tom Melham
University of Oxford

Marcin Szymczak
RWTH Aachen University

Abstract

We investigate the use of machine learning classifiers for detecting online abuse in empirical research. We show that uncalibrated classifiers (i.e. where the 'raw' scores are used) align poorly with human evaluations. This limits their use for understanding the dynamics, patterns and prevalence of online abuse. We examine two widely used classifiers (created by Perspective and Davidson et al.) on a dataset of tweets directed against candidates in the UK's 2017 general election. A Bayesian approach is presented to recalibrate the raw scores from the classifiers, using probabilistic programming and newly annotated data. We argue that interpretability evaluation and recalibration is integral to the application of abusive content classifiers.

1 Introduction

Computational tools for automatically detecting and categorizing abusive online content are now widely used for content moderation, to enforce and monitor regulatory and legal standards, and to study the dynamics of online abuse (Williams, 2019; Vidgen et al., 2019; Fortuna and Nunes, 2018). These tools enable abusive content to be assessed quantitatively, scalably and efficiently.

Recent research has drawn attention to several biases with existing classifiers and the datasets they are trained on, such as racial biases (Davidson and Weber, 2019; Sap et al., 2019), and evidence that they may be more attuned to detecting abuse against certain targets than others (Garg et al., 2019). Other research shows that existing tools can be fooled by 'obfuscatory' content, in which small changes are made so that the abuse is 'masked', even though it is clearly discernible to humans (e.g. changing 'niggas' to 'n!gg@z') (Gröndahl et al., 2018). Equally, many classifiers struggle with contextual statements, irony, humour and con-

tent that is non-abusive but 'incivil' (Vidgen and Derczynski, 2020).

Evaluating the explainability of classification systems for online abuse detection has become an important focus of research (Aluru et al., 2020; Wang, 2018; Švec et al., 2018). Explainable classifications can help to ensure systems are accountable, social biases are identified and addressed, and that model performance and generalisability is improved (Wachter et al., 2017; Biran and Cotton, 2017; Doran et al., 2018). In practice, explainability often requires statistical modelling to uncover the complex interactions between different input features that led to a result (Ribeiro et al., 2016). It may even require complete rethinking of how classifiers are developed, given the difficulties of post-hoc rationalisation and the potential for poor explanations to confuse end users (Rudin, 2018).

A related but previously under-researched problem in abuse classification is whether the scores returned by classifiers meaningfully encode differences in the likelihood that content is abusive. This issue can be seen as a problem of *interpretation*. In contrast with explainability this does not involve showing *why* a particular classification is given but, rather, ensuring that the classification itself is presented in understandable terms (Gilpin et al., 2019; Narayanan et al., 2018). To our knowledge only one piece of research has investigated this problem. The Perspective team at Jigsaw calibrated the scores of their toxicity classifier using isotonic regression (PerspectiveScoreNorm). The full details of the method are not published, but we understand that this calibration is primarily intended to ensure that, even as the production models are updated, the threshold of 0.8 remains a useful cutoff which for content moderation.

Ensuring that the scores from abusive content classifiers are interpretable would pose several benefits. First, the actual probabilities returned by

Proceedings of the Fourth Workshop on Natural Language Processing and Computational Social Science, pages 132–138
Online, November 20, 2020. ©2020 Association for Computational Linguistics
https://doi.org/10.18653/v1/P17

models can be used for empirical analyses, reducing the information lost from only using a categorical label decided by a threshold. This is crucial in cases where a lot of content lies near the cutoff, and is the primary motivation behind this work. Second, well-calibrated scores could help host platforms to curate and filter content. For instance, companies may only want their adverts near content that has a 99.99% chance of *not* being hateful. Well-calibrated models could be used to ensure this. Third, users who want to understand why their content has been taken down (or not) may want to review the scores. If they are poorly calibrated it could generate distrust and confusion.

We investigate the use of machine learning classifiers for detecting and analysing online abuse in empirical research. We present three contributions. First, we show that the scores from uncalibrated abusive content classifiers align poorly with human evaluations. Second, we present a method for recalibration which uses probabilistic programming, which also gives an indication of the confidence in the recalibration. Third, we show that not using a calibrated classifier can severely impact empirical analysis through a case study of abuse directed against MPs in the 2017 general election. All of our code and data is made available for other researchers to use.[1]

2   Research design

We evaluate the toxicity classifier from Perspective and the hate speech classifier provided by Davidson et al. (Davidson et al., 2017). Both classifiers, and the datasets they were trained on, have been extensively researched in machine learning and computational social sciences (e.g. Sap et al., 2019; Gröndahl et al., 2018; Davidson and Weber, 2019) and the Perspective classifier is widely used for content moderation. Better understanding of their limitations and flaws will help to inform responsible use of them , and support development of better systems in the future. To examine the classifiers, we study tweets directed at candidates on Twitter in the run up to the 2017 UK general election. We collected all mentions and replies to the 2,620 candidates from 16 May to 8 June 2017, creating a dataset of 8.93 million tweets. We apply both classifiers to the dataset, from which we construct two samples to be annotated.

2.1   Annotation of tweets for recalibration

Sample 1 contains 1,000 tweets, sampled uniformly from the probability distribution for the Perspective classifier scores (i.e. with 50 tweets from each 0.05 increment). Sample 2 contains 1,000 tweets, sampled uniformly from the probability distribution for the Davidson et al. classifier scores, also with 50 tweets from each 0.05 increment. The 1,000 tweets in each sample were given to annotators with the definitions of toxicity and hate provided by the original authors.

Annotators were not given the classifier scores, tweets were presented in random order, and they were not told the distribution of scores. Each sample was annotated by 5 different independent annotators (i.e. 10 in total). Annotators had all taken part in at least 6 weeks of hateful content annotation as part of other projects, and received 2 additional weeks of training and underwent regular discussion/training sessions. Annotators were all fluent in English (8 out of 10 were native speakers). They were equally split between male and female genders, all aged between 18 and 30, university educated and from a range of European countries.

Annotators differ in their perception of toxicity and hate. For Sample 1, the number of toxic tweets identified by annotators ranges from 12 to 103 and the inter-rater reliability, as measured by Fleiss' Kappa, is 0.37. For Sample 2, the number of hateful tweets identified by annotators ranges from 68 to 243 and the inter-rater reliability is 0.46. These low to moderate levels of agreement are in line with other annotation studies of abusive content, reflecting the difficulty of such tasks (Vidgen et al., 2019). They also reflect the relatively short guidelines provided by the creators of the Davidson classifier (Davidson et al., 2017) and the fact that for the Perspective classifier we had only the definition of toxicity: "a rude, disrespectful, or unreasonable comment that is likely to make you leave a discussion."[2] This gives considerable scope for annotators' interpretation of the content to differ.[3]

Figure 1a shows the receiver operating characteristic curves for the classifiers from Perspective and Davidson et al. over our annotated 1,000 tweet samples. The label for each tweet is decided by taking the majority vote across the 5 annotators. The AUC is 0.899 for Perspective and 0.745 for Davidson.

---

[1]See: https://zenodo.org/record/4075461#.X4Cc9i2ZOu4

[2]https://www.perspectiveapi.com/#/home
[3]See our online appendix for full annotation instructions.

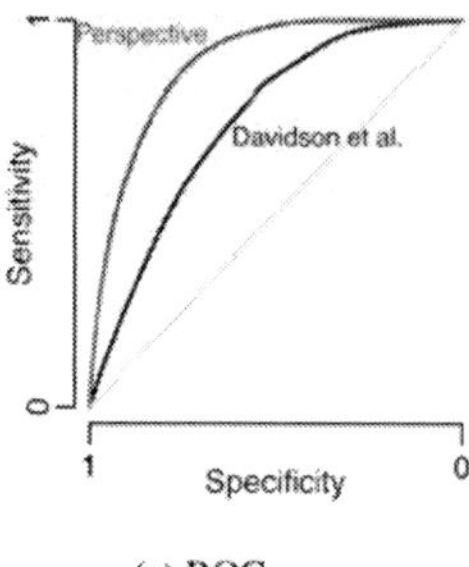

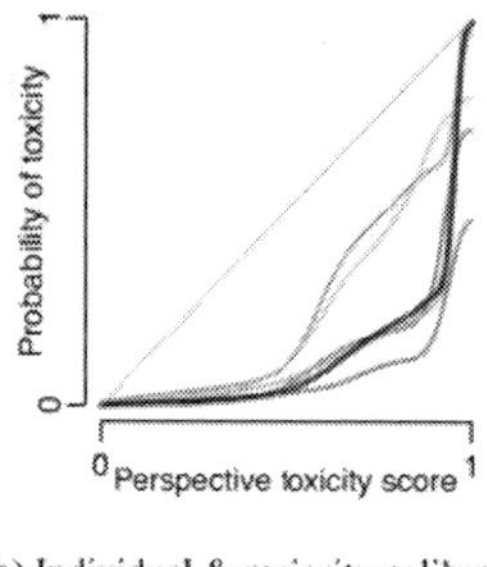

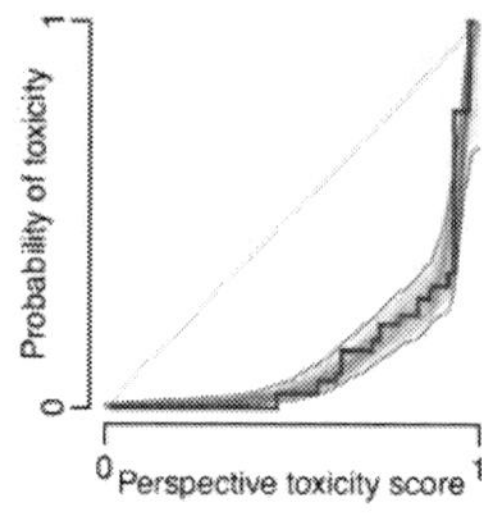

| (a) ROC curves | (b) Individual & majority calibration | (c) Stan vs isotonic regression |

Figure 1: (a) Receiver operating characteristic curves for the Perspective (Toxicity) and Davidson et al. classifiers on our samples. (b) Different recalibration curves for Perspective's toxicity classifier (colours for each individual and the majority vote in black). (c) The posterior distribution over calibration curves found by the Stan model (red), versus a standard piecewise-constant isotonic regression (purple).

3 Recalibrating the classifiers

3.1 Bayesian recalibration

In general, to recalibrate a classifier, one finds a recalibration curve that minimizes a particular cost function. The cost function is parameterized by true/false annotations $(a_1, \ldots, a_n)$ and classifier outputs $(p_1, \ldots, p_n)$, and it associates to each recalibration candidate $f : [0,1] \to [0,1]$ a cost (e.g. (Niculescu-Mizil and Caruana, 2005)). This has received considerable attention in machine learning and NLP research (Guo et al., 2017; Pleiss et al., 2017; Nguyen and O'Connor, 2015). We consider two methods for recalibration:

- isotonic regression as implemented in R and scikit-learn (Isotonic regression in R; SciKit), which finds a piecewise constant isotonic function minimizing the Brier score: $\frac{1}{n}(\sum_{a_i=\text{true}}(f(p_i))^2 + \sum_{a_i=\text{false}}(f(1-p_i))^2)$;

- a custom spline regression which uses Stan's Hamiltonian Monte Carlo simulator (Carpenter et al., 2017) to maximize the log of the likelihood of observing the true/false annotations $\left(\prod_{a_i=\text{true}} f(p_i) \cdot \prod_{a_i=\text{false}} f(1-p_i)\right)$ with respect to an uninformative prior distribution over splines.

To decide the true/false labels for recalibration, we take the majority vote from the five annotators for both Samples 1 and 2. (Our majority vote is intended to balance the background, identity and training of annotators, but we note that more advanced methods such as MACE (Hovy et al., 2013) could be used.)

Figure 1b shows a curve fit to the annotations provided by each annotator for Sample 1 against the classification scores returned by Perspective's toxicity classifier, using the spline regression (in Stan). The bold black curve is the recalibration curve from a majority vote. A well-calibrated curve lies close to the diagonal line, which means that the inferred probabilities are similar to the classifier's scores. All annotators give scores which are substantially lower than the Perspective classifier. We observed a similar result for the Davidson et al. classifier, which is not shown for space. This suggests that using the classifiers' raw scores will lead to an overestimation of the probability that content is abusive.

The two methods give similar results; Fig. 1c shows that the isotonic regression lies within the Stan confidence interval. Isotonic regression is faster to implement. However, the Stan implementation is better motivated from several perspectives. The maximization of log-likelihood is better motivated statistically, and for this application a focus on smooth recalibration curves is more useful. There are other calibration methods that use log-likelihood, such as Platt's recalibration (Platt, 1999) and temperature-based recalibration (Guo et al., 2017). Since our method is fitting a spline, rather than a sigmoid function, it is yet more flexible than these approaches. Moreover, our Stan implementation, being Bayesian, gives us a posterior distribution over possible calibration curves, indicating how confident we can be in the choice of calibration with the given annotations.

3.2 Recalibrated abuse

Figure 2 presents the recalibrated curves for both Perspective and Davidson et al. It shows that the original classifiers match poorly with human inter-

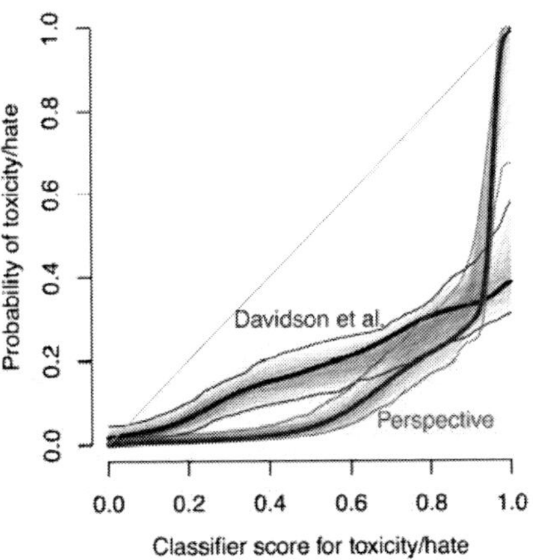

Figure 2: Recalibration curves for the Perspective and Davidson et al. classifiers. For each, the bold curve is maximum likelihood, and the 1%–99% interval is indicated.

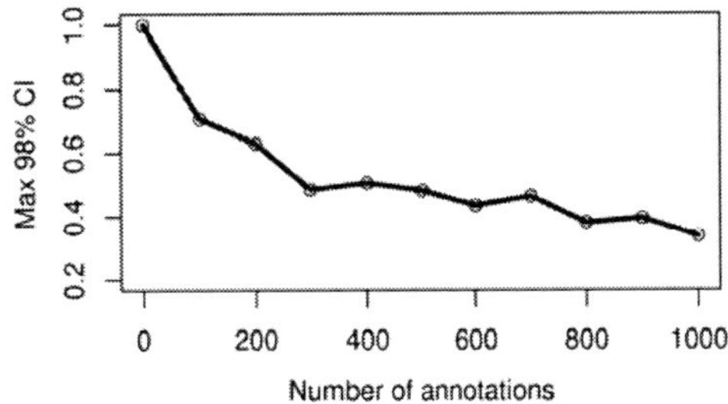

Figure 3: The maximum 98% confidence interval slowly decreases with the number of annotations.

pretations. For instance, a score of approximately 0.7 from Perspective aligns with only an inferred actual 0.2 probability of toxicity. The confidence interval is very tight for low toxicity scores, which is because nearly all the low-scored tweets were annotated as non-toxic; the confidence is less tight for low Davidson et al. scores because several low-scored tweets were annotated as hateful.

The Perspective classifier needs greater recalibration in the lower range of values than Davidson et al. but it has far better coverage of the inferred actual probabilities in the upper range. Notably, at no point does the inferred 'true' probability of abuse for the Davidson et al. classifier exceed 0.4. This suggests that, at least for this use case, the Davidson et al. classifier is a flawed way of measuring hate. This low upper limit may reflect how Davidson et al. constructed their training dataset, which involved sampling content through keywords and has been shown to contain several biases (Wiegand et al., 2019). Likely, the keywords and linguistic strategies used to express abuse differ in this new setting (i.e. tweets directed against UK candidates in the 2017 general election) compared with what the classifier was trained on.

The choice of 1,000 tweets is somewhat arbitrary, and we examine how the number of annotations that are used impacts recalibration (retaining a uniform distribution over the classification probabilities). Figure 3 shows how the maximum 98% confidence interval from Stan decreases as the number of annotations increases, showing the benefit of having more annotations. However, it also indicates that even relatively few annotations can be used for recalibration, with the rate of improvement slowing by 1,000 annotations. Confidence also varies across the calibration curves, with lower confidence in regions with greater annotator disagreement (approximately, in the 0.5 to 0.8 range for the Perspective classifier). It could be worth targeting annotator's efforts to these areas.

As a further validation, we held out 20% of the annotated tweets and found a calibration curve f for the remaining 80%. The Brier score for the uncalibrated held-out tweets was 0.25, but it fell to 0.06 after recalibrating with f, a vast improvement.

4   Analysis of online abuse in the 2017 UK election

To illustrate the importance of classifier calibration, we look at the temporal dynamics of abuse directed at two successful candidates in the 2017 UK election, Ivan Lewis and Diane Abbott. We show that recalibration is important for understanding the dynamics of abuse, such as when abuse 'events' take place, especially for candidates with a low volume of tweets. In this section we focus only on Perspective's toxicity classifier.

Figure 4 plots the number of toxic tweets directed at Lewis, using different thresholds (set at 0.5, 0.6, 0.7 and 0.8). As expected, the estimated prevalence of toxic tweets directed at Lewis depends on where this arbitrary threshold is set—he received only two tweets with toxicity > 0.8, but 10 with toxicity > 0.7, a 5-fold increase. More concerningly, the thresholds give a very different view of *when* he receives abuse. In our dataset, this is a problem for all candidates who receive few tweets. More broadly, this problem will occur for any segments of a dataset (e.g. groups, individuals or time periods) which have few entries.

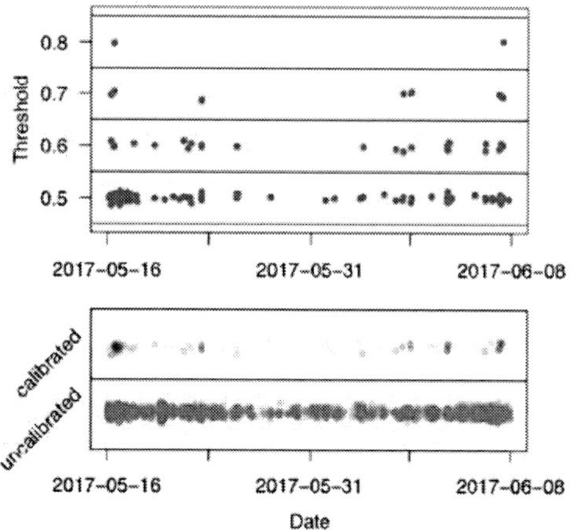

Figure 4: Timelines of toxicity received by Ivan Lewis. The upper panels use thresholds, the lower panels use the raw toxicity scores and the recalibrated scores. Each dot represents a toxic tweet. Opacity is proportional to the score. We deseason by stretching time by overall volume and use a vertical random jitter.

An alternative to applying a threshold is to directly analyse the classification probabilities. This is far more desirable as it is less biased and leads to less information loss. It can be achieved by summing the toxicity probabilities within each unit of time (e.g. every hour). The principle behind this is that if there are 50 tweets each with 0.2 probability of toxicity then it should be likely that ~10 will be toxic — and summing the probabilities best capture this. However, as the second panel of Figure 4 shows, the uncalibrated scores substantially overemphasize non-toxic tweets, and using them for this purpose would inflate the estimated prevalence of abuse. The probabilities can only be used if the classifier is calibrated, allowing for far more flexible and insightful social scientific analysis.

Lewis received only 3,700 tweets during the run up to the 2017 election. In contrast, Diane Abbott (Fig. 5) received 126,000. For candidates that receive many tweets, such as Abbot, the recalibrated probabilities show similar dynamics compared with using a 0.8 threshold (recommended by Perspective) and thus could be a reasonable choice (although they would still be biased by exactly where the threshold is set). However, for smaller samples this would lead to far less reliable results and could severely distort analyses.

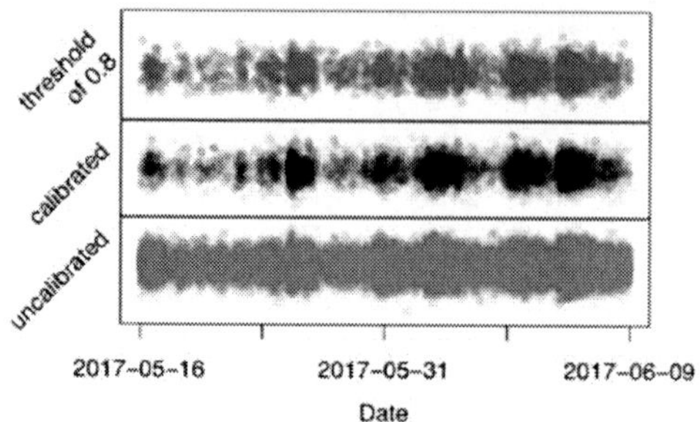

Figure 5: Timelines of toxicity received by Diane Abbott using different methods. (Because of the very large volume, the opacity of dots has been reduced by 80% overall.)

5 Discussion

Abusive content classifiers are increasingly being used for empirical analysis. Yet we show that they should be deployed with caution as their scores are often not interpretable. Although they are usually on an ordinal scale (i.e. a higher value means there is a higher chance of abuse), they are not interval (i.e. a score that is twice as great is twice as likely). If the scores do not meaningfully encode differences then content with a score that is twice as high is not necessarily twice as likely to be abusive—nor can it be interpreted as the 'strength' of abuse is twice as great. The probabilistic programming method we have presented addresses this problem, ensuring that classifiers better reflect human interpretations. Note that this procedure does not improve the 'performance' of classifiers, as measured by metrics such as AUROC, but is important because it makes them far more useable.

We propose that evaluation of interpretability (and recalibration) should be integral to abusive content classifier creation and application. One simple way of ensuring this is: (1) researchers apply their chosen classifier to the dataset they are analysing, (2) uniformly sample across the probabilities, (3) annotate the content based on the original guidelines, (4) evaluate the classifier scores using probablistic programming and (5) recalibrate them as needed. This process could be used for any similar NLP classification task, such as classification of incivil or aggressive language.

References

Sai Saketh Aluru, Binny Mathew, Punyajoy Saha, and Animesh Mukherjee. 2020. Deep Learning

Models for Multilingual Hate Speech Detection. *Arxiv:2004.06465v2*, pages 1–16.

Or Biran and Courtenay Cotton. 2017. Explanation and Justification in Machine Learning: A Survey. In *IJCAI Workshop on Explainable Artificial Intelligence*, pages 1–5.

Bob Carpenter, Andrew Gelman, Matthew D Hoffman, Daniel Lee, Ben Goodrich, Michael Betancourt, Marcus Brubaker, Jiqiang Guo, Peter Li, and Allen Riddell. 2017. Stan: A probabilistic programming language. *J. Statistical Software*, 76.

Thomas Davidson, Dana Warmsley, Michael Macy, and Ingmar Weber. 2017. Automated Hate Speech Detection and the Problem of Offensive Language. In *ICWSM*, pages 1–4.

Thomas Davidson and Ingmar Weber. 2019. Racial Bias in Hate Speech and Abusive Language Detection Datasets. In *3rd Workshop on Abusive Language Online (ACL)*, pages 1–11.

Derek Doran, Sarah Schulz, and Tarek R. Besold. 2018. What does explainable AI really mean? A new conceptualization of perspectives. *CEUR Workshop Proceedings*, 2071:1–8.

Paula Fortuna and Sérgio Nunes. 2018. A Survey on Automatic Detection of Hate Speech in Text. *ACM Computing Surveys*, 51(4):1–30.

Sahaj Garg, Ankur Taly, Vincent Perot, Ed H. Chi, Nicole Limtiaco, and Alex Beutel. 2019. Counterfactual fairness in text classification through robustness. In *AIES 2019 - Proceedings of the 2019 AAAI/ACM Conference on AI, Ethics, and Society*, pages 219–226.

Leilani H. Gilpin, David Bau, Ben Z. Yuan, Ayesha Bajwa, Michael Specter, and Lalana Kagal. 2019. Explaining explanations: An overview of interpretability of machine learning. *Proceedings - 2018 IEEE 5th International Conference on Data Science and Advanced Analytics, DSAA 2018*, pages 80–89.

Tommi Gröndahl, Luca Pajola, Mika Juuti, Mauro Conti, and N. Asokan. 2018. All You Need is "Love": Evading Hate-speech Detection. In *Proceedings of the 11th ACM Workshop on Artificial Intelligence and Security*, pages 2–12.

Chuan Guo, Geoff Pleiss, Yu Sun, and Kilian Q. Weinberger. 2017. On calibration of modern neural networks. *34th International Conference on Machine Learning, ICML 2017*, 3:2130–2143.

Dirk Hovy, Taylor Berg-Kirkpatrick, Ashish Vaswani, and Eduard Hovy. 2013. Learning Whom to Trust with MACE. In *Proceedings of NAACL-HLT*, pages 1120–1130.

Isotonic regression in R. 2015. isoreg function in R. https://www.rdocumentation.org/packages/stats/versions/3.6.2/topics/isoreg.

Menaka Narayanan, Emily Chen, Jeffrey He, Been Kim, and Sam Gershman. 2018. How do Humans Understand Explanations from Machine Learning Systems? An Evaluation of the Human-Interpretability of Explanation. *ArXiv pre-print*, pages 1–21. ArXiv:1802.00682v1.

Khanh Nguyen and Brendan O'Connor. 2015. Posterior calibration and exploratory analysis for natural language processing models. In *Proc. EMNLP 2015*, pages 1587–1598. Long version at arxiv:1508.05154.

Alexandru Niculescu-Mizil and Rich Caruana. 2005. Predicting good probabilities with supervised learning. In *Proc. ICML 2005*.

PerspectiveScoreNorm. 2020. Perspective API documentation: Score normalization and feedback. https://github.com/conversationai/perspectiveapi/blob/master/3-concepts/score-normalization.md.

John Platt. 1999. Probabilistic outputs for support vector machines and comparison to regularized likelihood methods. In *Advances in Large Margin Classifiers*, pages 61–74. MIT Press.

Geoff Pleiss, Manish Raghavan, Felix Wu, Jon Kleinberg, and Kilian Q. Weinberger. 2017. On fairness and calibration. *Advances in Neural Information Processing Systems*, 2017-December(Nips):5681–5690.

Marco Tulio Ribeiro, Sameer Singh, and Carlos Guestrin. 2016. Model-Agnostic Interpretability of Machine Learning. In *ICML Workshop on Human Interpretability in Machine Learning*, pages 91–96, New York.

Cynthia Rudin. 2018. Please Stop Explaining Black Box Models for High Stakes Decisions. In *NIPS*, pages 1–15.

Maarten Sap, Dallas Card, Saadia Gabriel, Yejin Choi, Noah A Smith, and Paul G Allen. 2019. The Risk of Racial Bias in Hate Speech Detection. In *ACL Proceedings*, pages 1668–1678.

SciKit. 2020. Scikit isotonic regression. https://scikit-learn.org/stable/modules/isotonic.html.

Andrej Švec, Matúš Pikuliak, Marián Šimko, and Mária Bieliková. 2018. Improving Moderation of Online Discussions via Interpretable Neural Models. In *Proceedings of the Second Workshop on Abusive Language Online (ACL)*, pages 60–65, Brussels. ACL.

Bertie Vidgen and Leon Derczynski. 2020. Directions in Abusive Language Training Data: Garbage In, Garbage Out. *Arxiv:2004.01670v2*, 1(1):1–26.

Bertie Vidgen, Rebekah Tromble, Alex Harris, Scott Hale, Dong Nguyen, and Helen Margetts. 2019. Challenges and frontiers in abusive content detection. In *3rd Workshop on Abusive Language Online*.

Sandra Wachter, Brent Mittelstadt, and Chris Russell. 2017. Counterfactual Explanations Without Opening the Black Box: Automated Decisions and the Gdpr. *Harvard Journal of Law & Technology*, 31:841–887.

Cindy Wang. 2018. Interpreting Neural Network Hate Speech Classifiers. In *Proceedings of the Second Workshop on Abusive Language Online (ACL)*, pages 86–92, Brussels. ACL.

Michael Wiegand, Josef Ruppenhofer, and Thomas Kleinbauer. 2019. Detection of Abusive Language: the Problem of Biased Datasets. In *NAACL-HLT*, pages 602–608, Minneapolis. ACL.

Matthew Williams. 2019. *Hatred behind the scenes: a report on the rise of online hate speech*. Mishcon de Reya, London.

Predicting independent living outcomes from written reports of social workers

Angelika Maier
Bielefeld University
Inspiration 1
33619 Bielefeld
amaier@uni-bielefeld.de

Philipp Cimiano
Bielefeld University
Inspiration 1
33619 Bielefeld
cimiano@cit-ec.uni-bielefeld.de

Abstract

In social care environments, the main goal of social workers is to foster independent living by their clients. An important task is thus to monitor progress towards reaching independence in different areas of their patients' life. To support this task, we present an approach that extracts indications of independence on different life aspects from the day-to-day documentation that social workers create. We describe the process of collecting and annotating a corresponding corpus created from data records of two social work institutions with a focus on disability care. We show that the agreement on the task of annotating the observations of social workers with respect to discrete independent levels yields a high agreement of .74 as measured by Fleiss' Kappa. We present a classification approach towards automatically classifying an observation into the discrete independence levels and present results for different types of classifiers. Against our original expectation, we show that we reach F-Measures (macro) of 95% averaged across topics, showing that this task can be automatically solved.

1 Introduction

Social workers are concerned with improving abilities and increasing confidence of their clients with the goal of supporting them in living their lives independently. A traditional taxonomy, called Metzler's taxonomy[1] (Metzler, 2001; Kommission, 2016), considers the following life categories in which independence is to be reached: *'everyday life'*, *'individual basic care'*, *'relationships'*, *'participation in cultural and social life'*, *'communica-*

tion', *'emotional and psychological development'* and *'health promotion and maintenance'*. Each category has specific subcategories, with overall 34 categories. Social workers document their observations with respect to the behaviour of clients in day-to-day records that capture the whole trajectory of their clients. Interviews carried out with social workers have revealed that they would profit substantially from automatic summarization of the trajectories of patients, in particular their progress over time on reaching independence in the different categories defined by Metzler.

Towards this goal, in this paper we investigate whether it is possible to automatize this task. We frame the task as a classification problem in which each observation in the records about the patient is classified into a discrete independence level. In particular, we distinguish the following five independence levels: *1 ('able to accomplish a certain task alone')*, *2 ('able to accomplish a given task with help')*, *3 ('partly able to accomplish a task with help')*, *4 ('unable to accomplish a certain task')*. The neutral label 5 applies for documentations that do not allow a conclusion regarding the level of independence.

In Table 1, we provide one example for each of those independence levels for different Metzler categories. These examples are derived from the actual data, slightly rephrased to ensure anonymity.

As one contribution of this paper, we describe the process of collecting a corpus on the basis of data from two social care institutions. The corpus has been annotated by social work students that for our purposes can be regarded as domain experts. After several annotation rounds, the annotator agreement reached 0.74 as measured by Fleiss' Kappa, corresponding to a substantial agreement.

Building on this corpus, we train different classifiers on the annotated data and show that the

---

[1]https://www.soziales.niedersachsen.de/startseite/behinderte_menschen/eingliederungshilfe_behinderte_menschen/bedarf-feststellung-des-bedarfs-gruppen-fuer-leistungsberechtigte-mit-vergleichbarem-bedarf-94870.html (as consulted online 11.10.2020), there, the taxonomy can be found in appendix 2.4

Proceedings of the Fourth Workshop on Natural Language Processing and Computational Social Science, pages 139–148
Online, November 20, 2020. ©2020 Association for Computational Linguistics
https://doi.org/10.18653/v1/P17

classifiers can reach a macro F-Measure of 95% averaged across the 34 Metzler categories on the task of predicting independence levels. The best results overall are obtained with a linear SVM (one-vs-one) classifier. The best result is achieved on Metzler's categories *M-6 ('Managing money')*, *M-11 ('Get up / Go to bed')*, *M-17 ('Organization of free time / private activities')*, *M-19 ('Encounters in social groups')*, *M-22 ('Compensation of sensory impairments and communication disorders')*, *M-24* and *M-25* on orientation in familiar and unfamiliar surroundings, *M-27* and *M-28* on coping with psychological disorders (100% F-measure), while the worst result is achieved on Metzler's category *M-21 ('Development of future perspectives, life planning')* (92% F-Measure). We rely on a feature ablation experiment to determine the importance of different features on the task.

1 is able to accomplish a certain task

Category	M-7
Documen-tation	Client has filled and dispatched the notification for health insurance.

2 is able to accomplish a certain task with help

Category	M-15
Documen-tation	Client was reminded of the visit of his brother. He went on a trip with his caretaker and his brother.

3 is partly able to accomplish a certain task with help

Category	M-8
Documen-tation	Client had dinner. The food was brought to her. Sometimes she led the spoon to her mouth by herself.

4 is not able to accomplish a certain task

Category	M-27
Documen-tation	Client stayed in her room this morning. Didn't want to come down for lunch and didn't want to go to the meeting center.

5 neutral / irrelevant for category

Category	M-23
Documen-tation	Client says he has a cold and is not feeling well.

Table 1: Examples for each of the independence levels for different Metzler categories.
M-7: Deal with financial matters and social law matters, M-15: Relationship with relatives, M-8: Nutrition, M-27: Coping with drive disorders, M-23: Time orientation

The paper is structured as follows: In Section 2, we discuss related work for the problem of predicting extra-linguistic personal attributes. In Section 3, we describe how the data was obtained from two different disability care institutions. In Section 4, the method is described, including the development of guidelines for annotation and a description of the annotation process. We also describe which classifiers we use to automatize the classification. Before concluding, we discuss our results.

2 Related Work

There has been considerable work on the task of predicting personal attributes of users on the basis of their written contributions, e.g. social media posts. Personal attributes are typically extra-linguistic attributes that are not explicitly mentioned in texts, but can be inferred on the basis of analysis of style, grammar or vocabulary. One can distinguish between physical personal attributes that manifest themselves physically (such as age, ethnicity, gender, etc) on the one hand, and psychological personal attributes including mood, emotion, stress level, sentiment, resilience etc. The independence level that we consider in our work does not fully belong to one of this categories. While independence level is not strictly speaking a physically manifested attribute such as age or gender, it is related to the (observable) behaviour of a person and has thus an obvservable manifestation. Yet, it has similar characteristics to a psychological variable in the sense that it is not objectively measurable and is subject to interpretation.

An older study was carried out by Baumrind (1967) in the field of child care to manually analyze written documentations in combination with the environment of children to assess child care behaviour as a basis to predict their preschool behaviour patterns. Among the different attributes considered, level of independence is considered.

Another group where the level of independence is of relevance are old people (Araújo and Ceolim, 2007; Karakaya et al., 2009). Karakaya et al. collected data for 33 elderly people living in a nursing home and 25 elderly living at home. They measured the functional mobility, depressive symptoms, level of independence, and quality of life for both groups for comparison. The level of independence was evaluated by the Kahoku Aging Longitudinal Study Scale (KALS), which evaluates activities of elderly people in 12 areas. Each activity was rated on a 4-point scale (0: dependent, 1-2: some help, 3: independent). In this scale, higher scores indicate higher level of independence. Our assessment of independence level follows in essence the proposal of the 4-point scale of Karakaya et al.

While there has been some work on (manual) independence level classification (e.g. the above mentioned works), we are the first to consider the automatic prediction using learned classifiers on textual documentations in the domain of disability care in social work. Furthermore, we investigate how the classification results vary depending on the Metzler category considered. An important difference to related work is that level of independence is not predicted from the self-reported experience of subjects, but from the written observations of a third party, in our case the social worker.

Due to the lack of work on automatic prediction of independence level, we discuss work on the related task of classifying personal attributes. There has been a lot of work on detecting personal attributes, in particular from social media posts from Facebook or Twitter (Kosinski et al., 2013; Yo and Sasahara, 2017).

Kosinski et al. (2013) use logistic and linear regression classifiers to detect psychological attributes related to *personality, intelligence, openness* and *happiness*, as well as physical attributes related to *sexual orientation, ethnicity, religious and political views, use of addictive substances, parental separation, age*, and *gender*, reaching accuracy levels between 85% and 88% on the data of 58,000 volunteers on Facebook. Yo and Sasahara (2017) tackle the prediction of the personal attributes *gender, occupation*, and *age groups* in tweets, reaching accuracy levels of 60-70%. A related task is the detection of stress levels, on which Lin et al. (2014) reach 83%-93% F-Measure on four different datasets derived from 350 million tweets data. Galatzer-Levy et al. (2018) extensively discuss the relevance of different machine learning algorithms and machine learning principles to the study of stress pathology, recovery, and resilience.

A related task is the classification of the emotion of a text or social media post. Bostan and Klinger (2018) compare models for prediction on annotated emotion corpora systematically, performing cross-corpus experiments by training classifiers on each dataset and evaluating them on others, reaching F-Measures (micro averaged) of 56% when training on all but one corpus and testing on a held-out corpus and 98% when training

and testing on the same corpus. They predict the emotions: *joy, anger, sadness, disgust, fear, trust, surprise, love, confusion, anticipation* and *no emotion* (noemo). Cevher et al. (2019) constructed the AMMER corpus, triggering emotions such as *fear, anger, annoyance, insecurity, joy* and *no emotion* in the experimental setting of a car driving situation. They make use of off-the-shelf algorithms and a bidirectional LSTM, reaching a F-Measure of 76% with Transfer Learning. Schuff et al. (2017) have re-annotated the SemEval 2016 Stance Data set (Mohammad et al., 2016) with the emotion labels *anger, anticipation, disgust, fear, joy, sadness, surprise* and *trust*. They apply Maximum Entropy, Support Vector Machines, a LSTM, a Bidirectional LSTM, and a Convolutional Neural Network (CNN) to provide baseline results for their corpus. They reach best results of 77% F-Measure with a bidirectional LSTM.

3 Data

The data was collected from 2 different stationary disability care facilities of a major European welfare provider located in the German State of North Rhine-Westphalia in the context of a common project with Bielefeld University. Following contractual obligations, the institution will not be named in this paper. The dataset was collected for clients that gave their explicit consent, yielding the complete documentation for 22 clients. The data comprises of 731,601 records with 295,812 observations documented by the social workers in natural language.

Client	Category	Date
1235	M-15	12. März 2016

Text
ANONYM hatte heute Besuch von seiner Mutter. Sie haben einen Spaziergang gemacht. engl: ANONYM's mother visited him today. They went for a walk.

Table 2: Example for a documentation of Metzler category *M-15 ('Shaping social relationships with relatives')*.

For each documentation, a client ID, a date, and a category is recorded. An example for a documentation is given in Table 2. Documentations can be very short containing only one or two words up to several sentences to provide a detailed description for the social workers of the following shift. The Metzler category of a documentation is assigned by the social worker.

The 34 categories describe measures of care applied and originate from the Metzler taxonomy that is standard in social care contexts for the purpose of documentation. The seven top level categories of the taxonomy and the respective number of subcategories are given in Table 3.

Area	Number of subcategories
Everyday life	7
Individual basic care	6
Relationships	3
Participation in cultural and social life	5
Communication	4
Emotional and psychic development	4
Health promotion and maintenance	5

Table 3: Top-level Metzler categories and number of subcategories.

4 Method

In this section we discuss the development of guidelines for annotation and provide a description of the annotation process. We also describe which classifiers we use to automatize the classification.

4.1 Guideline development

We used two small datasets, comprising of 677 and 500 documentations, respectively, for the development of guidelines. The guidelines include general annotation principles and examples for each level of independence for each Metzler category and a list of abbreviations that are repeatedly used in documentations (e.g. MA: Mitarbeiter (engl. employee or co-worker)). Due to contractual obligations, we are only allowed to share the general principles for annotation but not the examples (even if they were generalized and made unfamiliar for the annotation guidelines). In the example section of the guidelines, for each level of independence a short definition is given, as well as some typical phrasing for documentations of this level. Annotators were asked to rely only on the information in the social workers' written comment when classifying the level of independence. Further, they were asked not to judge or evaluate the effect of independence on the quality of life of the individual. For example, they were asked not to judge whether in their view the effect of a client being able to spend money independently was positive or not, that is, not to take into account whether the money was spent wisely or not.

4.2 Annotation Process

For the annotation, we employed 3 advanced bachelor students (semester 3 and higher) in the field of social work, with practical experience in disability care institutions. The annotation was done in two steps. The first 5,000 data points were annotated by four subjects: the first author and the 3 students. A second batch of data comprising of 8,313 data points was annotated by the students only. The annotation has been conducted with 'OMEN - a collaborative, annotation platform' [2]. For annotation, a single documentation and the respective Metzler category are presented and annotators had to choose the appropriate level of independence. The annotators were instructed to use a short version of the annotation guidelines as well as the Metzler category for reference during the annotation process. The training of the annotators and optimization of the guidelines has been conducted in two iterations. In order to estimate the inter-annotator agreement, Fleiss's kappa was calculated (Wirtz and Caspar, 2002). In the first annotation round of 677 documentations (about 20 documentations per Metzler category), the agreement between the annotators reached a κ-value of 0.59 (on document level). After discussion, a further independent annotation round of new 500 documentations (about 15 documentations per Metzler category) resulted in $\kappa = 0.66$, showing that the annotators converged in their understanding of the task. The results from the second round were also discussed and used for further modification of the guidelines. The 15,719 documentations selected for annotation were annotated in two steps. In the first subsequent independent annotation step involving 5,000 documentations, an agreement of $\kappa = 0.74$ was reached, which can be regarded as a substantial agreement

---

[2]https://github.com/FrankGrimm/omen

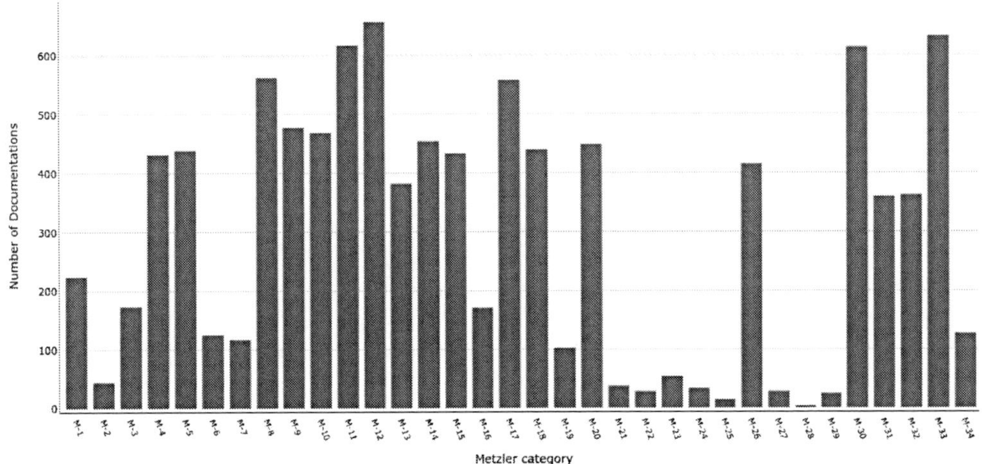

Figure 1: Number of documentations per Metzler category in annotated dataset selected with majority vote. N=10,071

in comparison to agreement by chance[3]. The remaining 8,313 documentations were annotated in a second subsequent annotation step by 3 annotators.

4.3 Classification models

On the basis of the annotated data described above, we train models to predict the level of independence in a supervised setting. For this purpose, we aggregate the annotated data with majority vote, i.e. only use documentations from the data annotated by 4 annotators where 3 or 4 of the annotators agree and only use documentations from the data annotated by 3 annotators where 2 or 3 of the annotators agree. The distribution of independence levels over the selected documentations can be found in Figure 2. Also, we report the number of documentations for each Metzler category in Figure 1.

We compare two settings: a setting where all the data is used to train one model that predicts level of independence irrespective of the Metzler category (category-agnostic classification) and one setting where there is one model per category (category-specific classification). We perform experiments with the following classification algorithms: linear Support Vector Machines (SVMs), AdaBoost, Random Forest, Logistic Regression, Perceptron, k-NN, Multinomial Naive Bayes and

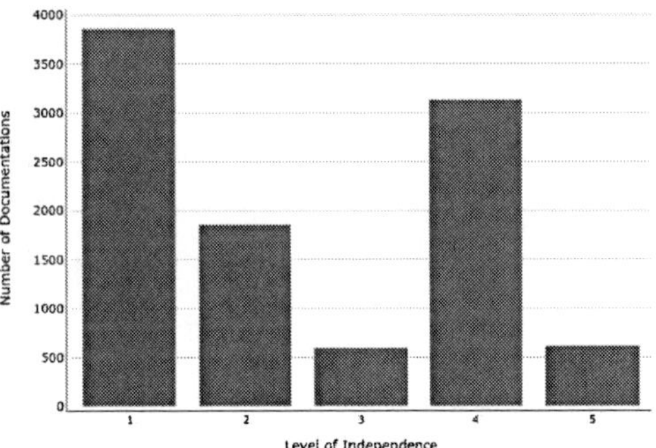

Figure 2: Number of documentations for each level of independence in annotated dataset selected with majority vote. N=10,071

Multi-layer Perceptron (MLP) as well as a convolutional neural network (CNN), with a convolutional window of 3.

We use the implemented version of these algorithms in the Python module scikit-learn (Pedregosa et al., 2011). For the CNN, we use the implementation in Keras (Chollet et al., 2015) with a convolutional window of 3, consisting of an embedding layer, two 1D convolutional layers, a dropout layer, a pooling layer and a dense layer. For the CNN, we use embeddings induced from our dataset rather than using pre-trained embeddings.

All names were substituted with the place-

---

[3]According to the scale of kappa value interpretation of Landis and Koch (1977)

holder 'ANONYM' before the annotation process. We pre-process the text data using standard pre-processing operations such as lemmatization, stemming and stopword removal. We use spaCy (Honnibal and Montani, 2017) to obtain the lemmata and POS-tags. All features are represented as tf.idf values in the models. POS-tags are glued to the words in a pre-processing step for this purpose. We compute embeddings specific for our dataset using all 295,812 documentations and all 636 unique texts for measures of care applied[4] (the wording over all data is very similar) to train our own word embeddings for our domain with the python module fasttext (Bojanowski et al., 2017). Also, we up-sample the datasets for training to have an equal distribution of the classes.

As a baseline, we consider models trained using unigram features weighted with tf.idf. We experimentally test different feature combinations including the following features for our models: trigrams, lemmata, stemmed words, word embeddings (only in CNN), POS-tags. This leads to 15 feature combinations (8 without POS tags and word embeddings for CNN).

5   Results

We adopt a 5-fold cross-validation setting in which in each fold we train with 80% of the data and evaluate on 20% of held-out data. We report the median F-measure over the five folds for each classifier. As a baseline, we rely on a model trained with unigrams weighted with tf.idf. We refer to this baseline as Bag-Of-Words (BOW) model. The only model with a different baseline is the CNN, where the convolutional window is of size 3, corresponding to the trigram features that we use on top of the BOW model. Therefore, we use the model with word embeddings that are trained on the raw text – rather than stemmed words or lemmata – as a baseline. The baseline score for the CNN is 6% F-Measure (macro) (median over five folds). The scores for the different classifiers using the BOW model are given in Table 4.

We report the F-Measure (macro) for the five best models in Table 5. The left part of the table shows the results for the category-specific setting in which we train one model per Metzler-category. The right part of the table shows the results for all

Baseline (BOW Model)	F1 (macro)
Linear SVM (one-vs-one)	0.86
Linear SVM (one-vs-rest)	0.85
Perceptron	0.85
LogisticRegression	0.85
KNN	0.81
Multinomial NB	0.80
RandomForestClassifier	0.69
AdaBoostClassifier	0.48
MLPClassifier	0.47

Table 4: Baseline scores with tf.idf of Bag-of-words : F-Measure (macro) (Median of 5-fold cross-validation) for models trained on all documentations; BOW=Bag-of-words

categories for the category-agnostic classification, that is the case where there is one single model that predicts independence levels independently of the Metzler category.

First of all, we observe that the Macro-average F_1 values in both settings are above the BOW baseline by 7% (category-specific setting) and 9% (category-agnostic setting) for the case of linear SVM and 7% and 10% for Perceptron, respectively. This trend is observed also for Logistic regression but not for KNN, where the value in the category-specific-setting increases 8% and drops 4% in the category-agnostic setting. For the CNN the value increases 82% in the category-specific setting and 52% in the category-agnostic setting. In general, we observe that the category-agnostic setting outperforms the category-specific setting for most classifiers , i.e. 2% for linear SVM, 3% for Perceptron, and 1% for Logistic regression. The exception is again the KNN classifier, where the value is 12% lower. Also, the CNN performs 30% better in the category-specific setting.

Considering the best-performing classifier, i.e. linear SVM (one-vs-one) for the specific categories, we observe that for 11 out of 34 categories, the category-agnostic setting performs better than the category-specific setting, for 9 categories both settings perform equally well and for 14 categories the category-specific setting performs better. The category-agnostic setting sometimes outperforms the category-specific setting in cases where there are a low number of (positive) examples for the corresponding category. This is the case for the categories *M-21*, *M-27* and *M-28*. In *M-28*, it is not possible to conduct 5-fold cross-validation

---

[4]Measures of care applied are another part of the data we obtained. It comprises of over 400,000 samples, but is more standardized than the documentations.

| | category-specific classification | | | | | category-agnostic classification | | | | | |
Metzler category	SVM OvO	Perceptron	LR	KNN	CNN	SVM OvO	Perceptron	LR	KNN	CNN	Support
All	**0.97***	0.96	0.94	0.90	0.75	n/a	n/a	n/a	n/a	n/a	10071
M-1	**0.95***	0.94	0.90	0.87	0.85	**0.95***	0.93	0.89	0.76	0.75	224
M-2	0.91	0.91	0.91	0.86	**0.94***	**0.94***	**0.94***	0.70	0.63	0.50	44
M-3	0.97	**0.98***	0.97	0.95	0.91	**0.93**	0.90	0.86	0.74	0.56	174
M-4	**0.96***	0.94	0.95	0.93	0.95	**0.96***	**0.96***	0.94	0.85	0.77	432
M-5	**0.95**	0.94	0.92	0.92	**0.95**	**0.98***	0.97	0.94	0.82	0.70	439
M-6	**1.00***	0.99	0.97	0.96	0.99	0.94	**0.96**	0.91	0.79	0.43	126
M-7	**0.87**	**0.87**	0.78	0.77	0.79	**0.97***	0.96	0.94	0.80	0.47	117
M-8	**0.98***	0.97	0.96	0.95	0.96	**0.96**	0.95	0.95	0.79	0.78	562
M-9	**0.96***	**0.96***	0.95	0.89	**0.96***	0.95	0.95	0.93	0.78	0.80	478
M-10	**0.97**	**0.97**	0.96	0.95	0.96	0.97	**0.98***	0.95	0.87	0.75	469
M-11	**1.00***	0.99	0.99	0.97	0.99	**0.92**	0.87	0.88	0.77	0.62	617
M-12	**0.97***	0.96	0.95	0.95	0.92	**0.96**	0.93	0.94	0.81	0.80	657
M-13	**0.96***	**0.96***	0.92	0.93	0.92	**0.96***	0.95	0.90	0.85	0.72	383
M-14	**0.99***	0.97	0.97	0.96	0.96	**0.94**	0.90	0.89	0.71	0.63	454
M-15	**0.99***	**0.99***	0.97	0.96	0.98	**0.99***	0.97	0.93	0.85	0.70	434
M-16	**0.93**	0.92	0.88	0.85	0.92	0.92	**0.94***	0.90	0.77	0.58	171
M-17	**1.00***	0.99	0.99	0.98	0.98	**0.95**	0.92	0.89	0.74	0.55	558
M-18	**0.98***	**0.98***	0.97	0.95	0.96	**0.97**	0.96	0.94	0.86	0.76	440
M-19	**1.00***	**1.00***	0.99	0.99	0.98	**1.00***	0.95	**1.00***	0.87	0.84	102
M-20	**0.96***	0.95	0.94	0.91	0.94	**0.96***	**0.96***	0.90	0.71	0.65	449
M-21	0.84	0.82	**0.83**	0.82	0.69	**0.92***	**0.92***	**0.92***	0.74	0.44	38
M-22	0.95	**1.00***	0.95	0.94	0.93	**1.00***	**1.00***	0.82	0.82	0.00	29
M-23	**0.94***	**0.94***	0.84	0.73	0.79	0.63	**0.88**	0.63	0.54	0.73	54
M-24	**1.00***	**1.00***	**1.00***	**1.00***	**1.00***	**1.00***	**1.00***	0.75	0.82	0.33	34
M-25	**1.00***	**1.00***	**1.00***	**1.00***	0.87	**1.00***	**1.00***	**1.00***	0.80	0.00	15
M-26	**0.98***	**0.98***	0.97	0.95	0.97	**0.95**	**0.95**	0.93	0.74	0.68	416
M-27	**0.78**	0.75	0.67	0.67	0.58	**1.00***	**1.00***	0.97	0.69	0.50	29
M-28	n/a	n/a	n/a	n/a	n/a	**1.00***	**1.00***	**1.00***	0.50	0.00	4
M-29	**0.92**	0.90	0.83	0.90	0.80	**0.93***	0.89	0.89	0.60	0.00	25
M-30	**0.98***	**0.98***	0.97	0.96	0.96	**0.97**	**0.97**	0.94	0.86	0.58	614
M-31	**0.93**	0.91	0.87	0.82	0.87	0.96	**0.97***	0.93	0.75	0.66	360
M-32	**0.98***	0.97	0.96	0.95	**0.98***	**0.96**	0.94	0.95	0.79	0.67	363
M-33	**0.99***	**0.99***	0.98	0.97	0.96	**0.94**	**0.94**	0.91	0.81	0.75	633
M-34	**0.93**	**0.93**	0.91	0.87	0.92	**0.98***	**0.98***	0.96	0.82	0.88	127
macro F_1	**0.93**	0.92	0.90	0.89	0.88	**0.95***	**0.95***	0.91	0.77	0.58	

Table 5: Best F-Measure (macro) (Median of 5-fold cross-validation) and category-wise F-Measure (macro) (Median of 5-fold cross-validation) with model trained on all Metzler categories for best 5 models and macro average over categories, * marking values for best models per category; OvO=one-vs-one, SVM= Linear Support Vector Machine, LR= Logistic Regression, , KNN= k-NN classifier, CNN=Convolutional Neural Network, Support= Absolut number of annotated documentations (before up-sampling)

Since the Metzler taxonomy is only available in german, we provide an english translation of the mapping for the categories that are not mentioned in the text or in Table 1 in Appendix A.1.

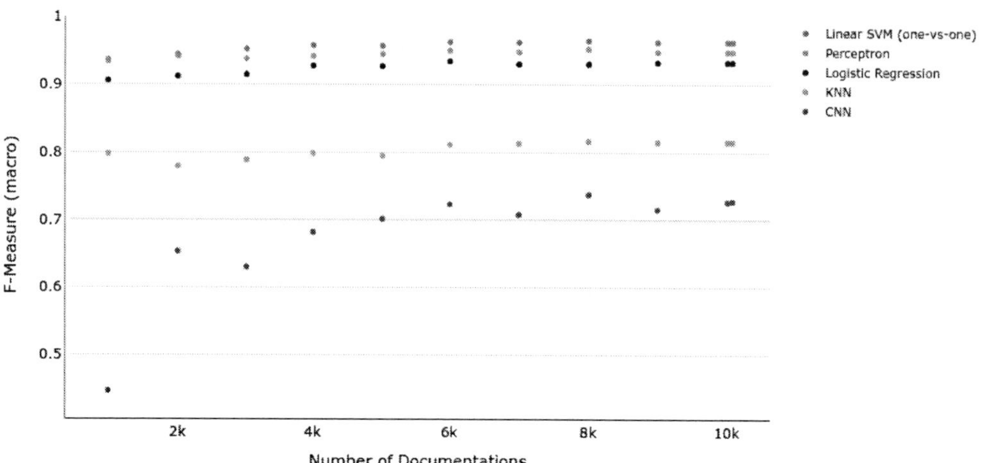

Figure 3: Impact of number of training samples in steps of 1,000 examples on the classification.

Feature combination	SVM OvO	Perceptron	LR	KNN	CNN
BOW	**0.89**	**0.89**	0.86	0.87*	-
ALL	0.89	**0.93***	0.91*	0.84	
-lemma	0.89	**0.92**	0.91*	0.85	-
-stem	**0.91**	**0.91**	0.89	0.84	-
-3grams	**0.93***	**0.93***	0.89	0.85	-
-POS	**0.89**	**0.89**	0.87	0.87*	0.75*

Table 6: Impact of leaving out different features on the classification performance, * marking values for best features per algorithm (3-grams = ngrams with n=3, POS= Part-Of-Speech tags, stem = stemmed words, lemma = lemmata)

with only 4 samples in the category-specific setting and the other categories occur so rarely that it is not possible to build an accurate category-specific classifier for them.

For category *M-23 ('time orientation')*, the category-agnostic setting has a rather low F-Measure in comparison to the other categories. One reason for this might be the fact that there are no examples for independence level *3 ('partly able to accomplish a task with help')* in *M-23*. Other categories where at least one label is missing are: *M-25 ('orientation in unfamiliar surroundings')*, *M-27* and *M-28*. Another reason for the better performance of the category-agnostic setting for some categories could be that these cate-

gories are more related to other sub-categories under the same top-level category, e.g. *M-2 ('Preparation of Snacks between main meals')* and *M-3 ('Preparation of main meals')* or categories *M-14* to *M-16* in the area *Relationships*. Categories with under 100 examples such as *M-27* and *M-28* on psychological disorders in addition to *M-2* seem to profit from their related categories in the category-agnostic setting and compensate for missing labels as well.

We experimentally investigate the impact of leaving out different features. In Table 6, we report the impact of leaving out different feature types from the full feature combination in comparison to the baseline models build with the unigram features weighted with tf.idf. For the SVM (one vs. one) a model with left out trigrams worked best. Only models with left out trigrams and left out stemmed words outperform the baseline. For Perceptron, the POS features have a great impact, because all models using POS outperform the baseline. The combinations of all features and leaving out lemmata worked best. The models build with Logistic regression outperform the baseline with every feature combination used on top of the unigrams. Here, the combination of all features except the trigrams worked best. For KNN no feature combination on top of the unigrams outperforms the baseline. Surprisingly, the worst F-Measures results from models using all features except the stemmed words. We also report the F-Measure for the CNN using stemmed words in combination with lemmata and inherent trigrams. The baseline for the CNN is 6%; using stemmed words and lemmata increases F-Measure by 69% compared with using the word embeddings trained on raw text.

Finally, we investigate the impact of increasing the training data size on the performance of the classifiers. Figure 3 shows how F-Measures are affected by adding training data in steps of 1,000 examples. The diagram shows that the performance convergences from about 6,000 examples onwards, yielding no significant improvement from there. We conclude thus that our result can not be improved much more by simply increasing the number of annotated samples.

6 Conclusion

We have presented an approach to automatically classify observations in written reports by social workers into discrete independence levels reflecting the level of independence of their clients. We have described the construction of a corpus with substantial agreement on the task, comprising of over 15,000 documents. We have presented results on the task with different classifiers, showing that we can obtain F-measures of 95% macro-averaged over the different Metzler categories that we considered. We have also shown that a category-agnostic model outperforms a category-specific approach with one model per category on average over all categories. Furthermore, for some categories featuring smaller amounts of examples, the category-agnostic classifier performs better. The CNN model did achieve good results on the task but did not outperform SVM with one vs. one. While we did not investigate how to integrate more complex syntactic features other than POS information, this is an obvious avenue for future work. A further interesting question is which other psychological attributes can be predicted on the basis of the documentations considered here. An obvious category to explore is the mood of clients. In addition to classifying independence levels, we intend to perform further studies on the annotated data: One task is to present the trajectories and derived information for independence level per Metzler category to social workers to understand if it provides useful insights for them. Furthermore, it would be interesting to investigate in how far the observations in written reports by social workers reflect the actual condition or opinion of a client.

Acknowledgments

This research is part of the project MAEWIN and was supported by the Digital Society research program funded by the Ministry of Culture and Science of the German State of North Rhine-Westphalia. More information on the project can be found at `https://www.uni-bielefeld.de/ fakultaeten/technische-fakultaet/ arbeitsgruppen/ semantic-computing/projekte/ maewin/` Many thanks to Frank Grimm for the development and technical support of the annotation tool.

References

Maria Odete Pereira Hidaldo de Araújo and Maria Filomena Ceolim. 2007. Assessment of the level of independence of elderly residents in long-term care institutions. *Revista da Escola de Enfermagem da USP*, 41(3):378–385.

Diana Baumrind. 1967. Child care practices anteceding three patterns of preschool behavior. *Genetic psychology monographs*.

Piotr Bojanowski, Edouard Grave, Armand Joulin, and Tomas Mikolov. 2017. Enriching word vectors with subword information. *Transactions of the Association for Computational Linguistics*, 5:135–146.

Laura Ana Maria Bostan and Roman Klinger. 2018. An analysis of annotated corpora for emotion classification in text. In *Proceedings of the 27th International Conference on Computational Linguistics, COLING 2018, Santa Fe, New Mexico, USA, August 20-26, 2018*, pages 2104–2119. Association for Computational Linguistics.

Deniz Cevher, Sebastian Zepf, and Roman Klinger. 2019. Towards multimodal emotion recognition in german speech events in cars using transfer learning. In *Proceedings of the 15th Conference on Natural Language Processing, KONVENS 2019, Erlangen, Germany, October 9-11, 2019*.

François Chollet et al. 2015. Keras. `https:// keras.io`.

Isaac R Galatzer-Levy, Kelly V Ruggles, and Zhe Chen. 2018. Data science in the research domain criteria era: relevance of machine learning to the study of stress pathology, recovery, and resilience. *Chronic Stress*, 2:2470547017747553.

Matthew Honnibal and Ines Montani. 2017. spacy 2: Natural language understanding with bloom embeddings, convolutional neural networks and incremental parsing. To appear.

Mehmet Gürhan Karakaya, Sevil Çuvalci Bilgin, Gamze Ekici, Nezire Köse, and Ayşe Saadet Otman. 2009. Functional mobility, depressive symptoms, level of independence, and quality of life of the elderly living at home and in the nursing home. *Journal of the American Medical Directors Association*, 10(9):662–666.

Gemeinsame Kommission. 2016. Niedersächsische anwendungshinweise zum hmb-w verfahren. verfahren der zuordnung von leistungsberechtigten zu gruppen für leistungsberechtigte mit vergleichbarem hilfebedarf (anlage 4 ffv lrv gem. §79 abs. 1 sgb 12). beschluss gk ffv lrv 8. sitzung.

Michal Kosinski, David Stillwell, and Thore Graepel. 2013. Private traits and attributes are predictable from digital records of human behavior. *Proceedings of the national academy of sciences*, 110(15):5802–5805.

J Richard Landis and Gary G Koch. 1977. The measurement of observer agreement for categorical data. *biometrics*, pages 159–174.

Huijie Lin, Jia Jia, Quan Guo, Yuanyuan Xue, Jie Huang, Lianhong Cai, and Ling Feng. 2014. Psychological stress detection from cross-media microblog data using deep sparse neural network. In *2014 IEEE International Conference on Multimedia and Expo (ICME)*, pages 1–6. IEEE.

Heidrun Metzler. 2001. Hinweise zum verständnis des fragebogens zum „hilfebedarf". *HMB-W./Version*, 5.

Saif Mohammad, Svetlana Kiritchenko, Parinaz Sobhani, Xiaodan Zhu, and Colin Cherry. 2016. Semeval-2016 task 6: Detecting stance in tweets. In *Proceedings of the 10th International Workshop on Semantic Evaluation (SemEval-2016)*, pages 31–41.

F. Pedregosa, G. Varoquaux, A. Gramfort, V. Michel, B. Thirion, O. Grisel, M. Blondel, P. Prettenhofer, R. Weiss, V. Dubourg, J. Vanderplas, A. Passos, D. Cournapeau, M. Brucher, M. Perrot, and E. Duchesnay. 2011. Scikit-learn: Machine learning in Python. *Journal of Machine Learning Research*, 12:2825–2830.

Hendrik Schuff, Jeremy Barnes, Julian Mohme, Sebastian Padó, and Roman Klinger. 2017. Annotation, modelling and analysis of fine-grained emotions on a stance and sentiment detection corpus. In *Proceedings of the 8th Workshop on Computational Approaches to Subjectivity, Sentiment and Social Media Analysis, WASSA@EMNLP 2017, Copenhagen, Denmark, September 8, 2017*, pages 13–23. Association for Computational Linguistics.

Markus A Wirtz and Franz Caspar. 2002. *Beurteilerübereinstimmung und Beurteilerreliabilität: Methoden zur Bestimmung und Verbesserung der Zuverlässigkeit von Einschätzungen mittels Kategoriensystemen und Ratingskalen*. Hogrefe.

Take Yo and Kazutoshi Sasahara. 2017. Inference of personal attributes from tweets using machine learning. In *2017 IEEE International Conference on Big Data (Big Data)*, pages 3168–3174. IEEE.

A Appendices

A.1 English translation for the mapping of Metzler categories in Table 5 that are not mentioned in text or in Table 1

M-1: shopping

M-4: laundry care

M-5: keeping own area tidy

M-9: body care

M-10: toilet use / personal hygiene

M-12: bathing / showering

M-13: put on / take off clothes

M-14: relationships in the immediate vicinity

M-16: relationships with friends / partners

M-18: participation in offers / events

M-20: exploring areas of life outside the home

M-26: Coping with fear / anxiety / tension

M-29: dealing with / reducing significantly self-endangering and extraneous behaviour

M-30: carrying out medical or therapeutic prescriptions

M-31: Arrangement and implementation of medical appointments

M-32: special nursing requirements

M-33: observation and monitoring of the state of health, M-34: health promoting lifestyle

Analyzing Political Bias and Unfairness in News Articles at Different Levels of Granularity

Wei-Fan Chen
Paderborn University
Department of Computer Science
cwf@mail.upb.de

Khalid Al-Khatib
Bauhaus-Universität Weimar
Faculty of Media, Webis Group
khalid.alkhatib@uni-weimar.de

Henning Wachsmuth
Paderborn University
Department of Computer Science
henningw@upb.de

Benno Stein
Bauhaus-Universität Weimar
Faculty of Media, Webis Group
benno.stein@uni-weimar.de

Abstract

Media organizations bear great reponsibility because of their considerable influence on shaping beliefs and positions of our society. Any form of media can contain overly biased content, e.g., by reporting on political events in a selective or incomplete manner. A relevant question hence is whether and how such form of imbalanced news coverage can be exposed. The research presented in this paper addresses not only the automatic detection of bias but goes one step further in that it explores how political bias and unfairness are manifested linguistically. In this regard we utilize a new corpus of 6964 news articles with labels derived from *adfontesmedia.com* and develop a neural model for bias assessment. By analyzing this model on article excerpts, we find insightful bias patterns at different levels of text granularity, from single words to the whole article discourse.

1 Introduction

Reporting news in a politically unbiased and fair manner is a key component of journalism ethics and standards. "Politically unbiased" means to report on an event without taking a *political position, characterization, or terminology*, and "fair", in this context, means to focus on original facts rather than on *analyses or opinion statements based on false premises*.[1] Although it is known that biased and unfair news do exist in the media, spreading misleading information and propaganda (Groseclose and Milyo, 2005), people are not always aware of reading biased content.

When fighting bias and unfairness, only the understanding of how these emerge (and how to avoid

them) can allow media organizations to maintain credibility and can enable readers to choose what to consume and what not. In pursuit of this goal, we recently studied how sentence-level bias in an article affects the political bias of the whole article (Chen et al., 2020). Also other researchers have proposed approaches to automatic bias detection (see Section 2 for details). However, the existing approaches lack an analysis of what makes up bias, and how it exposes in different granularity levels, from single words, to sentences and paragraphs, to the entire discourse.

To close this gap, we analyze political bias and unfairness in this paper within three steps:

1. We develop an automatic approach to detect bias and unfairness in news articles.

2. We study the bias distribution along different text granularity levels.

3. We explore various sequential patterns of how bias and unfairness become manifest in text.

We utilize two well-known websites that address media bias, *allsides.com* and *adfontesmedia.com*, in order to create a corpus with 6964 news articles, each of which is labeled for its topic, political bias, and unfairness. Based on this corpus, we devise a recurrent neural network architecture to learn classification knowledge for bias detection. We choose this network class because of its proven ability to capture semantic information at multiple levels: taking the model output for whole texts, we conduct an in-depth reverse feature analysis to explore media bias at the word, the sentence, the paragraph, and the discourse level. At the *word level*, we correlate the most biased sentences with LIWC categories (Pennebaker et al., 2015). At

---

[1] See http://www.adfontesmedia.com for a detailed characterization of political bias and unfairness.

Proceedings of the Fourth Workshop on Natural Language Processing and Computational Social Science, pages 149–154
Online, November 20, 2020. ©2020 Association for Computational Linguistics
https://doi.org/10.18653/v1/P17

the *sentence and paragraph level*, we reveal what parts of an article are typically most politically biased and unfair. At the *discourse level*, we reveal common sequential media bias patterns.

The results show that our model can utilize high-level semantic features of bias, and it confirms that they are manifested in larger granularity levels, i.e., on the paragraph level and the discourse level. At the word level, we find some LIWC categories to be particularly correlated with political bias and unfairness, such as *negative emotion*, *focus present*, and *percept*. At levels of larger granularity, we observe that the last part of an article usually tends to be most biased and unfairest.

2   Related Work

Computational approaches to media bias focus on factuality (Baly et al., 2018), political ideology (Iyyer et al., 2014), and information quality (Rashkin et al., 2017). Bias detection has been done at different granularity levels: single sentences (Bhatia and Deepak, 2018), articles (Kulkarni et al., 2018), and media sources (Baly et al., 2019). Recently, the authors of this paper studied how the two granularity levels "sentence" and "discourse" affect each other. An outcome of this research are insights and means of how sentence-level bias classifiers can be leveraged to better predict article-level bias (Chen et al., 2020).

Given these results, the paper in hand digs deeper by investigating how bias is actually manifested in a text at different granularity levels. Our approach resembles techniques where the attention mechanism in a model is used to output weights (which indicate feature importance) for each text segment (Bahdanau et al., 2014). Zhou et al. (2016), for instance, use word-level attention to focus on sentiment words, while Ji et al. (2017) use sentence-level attention to select valid sentences for entity relation extraction. Related to media bias, Kulkarni et al. (2018) show that the learned attention can focus on the biased sentences when detecting political ideology.

Regarding "attention" at multi-level granularity, Yang et al. (2016) propose a hierarchical attention network for document classification that is used at both word and sentence level. Yet, problems when using attention for such analyses are that the analysis unit (be it a word or a sentence) has to be defined before the training process, and that the set of classifiers which can output attention

is limited. By contrast, our unsupervised reverse feature analysis can be used with any classifier and at an arbitrary semantic level, even after the training process.

3   Media Bias Corpus

Although bias detection is viewed as an important task, we could not find any reasonably sized labeled corpus that suits our study, which is why we decided to built a new one. We started with the corpus of Chen et al. (2018) in order to obtain news articles with topics and political bias labels. We extended the corpus by crawling the latest articles from *allsides.com* and by adding the fairness labels provided by *adfontesmedia.com*. The new corpus is available at `https://github.com/webis-de/NLPCSS-20`.

Allsides.com   This website is a news aggregator that collects news articles about American politics, starting from June 1st, 2012. Each event comes with articles representing one of the three political camps: left, center, and right. Chen et al. (2018) crawled the website to extract 6447 articles. For our study, we extended their corpus by integrating all articles until March 15th, 2019, resulting in a total of 7775 articles. In addition to the political bias labels, we crawled the topic tags of each article.

Adfontesmedia.com   Since allsides.com focuses on political bias, we exploit adfontesmedia.com as another source for additional bias types. This portal maintains a "bias scale" quantifying the media bias of a broad set of US news portals. The bias assessments stem from media experts who annotate each portal with bias and fairness labels. Bentley et al. (2019) show that the portals' labels are highly correlated to findings from social scientists.

A New Media Bias Corpus   Based on the labels from adfontesmedia.com, we define three media bias types for news portals:

1. **Political Bias.** A portal is *neutral* if it is labeled as "skew left/right" or "neutral". It is *politically biased* if it is labeled with "most extreme left/right" or "hyperpartisan left/right".

2. **Unfairness.** A portal is considered *fair* if it is labeled as "original fact reporting", "fact reporting", "mix of fact reporting and analysis", "analysis", or "opinion". The portal is considered *unfair* if it is labeled as "selective story", "propaganda", or "fabricated info".

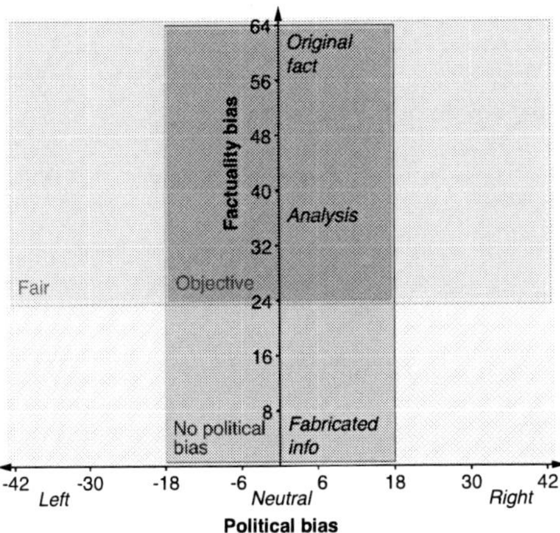

Figure 1: The bias chart from *adfontesmedia.com* (visually adjusted). The three rectangles represent the positive counterparts of the regions of the three bias types (*political bias*, *unfairness*, and *non-objectivity*).

Portal		Topic	
Name	Count	Name	Count
CNN	1021	presidential election	914
Fox News	1002	politics	525
New York Times	781	White House	515
...		...	
NPR News	1	domestic policy	2
The Nation	1	EPA	1
Vice	1	women's issues	1

Table 1: The top three and the bottom three portals along with the topics in our corpus.

3. **Non-Objectivity.** A portal is considered *objective* if it is politically unbiased and fair. Otherwise, it is considered as *non-objective*.

Figure 1 gives an overview of the labels; it is based on the bias chart at adfontesmedia: The political bias focuses on the x-axis of the chart, while the unfairness focuses on the y-axis of the chart. The non-objectivity is the combination of the two kinds of bias.

We label the collected articles according to this scheme. Since adfontesmedia.com does not cover all portals from allsides.com, the final corpus contains 41 portals with 6964 articles. The three largest portals are CNN (1021 articles), Fox News (1002 articles), and the New York Times (781 articles). Altogether, we count 111 different topics such as, "presidential election" (914 articles), "politics" (525 articles), and "white house" (515 articles). Table 1 lists the top three and the bottom three portals along

Media Bias	Training	Development	Test
Political Bias	39.25%	40.00%	42.82%
Unfairness	18.59%	17.48%	18.16%
Non-objectivity	39.84%	40.66%	43.31%

Table 2: The percentage of articles with each considered media bias type in the three datasets of our corpus.

with topics in our corpus.

4 Media Bias Analysis

This section presents our approach to study bias and unfairness at different levels of text granularity. At first, we develop classifiers for political bias, unfairness, and non-objectivity. Second, we do a reverse feature analysis study to explore the manifestation of bias at multiple levels of granularity and to identify different bias patterns.

4.1 Media Bias Classification

For the detection of bias in a text, we follow Chen et al. (2018) in keeping the word order, in order to be able to capture higher-level semantics. To this end, we develop classifiers with RNN served as the classical model for sequential inputs, where a cell is a GRU with a recurrent state size of 32. On top of the final hidden vector of GRUs is a prediction layer whose activation function is a softmax and the size is 2. We use the pre-trained word embedding of GloVe (Pennington et al., 2014) with a word embedding dimension of 50, the optimizer Adam, and a learning rate of 0.001. We train classifiers until no improvement in the development set is observed anymore; all classifiers are of the same structure and have the same hyperparameters.

To minimize the mnemonic information induced by the article topic, we split the dataset controlling the topics as an independent variable: we group the articles by their topic and select some groups to be in the test set, some to be in the development set, and the rest to be in the training set. We ensure that either the development set or the test set has at least 10% of the articles in the whole dataset, obtaining 5394 articles in the training set, 755 articles in the development set, and 815 articles in the test set.

Table 2 shows the distribution of the labels in the corpus. To avoid the exploitation of portal-specific features, each article is thoroughly checked and all information regarding the portal it was taken from (e.g., "CNN's Clare Foran and Phil Mattingly contributed to this report") is removed.

4.2 Reverse Feature Analysis

In addition to the effectiveness of our bias classification, we want to assess the kind of features that are learned. Formally, we use the developed classifiers to output the predicted bias probability p_{art} of the test articles, i.e., the probability of being *politically biased*, *unfair*, or *non-objective*. We iteratively remove text segments from the article and use the classifier to again predict the media bias probability p_{art-i}, where i denotes the index of the text segment in the article. The media bias strength of a text segment t_i is estimated as $p_{art} - p_{art-i}$. If a text segment is relevant for prediction, we expect to see a significant decrease from p_{art} to p_{art-i}.

Based on this estimation of media bias strength, we design three experiments to analyze and interpret the classifiers' predictions at the following levels of text granularity:

Word level (LIWC correlations) Related research suggests that media bias is manifested at a larger granularity level, including the paragraph level (Chen et al., 2018) and the clause level (Iyyer et al., 2014). To validate this, we use the LIWC categories to check the word level bias, because they have been used in Iyyer et al. (2014) to sample a set of sentences that may contain ideology bias.

In detail, for each sentence s_i, we compute its LIWC score of the category j as $|\{w_{i,k} \in c_j, k \in K\}| / |\{w_{i,k}, k \in K\}|$, where c_j denotes the words in LIWC category j, K denotes the bag-of-words in s_i, and $w_{i,k}$ denotes the k-th word in K. The Pearson correlation coefficient is used to measure the correlation between LIWC categories and media bias strength.

Sentence and paragraph-level (locations of media bias) Here we analyze the distribution of the media bias strength in the sentences and paragraphs (approximated as three continuous sentences). Basically, these values indicate which segment of a text mostly contains media bias.

Discourse level (media bias patterns) Here we analyze the patterns of the media bias strength across the different parts of an article's discourse. In particular, we split an article into four equally-sized parts and compute the average media bias strength of the sentences for each part. The splitting is comparable to the so-called "inverted pyramid" structure in journalism, where a news article starting by the summary, important details, general and background info (Pöttker, 2003).

	Political Bias	Unfairness	Non-objectivity
Majority	36.38%	45.01%	36.18%
RNN	75.60%	83.42%	75.42%
- Biased	69.41%	72.09%	69.57%
- Unbiased	81.80%	94.75%	81.13%

Table 3: The F_1 scores of RNN, majority baseline, and by-class performance of the three bias types.

5 Results and Discussion

In the following, we report and discuss the results of the experiments described in Section 4.

5.1 Media Bias Classification

First, we look at the automatic classification of media bias. Table 3 summarizes the performance of the developed RNNs in the three media bias classes. All classifiers outperform the majority baseline, achieving 75.60% for political bias, 83.42% for unfairness, and 75.42% for non-objectivity. Such a performance demonstrates the capability of the classifiers to detect topic-independent media bias features.

Looking closely at individual bias classes, we find that the RNN is good at predicting the absence of bias rather than bias. We interpret this because of the uneven distribution of the classes, especially in the unfairness (see Table 2).

5.2 Reverse Feature Analysis

Although the classifiers achieved good results, they are certainly not perfect. To account for the prediction errors, the following analysis uses only the predicted probabilities of those articles where the RNNs predicted the label correctly.

LIWC Correlations According to the Pearson correlations, most of the LIWC categories are not correlated with a high coefficient (neither in a positive or a negative way). However, the highest correlated categories are different among the three types of media bias. The categories that have the highest correlation with political bias are *negative emotion, anger*, and *affect*. This shows that politically biased articles tend to use emotional and opinionated words such as "disappoint", "trust", and "angry". For unfair articles, we see a higher correlation in *focus present*. Examples in this category are "admit", "become", and "determine". For non-objective articles, the bias is related to *percept* words such as "feel", "gloom", and "depict".

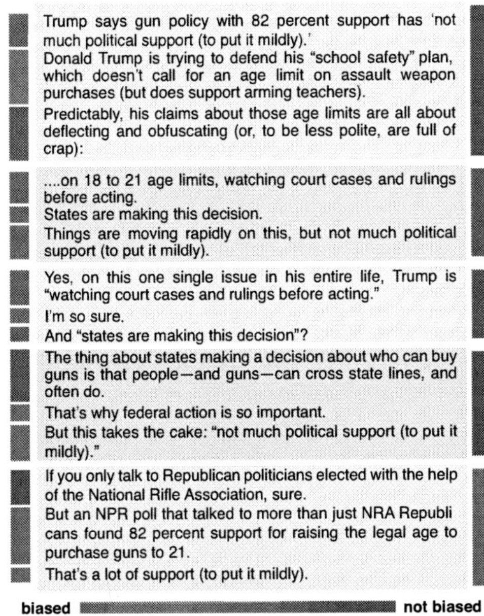

Figure 2: The media bias strength on sentence (left) and paragraph (right) level in an excerpt of one news article from the given corpus. Biased text segments are shown in red and unbiased text segments in blue.

Location of Media Bias Figure 2 visualizes the estimated media bias strength at the sentence and paragraph levels. As an example, we choose an article from Daily Kos, which is labeled as politically biased. In this article, we see a strong tendency to criticize Trump's claim, especially at the end of the article. At the paragraph level, our strength analysis of media bias successfully identifies the last paragraph as the most biased text segment. While at the sentence level, we see that the last two sentences are most biased in the last paragraph. The second sentence seems to be a bit biased, perhaps because of the word usage of "trying to defend". However, we see that the analysis fails to identify the third sentence as politically biased. Still, given that the sentence or paragraph level analysis is fully unsupervised, the reverse feature analysis seems to perform quite well.

Media Bias Patterns Figure 3 shows the identified media sequential patterns for the three bias types. We can notice that the media bias strengths for all articles in the second quarter are somewhat close. This is, in our opinion, because the second quarter of news articles usually contains some background information, which does not tend to

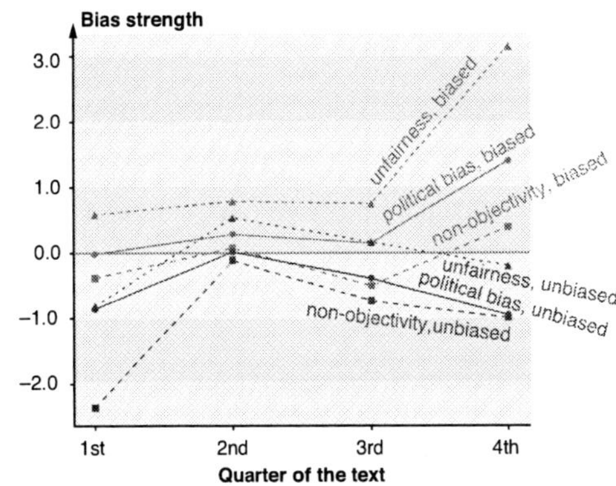

Figure 3: Patterns of the types of media bias as well as biased and unbiased text. Values are normalized to have a mean of zero and a standard deviation of one. Positive values indicate a stronger bias and negative values indicate that text has a lower bias or is unbiased.

be biased. We also see that all biased articles start with a neutral tone (close to mean) in the beginning and then emphasize the bias in the latter parts. Among the three media bias types, unfairness has the highest bias strength. Observing our corpus, we find that one typical way to be unfair is to report selected facts in a favor of some entity, which leads to completely different word usage. On the other hand, for political bias, describing facts with positive or negative expressions is a common indicator of bias there. Such a difference might be the reason for why the classifiers can better discover the unfair texts.

6 Conclusion

This paper has studied political bias and unfairness in news articles. We have trained sequential models for bias detection and have applied a reverse feature analysis to demonstrate that it is possible to reveal at what granularity level and how sequential patterns media bias is manifested. Specifically, we find that the last quarter seems to be the most biased part. A significant "by-product" of our research is a new corpus for bias analysis. And we believe this corpus can help, for example, investigate how journalists convey bias in a news article.

In the future, we will study how to utilize these results to detect bias or to rewrite the articles to remove and change bias. For example, based on the findings of this paper, the bias remover should pay more attention to the later paragraphs.

Acknowledgments

This work was partially supported by the German Research Foundation (DFG) within the Collaborative Research Center "On-The-Fly Computing" (SFB 901/3) under the project number 160364472.

References

Dzmitry Bahdanau, Kyunghyun Cho, and Yoshua Bengio. 2014. Neural machine translation by jointly learning to align and translate. *arXiv preprint arXiv:1409.0473*.

Ramy Baly, Georgi Karadzhov, Dimitar Alexandrov, James Glass, and Preslav Nakov. 2018. Predicting factuality of reporting and bias of news media sources. In *Proceedings of the 2018 Conference on Empirical Methods in Natural Language Processing*, pages 3528–3539.

Ramy Baly, Georgi Karadzhov, Abdelrhman Saleh, James Glass, and Preslav Nakov. 2019. Multi-task ordinal regression for jointly predicting the trustworthiness and the leading political ideology of news media. *arXiv preprint arXiv:1904.00542*.

Frank Bentley, Katie Quehl, Jordan Wirfs-Brock, and Melissa Bica. 2019. Understanding online news behaviors. In *Proceedings of the 37th Annual ACM Conference on Human Factors in Computing Systems*.

Sumit Bhatia and P Deepak. 2018. Topic-specific sentiment analysis can help identify political ideology. In *Proceedings of the 9th Workshop on Computational Approaches to Subjectivity, Sentiment and Social Media Analysis*, pages 79–84.

Wei-Fan Chen, Khalid Al Khatib, Benno Stein, and Henning Wachsmuth. 2020. Detecting media bias in news articles using gaussian bias distributions. In *Proceedings of the 2020 Conference on Empirical Methods in Natural Language Processing, Findings of ACL: EMNLP 2020*. To appear.

Wei-Fan Chen, Henning Wachsmuth, Khalid Al Khatib, and Benno Stein. 2018. Learning to flip the bias of news headlines. In *Proceedings of the 11th International Conference on Natural Language Generation*, pages 79–88.

Tim Groseclose and Jeffrey Milyo. 2005. A measure of media bias. *The Quarterly Journal of Economics*, 120(4):1191–1237.

Mohit Iyyer, Peter Enns, Jordan Boyd-Graber, and Philip Resnik. 2014. Political ideology detection using recursive neural networks. In *Proceedings of the 52nd Annual Meeting of the Association for Computational Linguistics*, volume 1, pages 1113–1122.

Guoliang Ji, Kang Liu, Shizhu He, and Jun Zhao. 2017. Distant supervision for relation extraction with sentence-level attention and entity descriptions. In *Proceedings of the Thirty-First AAAI Conference on Artificial Intelligence*.

Vivek Kulkarni, Junting Ye, Steve Skiena, and William Yang Wang. 2018. Multi-view models for political ideology detection of news articles. In *Proceedings of the 2018 Conference on Empirical Methods in Natural Language Processing*, pages 3518–3527.

James W Pennebaker, Ryan L Boyd, Kayla Jordan, and Kate Blackburn. 2015. The development and psychometric properties of LIWC2015.

Jeffrey Pennington, Richard Socher, and Christopher Manning. 2014. GloVe: Global vectors for word representation. In *Proceedings of the 2014 Conference on Empirical Methods in Natural Language Processing*, pages 1532–1543.

Horst Pöttker. 2003. News and its communicative quality: The inverted pyramid—when and why did it appear? *Journalism Studies*, 4(4):501–511.

Hannah Rashkin, Eunsol Choi, Jin Yea Jang, Svitlana Volkova, and Yejin Choi. 2017. Truth of varying shades: Analyzing language in fake news and political fact-checking. In *Proceedings of the 2017 Conference on Empirical Methods in Natural Language Processing*, pages 2931–2937.

Zichao Yang, Diyi Yang, Chris Dyer, Xiaodong He, Alex Smola, and Eduard Hovy. 2016. Hierarchical attention networks for document classification. In *Proceedings of the 2016 Conference of the North American Chapter of the Association for Computational Linguistics: Human Language Technologies*, pages 1480–1489.

Xinjie Zhou, Xiaojun Wan, and Jianguo Xiao. 2016. Attention-based lstm network for cross-lingual sentiment classification. In *Proceedings of the 2016 Conference on Empirical Methods in Natural Language Processing*, pages 247–256.

Mapping Local News Coverage: Precise location extraction in textual news content using fine-tuned BERT based language model

Sarang Gupta [*]
Data Science Institute
Columbia University, NY
`sg3637@columbia.edu`

Kumari Nishu [*]
Data Science Institute
Columbia University, NY
`kn2492@columbia.edu`

Abstract

Mapping local news coverage from textual content is a challenging problem that requires extracting precise location mentions from news articles. While traditional named entity taggers are able to extract geo-political entities and certain non geo-political entities, they cannot recognize precise location mentions such as addresses, streets and intersections that are required to accurately map the news article. We fine-tune a BERT-based language model for achieving high level of granularity in location extraction. We incorporate the model into an end-to-end tool that further geocodes the extracted locations for the broader objective of mapping news coverage.

1 Introduction

A media or news desert is an uncovered geographical area that has few or no news outlets and receives little coverage. Mapping locations mentioned in news articles is the primary step in identifying news deserts. A key challenge in the process is to manually peruse the corpus of news articles, identify the location mentions and assign spatial coordinates which can then be placed on a map to identify a newsroom's coverage.

While conventional Named Entity Recognition (NER) taggers such as those offered by spaCy (Honnibal and Montani, 2017), Natural Language Toolkit (NTLK) (Bird et al., 2009) and Stanford NLP (Finkel et al., 2005) group contain tags to identify organizations, geo-political entities (GPE) and certain non-GPE locations such as mountain ranges and bodies of water from text, they are not able extract precise location mentions such as addresses, streets or intersections in their entirety. For example, the sentence - *"The family will hold shivah from 7 to 9 p.m. Thursday, Oct. 13, and*

again Saturday, Oct. 15, at Temple Sinai, 5505 Forbes Ave., Pittsburgh." passed through the Stanford Named Entity Tagger, returns "Temple Sinai", 'Forbes Ave." and 'Pittsburgh" as separate location entities. However, to accurately map the location of interest, one requires the whole address - 'Temple Sinai, 5505 Forbes Ave., Pittsburgh.' to be returned as a single location.

In recent years, there has been an advent of powerful pre-trained deep learning based language models such as Google's Bidirectional Encoder Representations from Transformers (BERT) (Devlin et al., 2018), XLNet (Yang et al., 2019) and OpenAI's GPT-2 (Radford et al., 2018). These models can be fine-tuned for specific classification tasks in the absence of abundant training data and thus are often helpful with weak supervision (Ratner et al., 2017). We fine-tune the BERT model to extract precise location mentions in their entirety as iterated in the previous paragraph. We first build a dataset of about 10,000 sentences extracted from a corpus of 80,000 news articles spanning Jan 2018 to June 2019 published in Philadelphia Inquirer newspaper. We use Amazon Mechanical Turk (MTurk) to label the locations of interest in the sentences and fine-tune the BERT based NER tagger to classify the words in a text. Finally, we incorporate geocoding of the extracted locations into the pipeline.

In this work, we present an end-to-end system to extract geographic data from text. This tool could be particularly useful for newsrooms to map the coverage of their printed content helpful in identifying news deserts or by researchers and other organizations to extract precise location mention in text. Our main contributions are as follows: (1) Preparing a dataset containing sentences with words tagged as geopolitical entities, organizations, streets and addresses. (2) Fine-tuning an existing BERT based NER tagger to identify the aforemen-

---

[*] Equal contribution

Proceedings of the Fourth Workshop on Natural Language Processing and Computational Social Science, pages 155–162
Online, November 20, 2020. ©2020 Association for Computational Linguistics
https://doi.org/10.18653/v1/P17

tioned location entities. (3) Building an end-to-end system that consumes news content, transforms into BERT readable format and returns a list of the geocoded locations mentioned in the content.

The overall process is illustrated in Figure 1. We will first discuss our modelling approach followed by the process that we followed for geocoding the extracted locations.

2 Related Work

Named Entity Recognition (NER) is a well studied area in the field of Natural Language Processing (NLP). It aims to identify different types of entities such as people, organizations, nationalities and locations in text. Tools trained on conventional NER models such as Conditional Random Fields (Lafferty et al., 2001), Maximum Extropy (Ratnaparkhi, 2016) and LabeledLDA (Ramage et al., 2009) have been successful in identifying common named entities. However, challenge comes when high level of granularity is of interest in extracting location entities such as specific addresses, streets or intersections.

Lingad et al. (2013) evaluated the effectiveness of existing NER tools such as Stanford NER, OpenNLP and Yahoo! PlaceMaker on extracting locations from disaster-related tweets. Brunsting et al. (2016) presented an approach combining NER and Parts-of-Speech (POS) tagging to develop a set of heuristics to achieve higher granularity for location extraction in text.

There has been some work around the use of end-to-end neural architecture on several sequence labelling tasks including NER (Chiu and Nichols, 2015) and POS (Meftah and Semmar, 2018) tagging. Magnolini et al. (2019) explored the use of external gazetteers for entity recognition with neural models showing that extracting features from a rich model of the gazetteer and then concatenating such features with the input embeddings of a neural model outperforms conventional approaches.

Fine-tuning pre-trained language model for domain-specific machine learning tasks has become increasingly convenient and effective. Lee et al. (2019) introduced BioBERT, a BERT based biomedical language representation model for biomedical text mining and Xue et al. (2019) presented a fine-tuned BERT model for entity and relation extraction in Chinese medical text. Liu (2019) presented advances in extractive summarization using a fine-tuned BERT model.

To our knowledge, no previous work has been done to fine-tune a pre-trained language-based deep learning model to achieve the level of precision and granularity in location extraction that is required for the purpose of mapping news coverage. Furthermore, there does not exist an open source end-to-end tool to extract and geocode precise locations from a piece of text.

3 Model

Our approach to developing a named-entity tagger for the task of precise location extraction involves fine-tuning an existing neural network on a target dataset. Fine-tuning a model updates its pre-trained parameters, improving its performance on the downstream NLP task.

We treat the task of named-entity tagging in a sentence as that of token classification within a sequence, assigning each word (token) in the sentence (sequence) a label. The fine-tuning process for token classification involves: (1) Preparing the training dataset with expected labels for tokens within each sequence (2) Loading an existing model with pre-trained weights (3) Extending the model with a classification layer at the end with number of nodes equal to the number of classes in the task at hand (4) Training the model on the target dataset.

We will use Bidirectional Encoder Representations from Transformers (BERT), developed by Google AI in 2018 as the pre-trained model. BERT makes use of multiple multi-head attention layers to learn bidirectional embeddings for input tokens. It is trained for masked language modeling, where a fraction of the input tokens in a given sequence are masked and the task is to predict the masked word given its context (Devlin et al., 2018). Our decision to choose BERT is motivated by the fact that it is a general purpose language representation model pre-trained on millions of articles on English Wikipedia and BookCorpus. Given the diversity of topics present on these two training sets, we believe BERT would be able to generalize well to our dataset containing news articles. BERT's use of WordPiece tokenizer mitigates the out-of-vocabulary issue while tokenizing location names which are often proper nouns. With minimal architecture modification, BERT can be applied to our NER task.

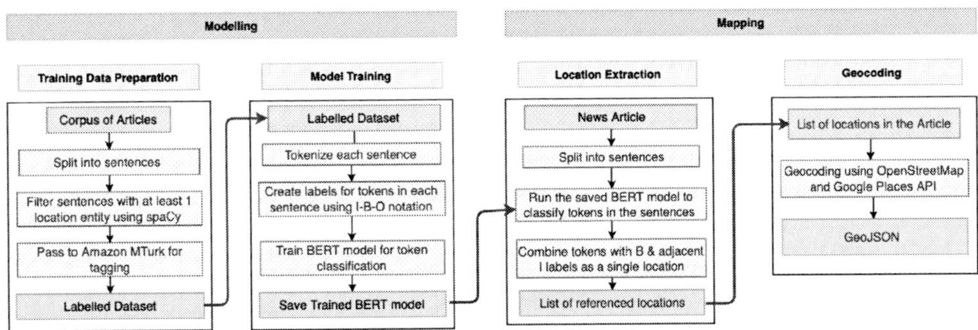

Figure 1: Overview of our methodology

3.1 Dataset Preparation

Our goal is to create a labelled dataset for token classification with each token labelled as being part of a location entity or not. For this purpose, we assembled a dataset of 10,000 sentences drawn from a corpus of 80,000 news articles ranging from January 2018 to June 2019 published in the Philadelphia Inquirer newspaper. The articles represented 'beats' including politics, opinions, sports, food and travel among others, published by a number of different authors. The articles originated from 10 different news sources which had their articles published on Philadelphia Inquirer website.

Since, majority of the sentences in the articles did not contain a location mention, sending the whole article for tagging on Amazon MTurk was not cost-efficient. To overcome this, we broke down the articles into individual sentences using spaCy's Sentencizer and devised a set of heuristics and custom rules on top of spaCy's NER system to capture sentences with mentions of addresses, streets and intersections. Through exploratory analysis and manually perusing the articles, we identified three patterns based on the syntactic relation between POS and NER tags present in the sentence:

Heuristic 1.

$$NER_{LOC} + POS_{PREP} + NER_{LOC}$$

Two location entities separated by a prepositional tag often highlighted a hierarchical location between two location entities. For example: In the phrase *'Arbor Street in Kensington.'* (Figure 2 - Top), refers to the street - Arbor Street, which is part of the neighborhood - Kensington.

Heuristic 2.

$$NER_{NUM} + POS_{NOUN} + POS_{PREP} + NER_{LOC}$$

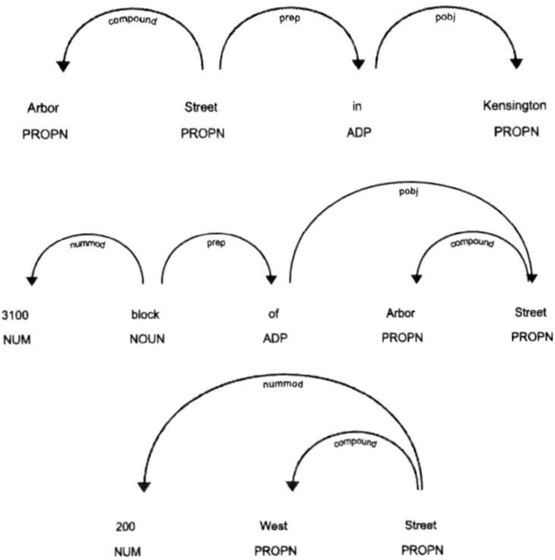

Figure 2: Heuristics to identify locations of interest

A number, noun and a prepositional tag preceding a place were collectively used to identify a precise location in the referenced place. For example, *'3100 block of Arbor Street.'* (Figure 2 - Middle)

Heuristic 3.

$$NER_{NUM} + POS_{LOC}$$

A number preceding a location entity, often a street, collectively referred to a building in a street or area. For example, *'200 West Street'* (Figure 2 - Bottom) refers to a building on the West Street.

Using the aforementioned, we filtered in sentences that contained at least one of the above patterns. Note that even though the defined heuristics are not exhaustive and can not define all possible syntactical patterns in which our locations of interest could exist in text, they offer an effective strategy to create labelled data for higher-level, less precise supervision required in transfer learning (Ratner et al., 2019). We augmented the dataset to include 20% of sentences that contained simple geo-polical entities (such as United States, Pennsylvania, Philadelphia etc.) as it is easier for a pre-trained language model to identify such mentions. A total of 10,000 sentences were randomly selected from this set.

As a second pass, the crowd workers on Amazon Mturk were instructed to identify locations of interest in the 10,000 sentences and mark their starting and ending character numbers in the sequence. The sentences were then tokenized using WordPiece tokenization (Wu et al., 2016) and the tokens were assigned labels using Inside-outside-beginning (I-O-B) notation (Ramshaw and Marcus, 1995). For instance, LOC_B represents the starting of a location entity and LOC_I represents subsequent tokens that are part of that location entity. An example is depicted in Figure 3 which shows tokens in a sentence tagged using the I-O-B notation.

3.2 Model Training

We used BERT's implementation provided by Hugging Face (Wolf et al., 2019) in PyTorch (Paszke et al., 2019). As the task was framed as a multi-label classification problem, a softmax layer comprising of 6 nodes (LOC_B, LOC_I, X, O, SEP, CLS) was added for token-level classification. The weights were initialized using BERT pre-trained for general purpose entity recognition (Link to GitHub repository of the pre-trained model). We fine-tuned both $BERT_{LARGE}$ and $BERT_{BASE}$ and used the original cased vocabulary of the respective models.

The models were trained using the BERTAdam (Adam (Kingma and Ba, 2014) optimizer with weight decay regularization for BERT) optimizer, with learning rate set to 3×10^{-5}. A weight decay rate of 0.01 to the main weight matrices alongside early stopping was used to add regularization. The average length of WordPiece tokenized sequence in our dataset was 40 (max: 241, min: 12, std: 16); we used a maximum sequence length of 128 for $BERT_{Base}$ and 64 for $BERT_{Large}$. A batch size of 32 was used for $BERT_{Base}$ and 16 for $BERT_{Large}$ and the models were trained for a total of 20 epochs. NVIDIA Tesla K80 and NVIDIA Tesla P100 GPUs on the Google Cloud Platform were used to fine-tune $BERT_{Base}$ and $BERT_{Large}$ respectively. Due to computational limitations, we could not train $BERT_{Large}$ with larger sequence lengths and batch sizes.

3.3 Experimental Results

In order to ensure the effectiveness of our experiment, we divided the dataset into training, development and test sets to maintain a ratio of 8:1:1. As the task was framed as a multi-label classification problem, we calculate common performance measures - Precision, Recall and F_1 scores (Liu et al., 2014) for each of our labels (LOC_B, LOC_I and O). The results are presented in *Table 1*.

Table 1: Results on the Test Set for $BERT_{Base}$ and $BERT_{Large}$

Model	Tag	Metric		
		Precision	Recall	F_1
$BERT_{Base}$	LOC_B	76.97	87.43	81.85
	LOC_I	74.83	71.97	73.38
	O	99.25	99.10	99.18
$BERT_{Large}$	LOC_B	78.27	81.01	79.62
	LOC_I	73.01	70.16	71.56
	O	98.14	98.22	98.18

As shown in *Table 1*, $BERT_{Base}$ performs better than $BERT_{Large}$ for all tags on all three evaluation metrics. We believe this is due to the fact that we used a shorter sequence length while training the $BERT_{Large}$ model, which ignores any location mentions after token 64.

To assess the overall performance of our model, we calculated the average precision, recall and F_1 scores weighted by the number of LOC_B and LOC_I labels in the test set. As there were a total of 2334 tokens tagged with the label LOC_B and 3355 tokens tagged with LOC_I in the test set, using weighted average scores helps in accounting for this imbalance. We obtain a weighted average F_1 of 76.83 on $BERT_{Base}$ and 74.87 on $BERT_{Large}$ (Table 2). Note that we have used a conservative approach in measuring the performance of the models. While all tokens might not be essential in identifying a location, our evaluation metrics requires the beginning (LOC_B) and all subsequent tokens (LOC_I) to be identified for the location to be marked as correct.

Figure 4 illustrates the comparison between our fine-tuned $BERT_{Base}$ model and standard NER tools such as those offered by spaCy and Stanford

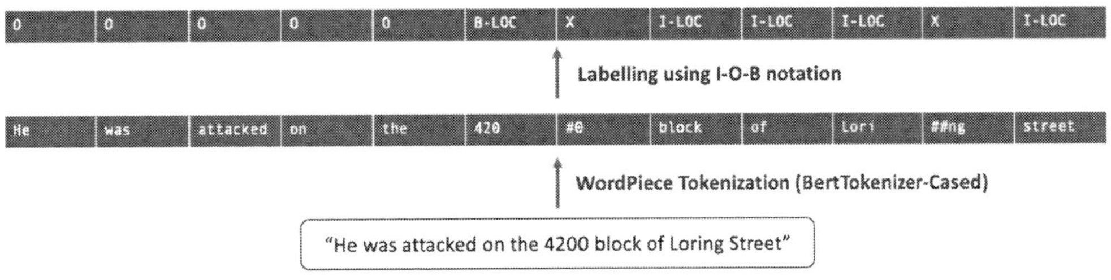

Figure 3: WordPiece Tokenization and Tagging

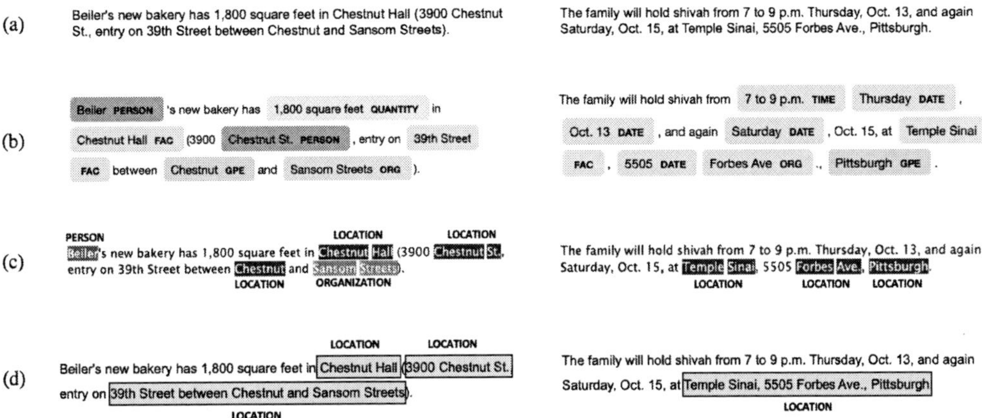

Figure 4: Illustration of different NER taggers (a) Original Sentence (b) SpaCy NER (c) Stanford NLP Group (d) Fine-tuned BERT$_{Base}$ Note: Desciption of SpaCy NER tags can be found at: `https://spacy.io/api/annotation`

Table 2: Weighted Average Scores on the Test Set for BERT$_{Base}$ and BERT$_{Large}$

Model	Metric (Weighted Average)		
	Precision	Recall	F_1
BERT$_{Base}$	75.70	78.28	76.83
BERT$_{Large}$	75.17	74.62	74.87

NLP group. Our model is able to extract precise location entities whereas the other tools split the entities into sub-entities.

4 Mapping

By deploying the fine-tuned BERT model, we present a system that (1) consumes textual news content (or any other text for that matter), (2) extracts the raw text of the locations referenced and (3) returns the corresponding geocodes. The geocodes can be plotted on a map using any standard mapping tool.

4.1 Location Extraction

The BERT models in (3) have been fine-tuned to perform entity recognition at a sentence level. Hence, the first step in location extraction is to split the content into individual sentences. Similar to the approach taken in the data preparation step, we use spaCy's Sentencizer to break the content into individual sentences. The sentences are then passed through the fine-tuned BERT model which return a list of precise location mentions in the sentence. The locations are regrouped at the content level.

4.2 Geocoding

Geocoding is the process of taking input text, such as an address or the name of a place, and returning a latitude/longitude location on the Earth's surface for that place. For instance, geocoding "Atlantic City" will yield 39.3643, 74.4229.

The locations are geocoded using geocoding APIs offered by Google Places and OpenStreetMap. The

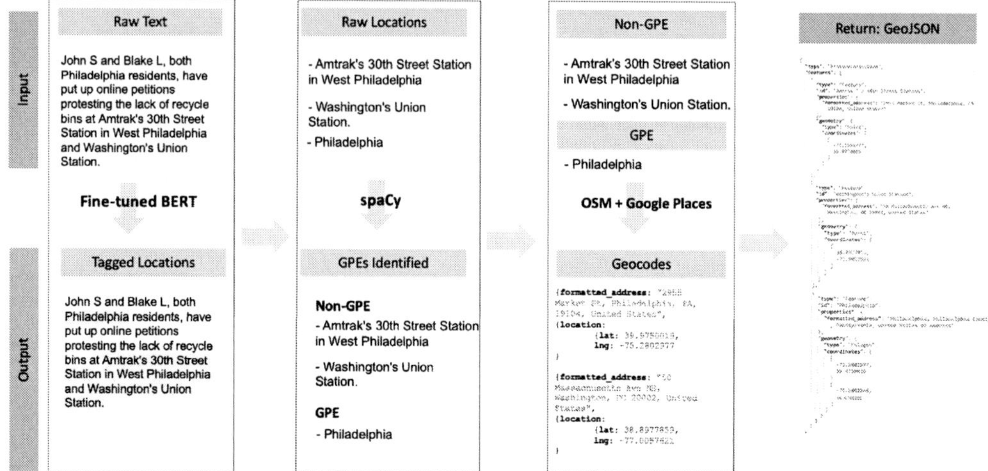

Figure 5: An example output of the mapping system

Text Search Service within the Google Places API returns information about a set of places based on a string, which makes it particularly useful for ambiguous address queries. However, due to limited number of free queries available every month, we utilize the open source OpenStreetMap API in conjunction with Google Places API to minimize the cost associated with geocoding. The OpenStreetMap API does not have an in-built text disambiguation service like Google Places' TextSearch but it is able to return geocodes for geo-political entities with high accuracy. To this extent, we use OpenSteetMap for geocoding locations which are geo-political entities and Google Places for other locations. Locations are identified as geo-political by passing the entity list through spaCy's NER tagger.

To facilitate disambiguation, we utilize the *location* and *radius* parameters in Google Places API and the *viewbox* parameter in the OpenStreetMap API which allows users to specify the preferred region of search. This is particularly useful for mapping local news coverage which is generally confined to a single region. Geo-political entities are geocoded as polygons with series of coordinates defining the enclosed area. For other locations a single point coordinate representing the centroid is returned. The final output is a GeoJSON containing a list of all extracted locations with their geocodes which can readily be consumed by a third-party mapping software.

In Figure 5, we can see an example of a input text and the corresponding GeoJSON output of the locations referenced in the text.

5   Conclusion and Future Work

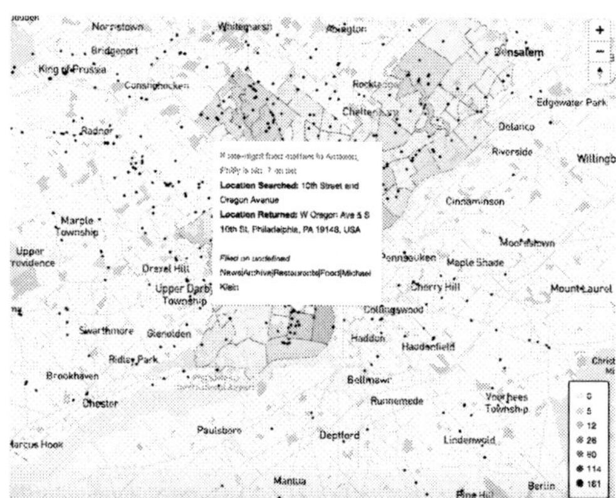

Figure 6: 1000 articles from Philadelphia Inquirer plotted on the map. The green polygons represent Philadelphia neighborhoods with color indicating number of times they have been referenced. Dots represents the locations referenced. The tooltip shows the metadata for the article that references one of the locations.

To map local news coverage, it is important to extract precise location mentions from textual news content. In this paper, we presented a fine-tuned BERT based language model to achieve high level of granularity that is required for this task. Compared to traditional NER taggers, our model is able to extract locations such as addresses, streets and intersections in their entirety, making it possible to accurately place them on a map. We also present an end-to-end system by deploying the model to extract locations from textual content and geocode them in a format that can be directly consumed by a mapping software for plotting.The system can be integrated with an interactive user interface to visualize location-related features of news content. An example is illustrated in Figure 6 of 1000 random news articles from Philadelphia Inquirer plotted using Mapbox API. The map shows the locations referenced in these news articles (denoted by the points) and the coverage across different Philadelphia neighborhoods (green polygons with color indicating the frequency).

Our work can be advanced and extended from many different perspectives. First, a more comprehensive dataset could be developed with specific tags for different location types. The BERT model can be further fine-tuned using this dataset to extract different location types from the text. Second, the disambigation of the extracted location can be further strengthened using contextual clues to enhance the accuracy of the geocoding process. Lastly, many other state-of-art pre-pretrained language models can be fine-tuned using our dataset and a comparison can be established to select the best performing model to be used for tagging.

Acknowledgments

We would like to thank the Brown Institute for Media Innovation at Columbia University and the Lenfest Institute for Journalism for providing us the resources to carry out this study and for their guidance throughout.

References

Steven Bird, Ewan Klein, and Edward Loper. 2009. *Natural Language Processing with Python*. O'Reilly Media Inc.

Shawn Brunsting, Hans De Sterck, Remco Dolman, and Teun van Sprundel. 2016. Geotexttagger: High-precision location tagging of textual documents using a natural language processing approach.

Jason Chiu and Eric Nichols. 2015. Named entity recognition with bidirectional lstm-snns. *Trans. Assoc. Comput. Linguist.*, 6.

Jacob Devlin, Ming-Wei Chang, Kenton Lee, and Kristina Toutanova. 2018. Bert: Pre-training of deep bidirectional transformers for language understanding.

Jenny Finkel, Trond Grenager, and Christoper Manning. 2005. Incorporating non-local information into information extraction systems by gibbs sampling.

Matthew Honnibal and Ines Montani. 2017. spacy 2: Natural language understanding with bloom embeddings, convolutional neural networks and incremental parsing. *To appear*.

Diederik P. Kingma and Jimmy Ba. 2014. Adam: A method for stochastic optimization.

John D. Lafferty, Andrew McCallum, and Fernando C. N. Pereira. 2001. Conditional random fields: Probabilistic models for segmenting and labeling sequence data. In *Proceedings of the Eighteenth International Conference on Machine Learning*, ICML '01, pages 282–289, San Francisco, CA, USA. Morgan Kaufmann Publishers Inc.

Jinhyuk Lee, Wonjin Yoon, Sungdong Kim, Donghyeon Kim, Sunkyu Kim, Chan Ho So, and Jaewoo Kang. 2019. Biobert: a pre-trained biomedical language representation model for biomedical text mining. *Bioinformatics*.

John Lingad, Sarvnaz Karimi, and Jie Yin. 2013. Location extraction from disaster-related microblogs.

Yang Liu. 2019. Fine-tune BERT for extractive summarization. *CoRR*, abs/1903.10318.

Yangguang Liu, Yangming Zhou, Shiting Wen, and Chaogang Tang. 2014. A strategy on selecting performance metrics for classifier evaluation. *International Journal of Mobile Computing and Multimedia Communications*, 6:20–35.

Simone Magnolini, Valerio Piccioni, Vevake Balaraman, Marco Guerini, and Bernardo Magnini. 2019. How to use gazetteers for entity recognition with neural models. In *Proceedings of the 5th Workshop on Semantic Deep Learning (SemDeep-5)*, Macau, China. Association for Computational Linguistics.

Sara Meftah and Nasredine Semmar. 2018. A neural network model for part-of-speech tagging of social media texts. In *Proceedings of the Eleventh International Conference on Language Resources and Evaluation (LREC 2018)*, Miyazaki, Japan. European Language Resources Association (ELRA).

Adam Paszke, Sam Gross, Francisco Massa, Adam Lerer, James Bradbury, Gregory Chanan, Trevor Killeen, Zeming Lin, Natalia Gimelshein, Luca Antiga, Alban Desmaison, Andreas Köpf, Edward Yang, Zach DeVito, Martin Raison, Alykhan Tejani, Sasank Chilamkurthy, Benoit Steiner, Lu Fang, Junjie Bai, and Soumith Chintala. 2019. Pytorch: An imperative style, high-performance deep learning library.

Alec Radford, Jeffrey Wu, Rewon Child, David Luan, Dario Amodei, and Ilya Sutskever. 2018. Language models are unsupervised multitask learners.

Daniel Ramage, David Hall, Ramesh Nallapati, and Christopher D. Manning. 2009. Labeled LDA: A supervised topic model for credit attribution in multi-labeled corpora. In *Proceedings of the 2009 Conference on Empirical Methods in Natural Language Processing*, pages 248–256, Singapore. Association for Computational Linguistics.

Lance A. Ramshaw and Mitchell P. Marcus. 1995. Text chunking using transformation-based learning.

Adwait Ratnaparkhi. 2016. *Maximum Entropy Models for Natural Language Processing*, pages 1–6. Springer US, Boston, MA.

Alex Ratner, Paroma Varma, Braden Hancock, and Chris Ré. 2019. Weak supervision: A new programming paradigm for machine learning.

Alexander Ratner, Stephen H. Bach, Henry Ehrenberg, Jason Fries, Sen Wu, and Christopher Ré. 2017. Snorkel. *Proceedings of the VLDB Endowment*, 11(3):269–282.

Thomas Wolf, Lysandre Debut, Victor Sanh, Julien Chaumond, Clement Delangue, Anthony Moi, Pierric Cistac, Tim Rault, Rémi Louf, Morgan Funtowicz, and Jamie Brew. 2019. Huggingface's transformers: State-of-the-art natural language processing.

Yonghui Wu, Mike Schuster, Zhifeng Chen, Quoc V. Le, Mohammad Norouzi, Wolfgang Macherey, Maxim Krikun, Yuan Cao, Qin Gao, Klaus Macherey, Jeff Klingner, Apurva Shah, Melvin Johnson, Xiaobing Liu, Lukasz Kaiser, Stephan Gouws, Yoshikiyo Kato, Taku Kudo, Hideto Kazawa, Keith Stevens, George Kurian, Nishant Patil, Wei Wang, Cliff Young, Jason Smith, Jason Riesa, Alex Rudnick, Oriol Vinyals, Greg Corrado, Macduff Hughes, and Jeffrey Dean. 2016. Google's neural machine translation system: Bridging the gap between human and machine translation. *CoRR*, abs/1609.08144.

Kui Xue, Yangming Zhou, Zhiyuan Ma, Tong Ruan, Huanhuan Zhang, and Ping He. 2019. Fine-tuning bert for joint entity and relation extraction in chinese medical text.

Zhilin Yang, Zihang Dai, Yiming Yang, Jaime Carbonell, Ruslan Salakhutdinov, and Quoc V. Le. 2019. Xlnet: Generalized autoregressive pretraining for language understanding.

Foreigner-directed speech is simpler than native-directed: Evidence from social media

Aleksandrs Berdicevskis

Språkbanken (The Swedish Language Bank), University of Gothenburg

`aleksandrs.berdicevskis@gu.se`

Abstract

I test two hypotheses that play an important role in modern sociolinguistics and language evolution studies: first, that non-native production is simpler than native; second, that production addressed to non-native speakers is simpler than that addressed to natives. The second hypothesis is particularly important for theories about contact-induced simplification, since the accommodation to non-natives may explain how the simplification can spread from adult learners to the whole community. To test the hypotheses, I create a very large corpus of native and non-native written speech in four languages (English, French, Italian, Spanish), extracting data from an internet forum where native languages of the participants are known and the structure of the interactions can be inferred. The corpus data yield inconsistent evidence with respect to the first hypothesis, but largely support the second one, suggesting that foreigner-directed speech is indeed simpler than native-directed. Importantly, when testing the first hypothesis, I contrast production of different speakers, which can introduce confounds and is a likely reason for the inconsistencies. When testing the second hypothesis, the comparison is always within the production of the same speaker (but with different addressees), which makes it more reliable.

1 Introduction

An important and relatively recent development in sociolinguistics, language evolution and typology is increased interest in sociocognitive determinants of linguistic complexity. Several influential theories (Dahl, 2004; Wray and Grace, 2007; McWhorter, 2007; Trudgill, 2011; Dale and Lupyan, 2012) link the likelihood of a language to maintain or to lose complexity to several social factors, most prominently, the proportion of non-native (L2) speakers in the population and population size. Their main claim can be formulated

as follows: large proportion of L2 speakers and large population size are likely to favour simplification (first of all, morphological simplification), presumably because they inhibit perfect language transmission. While interesting per se, this hypothesis can also be viewed as part of a larger question: to what extent do languages adapt to extralinguistic factors (Five Graces Group et al., 2009; Gibson et al., 2019).

There has been accumulated a solid body of evidence that at least partially supports this causal link. The evidence comes from typological studies (Lupyan and Dale, 2010; Sinnemäki, 2009; Bentz and Winter, 2013; Bentz et al., 2015; Szmrecsanyi and Kortmann, 2009), diachronic analyses (Carroll et al., 2012), computational modeling (Reali et al., 2014) and laboratory experiments (Atkinson et al., 2019; Raviv et al., 2019; Berdicevskis and Semenuks, 2020). Nonetheless, the evidence is not entirely consistent. Studies, for instance, yield different results with respect to whether both factors (population size and proportion of L2 speakers) are at play (Sinnemäki and Di Garbo, 2018) or only one of them (Koplenig, 2019), or whether population size does play a role, but solely because it is strongly correlated with the proportion of L2 speakers. Moreover, the alleged mechanism of simplification is not fully clear.

If we focus on the proportion of L2 speakers as the causal factor, then the hypothetical mechanism of its influence can be in very broad strokes represented as follows:

1. L2 speakers, acquiring the language as adults, often learn it imperfectly;

2. imperfect learning leads to simplified linguistic production;

3. simplification by L2 speakers spreads to the whole community.

Of these links, the first is the most accepted one, while the third causes the most doubt. Indeed, even

Proceedings of the Fourth Workshop on Natural Language Processing and Computational Social Science, pages 163–172

Online, November 20, 2020. ©2020 Association for Computational Linguistics

https://doi.org/10.18653/v1/P17

if L2s do speak a simplified version of a language, how and why does it affect native speakers? And if it does not, we would not expect the simplification to take place (unless the proportion of L2 speakers is extremely large, which is rarely the case).

It has been suggested (Atkinson et al., 2018) that one of the processes that can account for this "missing link" is foreigner-directed speech, which occurs when more proficient (L1) speakers accommodate their production to less proficient (L2) speakers. Atkinson et al. (2018) observe an equivalent of foreigner-directed speech in their artificial language-learning experiment which does lead to community-level language simplification. They argue convincingly that a similar process may occur in real languages, too, but it is an open question whether it actually does. Moreover, while foreigner-directed speech is being actively studied (Uther et al., 2007; Chun et al., 2016; Wiese, 2009; Lev-Ari et al., 2018; Rothermich et al., 2019), I am not aware of any study that would convincingly show, using a corpus of natural production, that foreigner-directed speech is indeed simpler than native-directed.

Coming back to link 2, it has neither been reliably established that production of L2 speakers is on average simpler than that of L1 speakers. In this paper, I attempt to fill in both these gaps using English, French, Italian and Spanish data extracted from a very large internet forum. The resulting corpus has several advantages over most of the existing learner corpora[1]. It represents naturally occurring written production; it is very large both in terms of number of tokens and number of speakers; the native language of every speaker is known; for many messages, it is possible to identify to whom they are addressed.

To sum up, I test two hypotheses:

1. non-native written speech is on average simpler than native;
2. written speech addressed to non-native speakers is on average simpler than that addressed to natives.

Hypothesis 2 can be further nuanced by asking whether the presence and degree of simplification depends on the addresser being an L1 speaker or an L2 speaker. For the theories about socially-facilitated language simplification, the most important sub-hypothesis is whether L1 speakers accom-

	ita	fra	spa	eng
L1 words (M)	3.6	6.8	23.1	71.1
L2 words (M)	1.0	3.8	5.7	54.7
L1 speakers (K)	3.1	5.0	17.4	17.4
L2 speakers (K)	1.9	5.9	7.6	39.2

Table 1: The WordReference corpus composition

modate, but I will test all the possibilities.

The operationalizations of *complexity* and *simpler* are discussed in Section 2.2.

2 Materials and methods

2.1 The WordReference corpus

All the data are extracted from WordReference forums[2], where users discuss various questions about languages. Importantly, every user has to provide their native language, and this information, alongside with the nickname, is publicly available (and, of course, visible to other users). Furthermore, for English, French, Italian and Spanish there exist forums "English Only", "Français Seulement", "Solo Italiano" and "Sólo Español", where all communication should occur only in the respective language, and this rule is generally observed.

The data were downloaded in March 2019. They were cleaned of hyperlinks, any traces of markup and all symbols that are neither alphanumeric characters used in the given language nor punctuation marks. Users may quote each other's messages to make it clear what they are responding to, and while sometimes this information can potentially be useful, it is difficult to process: sometimes users respond without quotes, sometimes one message can contain several quotes or nested quotes (A responding to B's cue which was written in response to C's cue etc). For this reason, all quotes are also erased. The resulting corpus size (excluding punctuation) is approximately 170M words (for more details see Table 1). Note that in terms of the number of words, L1 production prevails, even in the English subcorpus where the number of L2 speakers is noticeably higher.

The version of the corpus that is analyzed in this paper consists of four tab-separated files (each per language) with nine columns: message id; poster's nickname; poster's native language; the message itself; the id of the first message in the thread (if different from message id); topicstarter's nickname;

---

[1]The most comprehensive list can be found here: https://uclouvain.be/en/research-institutes/ilc/cecl/learner-corpora-around-the-world.html

[2]https://forum.wordreference.com/

topicstarter's native language; poster's status (L1 or L2); topicstarter's status. Statuses were inferred from native languages, but since users provide those as free text (and not by selecting a language from a predefined list), some errors are possible. If a user provides several native languages, he or she is considered to be L1 in all of them.

Most threads are started by non-native speakers (which is unsurprising), but the exact proportion of such threads varies: 66% for Italian, 87% for French, 61% for Spanish and 95% for English. Native speakers, however, also ask questions, which may address, for instance, technical terms, theoretical grammar, differences between language varieties (e.g. American vs British English), language variation, correct usage and pronunciation etc. Note that bilingual and multilingual users are also classified as native speakers as long as the forum language is one of the languages listed in their profile. It is possible that they should instead be treated as L2s, or as a separate category, or that differential treatment should be applied, but a thorough manual investigation would be required for an informed decision.

The corpus (openly available) has several important advantages. It contains naturally occurring written production both of L1 and L2 speakers. It is very large (probably the largest of currently existing learner corpora), both with respect to the number of tokens and the number of represented speakers. It contains some information about the interaction structure (which messages are posted in which thread and in which order). In principle, the social ties between forum users can also be reconstructed, cf. (Del Tredici and Fernández, 2018).

That said, the corpus has two important shortcomings. First, the data are noisy, and presumably the L2 production more so. This means that automatic annotation might introduce an unknown bias, especially if it is used for quantitative comparison of L1 and L2 production. Second, while the corpus contains huge amount of messages from many speakers, most messages are very short. These two disadvantages impose limitations on how complexity can be measured.

2.2 Measuring complexity

The research questions and the properties of the corpus yield several requirements to how complexity should be operationalized and quantified. With those requirements in mind, I opt for type-token ratio (TTR; the number of distinct words divided by the total number of words), a simple measure of lexicogrammatical diversity. First, unlike most other measures, it does not require any annotation. Automatic annotation of non-native speech poses several methodological problems (Díaz-Negrillo et al., 2013). Most importantly, it may introduce an unknown bias due to different performances on L1 and L2 (less standard) data. Controlling for this potential bias implies a substantial manual effort and is beyond the scope of this paper. Second, TTR is very responsive (Bentz et al., 2015) and thus well-suited for the analysis of the short texts. Third, TTR correlates quite well both with other, more advanced corpus-based measures and with manually compiled grammar-based measures of complexity (Bentz et al., 2016; Kettunen, 2014). Fourth, it performs no worse than average in a recent comparison of several corpus-based complexity measures (Berdicevskis et al., 2018).

The main drawback of TTR is that it is very sensitive to text size. To control for that, I use it to compare only the texts of the same size (taking the first n words of every message). A pilot study suggests that using more advanced TTR-based measures such as HD-D, MTLD (McCarthy and Jarvis, 2010; Koizumi and In'nami, 2012) or moving-average TTR (Covington and McFall, 2010), which are supposed to be more robust, affects the results yielded by plain TTR very litte. Since plain TTR is more interpretable, I opt for it.

An alternative approach would be to lump together all messages authored by one speaker, thus creating a slightly larger per-speaker subcorpora, which might make it possible to apply less responsive measures (e.g. word entropy), or even just applying the same measure, TTR, to larger chunks of text. The gain, however, would be small for most speakers, while the downside would be a step away from using a natural unit of analysis (message, a more or less coherent text with certain discursive properties) towards aggregation of data. Instead, I opt for using messages as datapoints and mixed-effect regression (see section 3) for fine-grained analysis without aggregation and with control for non-independence.

Yet another limitation of TTR (as well as most other measures that do not require annotation) is that it cannot distinguish between grammatical complexity (which is the main focus of the theories discussed in Section 1) and lexical complexity. That is, TTR can decrease because speakers use less different lemmas (lexical complexity), or less different inflected forms (grammatical complexity), or both. However, even with that limitation in mind, the quantitative test of hypotheses 1 and 2 are still valuable, and the individual contributions of lexical and grammatical complexity can be estimated in further studies.

3 Comparing complexities

3.1 L1 speakers vs L2 speakers

To test hypothesis 1 (non-native written speech is on average simpler than native), I extract all messages that are at least n words long and calculate TTR for the first n words of every such message. I do it for two values of n: 100 and 200. Smaller values are likely to yield non-robust estimates of TTR, larger values cut off too many messages and make the resulting sample too small. Thus, on the one hand, the 200-word threshold is likely to yield more robust results, but on the other hand, the 100-word thresholds yields more power and can be more informative. The differences between L1 and L2 speakers (for the 100-word threshold) are visualized on Figure 1 using violin plots.

To quantify the observed differences (which are obviously small) and test whether they are significant, I fit a mixed-effect linear regression model with TTR of the message as the dependent variable, speaker's STATUS (L1 vs L2) as main effect (predictor) and the random intercept for speaker id (nickname). The intercept controls for non-independence of the datapoints: several messages can be authored by the same speaker, and there might exist idiosyncratic differences in the complexity of linguistic production between individual speakers, which random effect takes into account. This mixed-effect approach is usually considered superior to methods like usual regression or t-tests, since it makes it possible to avoid aggregating data (averaging across messages and/or speakers).

I perform the calculations in R 4.0.2 (R Core Team, 2020), using the `lmerTest` package (Kuznetsova et al., 2017) to calculate p-values and `ggplot2` (Wickham, 2016) to estimate discrimination. In `lme4` (Bates et al., 2015) notation, the model looks as follows:

$$ttr \sim status + (1|speaker)$$

The results of the models for both 200- and 100-word thresholds (which are quite different) are summarized in Table1 2.

Obviously, the 100-word threshold yields much more datapoints (though presumably of lower quality). It also yields higher intercept values, which is understandable: as text length increases, TTR decreases, since new types appear at a lower rate than tokens. What is important are different values for slopes (i.e. the effect of STATUS). With the 200-word threshold, the threshold is positive (but not significantly different from zero) for all languages apart from English, where it is significant and negative (i.e. L2 speakers have simpler production, as expected). With the 100-word threshold, the slope is always significant, negative for Italian and positive for all other languages. Note that in all cases the slope is small.

3.2 Foreigner-directed speech

To test hypothesis 2 (non-native directed speech is simpler than native-directed), I extract all messages that are *second* in a thread, i.e. are *first responses* to a posted question (usually the first message in a thread is a question, and other messages are responses to it). I refer to the author of this second message (addresser) as the speaker, and to the author of the first message (addressee) as the topicstarter. The reason for taking only the second messages is that it is only for them we can be fully certain to whom they are addressed. Any other message can potentially be addressed to the topicstater (answering the original question) or the author(s) of one (or more) messages occurring between the original question and the response, or both, and there is no way to establish that automatically and reliably.

For all selected messages I repeat the procedure described in Section 3.1: if they are long enough, I calculate TTR for the first n words of every such message, n being 100 or 200. An additional threshold is that only speakers which has addressed at least one message to an L1 speaker and at least one to an L2 speaker are included. The differences between the complexity of speech addressed to L1 and L2 speakers (for the 100-word threshold) are visualized on Figures 2 (only when the addressers are L1 speakers) and 3 (only when the addressers are L2 speakers).

This time, we have two factors we are interested in: speaker's status and topicstarter's status (who

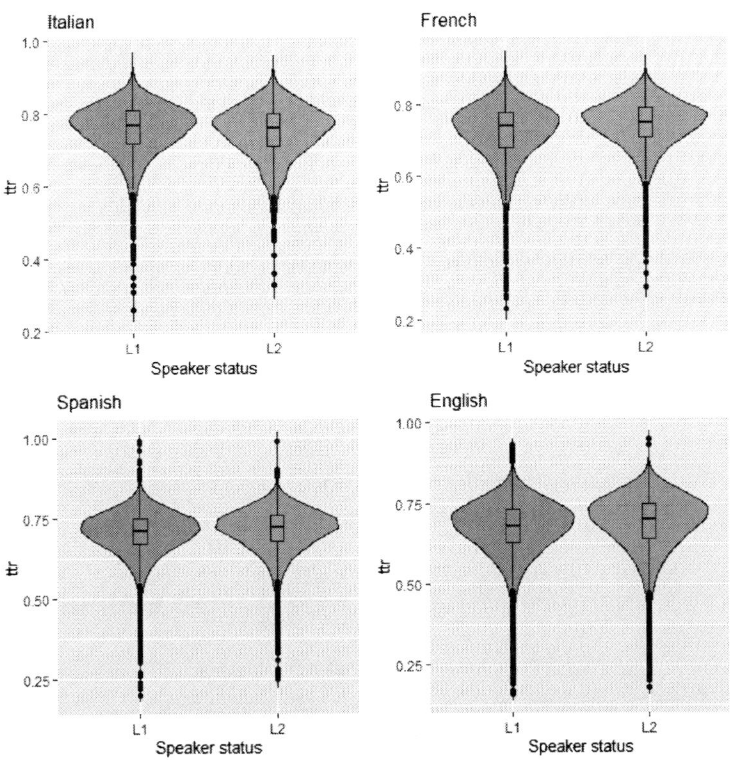

Figure 1: Complexity of L1 and L2 production (raw data, uncontrolled for speaker-specific effects; 100-word threshold)

Language	#messages	#speakers	α	β	SE	t (df)	p
Italian-200	2199	451	0.666	-0.005	0.006	-0.8 (358)	0.450
French-200	2742	573	0.628	0.009	0.005	1.9 (439)	0.064
Spanish-200	10675	2033	0.610	0.002	0.003	0.9 (1741)	0.350
English-200	29006	4561	0.585	-0.007	0.002	-3.4 (3461)	<0.001*
Italian-100	11033	1426	0.755	-0.008	0.003	-2.9 (1046)	0.004*
French-100	20787	2539	0.723	0.011	0.002	5.1 (1603)	<0.001*
Spanish-100	61001	6944	0.706	0.004	0.001	3.2 (4415)	0.002*
English-100	258016	18646	0.683	0.003	0.001	-3.3 (14930)	<0.001*

Table 2: Summary of the mixed-effects model for the two thresholds: TTR as predicted by STATUS (L1 vs L2) with random intercept for speaker. α = intercept, β = slope, all other columns pertain to slope. Asterisks denote significance at the 0.05 level.

Predictor	200-word threshold				100-word threshold			
	Coef	SE	*t* (df)	*p*	Coef	SE	*t* (df)	*p*
Italian	messages: 98, speakers: 61				messages: 686, speakers: 245			
(Intercept)	0.680	0.012	57 (82)	<0.001*	0.753	0.005	145 (380)	<0.001*
SP:L2	-0.016	0.032	-0.5 (85)	0.620	0.009	0.021	0 (336)	0.662
TS:L2	-0.030	0.015	-2 (88)	0.046*	-0.024	0.006	-4 (677)	<0.001*
SP:L2 x TS:L2	-0.021	0.047	-0.443 (92)	0.659	-0.011	0.022	0 (680)	0.623
French	messages: 166, speakers: 88				messages: 2130, speakers: 410			
(Intercept)	0.601	0.021	59 (162)	<0.001*	0.718	0.005	131 (1349)	<0.001*
SP:L2	0.073	0.040	2 (151)	0.072	0.031	0.018	2 (1420)	0.084
TS:L2	0.003	0.021	0 (157)	0.898	-0.013	0.005	-2 (2097)	0.016*
SP:L2 x TS:L2	-0.075	0.052	-1 (161)	0.154	-0.013	0.019	-1 (1954)	0.556
Spanish	messages: 550, speakers: 228				(messages: 4450, speakers: 864			
(Intercept)	0.606	0.005	133 (223)	<0.001*	0.702	0.002	321 (946)	<0.001*
SP:L2	-0.028	0.022	-1 (421)	0.191	-0.001	0.008	0 (2113)	0.925
TS:L2	-0.016	0.006	-3 (544)	0.006*	-0.013	0.002	-6 (4440)	<0.001*
SP:L2 x TS:L2	0.041	0.026	2 (538)	0.126	-0.003	0.010	0 (4430)	0.773
English	messages: 1629, speakers: 345				messages: 23284, speakers: 1720			
(Intercept)	0.573	0.007	83 (1338)	<0.001*	0.668	0.002	210 (5810)	<0.001*
SP:L2	-0.004	0.017	0 (1317)	0.804	0.017	0.007	2 (11200)	0.016*
TS:L2	-0.012	0.007	-2 (1625)	0.071	-0.007	0.002	-3 (23240)	0.002*
SP:L2 x TS:L2	0.004	0.018	2 (1625)	0.839	-0.020	0.007	-3 (22820)	0.005*

Table 3: Summary of the mixed-effects model for the 100-word threshold: TTR as predicted by STATUS (L1 vs L2) with random intercept for speaker. α = intercept, β = slope, all other columns pertain to slope. Asterisks denote significance at the 0.05 level.

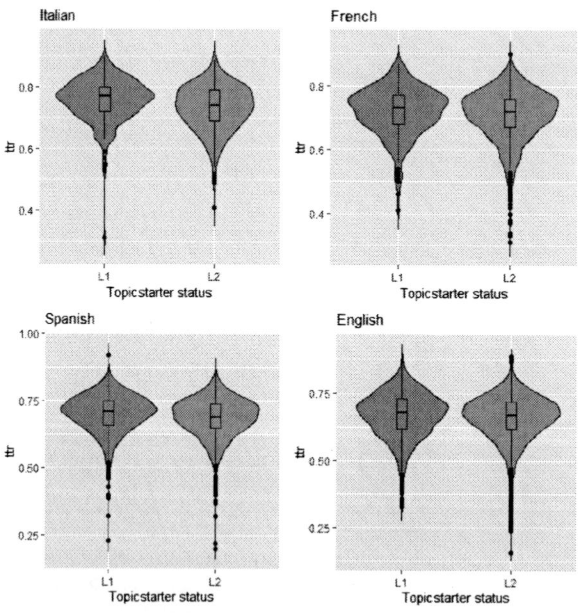

Figure 2: Complexity of L1 production addressed to L1 an L2 speakers (raw data, uncontrolled for speaker-specific effects; 100-word threshold)

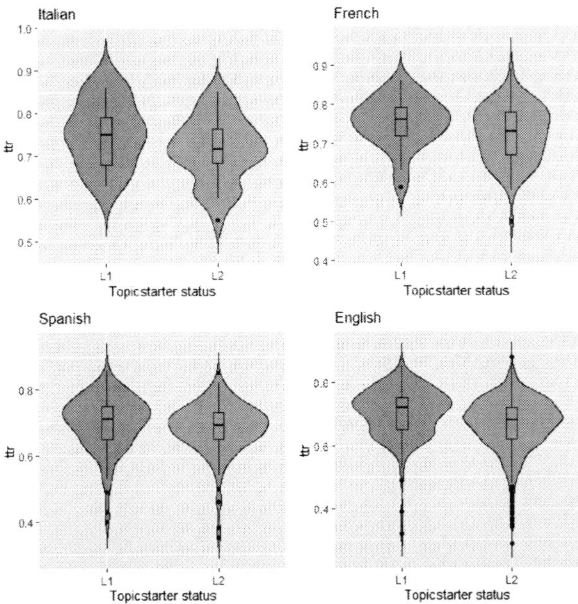

Figure 3: Complexity of L2 production addressed to L1 an L2 speakers (raw data, uncontrolled for speaker-specific effects; 100-word threshold)

speaks to whom). I fit a mixed-effect linear regression model with TTR of the message as the dependent variable, speaker's status (SP_STATUS), topicstarter's status (TS_STATUS) and their interaction as main effects and the random intercept for speaker id (nickname).

In lme4 notation:

$$ttr \sim sp\_status * ts\_status + (1|speaker)$$

Summaries of the models for both thresholds are provided in Table 3. When it comes to the effect of the topicstarter's (addressee's status), the models show much more unity than they did in section 3.1 for speaker's status. With 200-word threshold, the effect is negative (as expected) for Italian and Spanish and insignificant for French and English. With 100-word threshold, it is always negative and significant. The effect of the speaker's status if always insignificant apart from English with 100-word threshold, where it is positive (i.e., L2 production is more complex; cf. English-100 in Table 2. The interaction in this case is also significant and negative, implying that L2 speakers accommodate to other L2 speakers more than L1 speakers do (that is not the case for other languages and the other thresholds).

4 Discussion

I used the WordReference corpus data to test two hypotheses:

1. non-native written speech is on average simpler than native;
2. written speech addressed to non-native speakers is on average simpler than that addressed to natives.

Generally, the corpus data support hypothesis 2: the results vary across languages and threshold sizes, but the observed effects are either in the direction predicted by hypothesis or insignificant. However, they yield inconsistent results with respect to hypothesis 1. A skeptical reader may ask two questions. Suppose hypothesis 1 is not supported by the data because it is wrong (L2 production is not simpler than L1). Does hypothesis 2 still make sense then? Alternatively, suppose hypothesis 1 is not supported because the chosen method does not really work well on the available data and does not provide reliable complexity estimates. Can the results with respect to hypothesis 2 still be trusted? The answer to both questions is "probably yes".

The reason why the method described in the paper might work well for the comparison of L1-directed and L2-directed production, but not for the comparison of L1 and L2 production is that in

169

the latter case what is being compared is always the production of the same speaker (addressed to different persons). In the former case, the production of different speakers is compared, and that might introduce different confounds. It may, for instance, be that some L2 speakers use fewer different forms (TTR decreases), but some make many misspellings (TTR increases)[3]. Other systematic confounds may be present, e.g. that L2 speakers to a larger extent use quotes from textbooks (or some other sources they want to ask a question about) or rely on translation software etc. On the contrary, when the compared texts belong to the same speaker, we can assume that all parameters apart from that of interest (addressee's proficiency) are equivalent, which makes the comparison more reliable.

The same reasons make the comparisons across languages difficult. Cross-linguistic complexity comparisons were not relevant to the theoretical questions of this paper, but are of course still interesting and important. One obvious observation, however, can be made in this respect: English has noticeably lower TTR than the three Romance languages (as expected). In section 2.2, I raised the question whether the observed effects are due to the differences in lexical or grammatical complexity. For the cross-linguistic differences, the reason is likely to be in the domain of the grammar (English inflection is much poorer than Romance; while there is no reason to claim that about English lexicon), which suggests that the other differences are also at least partly due to grammatical complexity.

The answer to the first skeptical question is more hypothetical. If hypothesis 1 is wrong, hypothesis 2 may still be correct. It may be that while L2 speakers are less proficient, their production is not simpler (at least not as measured by TTR): for instance, it can be more variable, thus inflating complexity values. Nonetheless, L1 speakers are sensitive to the differences in proficiency and, being more capable of controlling their production, simplify it in order to accommodate to their interlocutors. That, however, is just a speculation.

The openly-available WordReference corpus can be used for further studies of foreigner-directed speech (and, of course, other phenomena related to non-native acquisition and usage). The understanding of the properties of L2 production can,

for instance, be nuanced by taking into account other relevant factors, such as speakers' mother tongues (Schepens et al., 2020) or social-network structure (Raviv et al., 2020).

5 Conclusions

Data from the WordReference corpus (a very large and diverse corpus of naturally occurring written speech in four languages) support the hypothesis that written speech addressed to non-native speakers is on average simpler than that addressed to natives (regardless of who is the addresser: a native or a non-native speaker). There is, however, some variation across languages and measurement thresholds. The same data, however, do not provide conclusive evidence with respect to hypothesis that non-native written speech is on average simpler than native. A probable reason is that the comparison of the production of different speakers is affected by various confounds and not as robust and reliable as comparison within one speaker's production.

The finding that foreigner-directed speech is simpler than native-directed is important for theories of contact-induced language simplification, since it may potentially explain how simplification spreads from non-native speakers to the whole population (including the coming generations).

The scripts that were used to create the corpus, extract the data and perform the statistical analysis, as well as the current version of the corpus are openly available[4].

Acknowledgments

I would like to thank the three anonymous reviewers for their comments and suggestions, and my colleagues at the Uppsala university and the University of Gothenburg, as well as the participants of the Evolang-2018 conference for feedback on various earlier versions of this work.

References

Mark Atkinson, Gregory J Mills, and Kenny Smith. 2019. Social group effects on the emergence of communicative conventions and language complexity. *Journal of Language Evolution*, 4(1):1–18.

Mark Atkinson, Kenny Smith, and Simon Kirby. 2018. Adult learning and language simplification. *Cognitive Science*, 42(8):2818–2854.

---

[3]One potential source of misspellings are diacritics, especially in French.

[4]https://github.com/AleksandrsBerdicevskis/word-reference-corpus

Douglas Bates, Martin Mächler, Ben Bolker, and Steve Walker. 2015. Fitting linear mixed-effects models using lme4. *Journal of Statistical Software, Articles*, 67(1):1–48.

Christian Bentz, Tatyana Ruzsics, Alexander Koplenig, and Tanja Samardžić. 2016. A comparison between morphological complexity measures: Typological data vs. language corpora. In *Proceedings of the Workshop on Computational Linguistics for Linguistic Complexity (CL4LC)*, pages 142–153, Osaka, Japan. The COLING 2016 Organizing Committee.

Christian Bentz, Annemarie Verkerk, Douwe Kiela, Felix Hill, and Paula Buttery. 2015. Adaptive communication: Languages with more non-native speakers tend to have fewer word forms. *PLOS ONE*, 10(6):1–23.

Christian Bentz and Bodo Winter. 2013. Languages with more second language learners tend to lose nominal case. *Language Dynamics and Change*, 3(1):1 – 27.

Aleksandrs Berdicevskis, Çağrı Çöltekin, Katharina Ehret, Kilu von Prince, Daniel Ross, Bill Thompson, Chunxiao Yan, Vera Demberg, Gary Lupyan, Taraka Rama, and Christian Bentz. 2018. Using universal dependencies in cross-linguistic complexity research. In *Proceedings of the Second Workshop on Universal Dependencies (UDW 2018)*, pages 8–17, Brussels, Belgium. Association for Computational Linguistics.

Aleksandrs Berdicevskis and Arturs Semenuks. 2020. Different trajectories of morphological overspecification and irregularity under imperfect language learning. In *The Complexities of Morphology*, pages 283–305. Oxford University Press.

Ryan Carroll, Ragnar Svare, and Joseph C Salmons. 2012. Quantifying the evolutionary dynamics of german verbs. *Journal of Historical Linguistics*, 2(2):153–172.

Eunjin Chun, Julia Barrow, and Edith Kaan. 2016. Native english speakers' structural alignment mediated by foreign-accented speech. *Linguistics Vanguard*, 1(open-issue).

Michael A. Covington and Joe D. McFall. 2010. Cutting the gordian knot: The moving-average type–token ratio (mattr). *Journal of Quantitative Linguistics*, 17(2):94–100.

Östen Dahl. 2004. *The growth and maintenance of linguistic complexity*. John Benjamins Publishing.

Rick Dale and Gary Lupyan. 2012. Understanding the origins of morphological diversity: The linguistic niche hypothesis. *Advances in Complex Systems*, 15(03n04):1150017.

Marco Del Tredici and Raquel Fernández. 2018. The road to success: Assessing the fate of linguistic innovations in online communities. In *Proceedings of the 27th International Conference on Computational Linguistics*, pages 1591–1603, Santa Fe, New Mexico, USA. Association for Computational Linguistics.

Ana Díaz-Negrillo, Nicolas Ballier, and Paul Thompson. 2013. *Automatic treatment and analysis of learner corpus data*, volume 59. John Benjamins Publishing Company.

The Five Graces Group, Clay Beckner, Richard Blythe, Joan Bybee, Morten H. Christiansen, William Croft, Nick C. Ellis, John Holland, Jinyun Ke, Diane Larsen-Freeman, and Tom Schoenemann. 2009. Language is a complex adaptive system: Position paper. *Language Learning*, 59(s1):1–26.

Edward Gibson, Richard Futrell, Steven P Piantadosi, Isabelle Dautriche, Kyle Mahowald, Leon Bergen, and Roger Levy. 2019. How efficiency shapes human language. *Trends in cognitive sciences*, 23(5):389–407.

Kimmo Kettunen. 2014. Can type-token ratio be used to show morphological complexity of languages? *Journal of Quantitative Linguistics*, 21(3):223–245.

Rie Koizumi and Yo In'nami. 2012. Effects of text length on lexical diversity measures: Using short texts with less than 200 tokens. *System*, 40(4):554 – 564.

Alexander Koplenig. 2019. Language structure is influenced by the number of speakers but seemingly not by the proportion of non-native speakers. *Royal Society open science*, 6(2):181274.

Alexandra Kuznetsova, Per B Brockhoff, Rune HB Christensen, et al. 2017. lmertest package: tests in linear mixed effects models. *Journal of statistical software*, 82(13):1–26.

Shiri Lev-Ari, Emily Ho, and Boaz Keysar. 2018. The unforeseen consequences of interacting with non-native speakers. *Topics in Cognitive Science*, 10(4):835–849.

Gary Lupyan and Rick Dale. 2010. Language structure is partly determined by social structure. *PLOS ONE*, 5(1):1–10.

Philip M McCarthy and Scott Jarvis. 2010. Mtld, vocd-d, and hd-d: A validation study of sophisticated approaches to lexical diversity assessment. *Behavior research methods*, 42(2):381–392.

John McWhorter. 2007. *Language interrupted: Signs of non-native acquisition in standard language grammars*. Oxford University Press.

R Core Team. 2020. *R: A Language and Environment for Statistical Computing*. R Foundation for Statistical Computing, Vienna, Austria.

Limor Raviv, Antje Meyer, and Shiri Lev-Ari. 2019. Larger communities create more systematic languages. *Proceedings of the Royal Society B*, 286(1907):20191262.

Limor Raviv, Antje Meyer, and Shiri Lev-Ari. 2020. The role of social network structure in the emergence of linguistic structure. *Cognitive Science*, 44(8):e12876.

Florencia Reali, Nick Chater, and Morten Christiansen. 2014. *THE PARADOX OF LINGUISTIC COMPLEXITY AND COMMUNITY SIZE*, pages 270–277. World Scientific.

Kathrin Rothermich, Havan L. Harris, Kerry Sewell, and Susan C. Bobb. 2019. Listener impressions of foreigner-directed speech: A systematic review. *Speech Communication*, 112:22 – 29.

Job Schepens, Roeland van Hout, and T. Florian Jaeger. 2020. Big data suggest strong constraints of linguistic similarity on adult language learning. *Cognition*, 194:104056.

Kaius Sinnemäki. 2009. Complexity in core argument marking and population size. In Geoffrey Sampson, David Gil, and Peter Trudgill, editors, *Language complexity as an evolving variable*, pages 126–140. Oxford University Press.

Kaius Sinnemäki and Francesca Di Garbo. 2018. Language structures may adapt to the sociolinguistic environment, but it matters what and how you count: A typological study of verbal and nominal complexity. *Frontiers in Psychology*, 9:1141.

Benedikt Szmrecsanyi and Bernd Kortmann. 2009. The morphosyntax of varieties of english worldwide: A quantitative perspective. *Lingua*, 119(11):1643 – 1663. The Forests behind the Trees.

Peter Trudgill. 2011. *Sociolinguistic typology: Social determinants of linguistic complexity*. Oxford University Press.

Maria Uther, Monja Knoll, and Denis Burnham. 2007. Do you speak e-ng-l-i-sh? a comparison of foreigner- and infant-directed speech. *Speech Communication*, 49(1):2 – 7.

Hadley Wickham. 2016. *ggplot2: Elegant Graphics for Data Analysis*. Springer-Verlag New York.

Heike Wiese. 2009. Grammatical innovation in multiethnic urban europe: New linguistic practices among adolescents. *Lingua*, 119(5):782 – 806.

Alison Wray and George W. Grace. 2007. The consequences of talking to strangers: Evolutionary corollaries of socio-cultural influences on linguistic form. *Lingua*, 117(3):543 – 578. The Evolution of Language.

Diachronic Embeddings for People in the News

Felix Hennig and **Steven R. Wilson**
University of Edinburgh
Edinburgh, UK
`F.M.P.Hennig@sms.ed.ac.uk,  steven.wilson@ed.ac.uk`

Abstract

Previous English-language diachronic change models based on word embeddings have typically used single tokens to represent entities, including names of people. This leads to issues with both ambiguity (resulting in one embedding representing several distinct and unrelated people) and unlinked references (leading to several distinct embeddings which represent the same person). In this paper, we show that using named entity recognition and heuristic name linking steps *before* training a diachronic embedding model leads to more accurate representations of references to people, as compared to the token-only baseline. In large news corpus of articles from *The Guardian*, we provide examples of several types of analysis that can be performed using these new embeddings. Further, we show that real world events and context changes can be detected using our proposed model, with a focus on the examples of UK prime ministers and role changes in the football domain.

1 Introduction

Diachronic embeddings are an extension to traditional word embeddings that capture changes in word representations over time. These approaches have been used for several computational social science studies focused on the analysis of language and its change over time. For example, Garg et al. (2018) used embeddings to study changes in gender and racial biases over decades of literary documents, and Szymanski (2017) used diachronic embeddings to solve temporal word analogies, leading to insights about political and social changes.

In computational studies of linguistic change, news corpora have been a popular resource because of their stylistic consistency from year-to-year and the availability of large amounts of text from each individual year or even month. In the news, changes in the usage of a word often correspond to changes in the world as well, allowing for inferences about what is happening in the world, and what journalists have been focused on from changes in the embeddings over time. Previous work has also analysed the changes that representations of specific entities undergo, such as corporations like Amazon and Apple or even names of people such as *Obama* or *Trump* (Yao et al., 2018).

However, linking the surname of a person directly to a specific individual is problematic in many cases. It does not allow us to have distinct embeddings for people with the same surname, such as *Bill* and *Hillary Clinton*. A surname might also be a word, such as "may". There is *Theresa May*, the person, but also the month *May* and the verb *may*, which are often treated as the same token for the purposes of creating word embeddings. Issues like these can interfere with downstream analyses based on diachronic embeddings, leading to cases where multiple distinct embeddings exist for the same person, causing information about them to be potentially overlooked. At the same time, multiple people may be represented by the same embedding, resulting in noisy results without a clear way to determine the full set of people represented by the embedding, or a way to disentagle each person's influence.

In this work, we tackle these problems by creating explicit, diachronic embeddings for references to individual people over time, which we embed in the same diachronic space as the remaining words. We do this by finding mentions of people in texts, then linking various surface forms of the same person together and aggregating these contexts. We use named entity recognition and use full names to alleviate the problems mentioned above. All work is done on a data set consisting of more than 2 million articles from *The Guardian*, a British newspaper which has not previously been used in

Proceedings of the Fourth Workshop on Natural Language Processing and Computational Social Science, pages 173–183
Online, November 20, 2020. ©2020 Association for Computational Linguistics
https://doi.org/10.18653/v1/P17

studies of diachronic embeddings. This provides an additional perspective to a number of studies which have exclusively focused on US-centric media outlets (Parker et al., 2011), especially the *New York Times* (Kutuzov et al., 2017; Yao et al., 2018; Szymanski, 2017). Further, we provide a set of case studies, showcasing some of the main issues with the baseline approach and the kinds of analyses that can be performed with our diachronic embeddings.[1]

2 Related Work

News corpora have seen a lot of attention from researchers in diachronic embeddings to make a variety of inferences about the real world. From finding temporal analogies (Zhang et al., 2015) – such as "iPod" being the 2000s equivalent of a "Walkman" in the 1990s – observing the change of the words "amazon" and "apple" (Yao et al., 2018) or tracing armed conflicts (Kutuzov et al., 2017). Yao et al. (2018) explicitly also show examples of persons in the media changing contexts as well as the changes in the association of a role to a person (president, mayor). We use their *DynamicWord2Vec* (DW2V) model to create the diachronic embeddings. Compared to other models which are typically based on alignment of trained embeddings spaces, DW2V aligns embedding spaces during training. Kutuzov et al. (2018) provide a good overview of the field.

Kutuzov et al. (2017) do event detection instead of gradual context changes, by tracking country names in the news over time and observing state changes between war and peace. They propose the aggregation of multiple words into "concept embeddings" and manage to improve the event detection score significantly this way. This is an example of a move away from strict word embeddings towards more high-level embeddings.

Previous analysis of people in corpora as mentioned above is strictly based on the simple mapping of a token to a person, usually the persons surname is used (Szymanski, 2017; Yao et al., 2018). While this is a workable solution, we seek to show how diachronic embeddings can be improved with more explicit linking of references to people.

A similar task to linking references of people in the news for diachronic embeddings is literary character detection (Vala et al., 2015) for modeling rela-

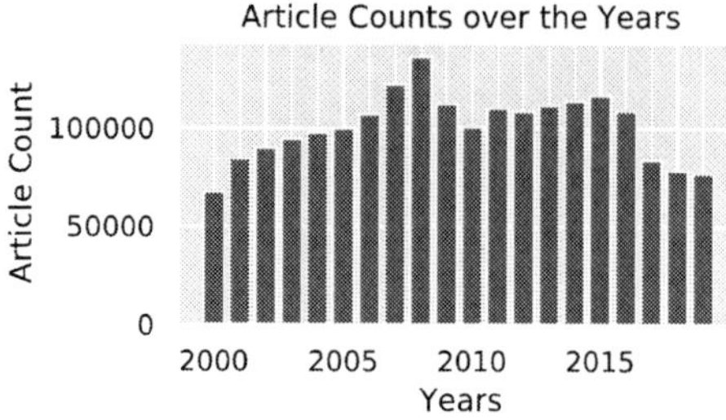

Figure 1: The article counts per year.

tionships between characters over time (Chaturvedi et al., 2016). However, proposed approaches such as the Book-NLP pipeline (Bamman et al., 2014) are focused on very long texts with set of recurring characters with less ambiguous names. In news data, on the other hand, it is common for completely unrelated people to share surnames (or even full names), and the same person may be mentioned in a large number of separate documents.

3 Data

We use a data set sourced from the British newspaper *The Guardian*. *The Guardian* provides all their content via an API called OpenPlatform[2], launched in 2009 (Anderson, 2009). This data source has seen only tangential use in the scientific community (Li et al., 2016; Guimarães and Figueira, 2017; Murukannaiah et al., 2017) and has not been used for diachronic models before.

The data set contains a total of $2,021,947$ articles spread over the years 2000 to 2019, containing 1.65 billion tokens. The documents[3] were retrieved from the API in March 2020. Each document consists of the article body and additional meta-information such as the section in which the article was published. We used spaCy[4] to tokenize the text, and the resulting data was a collection of token sequences, divided into yearly chunks.

Figure 1 shows the distribution of articles over the years, each year contains about $100,000$ articles, which is about 270 articles every day. The distribution of articles over sections is shown in Figure 2. Articles are distributed very broadly over topics ranging from media over sports to politics.

---

[1]Our pre-trained diachronic embeddings as well as the code to generate them are published at github.com/fhennig/DiachronicPeopleEmbeddings

[2]open-platform.theguardian.com

[3]Only documents with the types `article` and `liveblog` were included; this excludes other types of content like crossword puzzles.

[4]spacy.io

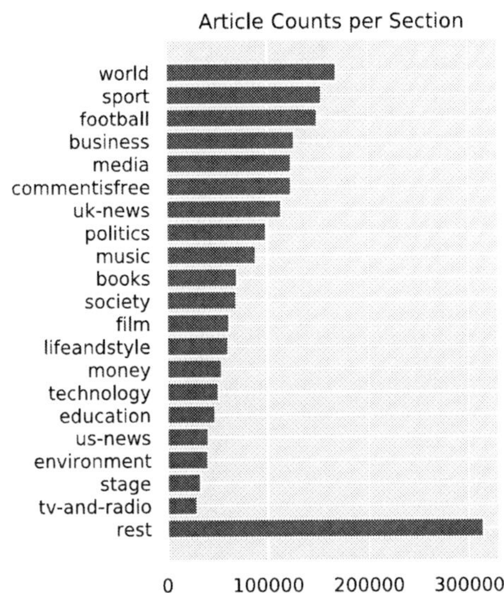

Figure 2: The article counts per section.

Notably, football is a distinct section from sports and contains about the same amount of articles.

4 Modelling People in the Text

While it is common for a person to be only referred to by their surname, a reference to a person in a text can take different forms, which should be linked to a single entity to allow the creation of consistent embeddings for people's names. Once a set of mentions have been linked to a person, a new text corpus is built where any span of tokens that is part of a mention is replaced by a pseudo-token representing the person.

4.1 Identifying Mentions

The baseline method for identifying the mention of a person in a text is to look for their surname, a single token. However, a person can also be referred to by their name, role or with co-references. We focus only on mentions by name, but go beyond the single-token method. We identify all occurrences of full or partial names and link them together based on context.

We identify names in the text using named entity recognition (NER) implemented in spaCy. It provides a neural NER model with an architecture based on Strubell et al. (2017), we used the default pretrained model for English: en_core_web_sm. The library creators report an accuracy of around

85% [5] for all entities, we only use the detection of persons for which no individual score is given.

The model detects full names (*Tony Blair*), partial names (*Blair*) mentions with title (*Mr. Blair*) and possessive mentions (*Blair's*). For subsequent linking of mentions, the possessive "'s" is ignored.

4.2 Merging Mentions

The subsequent linking of mentions relies on the structuring of the corpus into distinct documents, as well as the temporal structure to link local mentions more leniently – within an article or within a fixed time span. In writing, using references and shortening of names relies on saliency of the name to the reader, this is partially mimicked by the steps taken below.

Within an article, a person is often introduced by their full name, and subsequently only a part of their name – often the surname – is used to refer to them. In that case, the surname is non-ambiguously referring to the person identified by the full name in that same article. Therefore, within an article, we link any detected mention whose tokens are a subset of a previously seen mention in that article to that previous mention.

Across articles, mentions are then linked together based on exact match of their name, which typically means first and last name.

We observed that for very well-known people, there were quite a few articles which referred to them only by their surname, never mentioning their full name in the article. This is typically done for presidents and prime ministers, which are famous enough to be associated with their surname only. To merge these occurrences, for every month, every name that consists only of a single token is linked to the person whose name contains that token and has the most mentions in that month and the previous month. The same is done for names that start with *Mr* or *Mrs*. This helps mapping *Mr Johnson* and *Johnson* to *Boris Johnson*. This also produces a few false positives, such as *Mrs Blair* getting mapped to *Tony Blair*. Doing this matching at the month-level allows the ambiguous reference *Clinton* to be mapped to *Bill Clinton* in one time period and *Hillary Clinton* in another.

Once linking is complete, for every mention the span of tokens forming the mentions is replaced with a single token: the full unique name of the person that is referenced.

___

Mentions	People
> 5	458, 158
> 50	61, 828
> 500	7, 559
> 5,000	417
> 50,000	10

(a) Number of people that have more than a specific number of mentions, illustrating a logarithmic relationship.

Person	Count
Tony Blair	144,061
Donald Trump	143,149
David Cameron	119,176
Gordon Brown	116,895
Boris Johnson	84,744
Hillary Clinton	67,700
Chelsea	62,336
Commons	58,079
George Bush	58,018
George Osborne	56,646

(b) The 10 people with more than 50,000 mentions.

Table 1: The distribution of people and mentions, as well as the top 10 people by mention count.

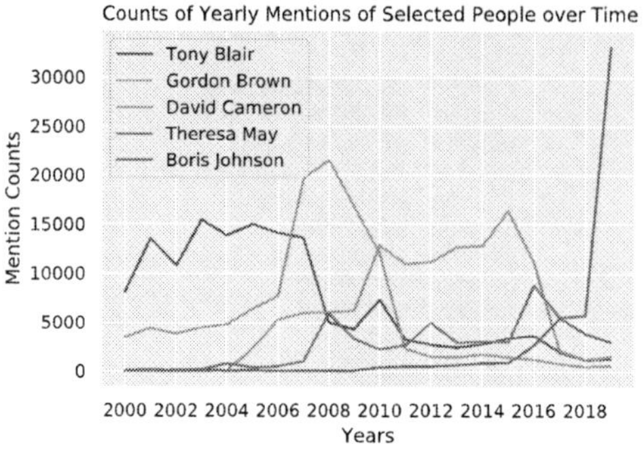

Figure 3: Mentions of the 5 prime ministers of the UK from 2000 to 2019.

4.3 Data Analysis

The identifying and linking of occurrences of people in the corpus allows for an initial analysis and provided useful insights for subsequent experiments with embedding models.

Persons in the Data Set Overall, there are 2,725,110 persons with 29,943,111 total mentions in our dataset.[6] Table 1a shows how many people have how many mentions. The distribution is logarithmic; like vocabularies of corpora, the distribution of people in the corpus follows Zipf's Law. A few people are mentioned very frequently, while most people are only referred to a few times.

Table 1b shows the 10 people that have at least 50,000 mentions. *Chelsea* and *Commons* are notable false positives; the quality of the name detection is discussed below. The other 8 people are all politicians: four from the UK and four from the US. In fact, the top 100 mentions are dominated by politicians, but athletes, in particular football players, make up a large portion, too.

The raw frequencies of mentions can be analysed to make approximate inferences about the world at a given point in time. Figure 3 shows the mentions of the prime ministers of the UK for the past two decades. The mentions show popularity trends corresponding to their terms as prime ministers. For *Tony Blair*, *Gordon Brown* and *David Cameron* these curves give a good overview of when they were in office, but after 2016 it is not entirely clear who would be prime minister; from the frequencies it does not look as if Theresa May would ever be

prime minister. We further analyse the prime ministers using our diachronic models in Section 5.2.2.

Quality of NER As mentioned above, the NER used has a reported accuracy of around 85%. "Facebook", "Twitter" and "Brexit" were falsely identified as persons, just like the previously mentioned "Commons" – likely detected as a name in the phrase "House of Commons", a British political institution. Besides the already reported "Chelsea", there are also "Tottenham", "Manchester United", "Fulham" and many other sports teams in the false positives. For the creation of the embeddings, these false positives are not an issue, because they are detected consistently.

There were also many instances of false positive detected names of the form "Manchester 1 - 1 Norwich", a match result. In this case, a detected mention like this cannot be merged and "ties up" the words "Manchester" and "Norwich", preventing them from contributing to any embeddings. In our investigation of a sample of these embeddings, however, we observed that this effect was not significant. Tokens such as "Manchester" are typically very common throughout the corpus and so we can still build reliable embeddings for them, even if some of their occurrences are missed due to being treated as names.

Duplicate and Ambiguous Names Our modelling of mentions was motivated by problems with the token based surname to person mapping, namely the prevalence of duplicate and ambiguous surnames. Using the detected and linked mentions as described above, we can assess the prevalence of both phenomena.

We evaluate duplicates year by year. Each year

---

[6]In order to avoid the inflation of counts of a person's name due to false positives in the linking process, only exact matching was used to link mentions *across articles* for the results presented in this section only (as opposed to heuristically linking surname-only mentions *across articles* as well). *Within-article* linking was still performed as usual.

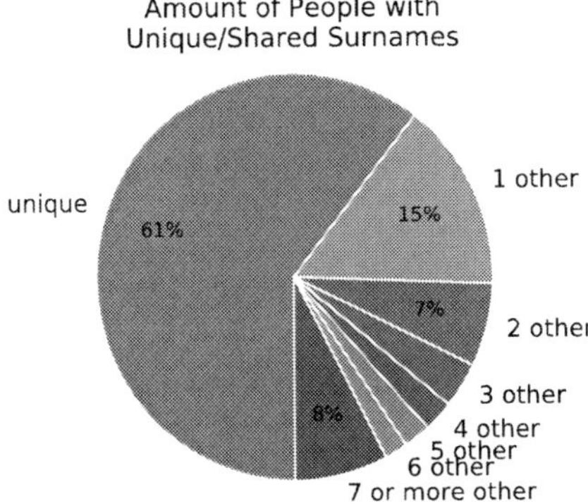

Figure 4: Percentages of people with shared/unique surnames. For each year, every person with at least 50 mentions was considered. Only names within the same year were used to identify duplicates.

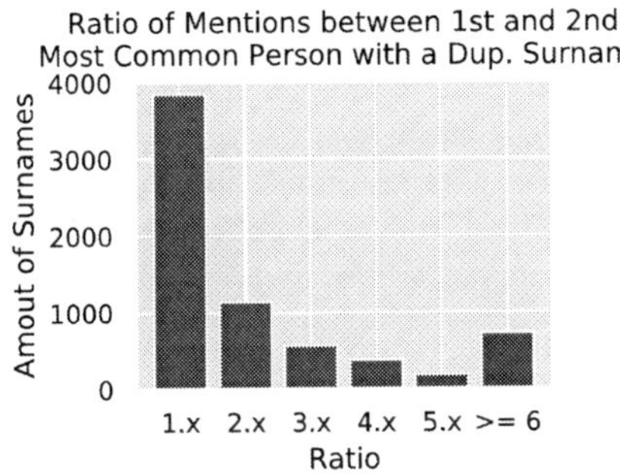

Figure 5: The plot shows the relative frequency of people that share a surname. I.e. if two people share the name *Johnson*, how many times more is the more common *Johnson* mentioned compared to the other?

we retrieve any person with at least 50 mentions and group them by surname. For every surname we then get a count of how many people share this surname. Figure 4 shows the aggregated distribution of these counts. More than a third of people do not have a unique surname.

For people with the same surname, we were also interested in whether they would all be mentioned approximately the same amount or if it is common for one person to dominate the total mentions of the surname.

Figure 5 shows the ratio of mentions between the most mentioned person with a surname and the second most. We observe that it is not uncommon for a single person to "dominate" a surname, dwarfing any mentions of other people with the same sur-

name. Although in most cases, the first and second most commonly mentioned person with a shared surname do not have a big difference in counts of mentions.

Some surnames are also proper nouns or adjectives, we call these *ambiguous* names. The prevalence of these names is difficult to quantify due to false positives in the NER, but in 2019, from all people with at least 200 mentions, *Philip Green*, *Arron Banks* and *Fiona Hill* have the surnames that are most likely to also be used as a regular word. In all three cases, their surnames is 50 times more likely to be used as a regular word than as their surname.

In token based models, both phenomena – duplicate and ambiguous surnames – can lead to a person being "invisible", because any individual part of their name is too common on its own in another context. In Section 5.2.1 we present an embedding example for each phenomenon.

5 Diachronic Model

Once persons have been identified and linked, we trained diachronic models with the *Dynamic-Word2Vec* (DW2V) model (Yao et al., 2018). The model learns embeddings for all time slices concurrently, encoding within-time-slice similarities of tokens as well as inter-time-slice similarities of tokens to themselves at the same time. This eliminates a subsequent alignment step and also makes embeddings more stable.

The experiments and analysis of the models investigate the following questions both qualitatively and quantitatively: (1) How well can the explicit person model generate traces for people, compared to a token based baseline? (2) How well do the traces model context changes in the real world?

5.1 Experimental Setup

The baseline model uses no person detection and is purely token based; subsequently called the `token` model. Our model – subsequently called the `person` model – embeds detected persons using within-article and cross-article merging as described in Section 4.

Both models use yearly slices, covering 20 years from 2000 to 2019 (inclusive). To define the vocabulary that is used, only words or names with more than 500 occurrences across the whole time span were considered. The vocabularies of both models differ, but both contain around 55,000 types. Many

Model:	person	token	token	token	person	person
Year	*Taylor Swift*	`taylor`	`swift`	`johnson`	*Boris Johnson*	*Dustin Johnson*
2010	Iggy Pop	adam	immediate	davies	mayor	Francesco Molinari
2011	Selena Gomez	davies	swiftly	alex	Bravo Boris	mcilroy
2012	Patti Smith	adam	speedy	ryan	Ed Miliband	Charl Schwartzel
2013	Beyoncé	craig	timing	nick	Iain Duncan Smith	Zach Johnson
2014	Lily Allen	jones	kim	joe	Iain Duncan Smith	Jim Furyk
2015	Madonna	smith	adele	adam	vince	Jason Day
2016	Justin Bieber	adam	beyoncé	tony	David Cameron	Jason Day
2017	Beyoncé	smith	recall	cameron	Theresa May	Jordan Spieth
2018	Beyoncé	mitchell	swiftly	jeremy	Jeremy Corbyn	Brooks Koepka
2019	Madonna	ross	drake	boris	Jeremy Corbyn	Phil Mickelson

Table 2: The table shows the closest words for different people/tokens in the two models, over the last 10 years. *Taylor Swift* is shown in the `person` model, and her first and last name as tokens in the baseline model, showing the ambiguity of the names by themselves. Similarly, the name *Johnson* is shown in the baseline model, and two specific Johnsons are shown in our `person` model.

common words are in both vocabularies, most differences are in the names, which appear as individual tokens in the `token` model and as compound names in the `person` model. Further details about the model training can be found in Appendix A.

5.2 Qualitative Analysis

Here, we first exemplify the problem of ambiguous and duplicate names, then show the modelling of the role of UK prime minister as an example of real world change represented in the model.

5.2.1 Taylor Swift, Boris and Dustin Johnson

Table 2 shows the closest word every year for the last 10 years, for the people *Taylor Swift*, *Boris Johnson* and *Dustin Johnson* in our `person` model, as well as the names `taylor`, `swift` and `johnson` as tokens in the baseline model.

Taylor Swift is an American pop musician, and provides an example of an ambiguous name that is difficult to find in the baseline model. In most years from 2010-2019, neither her first nor last name is associated with meaningful tokens in the baseline model; `taylor` is in the vicinity of various common names, and `swift` is mostly associated with other words related to the meaning "happening quickly or without delay". Our model places *Taylor Swift* into the neighborhood of other pop musicians throughout the years, such as Beyoncé and Madonna.

The name *Johnson* is provided as an example of a duplicate surname. In the baseline model, the surname is associated with various first and last names throughout the first 7 years of the shown time frame. In the last 3 years, associated tokens indicate *David Cameron* and *Jeremy Corbyn* – two British politicians, as well as the first name of *Boris*

Johnson. In these years, *Boris Johnson* was by far the most mentioned person with his surname. Looking at his neighboring words and people in our model, we see him associated with other politicians throughout the years or with his role ("mayor"). *Dustin Johnson* also shares the surname, he is an American golfer with a relatively small amount of mentions throughout the years. The baseline model does not show him at all, while our model associates him with other golfers, even people he played with (i.e. *Jordan Spieth* in 2017).

5.2.2 Prime Ministers of the UK

We present the change of the UK prime minister from 2000-2019 as an example of the representation of real world change in the model. We use the the vector of the incumbent prime minister in 2010 – the middle of the time range – as the vector for the role "prime minister". For all other years we retrieve the closest person or token to this vector. Table 3 shows the closest person/token in our new model and the baseline. Our model is mistaken only twice, while the baseline is wrong 8 times. Furthermore, the `token` model does not allow searching only for people and it is difficult to know how to associate tokens with names.

The biggest differences are seen for *Gordon Brown*, *Theresa May* and *Boris Johnson*. The `token` model does not retrieve *May* or *Johnson* at all, and retrieves *Gordon Brown* only one out of 3 years, and with his first instead of last name. From the neighborhood of the tokens in the embedding space we found that `brown` is predominantly associated with the color and `may` with its usage as a modal verb. `Johnson` is not ambiguous, but a very common surname.

Year	Our Model	baseline
2000	Tony Blair	hague (blair)
2001	Tony Blair	chancellor (blair)
2002	Tony Blair	blair
2003	Tony Blair	blair
2004	Michael Howard*	chancellor (blair)
2005	Tony Blair	chancellor (gordon)*
2006	Tony Blair	chancellor (gordon)*
2007	Gordon Brown	blair*
2008	Gordon Brown	gordon
2009	Gordon Brown	cameron*
2010	David Cameron	cameron
2011	David Cameron	cameron
2012	David Cameron	cameron
2013	David Cameron	cameron
2014	David Cameron	cameron
2015	Jeremy Corbyn*	cameron
2016	Theresa May	cameron*
2017	Theresa May	jeremy*
2018	Theresa May	jeremy*
2019	Boris Johnson	jeremy*

Table 3: The table shows the names/tokens closest to the vector for *David Cameron* and `cameron` respectively, in 2010. For the token based model, the token in parenthesis is the closest name, shown for a fairer comparison. The asterisk indicates incorrect associations.

5.2.3 Largest Change Spikes

Simple factual information such as a person's role can be found with the model, while spikes in the model can help us to detect real world *events*. The largest context changes in the model were identified by calculating cosine distance scores for every word to itself throughout the years. Inspection of samples from the largest spikes showed that these detected spikes corresponded to long term change events as well as one-off events. Examples for long term change events that we observed are the election of *Imran Khan* as prime minister of Pakistan in 2018 or the Scottish football player *David Marshall* joining the national team in 2004. *Imran Khan* also attended a series of sports events in 2015, which also showed as a significant context change in the model. However in this case it was only a one-off event. In general, career changes, promotions and team changes for athletes (long term changes) as well as accidents, wins of competitions or legal disputes (one-off events) were frequently observed causes of context change.

We also noticed that despite using the full name of a person, there are still duplicates that are falsely linked together. This happens when a person has a common first and last name, such as *David Marshall* or *Scott Walker*. Sporadic reporting about two different people in different domains then appears as a context change of a single person.

Overall, spikes are most pronounced in medium to low data settings, where just a few articles can already have a big influence on the context of a person. With a lot of articles, a person's context fluctuates less, but is more precise.

Examining surnames in the baseline model showed that uncommon first or last names still showed similar spikes as the `person` model, but many people could not be found at all in the baseline model due to their names being too common.

5.3 Quantitative Analysis

Quantitative analysis is a difficult task with diachronic models because there are no accepted gold standard embedding spaces to compare against. Yao et al. (2018) use the sections associated with the articles to group words together. They then identify clusters in the embedding space and compare them with the groupings created by the sections. Kutuzov et al. (2017) track countries in the news and use a manually created database of armed conflicts as a target to compare their model against.

We present two experimental setups, one following Yao et al. (2018) based on the sections of articles and one inspired by the change event detection by Kutuzov et al. (2017), comparing our model against gold standard change events in the football domain.

5.3.1 Section Analysis for Ambiguous Names

One way to measure the quality of embeddings in bulk is to assess the overlap of clusters in embedding space with clusters given by the sections assigned to each article in the corpus (Yao et al., 2018). Section labels were not used in the training process, and are semantically cohesive, so we expect that people from the same section should cluster together in embedding space, too.

We derive the dominant section of people per year by finding the section with the highest count of mentions for every person for that year. Persons with a dominant section that has less than 35% of their total mentions were not included due to the section association being too unclear (following Yao et al. (2018)). Every yearly person vector was also only included if the person had at least 100 mentions that year, to ensure some degree of stability in the embeddings (Burdick et al., 2018). Note that the sizes of sections by article count are heavily imbalanced. This translates also to the number of people in the sections: the number of people in a section can differ by two orders of magnitude.

Cl.	yearly		total	
	`t. model`	`p. model`	`t. model`	`p. model`
non-ambiguous names only				
10	0.6425	**0.6484**	0.6575	**0.6780**
15	0.6565	**0.6731**	0.6602	**0.6671**
20	0.6506	**0.6665**	0.6367	**0.6632**
25	0.6374	**0.6575**	0.6544	**0.6556**
ambiguous names included				
10	0.6472	**0.6478**	**0.6641**	0.6261
15	0.6559	**0.6698**	0.6588	**0.6748**
20	0.6501	**0.6645**	0.6537	**0.6785**
25	0.6400	**0.6586**	0.6523	**0.6630**

Table 4: Normalised mutual information scores for various experimental settings. The Cl. column represents the number of clusters. The "yearly" columns contains averaged clustering results by year. The "total" column contains clustering results of all vectors across all years in one space.

To make our model and the baseline directly comparable, full names had to be mapped to tokens in the baseline model; we used the surname of each person as their token. For a fair comparison, the mapping had to be injective, so only people with a unique[7] surname were included.

The vectors from all years can be clustered in a single vector space, or clustering can be done for each year and the results averaged over years. The full space emphasises cross-year alignment, whereas the yearly clustering emphasises local separation. We report results for both as `total` and `yearly`. For both settings, we always create three clusterings and average the results to smooth out effects of random initialisation. We used spherical k-means[8] to create the clusters. Two sets were evaluated:

(1) `non-ambiguous only`: For every mapped token, we ensured that the mapped token *also* appeared at least 35% of the time in the same section as the full name (15,622 vectors).

(2) `ambiguous names included`: All the names are included, regardless of the distribution of the associated token (20,084 vectors).

As an example, in 2019 the dominating section for *Theresa May* was `politics` with 63% prevalence. The word `may` appeared mostly in `politics` too, but only with 8% prevalence. Therefore, *Theresa May* is included in the second set, but not in the first.

Table 4 shows the results of the experiments.

[7]As we only included people with over 100 mentions, some non-unique surnames may be considered unique if only one person with the surname has more than 100 mentions.

[8]We use the implementation provided by the spherecluster Python package.

Across both data sets and both experimental setups, for various cluster sizes, the `person` model outperforms the `token` model except in the 10 cluster setup with the ambiguous names included.

It is interesting to see that the gains in the set containing the ambiguous names are not larger, as it would be expected. A potential reason could be that while, for example, `may` appears frequently in many sections, the generic contexts "cancel out", leaving the political context given by *Theresa May* as the dominant context for clustering, even though the immediate neighbourhood of the word does not contain words indicating that.

5.3.2 Football

As described above, context changes of a person show up as vector space movement in the model. We quantify this using football players that change their role from player to coach. This role change is an important event and there is a lot of reporting on the football domain, with detailed instead of broad reporting.

We use Wikidata (Vrandečić and Krötzsch, 2014) as the source for career change information. Wikidata is an open access, community maintained knowledge graph containing over 80 million nodes. To retrieve the relevant persons, we first selected people by name and then filtered the list based on specific properties to eliminate duplicates. Out of a list of names appearing in the football section of the corpus, 39 players were retrieved that became coaches in the years between 2001 and 2019. The full list can be found in appendix B.

Based on the assumption that their change from being a player to becoming a coach was their biggest change in their context, we looked for the biggest change in the embedding space throughout all years, in the `person` model. For 8 out of 39 people, their biggest change spike coincided with the year in which they were first a trainer. This gives a 21% accuracy, 4 times better than random guessing. For 5 additional people, during the year of their career change, a spike occurred that was larger than 1 standard deviation from the mean change.

6 Discussion of Results

In the analysis of the persons that appear in the corpus we showed the extend to which duplicate names are prevalent, showing that more than a third of people do not have a unique surname. In the examples from the embeddings we showed how these ambiguous and duplicated surnames prevent meaningful embeddings for these names in the baseline model. With the example of the UK prime minister we showed that our model identified the prime minister each year with 90% accuracy compared to 65% for the baseline model.

For people with unique but potentially ambiguous surnames, our model improved embeddings as well. Improvements were minor, but consistent across 15 out of 16 different experiments.

For the analysis of the change tracking in the model, the case of the prime minister of the UK showed that the explicit person embeddings improved the association markedly. A systematic look at change detection in role changes for football players showed performance four times better than the random baseline, but there is still room for improvement.

Context changes in the model can be linked to real world events, but not all real world changes appear in the model. This may be explained by selective reporting in the source corpus, as not all events that actually happen are reported on. Reporting is also selective in other ways: for a role change like an election and a new prime minister, the reporting focuses more on the new person overtaking the role than on the person being replaced. When a prime minister changes, there is a much more noticeable context change for the person getting into office than the person getting out of office. For athletes, team changes or role changes are also less easy to detect than complete out of context reporting, about for example sexual misconduct or drunk driving.

Overall, the detection and linking of names worked well and was a large improvement over using surnames only. It enabled us to identify certain people in the first place and disambiguate people with common surnames. The NER has a few false positives, but false positives are consistent (i.e. Twitter is misclassified as a person, but in every occurrence).

7 Conclusion

We have shown that full name identification of individuals in the news based on NER and heuristic linking is doable and provides meaningful insights linkable to real world developments. This approach is a simple yet effective improvement over a token based baseline. We quantified some common problems with the baseline approach, such as duplicate and ambiguous surnames. We provided some initial analysis of event detection both based on samples and a small quantitative experiment, showing promising results, and we provided an analysis of a previously understudied, British news corpus.

Future work on the model can incorporate improvements to NER models as well as expanding the detection of references to non-name references such as role references, co-references. Linking can be improved with a more sophisticated treatment of name variants and titles. These steps have been shown to improve character detection in literary texts (Vala et al., 2015). Lastly, gaps in reporting could be filled by relying on more than a single newspaper as a source of text.

References

Kevin Anderson. 2009. Guardian launches Open Platform tool to make online content available free. *The Guardian*.

David Bamman, Ted Underwood, and Noah A Smith. 2014. A bayesian mixed effects model of literary character. In *Proceedings of the 52nd Annual Meeting of the Association for Computational Linguistics (Volume 1: Long Papers)*, pages 370–379.

Laura Burdick, Jonathan K Kummerfeld, and Rada Mihalcea. 2018. Factors influencing the surprising instability of word embeddings. In *Proceedings of the 2018 Conference of the North American Chapter of the Association for Computational Linguistics: Human Language Technologies, Volume 1 (Long Papers)*, pages 2092–2102.

Snigdha Chaturvedi, Shashank Srivastava, Hal Daume III, and Chris Dyer. 2016. Modeling evolving relationships between characters in literary novels. In *Thirtieth AAAI Conference on Artificial Intelligence*.

Nikhil Garg, Londa Schiebinger, Dan Jurafsky, and James Zou. 2018. Word embeddings quantify 100 years of gender and ethnic stereotypes. *Proceedings of the National Academy of Sciences*, 115(16):E3635–E3644.

Nuno Ricardo Pinheiro da Silva Guimarães and Álvaro Pedro de Barros Borges Reis Figueira. 2017. Building a Semi-Supervised Dataset to Train Journalistic Relevance Detection Models. In *2017 IEEE 15th Intl Conf on Dependable, Autonomic and Secure Computing, 15th Intl Conf on Pervasive Intelligence and Computing, 3rd Intl Conf on Big Data Intelligence and Computing and Cyber Science and Technology Congress(DASC/PiCom/DataCom/CyberSciTech)*, pages 1271–1277.

Andrey Kutuzov, Lilja Øvrelid, Terrence Szymanski, and Erik Velldal. 2018. Diachronic word embeddings and semantic shifts: A survey. In *Proceedings of the 27th International Conference on Computational Linguistics*, pages 1384–1397, Santa Fe, New Mexico, USA. Association for Computational Linguistics.

Andrey Kutuzov, Erik Velldal, and Lilja Øvrelid. 2017. Tracing armed conflicts with diachronic word embedding models. In *Proceedings of the Events and Stories in the News Workshop*, pages 31–36, Vancouver, Canada. Association for Computational Linguistics.

Junyi Jessy Li, Kapil Thadani, and Amanda Stent. 2016. The Role of Discourse Units in Near-Extractive Summarization. In *Proceedings of the 17th Annual Meeting of the Special Interest Group on Discourse and Dialogue*, pages 137–147, Los Angeles. Association for Computational Linguistics.

Pradeep K. Murukannaiah, Chinmaya Dabral, Karthik Sheshadri, Esha Sharma, and Jessica Staddon. 2017. Learning a Privacy Incidents Database. In *Proceedings of the Hot Topics in Science of Security: Symposium and Bootcamp*, HoTSoS, pages 35–44, Hanover, MD, USA. Association for Computing Machinery.

Robert Parker, David Graff, Junbo Kong, Ke Chen, and Kazuaki Maeda. 2011. English Gigaword Fifth Edition LDC2011T07. Technical report, Linguistic Data Consortium.

Emma Strubell, Patrick Verga, David Belanger, and Andrew McCallum. 2017. Fast and Accurate Entity Recognition with Iterated Dilated Convolutions. *arXiv:1702.02098 [cs]*.

Terrence Szymanski. 2017. Temporal Word Analogies: Identifying Lexical Replacement with Diachronic Word Embeddings. In *Proceedings of the 55th Annual Meeting of the Association for Computational Linguistics (Volume 2: Short Papers)*, pages 448–453, Vancouver, Canada. Association for Computational Linguistics.

Hardik Vala, David Jurgens, Andrew Piper, and Derek Ruths. 2015. Mr. Bennet, his coachman, and the Archbishop walk into a bar but only one of them gets recognized: On The Difficulty of Detecting Characters in Literary Texts. In *Proceedings of the 2015 Conference on Empirical Methods in Natural Language Processing*, pages 769–774, Lisbon, Portugal. Association for Computational Linguistics.

Denny Vrandečić and Markus Krötzsch. 2014. Wikidata: A free collaborative knowledgebase. *Communications of the ACM*, 57(10):78–85.

Zijun Yao, Yifan Sun, Weicong Ding, Nikhil Rao, and Hui Xiong. 2018. Dynamic Word Embeddings for Evolving Semantic Discovery. *Proceedings of the Eleventh ACM International Conference on Web Search and Data Mining - WSDM '18*, pages 673–681.

Yating Zhang, Adam Jatowt, Sourav Bhowmick, and Katsumi Tanaka. 2015. Omnia Mutantur, Nihil Interit: Connecting Past with Present by Finding Corresponding Terms across Time. In *Proceedings of the 53rd Annual Meeting of the Association for Computational Linguistics and the 7th International Joint Conference on Natural Language Processing (Volume 1: Long Papers)*, pages 645–655, Beijing, China. Association for Computational Linguistics.

Appendix

A Diachronic Model Implementation Details

For the DW2V model Yao et al. (2018) provide their hyper-parameter settings as a starting point: $\lambda = 10, \tau = \gamma = 50$ and window size 5 for the PPMI matrices, 5 epochs of training. The absence of gold standard embeddings or other high-quality target data hinders a systematic hyper-parameter search. We briefly trained some models using slightly varied parameters to adjust to the different data size, but no large improvements could be found. The model creates two embeddings for each word, which we concatenate to form the final word embeddings. In comparison to the reference implementation, both the batches as well as the order in which the time slices are updated are randomised, to prevent any skewed embeddings that would be created by a fixed training order.

B Football Players and Coaches

2001	2014
Walter Mazzarri	Paul Scholes
Didier Deschamps	2015
Roberto Mancini	Jürgen Klopp
2003	David Wagner
Massimiliano Allegri	2016
2004	Zinedine Zidane
Ian Rush	Patrick Vieira
2005	Unai Emery
Henning Berg	Olof Mellberg
Paul Gascoigne	2017
2006	Harry Kewell
Gareth Southgate	2018
Antonio Conte	Thierry Henry
Diego Simeone	Marco Silva
2007	Joey Barton
Thomas Tuchel	Sol Campbell
Pep Guardiola	Garry Monk
Paul Le Guen	2019
2008	Jonathan Woodgate
Luis Enrique	Jürgen Klinsmann
2009	Scott Parker
Jaap Stam	Duncan Ferguson
Vincenzo Montella	Dick Advocaat
Mauricio Pochettino	Mikel Arteta
2011	Pepe Mel
Dietmar Hamann	
2013	
Laurent Blanc	

Table 5: Players that became coaches between 2001 and 2019

Table 5 shows the full list of players who later became coaches between 2001 and 2019, as retrieved from Wikidata. The analysis of these people was presented in section 5.3.2.

Social media data as a lens onto care-seeking behavior among women veterans of the US armed forces

Kacie Kelly
George W. Bush Institute
kkelly@bushcenter.org

Alex B. Fine
Qntfy
alex.fine@qntfy.com

Glen Coppersmith
Qntfy
glen@qntfy.com

Abstract

In this article, we examine social media data as a lens onto support-seeking among women veterans of the US armed forces. Social media data hold a great deal of promise as a source of information on needs and support-seeking among individuals who are excluded from or systematically prevented from accessing clinical or other institutions ostensibly designed to support them. We apply natural language processing (NLP) techniques to more than 3 million Tweets collected from 20,000 Twitter users. We find evidence that women veterans are more likely to use social media to seek social and community engagement and to discuss mental health and veterans' issues significantly more frequently than their male counterparts. By contrast, male veterans tend to use social media to amplify political ideologies or to engage in partisan debate. Our results have implications for how organizations can provide outreach and services to this uniquely vulnerable population, and illustrate the utility of non-traditional observational data sources such as social media to understand the needs of marginalized groups.

1 Introduction

Women comprise a small but rapidly growing portion of the US military veteran population. Indeed, women are one of the fastest-growing demographics in this population (Danan et al., 2017), and saw a two-fold increase between 1988 and 2008 (Manning, 2008). This trend is reflected in the use of Department of Veterans Affairs (VA) services: since 2000, the number of women seeking care at the VA has increased from around 150,000 to half a million. The rapid increase in the number of women veterans, coupled with increases in the rates at which these women use veteran healthcare resources, represents a profoundly significant development for veteran service organizations (VSOs) and veteran healthcare providers. While women veterans face many of the same challenges as their male counterparts during and after deployment, there are also notable differences in the types and rates of specific challenges faced by these two groups. Perhaps the most striking example concerns military sexual trauma (MST). A recent study found that, among veterans diagnosed with PTSD, 31% of women reported MST, compared to just 1% of men (Maguen et al., 2010). The same study found that MST was, in turn, highly comorbid with depression, anxiety, and eating disorders in women veterans. While the incidence of PTSD, particularly related to combat exposure, and substance use disorder seem to be greater among male veterans, women veterans are overall more likely to experience service-related disabilities than men (Frayne et al., 2007), and are also more likely than men to meet diagnostic criteria for depression and anxiety (Runnals et al., 2014). Finally, according to a recently released report from the VA, the suicide rate among women veterans increased by 6.5% between 2005 and 2017, which positions women veterans as the demographic group of veterans with the fasting-growing suicide rate (VA, 2019).

Not only do women veterans present a clinical picture that differs in systematic ways from that of their male counterparts, and therefore place distinctive demands on clinicians and other healthcare providers, women veterans are also a remarkably demographically diverse population. Relative to the general population, racial, ethnic, and sexual minorities are significantly over-represented among women veterans (Blosnich et al., 2013; Gates, 2010; Koo et al., 2015). Women in the US

Proceedings of the Fourth Workshop on Natural Language Processing and Computational Social Science, pages 184–192
Online, November 20, 2020. ©2020 Association for Computational Linguistics
https://doi.org/10.18653/v1/P17

armed forces also tend to be younger, on average, and are more likely to belong to racial and ethnic minorities than their male counterparts (Maguen et al., 2010).

1.1 Barriers to care for women veterans

Are VSOs and the VA up to the challenge posed by such a seismic shift in the composition of the population they are intended to serve? While 30% of women veterans are estimated to interact with VSOs, the literature on this front is somewhat equivocal, with some evidence suggesting that women veterans face specific structural barriers to care. Relative to their male counterparts, women veterans are more likely to shoulder caretaking responsibilities for children and other family members (Mattocks et al., 2012), often forcing them to seek after-hours healthcare services that are frequently unavailable. Familial and domestic responsibilities may exacerbate one of the most commonly-cited reasons among veterans for not seeking care, which is distance to the nearest VA clinic (Institute of Medicine, 2014). Moreover, a high percentage of women veterans, particularly those ages 18-44, report being unsure of whether they qualify for VA services or believing—in many cases erroneously—that they do not (Mattocks et al., 2012). In addition to such structural barriers to care-seeking, women veterans also sometimes report feeling generally unwelcome or unaccommodated at veteran-oriented care centers such as the VA. For instance, women veterans have reported a lack of gender-sensitivity in health care services provided at the VA, especially non-academically affiliated VA centers with smaller and more male-dominated caseloads (Runnals et al., 2014), and have reported feeling unwelcome at VA centers, which tend to be male-dominated (VA, 2015). Finally, women veterans report sexual harassment by male VA clients with dismaying frequency (Steinhauer, 2019).

1.2 Social media and the "clinical whitespace"

The rapid increase in the proportion of young women veterans, coupled with well-documented barriers to care experienced by women veterans, highlights the need for better insight into the day-to-day challenges facing women veterans. Because women veterans report feeling uncomfortable in settings such as the VA, and are using VA services at a lower rate than their male coun-

terparts (House Committee on Veterans Affairs, 2019), there are relatively few clinical encounters for healthcare providers to gain a deep understanding of the specific issues facing women, the barriers to care as they perceive them, and the compensating behaviors they are engaging in when care is not available or not perceived to be available. Moreover, much of the literature cited above is based on data from women receiving VA care. It is highly likely that much of the literature on barriers to care-seeking among women veterans is systematically under-representing the women who are most likely to avoid encounters with the VA and other VSOs. Such gaps in health data derived from clinical encounters have been previously referred to as the "clinical whitespace" (Coppersmith et al., 2017).

A large body of previous work suggests that this whitespace can be to some degree filled by large-scale analysis of public social media data, such as Twitter. Social media data constitutes a particularly rich and ecological data source for understanding a wide variety of physical and behavioral conditions through an epidemiological lens. Previous work has demonstrated the utility of social media and other sources of observational online data in identifying and understanding mental health conditions in a population (Coppersmith et al., 2018, 2015), tracking flu infections (Lamb et al., 2013), and screening for pancreatic cancer (Paparrizos et al., 2016), to name just a few examples. Here, we make the point—not previously made to our knowledge—that such data sources may prove particularly illuminating and necessary in efforts to understand the health of marginalized groups, whose "clinical whitespaces" may be even greater those of the general population. In the context of the current discussion, because women veterans are often excluded or marginalized in care settings—implicitly and explicitly—it is likely that emergent, informal social networks such as those that form through social media may prove to be a particularly important source of connection and source of information for women veterans.

In what follows, we use techniques from NLP and computational psychology to conduct an exploratory analysis into the motivations, beliefs, attitudes, and behaviors of women veterans based on the content of their social media posts. We present a series of analyses that, we believe, strongly suggest that women veterans use social media in systematically different ways from male veterans. Our results suggest that women veterans are more likely than men to use social media to discuss and form community around their experiences as veterans in ways that are constructive and positive. We argue that this finding has implications for how veteran-focused organizations educate, engage, and serve a diverse veteran population.

2 Methods

2.1 Data collection

The analyses reported below are based on a sample of approximately 3 million messages from 20,000 unique Twitter users.

Social media posts by US military veterans were collected from the Twitter API, using methods closely modeled on those described in (Beller et al., 2014). Beller and colleagues describe techniques for automatically identifying profession and other fine-grained social roles on the basis of self-disclosure. We began by manually constructing a corpus of words judged by subject matter experts[1] to indicate military experience (e.g., "veteran", "deployed", "USMC", "OIF" (Operation Iraqi Freedom), to name a few. We first searched messages and user descriptions for these words, then further refined the search using regular expressions to determine when these words occurred in contexts indicating that the author identified with the role or experience (e.g., "I'm a ___", "As a ___ I think"). Trained human annotators then manually inspected 10% of messages returned in this way to validate our search algorithm, which was found to have a 95% true positive rate. For each user who passed this filtering step, we collected additional public posts.

Following the initial data collection procedure described above, we applied age and gender classifiers to each user's data. These classifiers were previously trained on a separate sample of Twitter users who explicitly indicated their age or year of birth. Of the 20,000 users in our sample, 86% were male and 14% female (our gender classifier also includes an "other" category to capture individuals who do not conform to a gender binary).

---

[1] Specifically, we solicited input from a woman who served in the United States Air Force and subsequently trained as a clinical social worker, and who still works with military veterans and VSOs; as well as a retired colonel in the US Marine Corps currently working directly with a variety of VSOs.

Women veterans in the sample had a mean age of 29.7 years (SD=5.5), and men in our sample were closely matched, with a mean age of 29.8 years (SD=5.5). Our sample contains more women than the overall veteran population (9% in 2015, according to recent VA statistics (VA, 2017), but closely matches the demographics of currently-serving military, in which 16% of enlisted service members and 19% of officers are women (Council on Foreign Relations, 2020). This difference from the overall veteran population was expected, given that social media users skew younger than the general population.

3 Topic modeling

To begin with, we pursued a bottom-up, data-driven analysis of the data—namely, topic modeling—to assess differences in how men and women veterans use social media. Topic modeling is an unsupervised machine learning algorithm that discovers latent semantic structure in collections of text by finding coherent "topics". Intuitively, topics can be thought of as bundles of words with high probabilities of co-occurrence. Topic modeling is therefore more sensitive to subtle linguistic patterns than simply counting word frequencies. For instance, simple word frequency analyses might reveal that the word "party" occurs frequently in a discourse. This finding, however, would be open to interpretation, owing to the ambiguity of the word "party" and the lack of context of word frequency (sometimes called unigram frequency). By contrast, topic modeling might reveal that "party" frequently co-occurs with "America", "freedom", "liberty". These words would be said to form a "topic". Topic modeling assigns a distribution to word-topic combinations, such that for a given word or term, we can estimate the probability that that word came from a given topic with $p(term|topic)$. To prepare the data for topic modeling, we first removed all retweets, URLs, hashtags, and mentions. Topic modeling using latent Dirichlet allocation (LDA; (Blei et al., 2003)) was applied to the remaining 2.1 million posts that remained after data cleaning. Posts were then assigned a topic by finding the topic which maximizes the probability of all words in the post. Next, we computed the rate at which each user mentioned each topic by simply dividing the number of posts about each topic authored by the user by the total number of posts from the user; we will refer to this quotient as mention rate. We then computed an average topic mention rate for men and women by averaging by-user mention rates separately for the two groups. For ease of exposition, we asked human annotators to assign human-readable labels to the topics generated by our analysis. Creating such topic labels is often as much art as science, and runs the risk of entrenching the biases of the annotators. In this context, we'll note first that we created these labels *before* conducting the analyses reported below. Second, the goal of this work is ultimately to inform and educate non-technical stakeholders and empower them to use methods such as these to, for example, programmatically identify women veterans on social media who may benefit from the services of particular VSOs. We feel that it's important, in early phases of this work especially, to present these results in a way that makes them accessible to the intended end users.

We began by finding which topics were, overall, most frequent in the posts of women veterans and male veterans. We found that the same five topics were most common among men and women, and these are shown in Figure 1. We found that the most common topic among male veterans was "Partisan politics", corresponding to around 3.75% of all posts. For women, the most common topic was "Personal reflection", corresponding to about 3.52% of all posts.

To identify more subtle differences between the two groups, we then computed the difference in mention rate across men and women (women's mention rate - men's mention rate). In Figure 2, we plot the difference in topic mention rate for the five topics with the largest positive difference (i.e., topics mentioned more by women) as well as the five topics with the largest negative difference (i.e., topics mentioned more by men).

3.1 Topic modeling results and discussion

While both men and women frequently mention Civic Engagement and Partisan Politics, the former occurred substantially more frequently in women's tweets, while the opposite was true of the latter. Women-favored topics generally reflect more pro-social concerns (civic engagement), community and interpersonal relatedness, and the day-to-day business of running a family or business. By contrast, male-favored topics reflect an over-arching concern with abstract political topics,

conflict with other users, and sports. These results suggest that women veterans may be more likely than their male counterparts to use social media to form community and relationships in ways that are constructive and positive. By contrast, male veterans appear more likely to use social media to engage with news and controversial, divisive current events.

These results are suggestive, and accord very broadly with the hypothesis under discussion— namely, that social media may be used by women towards healthier or more pro-social ends, and may therefore serve as a particularly important platform for connecting with women veterans. However, these results do not directly address the key question of how women are talking about both their status as veterans and their health. In the section that follows, we take a different methodological tack to explore this question.

4 Mental health and veteran keywords

In order to more directly examine differences in social media use between women veterans and male veterans and how this might pertain to care-seeking, we asked whether there are gender differences in the use of specific keywords related to veteran's issues and health issues of common concern to veterans, such as post-traumatic stress. To identify these keywords, we used word embeddings to find the semantic nearest neighbors of seed terms deemed a priori relevant to these subjects, in collaboration with subject matter experts (see footnote 1). Word embeddings encode the words in a collection of text in terms of a numeric vector of all the contexts in which each word occurs. For instance, suppose we had a sample of English that consisted of the sentences "The visitor likes dogs" and "The dog likes visitors". Leaving aside singular/plural morphology, we would represent "visitor" and "dogs" in very similar terms, since they seem to occur in very similar types of contexts (after "the" or after "likes"), whereas "the" appears to occur in very different contexts. This is useful because it allows us to precisely define how similar two words are by computing the Euclidean distance between those two words in the encoding scheme. Here, we used word2vec (Mikolov et al., 2013) to compute embeddings for the words in our corpus. We then identified mental health-related keywords by finding the 50 terms most similar to "depression" and

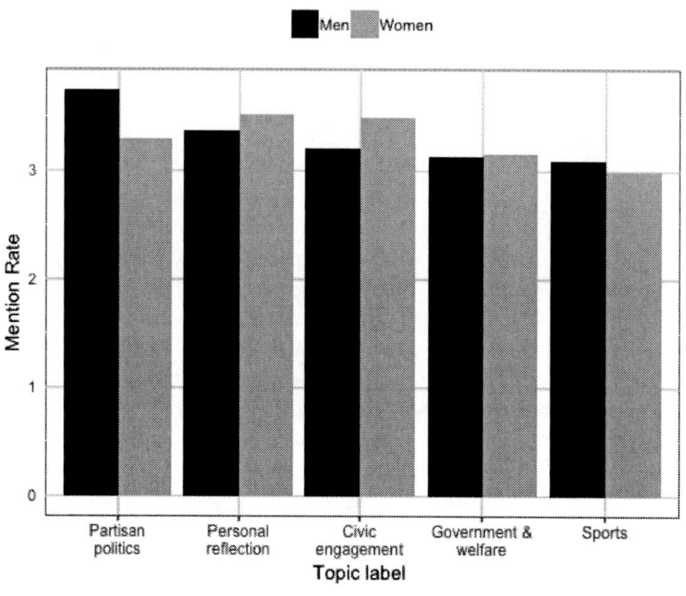

Figure 1: Mention rates of five most common topics among men and women.

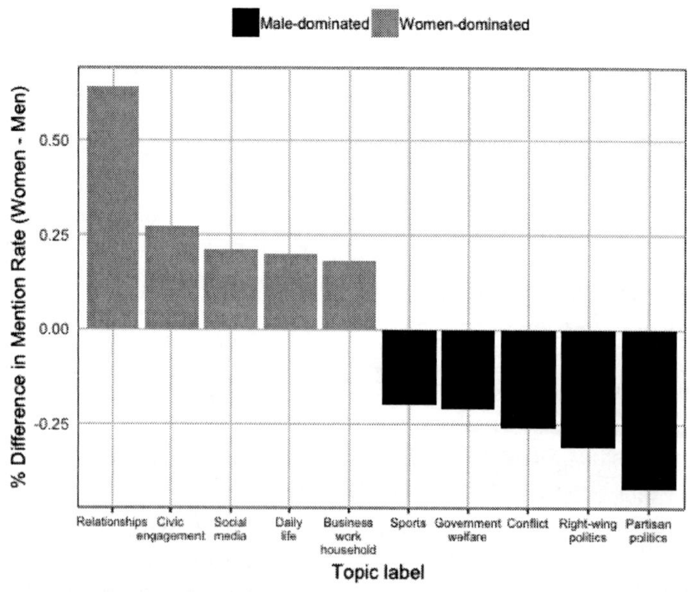

Figure 2: Topics with greatest differential mention rates between men and women.

188

"PTSD". We identified veteran-related keywords by finding the 50 terms (specifically, lemmatized words) most similar to "veteran" and "service". For the sake of illustration, we display the top 15 terms in each group in Table 1.

4.1 Keywords results and discussion

To compare rates of keyword use between men and women, we computed the average number of unique user mentions per day, per gender, and compared the rate of keyword mentions across genders. Because the sample is not balanced, with far more men than women, we normalize the mention rate by dividing average daily unique user mentions by the total number of users. The results of this comparison are shown in Figure 3.

Women were overall significantly more likely to mention keywords related to both veteran's issues and mental health than men ($p < .001$). Moreover, both groups were more likely to mention veteran-related keywords than mental health-related keywords ($p < .05$). The latter pattern did not differ across the two groups, and the interaction between keyword type and gender was not significant ($p > .5$). This finding indicates that women veterans are significantly more likely than their male counterparts to use social media platforms to discuss both their mental health and their experiences as veterans. These results have wide-ranging significance, which we will elaborate on below. In order to provide further insight into the gender-driven differences in the use of these keywords, we ranked, by gender, the frequency with which each keyword was mentioned and computed the difference in rank between men and women by subtracting each keyword's ranking among women from its ranking among men (i.e., large values indicate that a word is used more often among women). In Figure 4 we plot the ten most women- and men-biased keywords in the corpus.

Women-favored keywords were largely consonant with the findings above. Women were much more likely to mention the word "caregiver", for example. This resonates with our own findings as well as the findings from existing literature summarized above—namely, that women veterans are far more likely to serve in caretaking roles in their families, and that this is particularly relevant to their experience as veterans. Perhaps most strikingly, four out of the ten most women-biased keywords were directly related to health, wellbeing, or

care-seeking: "caregiver", "hosp", "asthma", and "drs" (Social Security Administration), "arthritis", "paramedic", "migraine". By contrast, only one of the ten most male-favored keywords relates to these topics in any straightforward way.

5 Discussion

These exploratory analyses provide an initial, rich set of indications that women veterans and male veterans use social media differently, and that these differences are relevant to the work of VSOs and the VA. Specifically, women veterans seem more likely than their male counterparts to use social media for finding community and for discussing or seeking information about healthcare. These findings have specific implications for the VSO community and the VA in considering opportunities for outreach to women veterans using social media platforms. Before proceeding further, however, we acknowledge that the method used to classify users according to gender, in their attempt to identify general patterns, could systematically mis-classify individuals whose social media behavior does not conform to gender norms, or to their own gender identity. This kind of systematic bias falls under the heading of what is often known as "algorithmic bias". We believe that the best remedy for algorithmic bias–or any other form of difficult-to-avoid bias–is to seek converging evidence from multiple methods and data sources, and thus avoid over-interpreting any one particular set of results.

Analyses like those reported here suggest several avenues for action to veteran organizations such as VSOs and mental health organizations that serve veteran populations. Specifically, our results suggest that social media-based outreach campaigns intended to promote self-care and treatment-seeking among veterans may be a particularly promising way to engage women veterans. Results from modeling efforts such as those reported here could be used to construct tailored audiences on platforms such as Facebook, Instagram, and Twitter. Indeed, pilot studies are underway to test the efficacy of constructing social media advertising campaigns for veteran-oriented, inpatient treatment based on the data reported here.

Moreover, topics, keywords, and n-grams (not explored here) constructed from corpora such as the one described in this paper are particularly well-suited to informing search-based advertising,

Veteran keywords	Mental health keywords
veteran	suicide
supporter	crime
family	murder
marines	medication
military	pain
army	ptsd
service	disability
unit	stress
commitment	depression
patriot	alcoholism
honorably	addiction
leader	anxiety
sir	nightmares
doctor	mysteriously
medical	disorder

Table 1: 15 terms most similar to "veteran" and "service" (left column) and "PTSD" and "mental health" (right column)

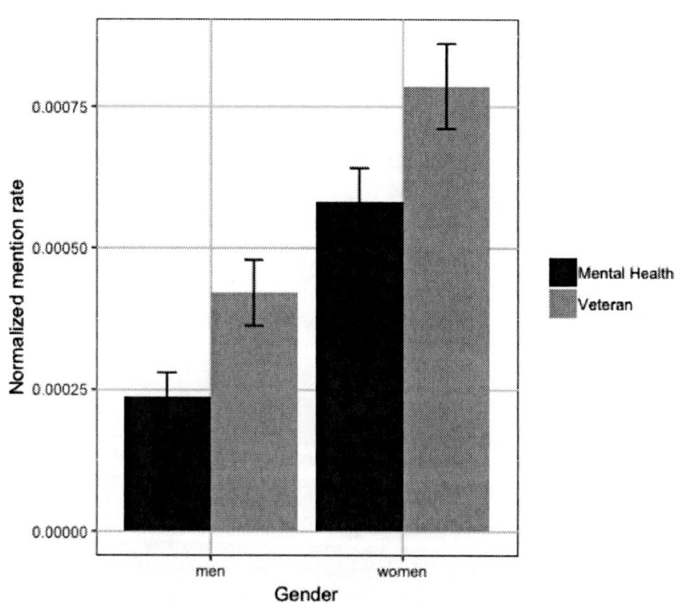

Figure 3: Normalized mention rate of veteran- and mental health-related keywords for men and women.

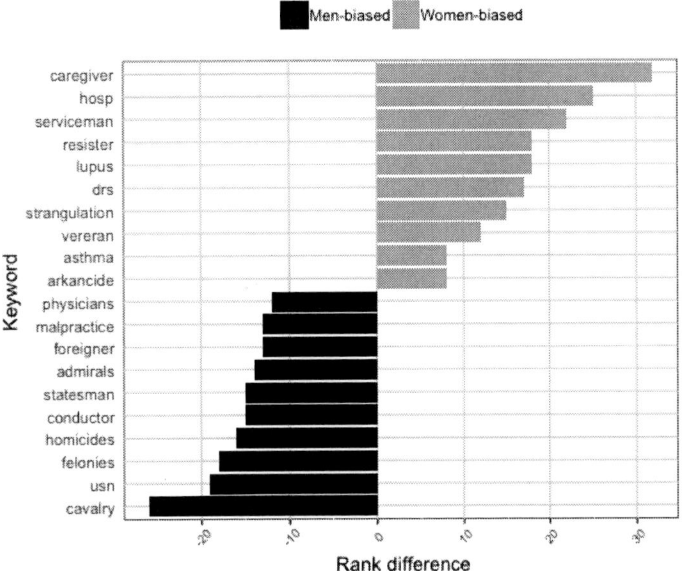

Figure 4: Top 10 most gender-distinctive keywords for women and men.

in which VSOs pay for the ability to promote services to internet users based on the strings they search on platforms such as Google. In general, commonly-used strings cost more. Data such as these, derived directly from the population of interest, would allow VSOs to deploy often highly-constrained advertising budgets to reach the individuals that stand to gain the most from their services. For example, we saw above that women veterans are likely to mention "pain" and "nightmares" in similar contexts as "depression". A targeted insight such as this would empower a nonprofit VSO to promote its services to women veterans and avoid spending large sums of money for strings explicitly containing the word "depression", the high cost of which is likely to be driven in part by life sciences companies with vastly larger advertising budgets.

Finally, evidence that women veterans may be more likely to use social media for care- and community-seeking suggests the intriguing possibility that telehealth services such as web-based mental health counseling may be particularly welcomed by this community.

Beyond engagement and outreach in the traditional sense, it is important to recognize that social media constitutes an important outlet for seeking care and information about care for women vet-

erans. It should therefore be a priority for VSOs and the VA to disseminate quality content for these platforms so that those using it for this purpose can find the right information at the right time and ultimately get connected to appropriate resources.

6 Conclusion

In this paper we presented a series of analyses strongly suggesting that women veterans of the US military use social media—specifically, Twitter—in a qualitatively different way from male veterans. Specifically, women veterans appear more likely to use social media platforms to engage in conversations about mental health and veteran-specific issues. These findings suggest that social media may be hugely important for veteran service organizations seeking to reach, connect with, and care for more women.

References

Charley Beller, Rebecca Knowles, Craig Harman, Shane Bergsma, Margaret Mitchell, and Benjamin Van Durme. 2014. I'ma belieber: Social roles via self-identification and conceptual attributes. In *Proceedings of the 52nd Annual Meeting of the Association for Computational Linguistics (Volume 2: Short Papers)*, pages 181–186.

David M. Blei, Andrew Y. Ng, and Michael I. Jordan.

2003. Latent Dirichlet allocation. *Journal of Machine Learning Research*, 3:993–1022.

John Blosnich, Melissa Ming Foynes, and Jillian C. Shipherd. 2013. Health disparities among sexual minority women veterans. *Journal of Women's Health*, 22(7):631–636.

Glen Coppersmith, Mark Dredze, Craig Harman, and Kristy Hollingshead. 2015. From ADHD to SAD: Analyzing the language of mental health on Twitter through self-reported diagnoses. In *Proceedings of the Workshop on Computational Linguistics and Clinical Psychology: From Linguistic Signal to Clinical Reality*, Denver, Colorado, USA. North American Chapter of the Association for Computational Linguistics.

Glen Coppersmith, Casey Hilland, Ophir Frieder, and Ryan Leary. 2017. Scalable mental health analysis in the clinical whitespace via natural language processing. In *Biomedical & Health Informatics (BHI), 2017 IEEE EMBS International Conference on*, pages 393–396. IEEE.

Glen Coppersmith, Ryan Leary, Patrick Crutchley, and Alex Fine. 2018. Natural Language Processing of Social Media as Screening for Suicide Risk. *Biomedical Informatics Insights*, 10:117822261879286.

Council on Foreign Relations. 2020. Demographics of the U.S. Military. `https://www.cfr.org/backgrounder/demographics-us-military`. Accessed: 2020-09-15.

Elisheva R. Danan, Erin E. Krebs, Kristine Ensrud, Eva Koeller, Roderick MacDonald, Tina Velasquez, Nancy Greer, and Timothy J. Wilt. 2017. An Evidence Map of the Women Veterans' Health Research Literature (2008–2015). *Journal of General Internal Medicine*, 32(12):1359–1376.

Susan M. Frayne, Wei Yu, Elizabeth M. Yano, Lakshmi Ananth, Samina Iqbal, Ann Thrailkill, and Ciaran S. Phibbs. 2007. Gender and use of care: Planning for tomorrow's veterans health administration. *Journal of Women's Health*, 16(8):1188–1199.

Gary J Gates. 2010. Lesbian , gay , and bisexual men and women in the US military : Updated estimates. Technical report, The Williams Institute.

House Committee on Veterans Affairs. 2019. VA 2030: A Vision for the Future of VA (Testimony of Dr. Patricia Hayes).

Institute of Medicine. 2014. Treatment for posttraumatic stress disorder in military and veteran populations: Final assessment. Technical report, Institute of Medicine, National Academy Press, Washington, D. C.

Kelly H. Koo, Claire L. Hebenstreit, Erin Madden, Karen H. Seal, and Shira Maguen. 2015. Race/ethnicity and gender differences in mental health diagnoses among Iraq and Afghanistan veterans. *Psychiatry Research*, 229(3):724–731.

Alex Lamb, Michael J. Paul, and Mark Dredze. 2013. Separating fact from fear: Tracking flu infections on Twitter. In *Proceedings of the Conference of the North American Chapter of the Association for Computational Linguistics (NAACL)*.

Shira Maguen, Li Ren, Jeane O. Bosch, Charles R. Marmar, and Karen H. Seal. 2010. Gender differences in mental health diagnoses among Iraq and Afghanistan veterans enrolled in veterans affairs health care. *American Journal of Public Health*, 100(12):2450–2456.

L. Manning. 2008. Women in the Military: Where They Stand. Technical report, Women's Research and Education Institute, Arlington, VA.

Kristin M. Mattocks, Sally G. Haskell, Erin E. Krebs, Amy C. Justice, Elizabeth M. Yano, and Cynthia Brandt. 2012. Women at war: Understanding how women veterans cope with combat and military sexual trauma. *Social Science and Medicine*, 74(4):537–545.

Tomas Mikolov, Ilya Sutskever, Kai Chen, Greg Corrado, and Jeffrey Dean. 2013. Distributed representations ofwords and phrases and their compositionality. *Advances in Neural Information Processing Systems*, pages 1–9.

John Paparrizos, Ryen W. White, and Eric Horvitz. 2016. Screening for pancreatic adenocarcinoma using signals from web search logs: Feasibility study and results. *Journal of Oncology Practice*, 12(8):737–744. PMID: 27271506.

Jennifer J. Runnals, Natara Garovoy, Susan J. McCutcheon, Allison T. Robbins, Monica C. Mann-Wrobel, Alyssa Elliott, Jennifer L. Strauss, Jean C. Beckham, Mira Brancu, Michelle Kelley, Suzanne E. Kerns, Monica Mann-Wrobel, Allison T. Robbins, Jennifer J. Runnals, Kristy Straits-Tröster, and Elizabeth Van Voorhees. 2014. Systematic Review of Women Veterans' Mental Health. *Women's Health Issues*, 24(5):485–502.

J. Steinhauer. 2019. Treated Like a 'Piece of Meat': Female Veterans Endure Harassment at the V.A.

VA. 2015. Study of Barriers for Women Veterans to VA Health Care. Technical report, Department of Veterans Affairs.

VA. 2017. Women Veterans Report: The Past, Present, and Future of Women Veterans. Technical report, Department of Veterans Affairs.

VA. 2019. National Veteran Suicide Prevention Annual Report. Technical report, VA Office of Mental Health and Suicide Prevention.

Understanding Weekly COVID-19 Concerns through Dynamic Content-Specific LDA Topic Modeling

**Mohammadzaman Zamani[1], H. Andrew Schwartz[1], Johannes Eichstaedt[2],
Sharath Chandra Guntuku[3], Adithya Virinchipuram Ganesan[1],
Sean Clouston[1], and Salvatore Giorgi[3]**
[1] Stony Brook University [2] Stanford University [3] University of Pennsylvania
mzamani@cs.stonybrook.edu

Abstract

The novelty and global scale of the COVID-19 pandemic has lead to rapid societal changes in a short span of time. As government policy and health measures shift, public perceptions and concerns also change, an evolution documented within discourse on social media. We propose a dynamic content-specific LDA topic modeling technique that can help to identify different domains of COVID-specific discourse that can be used to track societal shifts in concerns or views. Our experiments show that these model-derived topics are more coherent than standard LDA topics, and also provide new features that are more helpful in prediction of COVID-19 related outcomes including social mobility and unemployment rate.

1 Introduction

In early 2020, the entire world slowly became aware of a severe respiratory disease (Adhikari et al., 2020) with often catastrophic consequences (Zaim et al., 2020; Santesmasses et al., 2020). Since then, COVID-19 has infected millions of people worldwide and is on a trajectory to cause more than 1 million deaths globally before the end of 2020 (Medicine, 2020). Government and public health agencies have sought to mobilized and promote protective measures (Sen-Crowe et al., 2020) as scientific efforts rapidly build a foundation of knowledge to treat the disease, and economies have experienced rapid drops in employment (Zaim et al., 2020). These ongoing changes make the COVID-19 pandemic a time of immense and multifaceted social change that is rapidly evolving and largely, if imperfectly, narrated from millions of voices on social media.

User generated discourse like social media provide rich and continuous data on the evolution of significant world events - be it pandemics, hurricane relief, earthquakes, or wildfires (Thackeray et al., 2012). Given the rapidly evolving nature of such public health emergencies, the ability to extract and quantify the progression of topics can provide a unique window into the concurrent societal change. Realizing this objective is partially met through the goals of topic modeling, such as Latent Dirichlet Allocation (LDA; Blei et al. (2003)). However, tracking significant world events present 2 challenges to standard topic models: (1) the need for rapidly evolving topics rather than topics from a single snapshot of language at a time, and (2) the need to focus on event-relevant lexical patterns rather than general patterns.

Latent Dirichlet Allocation (LDA) is one of the most commonly used topic modeling methods, whereby probabilities of words belonging to topics (clusters of semantically related words) are derived from textual data. Not only can this provide a good set of features for predictive models (Brody and Elhadad, 2010; Zamani et al., 2018b), but also a tool for generating hypotheses and gaining insight in a manner easily interpretable by humans (Schwartz et al., 2013; Hu et al., 2012).

In this paper, we present and evaluate modifications to LDA, addressing the two aforementioned challenges, to focus on capturing topics that can characterize evolving interests specifically for COVID-19. Addressing such challenges enables several applications including monitoring the impact of a specific event on social, emotional, mental well-being and behaviours (Zamani et al., 2018a; Mirzaei et al., 2019). Building on previous work in online topic modeling (Canini et al., 2009), we propose the creation of short-interval *dynamic topics* that are updated on a regular basis (weekly or monthly). Furthermore, because words in social media posts cover a wide variety of domains (even when limited to posts containing COVID-19 keywords), we introduce a *content-specific* preprocessing step that focuses the lexicon on the domain. This limits the generation of incoherent or general domain topics — rather than a single general health

Proceedings of the Fourth Workshop on Natural Language Processing and Computational Social Science, pages 193–198
Online, November 20, 2020. ©2020 Association for Computational Linguistics
https://doi.org/10.18653/v1/P17

care topic, multiple health care topics may emerge, such as those related to vaccines and testing. This is especially important in the context of rapidly evolving public health emergencies like COVID-19, where conversations around physical distancing and protective measures have evolved as national policy has changed (Ross, 2020).

Our **contributions** include the formalization and evaluation of methods for topic modeling over (1) time series language data and (2) content focused lexical patterns; (3) open source data set of dynamic COVID-specific topics by week[1]; (4) demonstration that such topics can be used effectively as features to predict future US county-level mobility and unemployment.

2 Methods

2.1 Dynamic LDA topic modeling

LDA topic modeling estimates two sets of distributions: 1) representing each document as a multinomial distribution over T topics and 2) representing each topic with a multinomial distribution over W words. Blei, NG, and Jordan (2003) presented the LDA procedure to approximate the maximum-likelihood estimate for these distribution. Griffiths (Griffiths, 2002) presented a Gibbs Sampling based approach, which consists of a symmetric Dirichlet prior for both topics and words distributions followed by a Markov chain Monte Carlo inference. In this approach, at step i the topic assignment of word w_i is sampled according to the following conditional distribution:

$$P(z_i = j | \mathbf{z}_{-i}, \mathbf{w}) = \frac{n_{-i,j}^{(w_i)} + \beta}{n_{-i,j}^{(\cdot)} + W\beta} \frac{n_{-i,j}^{(d_i)} + \alpha}{n_{-i,.}^{(d_i)} + T\alpha} \tag{1}$$

where, $\mathbf{w}$ is the data set consisting of words $w_1, ..., w_n$, in which each w_i belongs to a document d_i. Also, sub-index $-i$ indicates that the token at position i is disregarded in the calculation, $\mathbf{z}_{-i}$ is the topic probability distribution over words, $n_{-i,j}^{(w_i)}$ is the number of times word w_i is assigned to topic j, $n_{-i,j}^{(\cdot)}$ is the total number of words assigned to topic j, $n_{-i,j}^{(d_i)}$ is the number of times a word in document d_i is assigned to topic j, and $n_{-i,.}^{(d_i)}$ is the total number of words in document d_i.

Inspired by these online Gibbs sampling approaches, we present a simple *dynamic topic modeling* for streams of data, when we are able to store a portion of data. The main difference with the aforementioned online sampler is that, in our scenario, we do not aim for estimating the topics distribution for the whole data set. In fact, we have a set of topics for each batch of data, and track changes over time as we receive a new batch of data. Since topics represent different concepts in the data set, we can trace how the existing concepts evolve, as well as discover vanishing or newly trending concepts.

In dynamic topic modeling for in-batch sampling we repeatedly use Gibbs sampling as in Equation 1 until we meet a stoppage criteria. However when it comes to cross-batch sampling we perform a more conservative sampling in order to transfer the topics posterior distribution obtained from the last batch into the topics prior distribution of the new batch. As shown in Equation 2, we use topics distribution over words from the previous batch but document distribution over topics from the current batch. This way we transfer the topics distribution over words to the current batch of data, while words in the same document still have a higher chance to be assigned to the same topics.

$$P(z_i^t = j | \mathbf{z}_{t-1}, \mathbf{w}_t) = \left(\frac{n_j^{(w_i)} + \beta}{n_j^{(\cdot)} + W\beta}\right)_{t-1} \left(\frac{n_{i,j}^{(d_i)} + \alpha}{n_{i,.}^{(d_i)} + T\alpha}\right)_t \tag{2}$$

Here, subindex t and $t-1$ determine that $n_j^{(w_i)}$, $n_j^{(\cdot)}$ and W are obtained from batch $t-1$ while $n_{i,j}^{(d_i)}$, $n_{i,.}^{(d_i)}$ and T are calculated from batch t.

2.2 Content-specific topic modeling

Content-specific (CS) topic modeling is a process for preparing text data for topic modeling, such that the desired topics are limited in thematic scope. In this paper we apply this method to automatically derive topics related to COVID-19, though this method has previously been applied to drinking (Giorgi et al., 2020) and diabetes tweets (Griffis et al., 2020). The entire process includes four steps: (1) tokenization and colocations; (2) identifying words most associated with our theme; (3) filtering documents to only the most discriminative words; and (4) the topic modeling process.

We start with a thematically coherent corpus, which in our case is a set of tweets containing COVID-19 keywords, from the streaming Twitter API: stayhome, stayathome, virus, coronovirus, coronavirus, covid, 2019-ncov, covd, outbreak,

---

[1] https://github.com/wwbp/weekly_covid_lda_topics

pandemic, corona, corono, washyourhand, hand-washing, and sarscov (Guntuku et al., 2020).

We note that COVID-19 tweets contain language that may not be associated with COVID-19; for example, "RT" will appear in a large sample of our tweets, though this may or may not be associated with COVID-19. Thus, we would like to identify COVID-19 language and restrict our LDA process to that. As such, we take a random sample of COVID-19 tweets and find a matched set of tweets not related to our theme (i.e., tweets *without* COVID-19 keywords). We combine the COVID-19 and matched data, tokenize each document, and identify collocations (i.e., word phrases which are more common than the individual words within the phrase).

Next, we create a tweet level binary outcome: 1 if the tweet contains COVID-19 keywords and 0 otherwise, in other words, 1 for COVID-19 tweets and 0 for matched tweets. We then calculate a weighted log odds ratio, using an informative Dirichlet prior to estimate the difference in frequency of a word across two corpora (i.e., COVID-19 and matched tweets) (Monroe et al., 2008; Jurafsky et al., 2014). The prior shrinks word frequencies towards those of a large background corpus, while the z-score of the log odds ratio controls variance in word frequencies. Taking the tokens most associated with the binary outcome, we filter each document in our COVID-19 corpus to contain only these tokens, and run topic modeling over this filtered corpus.

3 Data

We built a COVID-19 corpus from publicly available Twitter data (March 12, 2020 to the end of June 2020; 2.6 million tweets), pulled from the streaming API using a set of COVID-19 keywords. We also took a sample of tweets pulled from the random 1% stream, which did not contain the COVID-19 keywords, as our matched tweets. We break this corpus into two sets of weekly and monthly data sets. The former, which is used for the coherence and real time tracking experiments, spans 5 weeks of tweets and contains 150,000 tweets per week for each of the COVID-19 and matched tweets. The latter, used for prediction experiment, spans 4 months and contains 500,000 tweets per month.

For the prediction task, we collect two monthly US county COVID-19 related outcomes: We use the SafeGraph Places Patterns[1] data, which contains aggregated and anonymized foot traffic data for 6 million points across the US. We use three months of mobility data from April to June, 2020. We also collect two months (April and May, 2020) of yearly-adjusted unemployment rates as reported by the US Bureau of Labor Statistics (BLS)[2].

4 Experiments

We perform three tasks to evaluate our proposed method. First, we consider weekly topic *coherence* as an intrinsic evaluation metric. Next, we manually compare the evolution of hand selected topics to real-world events for *real time tracking*. Finally, as an extrinsic evaluation metric, we use our topics as feature for predicting monthly mobility and unemployment.

For each of our three experiments, we create 40 weekly and monthly topics (for each LDA method) using the Java-based Mallet software package (McCallum, 2002), which implements Gibbs sampling (Gelfand and Smith, 1990). For each LDA method, parameters are kept constant ($\alpha = 5/N$, $\beta = 0.1$), where N is the number of desired topics. Additionally, stop words are removed and the number of unique tokens is constant at 8,000. All text pre-processing as well as the *prediction* task is done with the Python package DLATK (Schwartz et al., 2017).

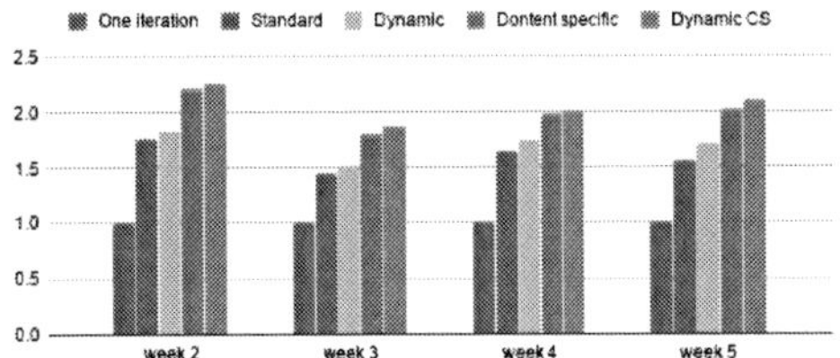

Figure 1: Normalized weekly point-wise mutual information coherence. Week 1 is excluded from this figure as dynamic CS and dynamic are the same as CS and standard, respectively, in Week 1.

Coherence We compare the average coherence (see appendix for formal definition) of topics across four LDA methods plus a baseline: standard LDA, CS, dynamic, and dynamic CS. For a topic t the

[1]https://www.safegraph.com/dashboard/covid19-commerce-patterns

[2]https://www.bls.gov/bls/newsrels.htm#OEUS

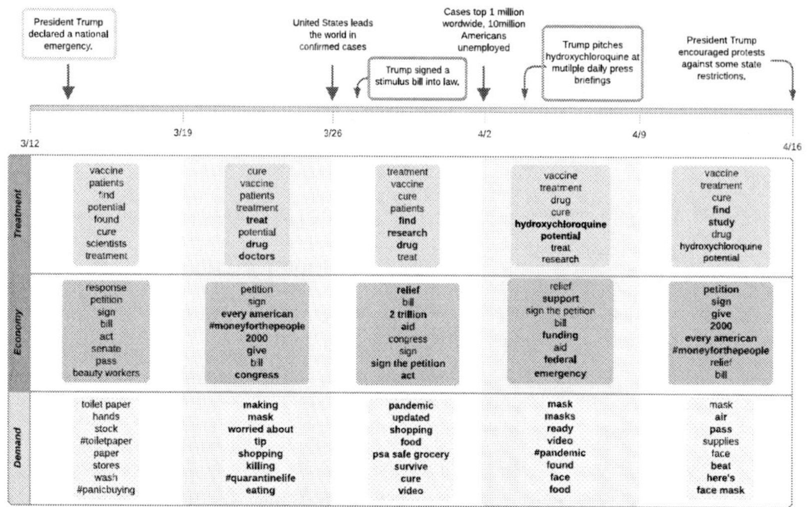

Figure 2: Timeline of COVID-19 events and topics over a five week period. Topics are visualized using the top 8 weighted words per week, bolded words are new to the top 8 topic words at that time point.

	m2→m3	m3→m4	m4→m5	Average
unigrams	0.15	0.20	0.34	0.23
unigrams + Standard LDA	0.19	0.25	0.43	0.29
unigrams + Dynamic	0.20	0.26	0.43	0.30
unigrams + CS	0.23	0.26	**0.46**	**0.32**
unigrams + Dynamic CS	**0.30**	0.26	**0.47**	**0.34**

(a) Social Mobility

	m2→m3	m3→m4	Average
unigrams	0.21	0.27	0.24
unigrams + Standard LDA	0.28	0.36	0.32
unigrams + Dynamic	0.27	**0.42**	0.34
unigrams + CS	0.24	0.38	0.31
unigrams + Dynamic CS	**0.31**	**0.40**	**0.36**

(b) Adjusted unemployment rate

Table 1: Prediction accuracies (Pearson r): language features from month n predict outcomes at month $n+1$. Bold indicates significant improvement over unigrams + standard method, according to paired t-tests.($p < .05$).

coherence score can be obtained as the summation of coherence score of each pair of words from the top selected words of that topic. For the coherence of pair of words there are various options, where we use point-wise mutual information (PMI) as suggested by (Newman et al., 2010):

$$Coherence(t) = \sum_{i<j} log \frac{p(w_i, w_j)}{p(w_i)p(w_j)} \quad (3)$$

where, w_i and w_j are from the top words of the topic t.

Our baseline is a single iteration of Gibbs sampling for standard LDA and is used for normalizing all scores.

Figure 1 shows the results of our *coherence* task. Not surprisingly, all four LDA methods outperform the single iteration baseline. We see a small increase in coherence when using the dynamic approach over standard LDA. Significant increases (above both the standard and dynamic approaches) occur when using the CS method, as determined by a t-test ($p < 0.05$). Finally, we see marginal increases in coherence (above the CS method) when using the the dynamic CS approach.

Real Time Tracking For the tracking task, the goal is to see if our topics are evolving alongside real world events. As such, we hand select three topics, labeled as *treatment*, *economy* and *demand* and show their evolution over a 5 weeks period. The timeline in Figure 2 shows the top eight weighted words within each topic, in addition to plotting notable COVID-19 events.

The *demand* topic starts with mentions of toilet paper and panic buying and moving to masks and general supplies. The *treatment* topic mentions hydroxychloroquine around the time the FDA approved emergency use (March 29) and when Trump was frequently mentioning the drug (April 3 through 5). Finally, the *economy* topic starts with calls for emergency federal help ("sign", "act", "pass") and then moves onto more specific information around the stimulus bill ("2 trillion" and "congress") before stabilizing.

Prediction Using a 10-fold cross validation setup, we predict two monthly COVID-19 related outcomes: social mobility and unemployment rates. We extract monthly topic representations (standard, dynamic, CS and dynamic CS) for US counties who have written at least 7,500 words per month (i.e., each observation is a US county and is represented as a bag-of-topics).

Here, we use language features for a given month to predict the outcomes for the following month (e.g., topics from March are used to predict outcomes in April). For each month, we perform a 10-fold cross-validation of a regularized ridge regression and report the Pearson r between our predicted values and the actual rates. We use unigram features as the baseline and compared our gain by adding standard LDA features vs. dynamic CS LDA features. Results in Table 1 suggest that while topic features are adding on top of unigrams, the dynamic CS features perform significantly better.

5 Discussion

Discussions on social networks are rapidly changing, especially those centered around COVID-19. As such, the goal of the current study was to see if we could reasonably monitor those changes over time using a novel LDA topic-modeling approach, namely dynamic content-specific LDA. Results showed that we could reliably track topic evolution and leverage those dynamics to predict changes in real work outcomes (mobility and unemployment) We found that many such observations could be readily tracked, suggesting that we could reliably track discussions, even when the specific words or concerns used to reference that topic change.

This has a direct application to COVID-19 as it may help determine appropriate shifts in public health strategy as topics evolve towards consensus. Additionally, insofar as topics involve and reliably track symptoms, then evolution in reported symptoms may help in efforts to map out differences in strains or in disease evolution. It is also worthwhile to note that this model can be used to track *any* evolving discussion over time. Indeed, many discussions both in the field of public health or medicine and in other fields, such as understanding financial shifts or changes to public acceptance of known falsehoods or conspiracies, are discussed regularly online and may be tracked as they evolve. The evolution of such discussions can be telling, we think, and the mapping of that evolution warrants

further interrogation.

A central goal in epidemiological modeling is monitoring psychiatric and health outcomes, and their correlates, as they shift over time. This study helps us to better identify and track the discourse around COVID-19 via an online social network and also helped to characterize changes in topics as they evolved over time. As such, LDA topic analysis identified and helped to characterize changing interests in both COVID-19 and its societal effects as they emerged over time. This study suggests that further research should seek to understand how these topics are associated with the distribution of COVID-19 cases and changes in mental health.

References

Sasmita Poudel Adhikari, Sha Meng, Yu-Ju Wu, Yu-Ping Mao, Rui-Xue Ye, Qing-Zhi Wang, Chang Sun, Sean Sylvia, Scott Rozelle, Hein Raat, et al. 2020. Epidemiology, causes, clinical manifestation and diagnosis, prevention and control of coronavirus disease (covid-19) during the early outbreak period: a scoping review. *Infectious diseases of poverty*, 9(1):1–12.

David M Blei, Andrew Y Ng, and Michael I Jordan. 2003. Latent dirichlet allocation. *Journal of machine Learning research*, 3(Jan):993–1022.

Samuel Brody and Noemie Elhadad. 2010. An unsupervised aspect-sentiment model for online reviews. In *Human language technologies: The 2010 annual conference of the North American chapter of the association for computational linguistics*, pages 804–812.

Kevin Canini, Lei Shi, and Thomas Griffiths. 2009. Online inference of topics with latent dirichlet allocation. In *Artificial Intelligence and Statistics*, pages 65–72.

Alan E Gelfand and Adrian FM Smith. 1990. Sampling-based approaches to calculating marginal densities. *Journal of the American statistical association*, 85(410):398–409.

Salvatore Giorgi, David B Yaden, Johannes C Eichstaedt, Robert D Ashford, Anneke EK Buffone, H Andrew Schwartz, Lyle H Ungar, and Brenda Curtis. 2020. Cultural differences in tweeting about drinking across the us. *International Journal of Environmental Research and Public Health*, 17(4):1125.

Heather Griffis, David A Asch, H Andrew Schwartz, Lyle Ungar, Alison M Buttenheim, Frances K Barg, Nandita Mitra, and Raina M Merchant. 2020. Using social media to track geographic variability in language about diabetes: Infodemiology analysis. *JMIR diabetes*, 5(1):e14431.

Tom Griffiths. 2002. Gibbs sampling in the generative model of latent dirichlet allocation.

Sharath Chandra Guntuku, Garrick Sherman, Daniel C Stokes, Anish K Agarwal, Emily Seltzer, Raina M Merchant, and Lyle H Ungar. 2020. Tracking mental health and symptom mentions on twitter during covid-19. *Journal of general internal medicine*, pages 1–3.

Yuheng Hu, Ajita John, Fei Wang, and Subbarao Kambhampati. 2012. Et-lda: Joint topic modeling for aligning events and their twitter feedback. In *AAAI*, volume 12, pages 59–65.

Dan Jurafsky, Victor Chahuneau, Bryan R Routledge, and Noah A Smith. 2014. Narrative framing of consumer sentiment in online restaurant reviews. *First Monday*.

Andrew Kachites McCallum. 2002. Mallet: A machine learning for language toolkit (2002).

Johns Hopkins University & Medicine. 2020. Coronavirus resource center.

Mehrdad Mirzaei, Shaghayegh Sahebi, and Peter Brusilovsky. 2019. Annotated examples and parameterized exercises: Analyzing students' behavior patterns. In *International Conference on Artificial Intelligence in Education*, pages 308–319. Springer.

Burt L Monroe, Michael P Colaresi, and Kevin M Quinn. 2008. Fightin'words: Lexical feature selection and evaluation for identifying the content of political conflict. *Political Analysis*, 16(4):372–403.

David Newman, Youn Noh, Edmund Talley, Sarvnaz Karimi, and Timothy Baldwin. 2010. Evaluating topic models for digital libraries. In *Proceedings of the 10th annual joint conference on Digital libraries*, pages 215–224.

Katherine Ross. 2020. Why weren't we wearing masks from the beginning? dr. fauci explains. *TheStreet*.

Didac Santesmasses, José Pedro Castro, Aleksandr A Zenin, Anastasia V Shindyapina, Maxim V Gerashchenko, Bohan Zhang, Csaba Kerepesi, Sun Hee Yim, Peter O Fedichev, and Vadim N Gladyshev. 2020. Covid-19 is an emergent disease of aging. *MedRxiv*.

H Andrew Schwartz, Johannes C Eichstaedt, Margaret L Kern, Lukasz Dziurzynski, Stephanie M Ramones, Megha Agrawal, Achal Shah, Michal Kosinski, David Stillwell, Martin EP Seligman, et al. 2013. Personality, gender, and age in the language of social media: The open-vocabulary approach. *PloS one*, 8(9):e73791.

H Andrew Schwartz, Salvatore Giorgi, Maarten Sap, Patrick Crutchley, Lyle Ungar, and Johannes Eichstaedt. 2017. Dlatk: Differential language analysis toolkit. In *Proceedings of the 2017 Conference on Empirical Methods in Natural Language Processing: System Demonstrations*, pages 55–60.

Brendon Sen-Crowe, Mark McKenney, and Adel Elkbuli. 2020. Social distancing during the covid-19 pandemic: Staying home save lives. *The American journal of emergency medicine*.

Rosemary Thackeray, Brad L Neiger, Amanda K Smith, and Sarah B Van Wagenen. 2012. Adoption and use of social media among public health departments. *BMC public health*, 12(1):1–6.

Sevim Zaim, Jun Heng Chong, Vissagan Sankaranarayanan, and Amer Harky. 2020. Covid-19 and multi-organ response. *Current Problems in Cardiology*, page 100618.

Mohammadzaman Zamani, Anneke Buffone, and H Andrew Schwartz. 2018a. Predicting human trustfulness from facebook language. *arXiv preprint arXiv:1808.05668*.

Mohammadzaman Zamani, H Andrew Schwartz, Veronica E Lynn, Salvatore Giorgi, and Niranjan Balasubramanian. 2018b. Residualized factor adaptation for community social media prediction tasks. *arXiv preprint arXiv:1808.09479*.

Emoji and Self-Identity in Twitter Bios

Jinhang Li,[*] **Giorgos Longinos,**[*] **Steven R. Wilson** and **Walid Magdy**
School of Informatics
The University of Edinburgh
Edinburgh, United Kingdom
{j.li-183,g.longinos}@sms.ed.ac.uk
steven.wilson@ed.ac.uk, wmagdy@inf.ed.ac.uk

Abstract

Emoji are widely used to express emotions and concepts on social media, and prior work has shown that users' choice of emoji reflects the way that they wish to present themselves to the world. Emoji usage is typically studied in the context of posts made by users, and this view has provided important insights into phenomena such as emotional expression and self-representation. In addition to making posts, however, social media platforms like Twitter allow for users to provide a short bio, which is an opportunity to briefly describe their account as a whole. In this work, we focus on the use of emoji in these bio statements. We explore the ways in which users include emoji in these self-descriptions, finding different patterns than those observed around emoji usage in tweets. We examine the relationships between emoji used in bios and the content of users' tweets, showing that the topics and even the average sentiment of tweets varies for users with different emoji in their bios. Lastly, we confirm that homophily effects exist with respect to the types of emoji that are included in bios of users and their followers.

1 Introduction

With the rise of social media usage and online text-based communication, emoji, a simple but powerfully expressive set of visual characters (Danesi, 2016), have become a hugely popular means to express emotions, moods, and feelings over computer-mediated communication (Kelly and Watts, 2015). In the era of big data, with more and more people engaging with social media, researchers have begun to study the ways in which social media users include emoji in their posts, finding that emoji usage is associated with things like personality (Li et al., 2018), culture (Guntuku et al., 2019),

---

[*] Authors contributed equally.

and socio-geographical differences (Barbieri et al., 2016).

Prior work has typically focused on how people use emoji within the posts that they make online (Ljubešić and Fišer, 2016; Robertson et al., 2018), or the way that they can be used as reactions to other content (Tian et al., 2017). However, emoji are also commonly used within user's self-created profiles. In this work, we specifically examine the inclusion of emoji in Twitter bios, which are short (160 characters maximum) texts describing a Twitter account. These bios are featured prominently on a user's profile page, and given their limited length, users often use this space succinctly express the essential information about their accounts. Therefore, we expect that the choice of emoji used in these bios will have a strong connection to a user's online self-identity, or the way that they seek to portray themselves to others on a social media platform.

The goal of this paper is to give an overview of how emoji are used in Twitter bios from a computational linguistics perspective, that is, we treat emoji as a special category of tokens and make use of natural language processing methods to understand the major trends in the ways that people use emoji in their bios and what this says about both the things they tweet about and their follower network. Our results provides insights into the variety of ways in which people choose to present themselves online in their Twitter bios that may be overlooked when only considering non-emoji word tokens or only considering the ways that people use emoji in the content of tweets. More specifically, we ask, and subsequently describe the work done to answer, the following research questions:

RQ1. How are emoji used in Twitter bios? As a first step, we seek to characterize the ways in which users use emoji in their bios. We look at the types of emoji that most commonly used in Twitter bios,

Proceedings of the Fourth Workshop on Natural Language Processing and Computational Social Science, pages 199–211
Online, November 20, 2020. ©2020 Association for Computational Linguistics
https://doi.org/10.18653/v1/P17

and the position within the bios that emoji appear. We compare our findings to trends from the usage of emoji in tweets by the same set of users and note the differences.

RQ2. What is the relationships between the emoji in a user's bio and the content that the user posts? Next, we explore the correlations that exist between the choice of emoji to be included in a user's bio and the content that that user tweets about. We consider this from the perspectives of word-level patterns, topic usage, and overall tweet sentiment.

RQ3. Do users and their followers use emoji in their bios in a similar way? Last, we investigate the homophily of emoji usage with bios by studying the follower networks of our core set of users. We look at the similarities in both the absence or presence of emoji in users' bios as well as particular choices of emoji used.

2 Background

2.1 Online Self-Identity

Self-identity, or self-concept, is a collection of firm and noticeable beliefs about oneself (Sparks and Shepherd, 1992). From a general perspective, self-identity gives the answers to the question "Who am I?". Many components make up self-identity together. The self-categorization theory asserts that the self-identity consists of at least two types of self-categorization: personal identity (what makes me unique?) and social identity (which groups do I belong to?) (Guimond et al., 2006).

As social attributes are inherent, people reveal their self-identity when they communicate with others or interact with the outside world (Fisher et al., 2014). Expressing themselves is also a way for people to establish connections and bonds with the world. Therefore, social media provides a natural opportunity to study self-identity. Previous studies have shown that specific personality characteristics can be measured by analyzing linguistic behavior on social media using natural language processing techniques (Plank and Hovy, 2015). Other work analyzed the words, phrases, and topics collected from the Facebook messages, and linked these to personality traits and demographics of users (Schwartz et al., 2013). Twitter bios have been shown to be are particularly useful in discovering other aspects of self-identity such as political and religious affiliations (Rogers and Jones, 2019).

2.2 Self-representation in Emoji

While many studies related to online self-identity are based on the analysis of textual features, others have turned to emoji as important signals of users' identities. In one study, researchers looked at Twitter names and bios, uncovering stark differences in the emoji use of groups supporting and opposed to white nationalism (Hagen et al., 2019). Graells-Garrido et al. (2020) found that in two South American countries, different colour variations of heart emoji indicated users' opinions about abortions: tweets containing the green heart emoji '💚' were more likely to convey support of women's rights, while the blue heart emoji '💙' was more associated with stronger restrictions of abortions. In another study, researchers explored differences in emoji usage across cultures, finding that users from western countries tend to use more emoji than users from eastern countries (Guntuku et al., 2019). Although there were specific emoji that were found to be culturally specific (e.g. cooked rice '🍚'), it was suggested that many common emoji have similar meanings across cultures.

It has been shown that usage of some emoji are also correlated with aspects of identity such as personality traits (Völkel et al., 2019), and the use of skin-tone modifiers in emoji has been linked to greater feelings of self-representation online, with no evidence that the skin-tones in emoji correlated with the expression of racist views online (Robertson et al., 2018, 2020). Other work found gender stereotypes in the use of male and female emoji modifiers: male modifiers were more frequently used in emoji related to business and technology while female modifiers were used in emoji related to love and makeup more often (Barbieri and Camacho-Collados, 2018).

3 Data

For our study, we sampled users from Twitter who tweeted between April and July 2020. Using the Twitter streaming API, we began collecting tweets and storing all user-level information available for

Dataset	Users	Tweets	Retweets
EmojiBio	20,000	2,998,219	1,568,661
NonEmojiBio	2,000	491,646	247,800
Followers	7,105,521	425,704,661	169,935,436

Table 1: Number of users, tweets, and retweets (subset of tweets) in our datasets.

Bios		Tweets	
Emoji	Appearances	Emoji	Appearances
(emoji)	1311	(emoji)	115999
(emoji)	1152	(emoji)	65410
(emoji)	965	(emoji)	48411
(emoji)	720	(emoji)	40892
(emoji)	559	(emoji)	34368
(emoji)	547	(emoji)	33766
(emoji)	543	(emoji)	33173
(emoji)	490	(emoji)	23037
(emoji)	467	(emoji)	17040
(emoji)	326	(emoji)	16929

Table 2: The most frequently used emoji in the bios and tweets of the emojiBio dataset.

Group Name	Num. Emojis	In Bios	User ratio	Examples
People & Body	2485	745	20.0%	(emoji)
Symbols	301	229	15.4%	(emoji)
Objects	299	219	15.9%	(emoji)
Flags	275	215	16.5%	(emoji)
Travel & Places	264	206	14.9%	(emoji)
Smileys & Emotion	162	151	**44.3%**	(emoji)
Animals & Nature	147	132	18.9%	(emoji)
Food & Drink	131	117	5.5%	(emoji)
Activities	95	82	15.2%	(emoji)

Table 3: Emoji groups present in Unicode Emoji v13.0, number of unique emoji in the group, number of unique emoji used at least once in a bio in the userBios dataset, the percentage of users who use at least one emoji from the corresponding group in their bio, and examples of emoji from the group.

each tweet, including the bio. In order to filter out both fake or less well-established accounts, we removed all accounts that had less than 100 followers, and to remove celebrity or other widely popular accounts, we filtered out those with more than 1000 followers. From the remaining set of users, we randomly sampled 20,000 users which have at least one emoji in their bios, and collected their most recent 200 tweets, as available, labeling this dataset "emojiBio". We also collected 200 tweets each for a set of 2,000 users who did *not* use any emoji in their bio as a control group, which we label the "nonEmojiBio" dataset. Finally, the "Followers" dataset contains the user-level information and recent tweets of the followers of the users of both the emojiBio and nonEmojiBio datasets. Details about the size of the datasets are presented in Table 1.

As our dataset contains text written in many langauges, we first used the pre-trained fastText language identification model (Joulin et al., 2016a,b) to detect the language that each tweet or bio was written in. The most common languages in our datasets were English, Japanese, Spanish, and Portuguese, followed by others. After identifying the langauges, we tokenized the English-language texts using the NLTK (Loper and Bird, 2002) TweetTo-kenizer[1] and the texts detected as being written in other languages using the Polyglot multilingual tokenizer.[2]

4 Emoji Usage in Bios

First, we sought to characterize the use of emoji in users' bios, so we turn to just the emojiBio dataset.

We contrast the most commonly used emoji[3] in bios and in tweets in Table 2, finding that facial expression emoji ('(emoji)', '(emoji)', '(emoji)', '(emoji)', '(emoji)', '(emoji)') are more frequently used in tweets, while different variations of heart emoji ('(emoji)', '(emoji)', '(emoji)', '(emoji)', '(emoji)', '(emoji)') are more frequently used in bios. Another emoji that is regularly used in bios is the rainbow emoji '(emoji)'. The sparkles emoji '(emoji)' and the female sign emoji '(emoji)' (not in top 10) are frequently used in both bios and tweets. We also checked the average position of emoji within users' bios and tweets, and found that in both cases, most emoji appear at the end of the text. These emoji at the end commonly signify the overall meaning or sentiment of the text. However, we noticed that the emoji in bios are, on average, used closer to the middle of the text than emoji that are used in tweets. There is also a nontrivial number of emoji used at the *start* of texts, which happens more often in bios than in tweets. Additionally, we found that is more common for users to use a single emoji as the entire content of a bio than as the entire content of a tweet (more details in Appendix B).

Unicode Emoji 13.0 contains a total of 4,159 emoji in nine groups according to categories. We carried out analysis on emoji based on their predefined groups, and the results are shown in the Table 3. We found that the number of unique emoji in a category is directly correlated with the number of unique emoji from that group that appear in users' bios. However, after calculating the proportion of

---

[1] https://www.nltk.org/api/nltk.tokenize.html
[2] https://polyglot.readthedocs.io/

[3] In their Unicode representations, some emoji with the same visual pattern are represented by different code points for historical reasons, code points can be divided into fully-qualified, minimally-qualified or unqualified (https://www.unicode.org/reports/tr51/). In this paper, we only present the qualified version of a given emoji pattern when reporting results.

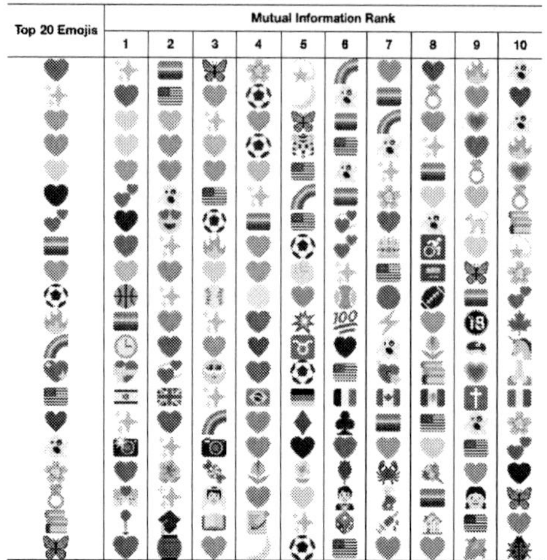

Table 4: Mutual information score rank of emoji in the bios group by top 20 emoji.

Table 5: Mutual information score rank of tokens in the bios group by top 20 emoji, and translate non-English in parentheses.

Top 20 Emojis	Mutual Information Rank				
	1	2	3	4	5
❤️	flamengo	apaixonada (in love)	god	love	kids
✨	フォロー (follow)	たい (want)	気軽 (feel free)	よろしく (nice to meet you)	無言 (silent)
💜	cabj	boca	juniors	هلال (crescent moon)	blue
💙	bts	ct7	army	account	fan
❤️	cabj	boca	juniors	news	galatasaray
🖤	flamenguista	浴 (like)	flamengo	ucf	الاتحاد (the Union)
💘	大好き (like very much)	フォロー (follow)	無言 (silent)	pop	参戦 (participation in a war)
🏳️‍🌈	bi	gay	lgbt	queer	artist
💗	pibas	scp	got7	nct	jaehyun
⚽	jugador (player)	soccer	football	fútbol (soccer)	atleta (athlete)
✳️	円 (circle)	fire	خاص (special)	knight	vila (village)
📞	生活 (life)	genderfluid	ロー (law)	定時 (on time)	東 (east)
💕	ありがとう (thank you)	gnc	bbb20	website	フィギュア (figure)
🇺🇸	maga	trump	american	conservative	kag
♥️	انسان (man)	caballero (gentleman)	ادعو (pray for)	قول (say)	الله (Allah)
👻	sc	ig	snapchat	snap	mma
🌸	crossing	桜 (cherry blossoms)	垢 (account)	ライブ (live)	もっと (more)
💍	married	元 (former)	clan	crisa	motion
📚	bookstan	derecho (right)	uca	educación (education)	libros (books)
🦋	diary	vtuber	ライブ (live)	york	木 (wood)

the users who use at least one emoji from each group, we noticed that most users used emoji from the Smileys & Emotion group in bios, with a total of 44.3% of the 20,000 users, followed by the People & Body group with 20% of users including at least one emoji from that group. On the contrary, the number of users who used the emoji of the Food & Drink group is the least, accounting for only 5% of the total users. This suggests that users choose to represent themselves with more facial expressions, people-centric emoji, and emotions, which are connected to aspects of self-identity. We also found that many users use their bios to present their interests to others – some users use these types of emoji to express their love for certain singers or sports clubs.

Next, we examine the relationships between sets of emoji that users include in their bios. We selected the top 20 emoji used in bios and computed the mutual information between the presence of these emoji in a user's bio and the presence of any other emoji. The emoji with the highest mutual information scores are presented in Table 4.[4] . We found that high-frequency emoji also had high mutual information scores for many other emoji, such as heart emoji of various colors: '💚', '🤍','❤️'. This indicates that these high requency emoji are not used indiscriminately, but in particular ways

and have patterns in the ways that they co-occur with other emoji. Another finding is that emoji which are similar to the original emoji have high scores. This finding suggests that similar or the same types of emoji are more likely to be used together. For example, in row 10, four types of ball emoji: basketball '🏀', baseball '⚾', tennis '🎾', and American football '🏈', appear in the ten emoji that provide the most mutual information for soccer ball emoji '⚽'. People who like football may also enjoy other ball sports, and using these ball emoji in the bios at the same time indicates that they are ball sports enthusiasts (either as players or spectators). Another example is that in the 14th row, there are eight national flag emoji out of the ten emoji that have the highest mutual information with the American flag emoji '🇺🇸'. People may use multiple flags in the bios to imply their residences and national origin. Finally, we noticed that users tend to use emoji together that fit a specific context. For example, for the ring emoji '💍' in row 18, the most relevant emoji are kiss '💋', person with veil '👰', man in tuxedo '🤵', and pregnant woman '🤰'. People may use these emoji in the bios to express their relationship status, potentially indicating whether they are engaged, married, or expecting a child.

We also calculated the mutual information score of non-emoji tokens and the top 20 emoji, as shown in Table 5. Our dataset is multilingual, so the tokens obtained are also multilingual. We removed some tokens that do not capture any specific content information, such as some honorifics in Japanese. We found that the usage of emoji is related to words with similar meanings as the emoji, consistent with our previous findings that emoji with similar mean-

---

[4]The first emoji represent a red heart, and the fifteenth emoji represent a heart suit. They are two emoji patterns with entirely different meanings and also subtle differences in the shape and color.

	EmojiBio		NonEmojiBio	
	Bios	**Tweets**	**Bios**	**Tweets**
Average Number of Emoji	3.05	0.73	0	0.39
Average Number of Hashtags	0.23	0.06	0.19	0.08
Average Number of Words	8.51	6.75	9.49	7.74

Table 6: The average number of emoji, words (excluding stopwords) and hashtags in the bios and tweets of the emojiBio and nonEmojiBio datasets

ings had high mutual information. An example of this in the word-level results is in row 10 of Table 5, the tokens most related to soccer ball emoji '⚽' are words in different languages with similar meanings related to soccer and player. This finding further confirms that people prefer to use relevant emoji in a specific context. There are many other examples with similar trends, such as the rainbow flag emoji '🏳️‍🌈' in row 8 and the American flag emoji '🇺🇸' in row 14. Further, we observed that the heart emoji used in bios are more related to showing the love for celebrities or sports clubs, for example, "flamengo" (Row 1) is a sports club (shorthand name for Clube de Regatas do Flamengo), and "bts" (Row 4) is a Korean male singing group.

5 The Relationship between Emoji in Bios and Tweeted Content

Next, we explore the relationship between Emoji usage in bios and tweeted content. We start by comparing the overall trends in twitter usage between the sets of users with and without emoji in their bios in order to investigate whether there are notable differences in the volume of emoji, hashtags, and words (excluding emoji, hashtags, and stopwords) used by each group (Table 6).

In terms of the quantity of words and hashtags, there are no significant differences between the emojiBio and nonEmojiBio datasets. In the emojiBio dataset, we noticed that there is increased usage of emoji in bios compared to tweets (3.05 emoji in bios compared to 0.73 in tweets). The fact that the character limit for tweets is more flexible than the limit for bios makes this result even more impressive. In the nonEmojiBio dataset, the average number of emoji that appear in tweets drops to 0.39, which is roughly half the rate of emoji usage in tweets found in the emojiBio group. In terms of hashtags, there is again an increased usage in bios which is similar between the two datasets. In terms of words, users who do not have emoji in their bios tend to use a slightly higher amount of words in their bios and tweets. Specifically, the users in the

nonEmojiBio group used roughly 1 more word, on average, than their emojiBio counterparts, in both tweets and bios.

In addition to differences in the number of words, hashtags, and emoji used, we expect that aspects of a user's identity that are revealed through emoji in their bios will be reflected in measurable ways in the *content* that they choose to tweet about. We perform a case study in which we select two particular interesting emoji that were common in users' bios, and compare the content of the tweets from users who had these emoji in their bios using both topic modeling and sentiment analysis.

The emoji that we focus on for this case study are the rainbow emoji '🌈', and the American flag emoji '🇺🇸'. These emoji are both used with similar frequencies, but are rarely used together and represent distinct groups of users which we seek to understand through the lens of the twitter content that they generate. In our emojiBio dataset, the number users using these in bios are close at 324 ('🌈') and 302 ('🇺🇸'), while only two of the users use both emoji at the same time in their bios, so these two emoji can distinguish users well. These emoji also belong to different emoji subgroups within Unicode Emoji 13.0: the rainbow '🌈' belongs to the sky & weather subgroup under the Travel & Places group, and the American flag '🇺🇸' belongs to the country-flag subgroup under the Flags group.

Among the 324 users who use rainbow emoji '🌈', 155 users use English in the bios, 46 Japanese, 33 Portuguese, and 31 Spanish. For comparison, among the 302 users who use the American flag '🇺🇸', 245 use English as the language in bios, 15 Spanish, 12 Japanese, and 9 Portuguese. The tweets involved also are multilingual, but are mostly written in English. For the analyses in this section, we first translated all non-English tweets into English using the Google Translate API.[5] Considering that the topic modeling and sentiment analysis methods that we use mostly rely on bag-of-words representations of the text, issues with the grammatical accuracy of translated tweets will not have as large of an impact. After the translation, we have two sets of tweets corresponding to the two groups of users who used the emoji of '🌈' and '🇺🇸'. The number of tweets for each group are 61,239 and 58,376, respectively.

We performed topic modeling using Latent Dirichlet Allocation (Blei et al., 2003) on the tweets

---

[5]https://cloud.google.com/translate

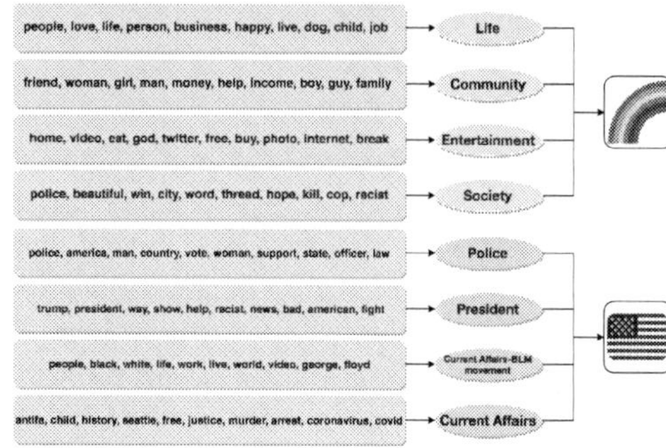

Figure 1: The most relevant tokens for topics inferred from the tweets from users who use the 'rainbow' emoji and the 'United States flag' emoji in their bios.

of users who used the emoji '🌈' and '🇺🇸' in their bios. We used the coherence score provided by the gensim Python library[6] to select the number of topics. We train a separate topic model for each group of users, and select four topics for each model. In Figure 1, we visualize the process of inferring topics by zooming in on the most relevant tokens for each of the topics within the set of tweets written by each group of users. The weights between topics are unequal, decreasing from top to bottom as presented in the figure. The topics of tweets from users who use rainbow emoji '🌈' in the bios include words related to concepts like life, community, entertainment, and society. We notice some topics that contain more pleasant words, some related to gender identity, others to life and pets. The fourth topic appears to be related to issues of police brutality. However, on the whole, the tweets posted by users who use the American flag emoji '🇺🇸' in the bios are more heavy and serious. They are more concerned about topics related to police, president, and current affairs. Because of the massive surge in the #blacklivesmatter movement, caused by the death of George Floyd in the United States, broke out at the end of May 2020, and we downloaded user tweets during this time, there is a clear topic for this current affair. Besides, other current affairs discussed include Antifa and COVID, but these were part of the same topic. Comparing the two sets of different topics, we found that the different emoji included by the users in their bios are related to distinct topics, which also may reflect the self-identities of the users who used these emoji.

____

[6]https://radimrehurek.com/gensim/

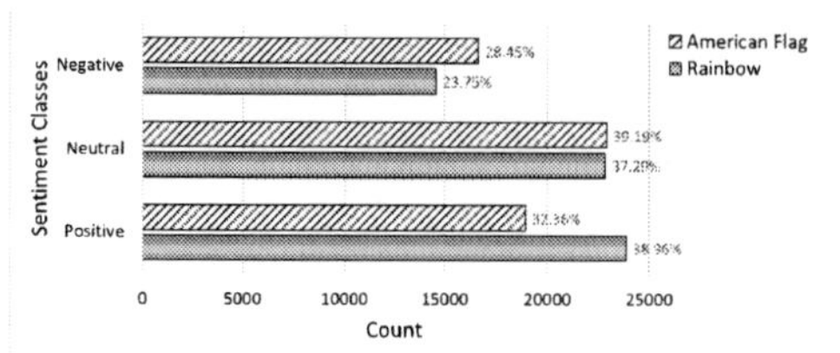

Figure 2: Sentiment analysis of the tweets from users who use emoji '🌈' and '🇺🇸' in bios separately.

The rainbow emoji '🌈' often represents gay pride, as well as happiness and peace in general, so the corresponding tweets also mostly reflect the love of these users for life and others. In contrast, users who use the American flag '🇺🇸' are more concerned about national politics and current affairs within the United States.

We also conducted a sentiment analysis on these two sets of tweets, using the Vader sentiment analysis tool (Hutto and Gilbert, 2014), giving the results presented in Figure 2. According to the figure, for the two datasets, the distribution of sentiment is fairly consistent overall, with more positive content than negative. While the amount of neutral sentiment in the two datasets is almost the same, the users with rainbow emoji '🌈' in their bios tweeted more positive content overall, compared the the users with the US Flag emoji '🇺🇸' in their bios. Close to 40% of the tweets from users who use rainbow emoji '🌈' in bios are positive, and less than 25% are negative. In contrast, less than 35% of tweets sent by users using the American flag '🇺🇸' in bios are positive, and close to 30% are negative.

These sentiment analysis results are mostly consistent with the results of the topic modeling. The tweets sent by users who use rainbow emoji '🌈' are more happy and light than those sent by users who use the American flag emoji '🇺🇸' in the bios. This case study suggests that users using different emoji in bios can reflect aspects of both their national identity and their personality. More specifically, this analysis shows that groups using some emoji in the bios generate more positive content than groups using other emoji.

6 Homophily Effects in Emoji Usage in Bios

For our final set of analyses, we explored the extent to which users and their followers use emoji in their bios in similar ways. At a very basic level, regarding the absence or presence of emoji in the

💚		⚽		🇺🇸		🐶	
💚	**7420**	💚	6529	🇺🇸	**26199**	💚	2028
💜	7361	⚽	**4054**	💚	5422	✨	1943
💛	5509	💚	3817	🚫	2582	💛	1375
💙	4902	✨	2128	⭐	2421	🐶	**1331**
✨	4897	🖤	1865	🌊	2262	💜	1150
🤍	3335	😍	1816	✝️	1933	🤍	913
❤️	2941	🔴	1523	✨	1929	🖤	828
💕	2880	👑	1495	💚	1861	🖤	791
🖤	2042	💜	1363	🙏	1837	🌊	782
😍	2042	💗	1319	💯	1568	💜	693

Table 7: Top 10 emoji used by followers of users with particular emoji in bios and their counts. Bold indicates the count for the same emoji that was used by the reference user. We observe that it is very common for a user and their followers to use the same kinds of emoji in their bios.

followers' bios, there was a considerable difference between the emojiBio and nonEmojiBio datasets. The followers of users that have emoji in their bios (emojiBio) have emoji in their bios as well 32.47% of the time. For the followers of users that do not have emoji in their bios (nonEmojiBio), this average percentage drops to 23.23%.

Next, we selected three representative emoji from the set of most frequently used emoji in the emojiBio dataset, namely, green heart emoji '💚', soccer ball emoji '⚽', and American flag emoji '🇺🇸'. Also, to eliminate bias caused by only considering high-frequency emoji, we selected the low-frequency dog face emoji '🐶' used by a total of just 157 users in our emojiBio dataset. In Table 7, we list the ten most frequently used emoji in the bios by the followers (from our Followers dataset) of the users who use these four specific emoji and mark the emoji that are the same as the users in bold text.

The green heart '💚' and the American flag '🇺🇸' are the emoji that are used most frequently by followers of users who also include these emoji. The soccer ball emoji '⚽' ranks third, and the dog face emoji '🐶' ranks fifth, only with several high-frequency emoji in front of them. There is a strong homophily relationship that indicates that the users use the same emoji with their followers in bios. Using the same emoji also reflects that emoji in the bios can reflect the users' self-identity in terms of group belonging, or their social identity. As an illustration, users using dog face emoji in bios may want to signal that they are dog lovers, and they

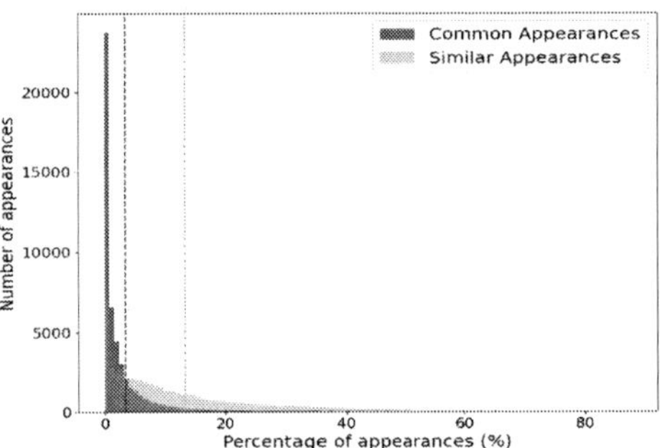

Figure 3: The distribution of the percentage of common and similar emoji appearances in the followers' bios. The lines in the graph represent the average percentage of common and similar emoji appearances.

Common Emoji Appearances		Similar Emoji Appearances	
Emoji	Percentage (%)	Emoji	Percentage (%)
🔞	14.75	🖤	34.77
🏳	13.72	💕	34.31
💚	13.33	🙏	33.91
💙	10.46	🤍	33.81
⚛️	10.4	❤️	30.32

Table 8: The emoji with the highest percentage of common (exact match) and similar appearances between the users' and the followers' bios.

may also chose to make online connections with others who are similar, leading to many other dog lovers in their networks.

We also take a particular look at the high-frequency emoji used by followers of users who use the American flag '🇺🇸'. Prior work on emoji and American political movements on Twitter (Hagen et al., 2019) pointed out that water ("blue") wave emoji '🌊' is related to the US Democratic party, and pointed out that this emoji is frequently associated with hashtag #resist to express anti-white nationalist sentiments. We also observe the use of the red heart '❤️' and blue heart '💙' emoji, two colors are are often associated with the US republican and democratic parties, respectively. These followers may be expressing their political opinions: they use the American flag emoji along with other more specific emoji express their particular views. Lastly, we notice several emoji related to religion in this column, indicating expressions of religious as well as political affiliations.

In addition to the focused study on these four emoji, we also examined whether the emoji used in bios of Twitter users are either the same, or generally similar to those used by their followers in the entire dataset. To assess similarity we trained our own emoji embeddings with a skip-gram model (Mikolov et al., 2013) using the tweets and bios of the emojiBio dataset, and subsequently we created a similarity lexicon of emoji based on the cosine similarity between the vectors, considering one emoji to be similar to another if it was within the top ten nearest neighbors in the learned embeddings space. We found that the average percentages for common (i.e., exact matches) and similar emoji appearances between the users of the emojiBio dataset and their followers are 3.45% and 13.30%, respectively. The respective distributions of the percentage for common and similar emoji appearances are presented in Figure 3. We used permutation tests to confirm that the difference between these two values was statistically significant, and therefore conclude that the followers of a given user seem to have a considerably high probability to use the same, or similar emoji in their bios as the users they follow. Table 8 shows the five emoji for which followers used the same, or similar emoji as the users that they follow.

7 Discussion

We now give answers to our original research questions based on our results:

RQ1. How are emoji used in Twitter bios? Our results showed that emoji are used in unique ways within users' bios on Twitter, even compared to the ways in which they are used in tweets. In general, emoji are positioned earlier in bios than in tweets, while there is a higher percentage of bios that start with an emoji compared to tweets. Also, it is more common for an emoji to be the only content of a bio than the only content of a tweet.

Moreover, facial expression emoji are the dominant type of emoji in tweets, while different variations of heart emoji are dominant in bios. Specifically, the most popular emoji in bios are from the Smileys & Emotion group, while the least frequently used emoji are from the Food & Drink group. Furthermore, we noted that the most frequently used emoji in bios have a high mutual information with other emoji that are similar to them, or from the same category (e.g. hearts, balls, flags), or related to the same concept (e.g. relationship status). In their bios, people tend to use emoji to show their support for musical groups or sports teams (or sports in general), as well as things like countries that they come from or are currently living in.

RQ2. What is the relationships between the emoji in a user's bio and the content that the user posts? Compared to users who do not have any emoji in their bios, users with emoji in their bios use about twice as many emoji in their tweets, on average. They also use less words in both their tweets and bios. In our case study, topic models built from the tweets of the users that use the rainbow '🏳️‍🌈' and the American flag '🇺🇸' emoji in their bios showed that users who have the rainbow emoji '🏳️‍🌈' in their bios tweet about life, community, entertainment, and society, whereas users who have the rainbow emoji '🏳️‍🌈' in their bios tweet about police, president, and current affairs. Also, it was shown that tweets of users that have the rainbow emoji '🏳️‍🌈' in bios convey a more positive sentiment on average compared to users that use the American flag '🇺🇸' in their bios. This is just one example to showcase the fact that the types of emoji that people choose to include in their bios reflect larger views, opinions, and sentiments that are expressed in the content of their tweets.

RQ3. Do users and their followers use emoji in their bios in a similar way? The usage of emoji in bios also led us to some conclusions related to homophily effects in Twitter. First, our results indicate that followers of users who have emoji in their bios, are more likely to have emoji in their bios as well. We also found that users tend to use the same, or similar emoji in their bios as the users they follow. For example, followers of users with the green heart emoji in their bios also had other colored hearts in their bios, with the green heart being the most common used by the followers. These findings suggest that there are indeed similarities within user networks in the ways in which emoji are used in Twitter bios.

8 Conclusion

We have presented an overview of the ways in which Twitter users include emoji in their bios, and what kinds of things we can learn about those users from the particular emoji that they use. Using a range of approaches, we have shown that emoji are an important component to consider when examining the ways in which users present themselves to others in online settings like Twitter. The emoji that users choose to include reveal important aspects of their self-identities, such as the teams and musicians that they support, the activities they enjoy, their national and political identities, and show their similarities with their followers in these same aspects. At the same time, we have only brushed the surface of the types of in-depth analyses that could be performed by consider specific sets of emoji and examining how these relate to the identities of the users who include them in their bios. This work can provide an important complementary view to other work on online-self identity that mainly focuses only on the plain text content.

References

Francesco Barbieri and Jose Camacho-Collados. 2018. How gender and skin tone modifiers affect emoji semantics in twitter. In *Proceedings of the Seventh Joint Conference on Lexical and Computational Semantics*, pages 101–106.

Francesco Barbieri, German Kruszewski, Francesco Ronzano, and Horacio Saggion. 2016. How cosmopolitan are emojis? exploring emojis usage and meaning over different languages with distributional semantics. In *Proceedings of the 24th ACM international conference on Multimedia*, pages 531–535.

David M Blei, Andrew Y Ng, and Michael I Jordan. 2003. Latent dirichlet allocation. *Journal of machine Learning research*, 3(Jan):993–1022.

Marcel Danesi. 2016. *The semiotics of emoji: The rise of visual language in the age of the internet.* Bloomsbury Publishing.

Michael Fisher, Martin Abbott, and Kalle Lyytinen. 2014. The concept of self-identity. In *The Power of Customer Misbehavior*, pages 61–67. Springer.

Eduardo Graells-Garrido, Ricardo Baeza-Yates, and Mounia Lalmas. 2020. Every colour you are: Stance prediction and turnaround in controversial issues. *arXiv preprint arXiv:2005.10019.*

Serge Guimond, Armand Chatard, Delphine Martinot, Richard J Crisp, and Sandrine Redersdorff. 2006. Social comparison, self-stereotyping, and gender differences in self-construals. *Journal of personality and social psychology*, 90(2):221.

Sharath Chandra Guntuku, Mingyang Li, Louis Tay, and Lyle H Ungar. 2019. Studying cultural differences in emoji usage across the east and the west. In *Proceedings of the International AAAI Conference on Web and Social Media*, volume 13, pages 226–235.

Loni Hagen, Mary Falling, Oleksandr Lisnichenko, AbdelRahim A Elmadany, Pankti Mehta, Muhammad Abdul-Mageed, Justin Costakis, and Thomas E Keller. 2019. Emoji use in twitter white nationalism communication. In *Conference Companion Publication of the 2019 on Computer Supported Cooperative Work and Social Computing*, pages 201–205.

Clayton J Hutto and Eric Gilbert. 2014. Vader: A parsimonious rule-based model for sentiment analysis of social media text. In *Eighth international AAAI conference on weblogs and social media.*

Armand Joulin, Edouard Grave, Piotr Bojanowski, Matthijs Douze, Hérve Jégou, and Tomas Mikolov. 2016a. Fasttext.zip: Compressing text classification models. *arXiv preprint arXiv:1612.03651.*

Armand Joulin, Edouard Grave, Piotr Bojanowski, and Tomas Mikolov. 2016b. Bag of tricks for efficient text classification. *arXiv preprint arXiv:1607.01759.*

Ryan Kelly and Leon Watts. 2015. Characterising the inventive appropriation of emoji as relationally meaningful in mediated close personal relationships. *Experiences of technology appropriation: unanticipated users, usage, circumstances, and design*, 20.

Weijian Li, Yuxiao Chen, Tianran Hu, and Jiebo Luo. 2018. Mining the relationship between emoji usage patterns and personality. *arXiv preprint arXiv:1804.05143.*

Nikola Ljubešić and Darja Fišer. 2016. A global analysis of emoji usage. In *Proceedings of the 10th Web as Corpus Workshop*, pages 82–89.

Edward Loper and Steven Bird. 2002. Nltk: The natural language toolkit. In *Proceedings of the ACL-02 Workshop on Effective Tools and Methodologies for Teaching Natural Language Processing and Computational Linguistics*, pages 63–70.

Tomas Mikolov, Kai Chen, Greg Corrado, and Jeffrey Dean. 2013. Efficient estimation of word representations in vector space. *arXiv preprint arXiv:1301.3781.*

Barbara Plank and Dirk Hovy. 2015. Personality traits on twitter—or—how to get 1,500 personality tests in a week. In *Proceedings of the 6th Workshop on Computational Approaches to Subjectivity, Sentiment and Social Media Analysis*, pages 92–98.

Alexander Robertson, Walid Magdy, and Sharon Goldwater. 2018. Self-representation on twitter using emoji skin color modifiers. In *Proceedings of the International AAAI Conference on Web and Social Media (ICWSM).*

Alexander Robertson, Walid Magdy, and Sharon Goldwater. 2020. Emoji skin tone modifiers: Analyzing variation in usage on social media. *ACM Transactions on Social Computing*, 3(2):1–25.

Nick Rogers and Jason J Jones. 2019. Using twitter bios to measure changes in social identity: Are americans defining themselves more politically over time?

H Andrew Schwartz, Johannes C Eichstaedt, Margaret L Kern, Lukasz Dziurzynski, Stephanie M Ramones, Megha Agrawal, Achal Shah, Michal Kosinski, David Stillwell, Martin EP Seligman, et al. 2013.

Personality, gender, and age in the language of social media: The open-vocabulary approach. *PloS one*, 8(9):e73791.

Paul Sparks and Richard Shepherd. 1992. Self-identity and the theory of planned behavior: Assesing the role of identification with" green consumerism". *Social psychology quarterly*, pages 388–399.

Ye Tian, Thiago Galery, Giulio Dulcinati, Emilia Molimpakis, and Chao Sun. 2017. Facebook sentiment: Reactions and emojis. In *Proceedings of the Fifth International Workshop on Natural Language Processing for Social Media*, pages 11–16.

Sarah Theres Völkel, Daniel Buschek, Jelena Pranjic, and Heinrich Hussmann. 2019. Understanding emoji interpretation through user personality and message context. In *Proceedings of the 21st International Conference on Human-Computer Interaction with Mobile Devices and Services*, pages 1–12.

Appendix

A   Differences across languages

A language identification analysis was conducted for the combined data of the emojiBio and nonEmojiBio datasets to identify the most frequently used languages in the tweets and bios. The analysis was conducted using the fastText language identification tool (Joulin et al., 2016b), (Joulin et al., 2016a) and the language distribution is presented in Figure 4.

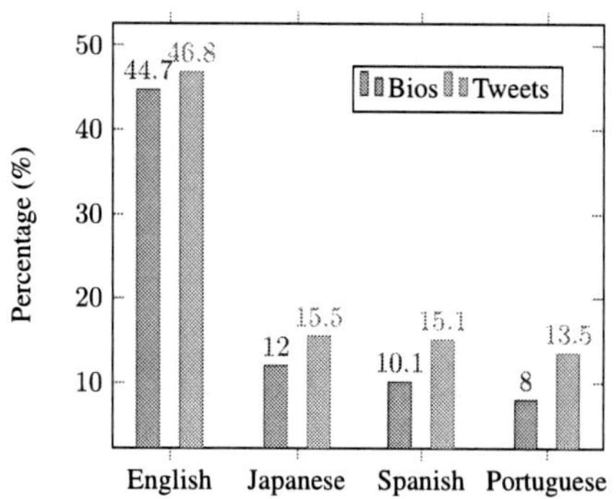

Figure 4: Language distribution in the tweets and bios of the emojiBio and nonEmojiBio datasets combined.

B   Positioning Analysis

The positioning analysis distribution for bios and tweets is presented in Figure 5. The results of the positioning analysis indicate that emoji appear earlier in bios than in tweets. For each emoji, its positional value was calculated by computing its distance from the first character of the text and dividing it by the overall length of the text. Therefore, emoji that were used at the beginning of the text had a positional value of 0, whereas emoji that were used at the end of the text had a positional value of 1.

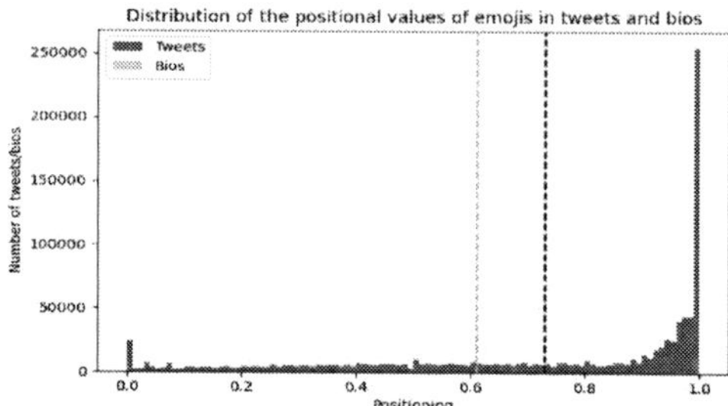

Figure 5: The distribution of the positional values of emoji in the tweets and bios of the emojiBio dataset. The vertical lines in the graphs represent the mean positional value for tweets (blue) and bios (orange).

C   Group Analysis

In the group analysis, we divided the bios into four groups according to the language used, and we calculated the mutual information score for all emoji that appeared. Table 9 shows the 25 emoji with the highest scores in each group. We observed that in all language groups, there were multiple national flag emoji amongst the results. In most cases, those flags belong to countries where the respective language is spoken as a first or second language by a considerable portion of the population.

While emoji grouping is analyzed in Chapter 4, it is also important to consider that Unicode Emoji also provides standards for subgroups of emoji. Specifically, each emoji belongs to a group and also belongs to a subgroup under the group, which makes the classification more specific. For example, the grinning face emoji '😀' belongs to the face-smiling subgroup under the Smileys & Emotion group. Each group contains a different number of subgroups, and overall there are 98 subgroups. We counted the total number of times the emoji from each subgroup appeared in users' bios and sorted them in descending order. Table 10 demonstrates the ten most popular subgroups.

The results suggest that the most frequently used subgroup is emotion while the face-smiling subgroup also belongs to the same category (Smileys & Emotion), showing that people are commonly using emoji to express their sentiments in bios. The

Language	English		Japanese		Spanish		Portuguese	
Rank	Emoji	Score	Emoji	Score	Emoji	Score	Emoji	Score
1	(emoji)	0.0048	(emoji)	0.0080	(emoji)	0.0043	(emoji)	0.0085
2	(emoji)	0.0036	(emoji)	0.0060	(emoji)	0.0037	(emoji)	0.0067
3	(emoji)	0.0036	(emoji)	0.0053	(emoji)	0.0033	(emoji)	0.0039
4	(emoji)	0.0031	(emoji)	0.0048	(emoji)	0.0028	(emoji)	0.0029
5	(emoji)	0.0029	(emoji)	0.0048	(emoji)	0.0024	(emoji)	0.0025
6	(emoji)	0.0027	(emoji)	0.0048	(emoji)	0.0017	(emoji)	0.0017
7	(emoji)	0.0025	(emoji)	0.0048	(emoji)	0.0010	(emoji)	0.0016
8	(emoji)	0.0025	(emoji)	0.0045	(emoji)	0.0010	(emoji)	0.0015
9	(emoji)	0.0025	(emoji)	0.0042	(emoji)	0.0009	(emoji)	0.0014
10	(emoji)	0.0025	(emoji)	0.0038	(emoji)	0.0009	(emoji)	0.0014
11	(emoji)	0.0024	(emoji)	0.0038	(emoji)	0.0008	(emoji)	0.0014
12	(emoji)	0.0022	(emoji)	0.0035	(emoji)	0.0008	(emoji)	0.0012
13	(emoji)	0.0021	(emoji)	0.0031	(emoji)	0.0008	(emoji)	0.0012
14	(emoji)	0.0019	(emoji)	0.0029	(emoji)	0.0008	(emoji)	0.0011
15	(emoji)	0.0018	(emoji)	0.0029	(emoji)	0.0008	(emoji)	0.0011
16	(emoji)	0.0017	(emoji)	0.0027	(emoji)	0.0008	(emoji)	0.0010
17	(emoji)	0.0017	(emoji)	0.0027	(emoji)	0.0007	(emoji)	0.0010
18	(emoji)	0.0017	(emoji)	0.0027	(emoji)	0.0007	(emoji)	0.0010
19	(emoji)	0.0016	(emoji)	0.0027	(emoji)	0.0007	(emoji)	0.0010
20	(emoji)	0.0016	(emoji)	0.0023	(emoji)	0.0007	(emoji)	0.0009
21	(emoji)	0.0016	(emoji)	0.0022	(emoji)	0.0007	(emoji)	0.0009
22	(emoji)	0.0015	(emoji)	0.0021	(emoji)	0.0007	(emoji)	0.0009
23	(emoji)	0.0015	(emoji)	0.0021	(emoji)	0.0007	(emoji)	0.0008
24	(emoji)	0.0014	(emoji)	0.0021	(emoji)	0.0007	(emoji)	0.0007
25	(emoji)	0.0014	(emoji)	0.0019	(emoji)	0.0006	(emoji)	0.0007

Table 9: Mutual information score rank of emoji in bios, group by language

Subgroup	Num	Examples
emotion	8448	(emoji) (emoji) (emoji)
country-flag	3870	(emoji) (emoji) (emoji)
sky & weather	2361	(emoji) (emoji) (emoji)
animal-mammal	1700	(emoji) (emoji) (emoji)
event	1407	(emoji) (emoji) (emoji)
plant-flower	1224	(emoji) (emoji) (emoji)
zodiac	1110	(emoji) (emoji) (emoji)
clothing	1092	(emoji) (emoji) (emoji)
game	971	(emoji) (emoji) (emoji)
face-smiling	844	(emoji) (emoji) (emoji)

Table 10: The distribution of emoji in bios, based on predefined subgroups.

second most frequently used subgroup is country-flag, which implies that users regularly use emoji in their bios to reveal their nationality or the countries where they have lived. Animal-mammal and plant-flower are also frequently used. These emoji are used to express the love of users for animals or plants, but also for decoration reasons, to make bios more attractive. Another interesting finding was that the zodiac subgroup ranks seventh. This finding shows that people like to use symbolic emoji to tell others about their zodiac, which they consider as a part of their self-identity.

To confirm that the emoji could be accurately grouped in clusters, we conducted a statistical analysis based on the results of the mutual information scores for the 20 most frequently used emoji in bios.

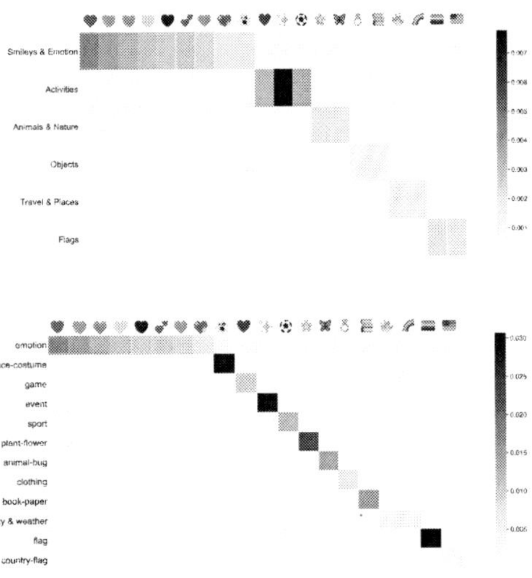

Figure 6: The average mutual information score between the 20 most frequently used emoji in bios and each group and subgroup, respectively.

Specifically, we divided the 20 most frequently used emoji into groups and subgroups, and we plotted two heat maps which illustrate the categorization of emoji, as shown in the Figure 6. While calculating the mutual information scores between a group and a specific emoji, we did not consider that emoji as part of the group, to ensure normalization. The results show that each emoji achieved a higher mutual information score with the group or subgroup in which it belongs. This suggests that emoji in bios are more commonly used with other emoji from the same group or subgroup.

D Topic Modeling

We conducted supplementary experiments on the topic modeling analysis of Chapter 5. Specifically, we used the LDAvis tool to visualize the results, and the topic distributions are shown in Figure 7. The topic distributions visualize the weight of each topic and the connection between different topics. More precisely, the circles represent the topics, and the distance between the circle centers determine the connection between the topics. More prevalent topics are represented by larger circles.

E Frequency Analysis

The results of the frequency analysis showed that the popularity of words and hashtags varies greatly between bios and tweets. Table 11 presents the most frequently appearing English words and hash-

	Bios		
Word	**Appearances**	**Hashtag**	**Appearances**
love	645	#bts	33
fan	473	#resist	28
life	375	#maga	22
account	371	#exo	21
insta	273	#bernie	16
instagram	218	#blacklivesmatter	15
flamengo	216	#jimin	14
god	212	#wwgwga	11
dm	212	#blm	11
follow	198	#mufc	10
	Tweets		
Word	**Appearances**	**Hashtag**	**Appearances**
like	22843	#peing	868
love	16025	#nintendoswitch	802
get	14019	#blacklivesmatter	790
people	13541	#newprofilepic	739
know	11671	#acnh	656
good	10867	#covid	563
time	9881	#animalcrossing	561
go	9791	#otgalafinal	458
lol	9504	#sanditon	349
got	9241	#psshare	345

Table 11: The most frequently appearing English words and hashtags in the bios and tweets of the emojiBio dataset.

	Bios		
Word	**Appearances**	**Hashtag**	**Appearances**
fan	53	#phish	4
love	48	#maga	4
account	36	#taehyung	3
life	28	#resistance	3
twitter	22	#kag	3
like	22	#ynwa	2
good	20	#trump	2
world	19	#research	2
god	19	#mufc	2
people	17	#bernie	2
	Tweets		
Word	**Appearances**	**Hashtag**	**Appearances**
like	3826	#chismesfarándulachilena	288
people	2500	#meigen	182
get	2315	#shindanmaker	160
love	2202	#covid	151
good	2036	#blacklivesmatter	135
know	1921	#survivor	127
time	1656	#nintendoswitch	121
think	1633	#digitalmarketing	104
go	1625	#lockdownhouseparty	102
see	1526	#bitcoin	92

Table 12: The most frequently appearing English words and hashtags in the bios and tweets of the nonEmojiBio dataset.

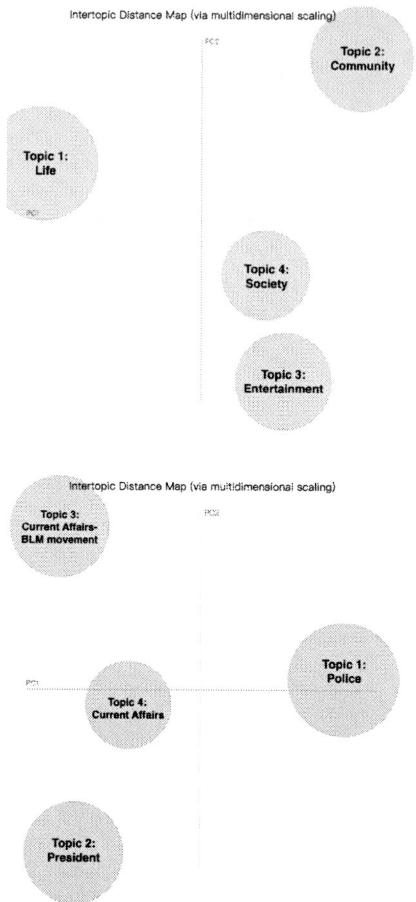

Figure 7: Topic distributions for the tweets of the users who the '' and '' emoji in their bios.

tags in the bios and tweets of the emojiBio dataset. While the frequency analysis was conducted on multilingual data, we present only the most frequently appearing English words for consistency reasons, since there are many different English translations for words in other languages.

In terms of words, the more frequently used words in bios are nouns, in contrast with tweets, where verbs appear more frequently. The most frequently used words in bios are mostly related to the social media activity of the user (account, insta, instagram, dm, follow) and their religious or spiritual beliefs (love, life, god). On the contrary, in tweets, we can see verbs related to positive sentimental expression (like, love) or the conduction of an activity (get, go, got).

The hashtags that more frequently appear in

bios are related to music artists or bands (#bts, #exo, #jimin), presenting the user's music preferences, to political beliefs or election candidates (#resist, #maga, #bernie) and the anti-violence protest group "Black Lives Matter" (#blacklivesmatter, #blm). The hashtags related to "Black Lives Matter" are commonly found also in tweets, together with hashtags related to gaming consoles and video games (#nintendoswitch, #animalcrossing, #acnh, #psshare), TV series (#sanditon) and music competitions (#otgalafinal). Users also use hashtags to tweet about Peing - an "anonymous Q&A box" service on Twitter (#peing) and to notify others about an update of their profile picture (#newprofilepic). Additionally, users frequently use a hashtag in their tweets which is related to the COVID-19 pandemic (#covid).

Overall, the results for the words and hashtags frequency analysis per element of the nonEmojiBio dataset do not have significant differences compared to the results of the emojiBio dataset. Also, despite the decreased usage of emoji in tweets by these users, the distribution of the frequencies are very similar compared to the emojiBio dataset, since facial expression emoji are dominant again. The complete results for the frequency analysis of the nonEmojiBio dataset are presented in Table 12, but they should be interpreted with caution since the nonEmojiBio dataset is considerably smaller.

Analyzing Gender Bias within Narrative Tropes

Dhruvil Gala[*] Mohammad Omar Khursheed[*] Hannah Lerner
Brendan O'Connor Mohit Iyyer

University of Massachusetts Amherst
{dgala,mkhursheed,hmlerner,brenocon,miyyer}@umass.edu

Abstract

Popular media reflects and reinforces societal biases through the use of *tropes*, which are narrative elements, such as archetypal characters and plot arcs, that occur frequently across media. In this paper, we specifically investigate *gender bias* within a large collection of tropes. To enable our study, we crawl tvtropes.org, an online user-created repository that contains 30K tropes associated with 1.9M examples of their occurrences across film, television, and literature. We automatically score the "genderedness" of each trope in our TVTROPES dataset, which enables an analysis of (1) highly-gendered topics within tropes, (2) the relationship between gender bias and popular reception, and (3) how the gender of a work's creator correlates with the types of tropes that they use.

1 Introduction

Tropes are commonly-occurring narrative patterns within popular media. For example, the **evil genius** trope occurs widely across literature (Lord Voldemort in *Harry Potter*), film (Hannibal Lecter in *The Silence of the Lambs*), and television (Tywin Lannister in *Game of Thrones*). Unfortunately, many tropes exhibit gender bias[1], either explicitly through stereotypical generalizations in their definitions, or implicitly through biased representation in their usage that exhibits such stereotypes. Movies, TV shows, and books with stereotypically gendered tropes and biased representation reify and reinforce gender stereotypes in society (Rowe, 2011; Gupta, 2008; Leonard, 2006). While **evil genius** is not an

---

[*]Authors contributed equally.

[1]Our work explores gender bias across two identities: cisgender male and female. The lack of reliable lexicons limits our ability to explore bias across other gender identities, which should be a priority for future work.

explicitly gendered trope (as opposed to, for example, **women are wiser**), the online tvtropes.org repository contains 108 male and only 15 female instances of **evil genius** across film, TV, and literature.

To quantitatively analyze gender bias within tropes, we collect TVTROPES, a large-scale dataset that contains 1.9M examples of 30K tropes in various forms of media. We augment our dataset with metadata from IMDb (year created, genre, rating of the film/show) and Goodreads (author, characters, gender of the author), which enable the exploration of how trope usage differs across contexts.

Using our dataset, we develop a simple method based on counting pronouns and gendered terms to compute a *genderedness score* for each trope. Our computational analysis of tropes and their genderedness reveals the following:

- **Genre impacts genderedness:** Media related to sports, war, and science fiction rely heavily on male-dominated tropes, while romance, horror, and musicals lean female.

- **Male-leaning tropes exhibit more topical diversity:** Using LDA, we show that male-leaning tropes exhibit higher topic diversity (e.g., science, religion, money) than female tropes, which contain fewer distinct topics (often related to sexuality and maternalism).

- **Low-rated movies contain more gendered tropes:** Examining the most informative features of a classifier trained to predict IMDb ratings for a given movie reveals that gendered tropes are strong predictors of low ratings.

- **Female authors use more diverse gendered tropes than male authors:** Using author gender metadata from Goodreads, we show that female authors incorporate a more diverse set of female-leaning tropes into their works.

212

Proceedings of the Fourth Workshop on Natural Language Processing and Computational Social Science, pages 212–217
Online, November 20, 2020. ©2020 Association for Computational Linguistics
https://doi.org/10.18653/v1/P17

	Titles (w/ metadata)		Tropes	Examples
Literature	15,495	(5,208)	27,229	679,618
Film	17,019	(8,816)	27,450	751,594
TV	7,921	(4,192)	27,134	488,632
Total	40,435	(18,216)	29,457	1,919,844

Table 1: Statistics of TVTROPES.

Our dataset and experiments complement existing social science literature that qualitatively explore gender bias in media (Lauzen, 2019). We publicly release TVTROPES[2] to facilitate future research that computationally analyzes bias in media.

2   Collecting the TVTROPES dataset

We crawl `TVTropes.org` to collect a large-scale dataset of 30K tropes and 1.9M examples of their occurrences across 40K works of film, television, and literature. We then connect our data to metadata from IMDb and Goodreads to augment our dataset and enable analysis of gender bias.

2.1   Collecting a dataset of tropes

Each trope on the website contains a *description* as well as a set of *examples* of the trope in different forms of media. Descriptions normally consist of multiple paragraphs (277 tokens on average), while examples are shorter (63 tokens on average). We only consider titles from film, TV, and literature, excluding other forms of media, such as web comics and video games. We focus on the former because we can pair many titles with their IMDb and Goodreads metadata. Table 1 contains statistics of the TVTROPES dataset.

2.2   Augmenting TVTROPES with metadata

We attempt to match[3] each film and television listed in our dataset with publicly-available IMDb metadata, which includes year of release, genre, director and crew members, and average rating. Similarly, we match our literature examples with metadata scraped from Goodreads, which includes author names, character lists, and book summaries. We additionally manually annotate author gender from Goodreads author pages. The second column of Table 1 shows how many titles were successfully matched with metadata through this process.

2.3   Who contributes to TVTROPES?

One limitation of any analysis of social bias on TVTROPES is that the website may not be representative of the true distribution of tropes within media. There is a confounding *selection bias*—the media in TVTROPES is selected by the users who maintain the `tvtropes.org` resource. To better understand the demographics of contributing users, we scrape the pages of the 15K contributors, many of which contain unstructured biography sections. We search for biographies that contain tokens related to gender and age, and then we manually extract the reported gender and age for a sample of 256 contributors.[4] The median age of these contributors is 20, while 64% of them are male, 33% female and 3% bi-gender, genderfluid, non-binary, trans, or agender. We leave exploration of whether user-reported gender correlates with properties of contributed tropes to future work.

3   Measuring trope genderedness

We limit our analysis to male and female genders, though we are keenly interested in examining the correlations of other genders with trope use. We devise a simple score for trope genderedness that relies on matching tokens to male and female lexicons[5] used in prior work (Bolukbasi et al., 2016; Zhao et al., 2018) and include gendered pronouns, possessives (*his*, *her*), occupations (*actor*, *actress*), and other gendered terms. We validate the effectiveness of the lexicon in capturing genderedness by annotating 150 random examples of trope occurrences as male (86), female (23), or N/A (41). N/A represents examples that do not capture any aspect of gender. We then use the lexicon to classify each example as male (precision = 0.85, recall = 0.86, and F1 score = 0.86) or female (precision = 0.72, recall = 0.78, and F1 score = 0.75).

To measure genderedness, for each trope i, we concatenate the trope's description with all of the trope's examples to form a document X_i. Next, we tokenize, preprocess, and lemmatize X_i using NLTK (Loper and Bird, 2002). We then compute the number of tokens in X_i that match the male lexicon, $m(X_i)$, and the female lexicon, $f(X_i)$. We also compute $m(\text{TVTROPES})$ and $f(\text{TVTROPES})$, the total number of matches for each gender across

---

[2] `http://github.com/dhruvilgala/tvtropes`

[3] We match by both the work's title and its year of release to avoid duplicates.

[4] We note that some demographics may be more inclined to report age and gender information than others.

[5] The gender-balanced lexicon is obtained from Zhao et al. (2018) and comprises 222 male-female word pairs.

Male Tropes	g	Female Tropes	g
Motivated by Fear	-1.8	Ms. Fanservice	3.4
Robot War	-1.6	Socialite	3.1
Cure for Cancer	-1.5	Damsel in Distress	2.7
Evil Genius	-1.3	Hot Scientist	2.2
Grand Finale	-1.2	Ditzy Secretary	2.0

Table 2: Instances of highly-gendered tropes.

all trope documents in the corpus. The *raw genderedness score* of trope i is the ratio $d_i =$

$$\underbrace{\frac{f(X_i)}{f(X_i) + m(X_i)}}_{r_i} \bigg/ \underbrace{\frac{f(\text{TVTROPES})}{f(\text{TVTROPES}) + m(\text{TVTROPES})}}_{r_{\text{TVTROPES}}}.$$

This score is a trope's proportion of female tokens among gendered tokens (r_i), normalized by the global ratio in the corpus (r_{TVTROPES}=0.32). If d_i is high, trope i contains a larger-than-usual proportion of female words.

We finally calculate the the *genderedness score* g_i as d_i's normalized z-score.[6] This results in scores from -1.84 (male-dominated) to 4.02 (female-dominated). For our analyses, we consider tropes with genderedness scores outside of $[-1, 1]$ (one standard deviation) to be highly gendered (see Table 2 for examples).

While similar to methods used in prior work (García et al., 2014), our genderedness score is limited by its lexicon and susceptible to gender generalization and explicit marking (Hitti et al., 2019). We leave exploration of more nuanced methods of capturing trope genderedness (Ananya et al., 2019) to future work.

4 Analyzing gender bias in TVTROPES

Having collected TVTROPES and linked each trope with metadata and genderedness scores, we now turn to characterizing how gender bias manifests itself in the data. We explore (1) the effects of genre on genderedness, (2) what kinds of topics are used in highly-gendered tropes, (3) what tropes contribute most to IMDb ratings, and (4) what types of tropes are used more commonly by authors of one gender than another.

4.1 Genderedness across genre

We can examine how genderedness varies by genre. Given the set of all movies and TV shows in TVTROPES that belong to a particular genre, we

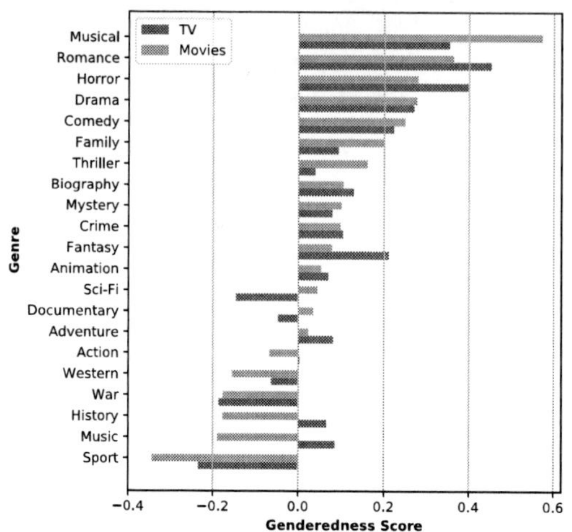

Figure 1: Genderedness across film and TV genres.

extract the set of all tropes used in these works. Next, we compute the average genderedness score of all of these tropes. Figure 1 shows that media about sports, war, and science fiction contain more male-dominated tropes, while musicals, horror, and romance shows are heavily oriented towards female tropes, which is corroborated by social science literature (Lauzen, 2019).

4.2 Topics in highly-gendered tropes

To find common topics in highly-gendered male or female tropes, we run latent Dirichlet analysis (Blei et al., 2003) on a subset of highly-gendered trope descriptions and examples[7] with 75 topics. We filter out tropes whose combined descriptions and examples (i.e., X_i) have fewer than 1K tokens, and then we further limit our training data to a balanced subset of the 3,000 most male and female-leaning tropes using our genderedness score. After training, we compute a gender ratio for every *topic*: given a topic t, we identify the set of all tropes for which t is the most probable topic, and then we compute the ratio of female-leaning to male-leaning tropes within this set.

We observe that 45 of the topics are skewed towards male tropes, while 30 of them favor female tropes, suggesting that male-leaning tropes cover a larger, more diverse set of topics than female-leaning tropes. Table 3 contains specific examples of the most gendered male and female topics. This experiment, in addition to a qualitative inspection of the topics, reveals that female topics

---

[6] $g_i \approx 0$ when $r_i = r_{\text{TVTROPES}}$

[7] We use Gensim's LDA library (Řehůřek and Sojka, 2010).

Topics (Most salient terms)	
Male	ship earth planet technology system build weapon destroy alien
	super strong strength survive slow damage speed hulk punch armor
	god jesus religion church worship bible believe angel heaven belief
	skill rule smart training problem student ability level teach genius
	money rich gold steal company city sell business criminal wealthy
Female	relationship married marry wife marriage together husband wedding
	beautiful blonde attractive beauty describe tall brunette eyes ugly
	naked sexy fanservice shower nude cover strip pool bikini shirt
	parent baby daughter pregnant birth kid die pregnancy raise adult
	food drink eating cook taste weight drinking chocolate wine

Table 3: Topic assignments in highly-gendered tropes.

High Rated		Low Rated	
Trope	g	**Trope**	g
Edutainment Show	1.2	Alpha Bitch	2.7
Cooking Stories	1.0	Sexy Backless Outfit	2.6
British Brevity	-0.9	Fanservice	1.9
Wedding Smashers	0.8	Shower Scene	1.4
Just Following Orders	-0.7	Sword and Sandal	-1.0

Table 4: Gendered tropes predictive of IMDb rating.

(maternalism, appearance, and sexuality) are less diverse than male topics (science, religion, war, and money). Topics in highly-gendered tropes capture all three dimensions of sexism proposed by Glick and Fiske (1996) – female topics about motherhood and pregnancy display gender differentiation, topics about appearance and nudity can be attributed to heterosexuality, while male topics about money and strength capture paternalism. The bias captured by these topics, although unsurprising given previous work (Bolukbasi et al., 2016), serves as a sanity check for our metric and provides further evidence of the limited diversity in female roles (Lauzen, 2019).

4.3 Identifying implicitly gendered tropes

We identify *implicitly gendered tropes* (Glick and Fiske, 1996)—tropes that are not defined by gender but nevertheless have high genderedness scores— by identifying a subset of 3500 highly-gendered tropes whose titles do not contain gendered tokens.[8] A qualitative analysis reveals that tropes containing the word "genius" (**impossible genius, gibbering genius, evil genius**) and "boss" (**beleaguered boss, stupid boss**) lean heavily male. There are interesting gender divergences within a high-level topic: within "evil" tropes, male-leaning tropes are diverse (**necessarily evil, evil corporation, evil army**), while female tropes focus on sex (**sex is evil, evil eyeshadow, evil is sexy**).

4.4 Using tropes to predict ratings

Are gendered tropes predictive of media popularity? We consider three roughly equal-sized bins of IMDb ratings (Low, Medium, and High).[9] For each IMDb-matched title in TVTROPES, we construct a binary vector $z \in \{0,1\}^T$, where T is the number of unique tropes in our dataset.[10] We set z_i to 1 if trope i occurs in the movie, and 0 otherwise. Tropes are predictive of ratings: a logistic regression classifier[11] achieves 55% test accuracy with this method, well over the majority class baseline of 36%. Table 4 contains the most predictive gendered tropes for each class; interestingly, low-rated titles have a much higher average *absolute* genderedness score (0.73) than high-rated ones (0.49), providing interesting contrast to the opposing conclusions drawn by Boyle (2014). While IMDB ratings offer a great place to start in correlating public perception with genderedness in tropes, we may be double-dipping into the same pool of internet movie reviewers as TVTROPES. We leave further exploration of correlating gendered tropes with box office results, budgets, awards, etc. for future work.

4.5 Predicting author gender from tropes

We predict the author gender[12] by training a classifier for 2521 Goodreads authors based on a binary feature vector encoding the presence or absence of tropes in their books. We achieve an accuracy of 71% on our test set (majority baseline is 64%). Interestingly, the top 50 tropes most predictive of male authors have an average genderedness of 0.04, while those most correlated with female authors have an average of 0.89, indicating that books by female authors contain more female-leaning tropes. Eighteen female-leaning tropes ($g_i > 1$), varying in scope from the non-traditional **feminist fantasy** to the more stereotypical **hair of gold heart of gold**, are predictive of female authors. In contrast, only

---

[8]This process contains noise due to our small lexicon: a few explicitly gendered, often problematic tropes such as **absolute cleavage** are not filtered out.

[9]Low: (0-6.7], Medium: (6.7-7.7], High: (7.7-10]

[10]We consider titles and tropes with 10+ examples.

[11]We implement the classifier in scikit-learn (Pedregosa et al., 2011) with L-BFGS solver, L2 regularization, inverse regularization strength C=1.0 and an 80-20 train-test split.

[12]We annotate the author gender label by hand, to prevent misgendering based on automated detection methods, and we would also like to further this research by expanding our Goodsreads scrape to include non-binary authors.

Male Author		Female Author	
Trope	g	Trope	g
Undressing the Unconscious	1.3	Cool Old Lady	2.7
First Girl Wins	1.3	Plucky Girl	2.5
Did Not Get the Girl	0.9	Feminist Fantasy	2.2
God is Evil	-0.8	Young Adult Literature	1.7
Retired Badass	-0.8	Extremely Protective Child	1.2

Table 5: Gendered tropes predictive of author gender.

two such character-driven female-dominated tropes are predictive of male authors; the stereotypical **undressing the unconscious** and **first girl wins**; see Table 5 for more. Furthermore, out of 115K examples of tropes in female-authored books, 17K are highly female, while just 2.2K are male-dominated. Since many of these gendered tropes are character-driven, this implies wider female representation in such gendered instances, previously shown in Scottish crime fiction (Hill, 2017). Overall, female authors frequently use both stereotypical and non-stereotypical female-oriented tropes, while male authors limit themselves to more stereotypical kinds. However, it is important to note the double selection bias at play in both selecting which books are actually published, as well as which published books are reviewed on Goodreads. While there are valid ethical concerns with a task that attempts to predict gender, this task only analyzes the tropes most predictive of author gender, and the classifier is not used to do inference on unlabelled data or as a way to identify an individual's gender.

5   Related Work

Our work builds on computational research analyzing gender bias. Methods to measure gender bias include using contextual cues to develop probabilistic estimates (Ananya et al., 2019), and using gender directions in word embedding spaces (Bolukbasi et al., 2016). Other work engages directly with `tvtropes.org`: Kiesel and Grimnes (2010) build a wrapper for the website, but perform no analysis of its content. García-Ortega et al. (2018) create PicTropes: a limited dataset of 5,925 films from the website. Bamman et al. (2013) collect a set of 72 character-based tropes, which they then use to evaluate induced character personas, and Lee et al. (2019) use data crawled from the website to explore different sexism dimensions within TV and film.

Analyzing bias through tropes is a popular area of research within social science. Hansen (2018) focus in on the titular princess character in the video game The Legend of Zelda as an example of the

Damsel in Distress trope. Lacroix (2011) study the development and representation in popular culture of the Casino Indian and Ignoble Savage tropes.

The usage of biased tropes is often attributed to the lack of equal representation both on and off the screen. *Geena Davis Inclusion Quotient* (Google, 2017) quantifies the speaking time and importance of characters in films, and finds that male characters have nearly twice the presence of female characters in award-winning films. In contrast, our analysis looks specifically at tropes, which may not correlate directly with speaking time. Lauzen (2019) provides valuable insight into representation among film writers, directors, crew members, etc. Perkins and Schreiber (2019) study an ongoing increase in the representation of women in independent productions on television, many of which focus on feminist content.

6   Future Work

We believe that the TVTROPES dataset can be used to further research in a variety of areas. We envision setting up a task involving trope detection from raw movie scripts or books; the resulting classifier, beyond being useful for analysis, could also be used by media creators to foster better representation during the writing process. There is also the possibility of using the large number of examples we collect in order to generate augmented training data or adversarial data for tasks such as coreference resolution in a gendered context (Rudinger et al., 2018). The expansion of our genderedness metric to include non-binary gender idenities, which in turn would involve creating similar lexicons as we use, is an important area for further exploration.

It would also be useful to gain further understanding of the multiple online communities that contribute information about popular culture; for example, an analysis of possible overlap in contributors to TVTROPES and IMDb could better account for sampling bias when analyzing these datasets.

7   Acknowledgements

We would like to thank Jesse Thomason for his valuable advice.

References

Ananya, Nitya Parthasarthi, and Sameer Singh. 2019. GenderQuant: Quantifying mention-level genderedness. In *Proceedings of the 2019 Conference of the North American Chapter of the Association for*

Computational Linguistics: Human Language Technologies, Volume 1 (Long and Short Papers), pages 2959–2969, Minneapolis, Minnesota. Association for Computational Linguistics.

David Bamman, Brendan O'Connor, and Noah A. Smith. 2013. Learning latent personas of film characters. In *Proceedings of the 51st Annual Meeting of the Association for Computational Linguistics (Volume 1: Long Papers)*, pages 352–361, Sofia, Bulgaria. Association for Computational Linguistics.

David M Blei, Andrew Y Ng, and Michael I Jordan. 2003. Latent dirichlet allocation. *Journal of machine Learning research*, 3.

Tolga Bolukbasi, Kai-Wei Chang, James Y. Zou, Venkatesh Saligrama, and Adam Kalai. 2016. Man is to computer programmer as woman is to homemaker? debiasing word embeddings. *CoRR*, abs/1607.06520.

Karen Boyle. 2014. Gender, comedy and reviewing culture on the internet movie database. *Participations*, 11(1):31–49.

David García, Ingmar Weber, and Venkata Rama Kiran Garimella. 2014. Gender asymmetries in reality and fiction: The bechdel test of social media. *CoRR*, abs/1404.0163.

Rubén H. García-Ortega, Juan J. Merelo-Guervós, Pablo García Sánchez, and Gad Pitaru. 2018. Overview of pictropes, a film trope dataset.

Peter Glick and Susan Fiske. 1996. The ambivalent sexism inventory: Differentiating hostile and benevolent sexism. *Journal of Personality and Social Psychology*, 70:491–512.

Google. 2017. *Using technology to address gender bias in film*.

Charu Gupta. 2008. (mis) representing the dalit woman: Reification of caste and gender stereotypes in the hindi didactic literature of colonial india. *Indian Historical Review*, 35(2).

Jared Capener Hansen. 2018. Why can't zelda save herself? how the damsel in distress trope affects video game players.

Lorna Hill. 2017. Bloody women: How female authors have transformed the scottish contemporary crime fiction genre. *American, British and Canadian Studies*, 28(1):52 – 71.

Yasmeen Hitti, Eunbee Jang, Ines Moreno, and Carolyne Pelletier. 2019. Proposed taxonomy for gender bias in text; a filtering methodology for the gender generalization subtype. In *Proceedings of the First Workshop on Gender Bias in Natural Language Processing*, pages 8–17, Florence, Italy. Association for Computational Linguistics.

Malte Kiesel and Gunnar Aastrand Grimnes. 2010. Dbtropes - a linked data wrapper approach incorporating community feedback. In *European Knowledge Acquisition Workshop (EKAW)*.

Celeste C. Lacroix. 2011. High stakes stereotypes: The emergence of the "casino indian" trope in television depictions of contemporary native americans. *Howard Journal of Communications*, 22(1):1–23.

Martha M Lauzen. 2019. It'sa man's (celluloid) world: Portrayals of female characters in the top grossing films of 2018'. *Center for the Study of Women in Television and Film, San Diego State University*.

Nayeon Lee, Yejin Bang, Jamin Shin, and Pascale Fung. 2019. Understanding the shades of sexism in popular TV series. In *Proceedings of the 2019 Workshop on Widening NLP*, pages 122–125, Florence, Italy. Association for Computational Linguistics.

David J Leonard. 2006. Not a hater, just keepin'it real: The importance of race-and gender-based game studies. *Games and culture*, 1(1).

Edward Loper and Steven Bird. 2002. Nltk: The natural language toolkit. In *In Proceedings of the ACL Workshop on Effective Tools and Methodologies for Teaching Natural Language Processing and Computational Linguistics. Philadelphia: Association for Computational Linguistics*.

F. Pedregosa, G. Varoquaux, A. Gramfort, V. Michel, B. Thirion, O. Grisel, M. Blondel, P. Prettenhofer, R. Weiss, V. Dubourg, J. Vanderplas, A. Passos, D. Cournapeau, M. Brucher, M. Perrot, and E. Duchesnay. 2011. Scikit-learn: Machine learning in Python. *Journal of Machine Learning Research*, 12:2825–2830.

Claire Perkins and Michele Schreiber. 2019. Independent women: from film to television. *Feminist Media Studies*, 19(7):919–927.

Radim Řehůřek and Petr Sojka. 2010. Software Framework for Topic Modelling with Large Corpora. In *Proceedings of the LREC 2010 Workshop on New Challenges for NLP Frameworks*, pages 45–50, Valletta, Malta. ELRA. http://is.muni.cz/publication/884893/en.

K. Rowe. 2011. *The Unruly Woman: Gender and the Genres of Laughter*. University of Texas Press.

Rachel Rudinger, Jason Naradowsky, Brian Leonard, and Benjamin Van Durme. 2018. Gender bias in coreference resolution. In *Proceedings of the 2018 Conference of the North American Chapter of the Association for Computational Linguistics: Human Language Technologies, Volume 2 (Short Papers)*, pages 8–14.

Jieyu Zhao, Yichao Zhou, Zeyu Li, Wei Wang, and Kai-Wei Chang. 2018. Learning gender-neutral word embeddings. *CoRR*, abs/1809.01496.

Association for Computational Linguistics
209 N. Eighth Street
Stroudsburg, Pennsylvania 18360

ISBN 978-1-7138-1998-1